W9-ADK-486

WITHDRAWN
WELLESLEY FREE LIBRARY

WELLESLEY FREE LIBRARY

ASSASSINATION CLASSROOM

YUSEI MATSUI

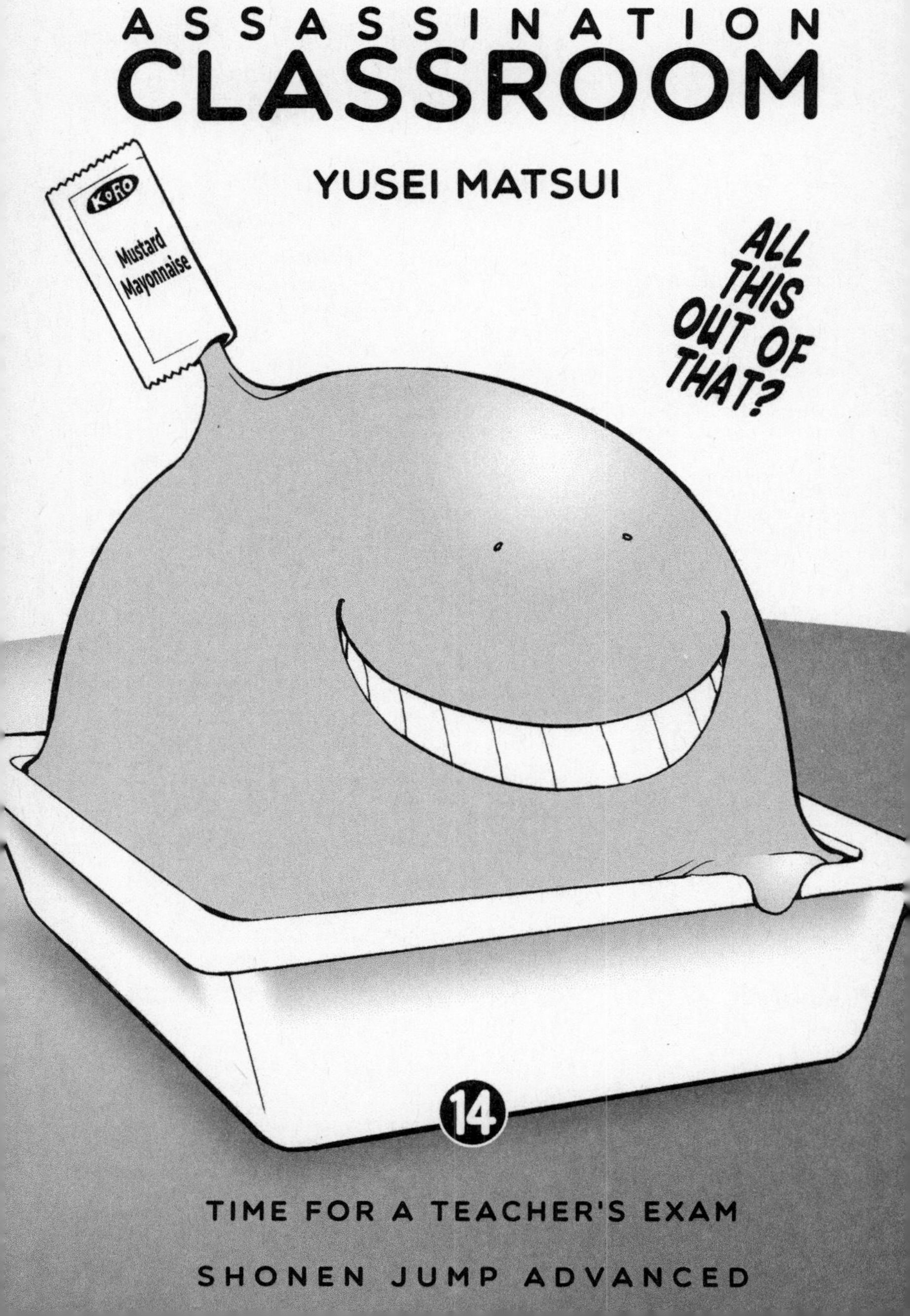
KoRO
Mustard Mayonnaise
ALL THIS OUT OF THAT?

14

TIME FOR A TEACHER'S EXAM

SHONEN JUMP ADVANCED

I EXPECT TO SEE YOU EXECUTE THE BEST ASSASSINATION ATTEMPT YOU ARE CAPABLE OF.
MAKE THE MOST OF YOUR KNOWLEDGE, INGENUITY AND HARD WORK.
THIS IS MY IDEA OF THE MOST FUN EVER.

Story Thus Far

Kunugigaoka Junior High, Class 3-E is led by a monster who has disintegrated the moon and is planning to do the same to the Earth next March.

Although we have a lot of data on his weaknesses, we are still far from successfully assassinating Koro Sensei...

Koro Tribune

December Issue

Published by: Class 3-E Newspaper Staff

Even the armies of the world, with the latest technology, can't kill the super creature Koro Sensei and collect the maximum 30 billion yen (300 million dollar) bounty! So it comes down to his students, the so-called "End Class." Thanks to Koro Sensei's dedication to them, they grow to become fine students who can even outshine the top students in their school. Likewise, their martial skills rapidly improve with the help of Mr. Karasuma from the Ministry of Defense, molding them into a professional team of assassins. The first trimester has gone by and the clock is ticking. Will they be able to successfully assassinate Koro Sensei?!

Breaking news! Koro Sensei completely revealed in his birthday suit!

THAT MEANS...
...HE'S BUTT-NAKED?
Don't blush! He'll notice us.

Koro Sensei

A mysterious, man-made, octopus-like creature whose name is a play on the words "koro senai," which means "can't kill." He is capable of flying at Mach 20 and his versatile tentacles protect him from attacks and aid him in everyday activities. Nobody knows who created him or why he wants to teach Class 3-E, but he has proven to be an extremely capable teacher.

Kaede Kayano

Class E student. She's the one who named Koro Sensei. She sits at the desk next to Nagisa, and they seem to get along well.

Uh-huh.

Nagisa Shiota

Class E student. Skilled at information gathering, he has been taking notes on Koro Sensei's weaknesses. He has a hidden talent for assassinations and even the Assassin Broker Lovro sees his potential.

Nagisa's mother is seriously scary...

I'LL KNOCK SOME SENSE INTO YOU!

Hinano Kurahashi

pick up!

As an animal lover, you might expect her to be an animal rights activist, but she can wring a chicken's neck or scale a fish all with a flirty smile on her face. You can tell how much she loves animals by the way she says "Thank you!" before eating them.

Karma Akabane

Class E student. A natural genius who gets top grades too. His failure in the final exam of the first semester has forced him to grow up and take things a bit more seriously.

Tadaomi Karasuma

Member of the Ministry of Defense and the Class E students' P.E. teacher. Though serious about his duties, he is successfully building good relationships with his students.

Rio Nakamura

Class E student. She was considered a prodigy back in elementary school but she longed to be "ordinary," so she pretended to be a poor student. Now she has a dream she's aiming for, so she might get more serious.

Terasaka's career choice!

Karma told everybody that politician was Terasaka's second choice. But since everyone teased him about it, Terasaka took it back right away. Nevertheless, it looks like he has already won 27 votes toward his future career.

Irina Jelavich

A sexy assassin hired as an English teacher. She's known for using her "womanly charms" to get close to a target. She often flirts with Karasuma, but hasn't had any success so far.

"You have to be a super-creature to ride!

The most dangerous ride in the world!

CORDLESS BUNGEE JUMP

Gakuho Asano

The principal of Kunugigaoka Academy, who built this academically competitive school based on his faith in rationality and hierarchy.

Assassination Class Roster

Always assassinate your target using a method that brings a smile to your face.

I am open for assassinations at any time. But don't let them get in the way of your studying.

I won't harm students who try to assassinate me. But if your skills are rusty, expect a good scrubbing.

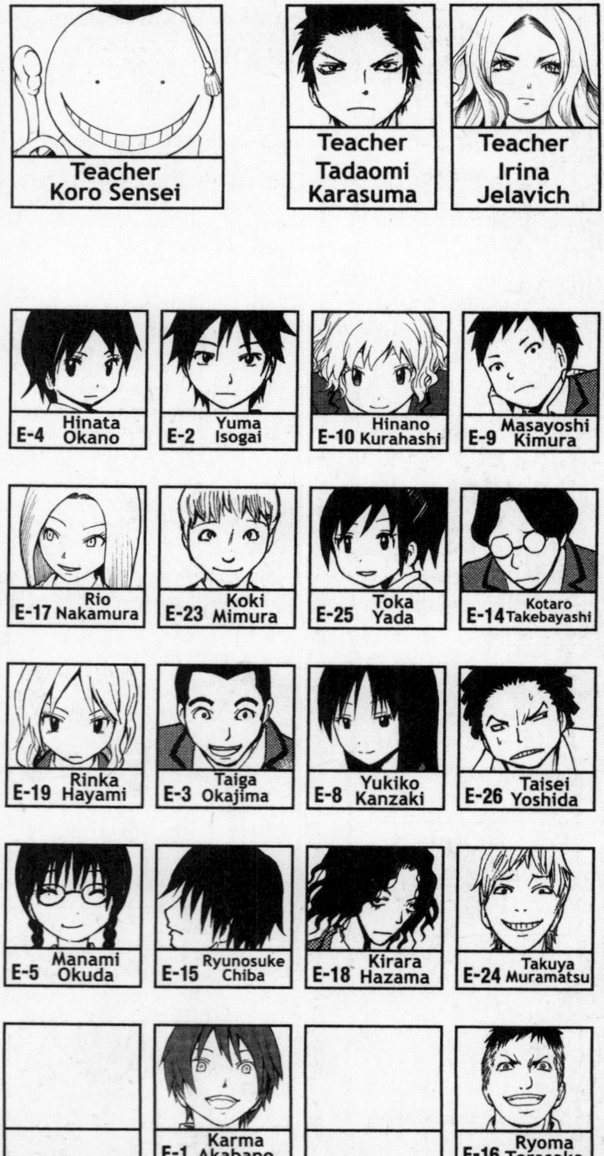

Teacher Irina Jelavich
Teacher Tadaomi Karasuma
Teacher Koro Sensei
E-9 Masayoshi Kimura
E-10 Hinano Kurahashi
E-2 Yuma Isogai
E-4 Hinata Okano
E-14 Kotaro Takebayashi
E-25 Toka Yada
E-23 Koki Mimura
E-17 Rio Nakamura
E-26 Taisei Yoshida
E-8 Yukiko Kanzaki
E-3 Taiga Okajima
E-19 Rinka Hayami
E-24 Takuya Muramatsu
E-18 Kirara Hazama
E-15 Ryunosuke Chiba
E-5 Manami Okuda
E-16 Ryoma Terasaka
E-1 Karma Akabane

Individual Statistics

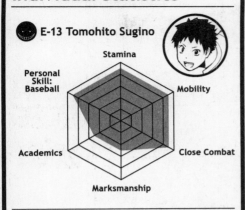

E-13 Tomohito Sugino

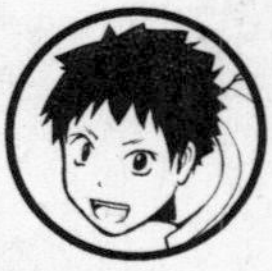

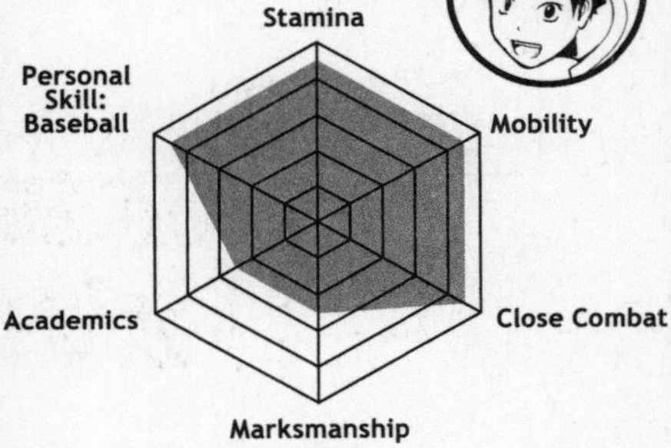
Stamina
Mobility
Close Combat
Marksmanship
Academics
Personal Skill: Baseball

E-14 Kotaro Takebayashi

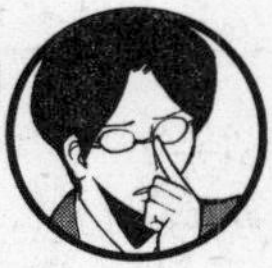

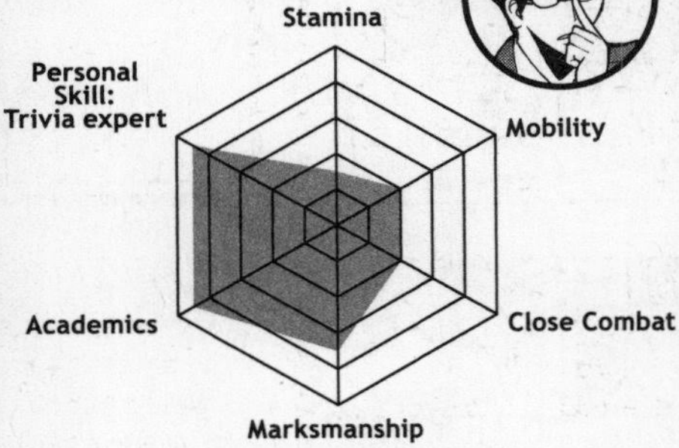
Stamina
Mobility
Close Combat
Marksmanship
Academics
Personal Skill: Trivia expert

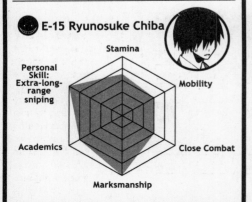

E-15 Ryunosuke Chiba

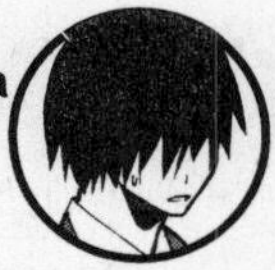

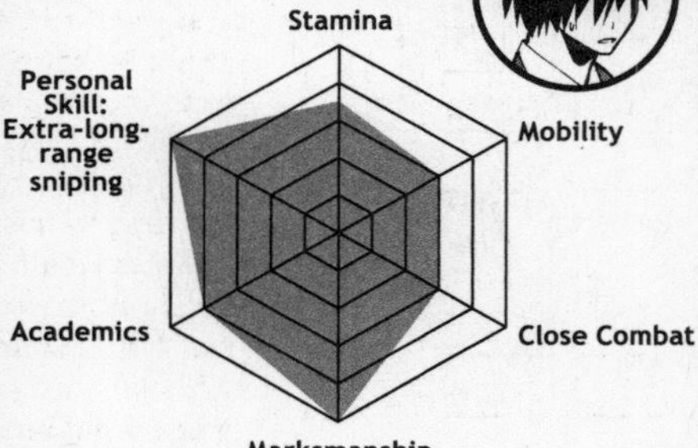
Stamina
Mobility
Close Combat
Marksmanship
Academics
Personal Skill: Extra-long-range sniping

Kunugigaoka Junior High

3-E

Koro Sensei Class Seating Arrangement

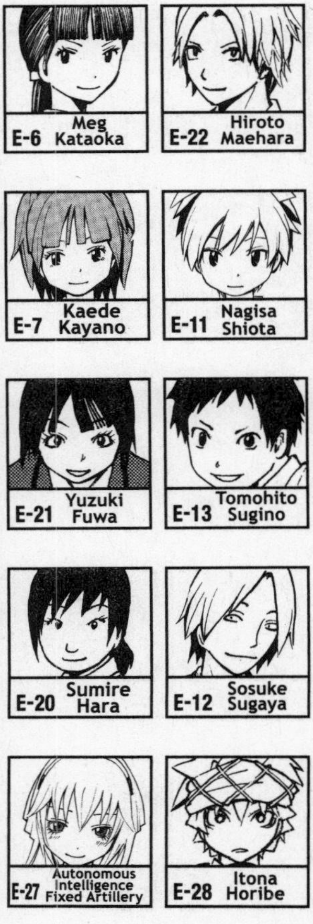
E-6 Meg Kataoka
E-22 Hiroto Maehara
E-7 Kaede Kayano
E-11 Nagisa Shiota
E-21 Yuzuki Fuwa
E-13 Tomohito Sugino
E-20 Sumire Hara
E-12 Sosuke Sugaya
E-27 Autonomous Intelligence Fixed Artillery
E-28 Itona Horibe

ASSASSINATION
CLASSROOM 14 CONTENTS

(ANSWER SHEET)

CLASS 116	Time for Guests	009
CLASS 117	Time for an Unexpected Guest	029
CLASS 118	Time for Fate	049
CLASS 119	Time for Final Exams—2nd Period	069
CLASS 120	Time for Bloodlust	089
CLASS 121	Time for a Solution	109
CLASS 122	Time Squared	129
CLASS 123	Time for a Revelation	151
CLASS 124	Time for a Teacher's Exam	171

| de | 3 | Class | E | Name | CONTENTS | Score | |

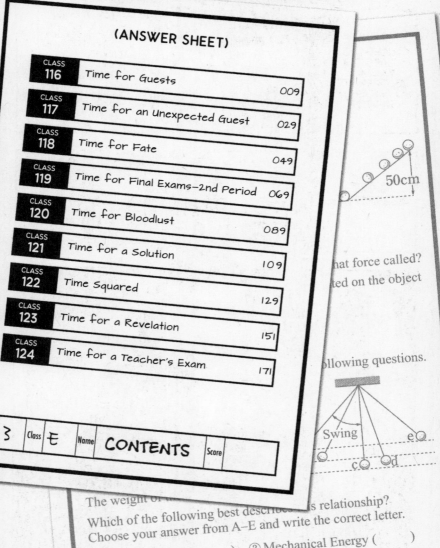

50cm

hat force called?

ted on the object

llowing questions.

Swing

The weight of ... s relationship?
Which of the following best describes ...
Choose your answer from A–E and write the correct letter ( )

①Kinetic Energy ( ) ②Mechanical Energy ( )

A: $e < b = c = d$ **B:** $b = c = d < e$ **C:** $c < d < b < e$

D: $e < b < d < c$ **E:** $b = c = d = e$

(Question 3): Answer the following question about an
experimental apparatus used to study weather fronts.
... in the middle of a tank of water as

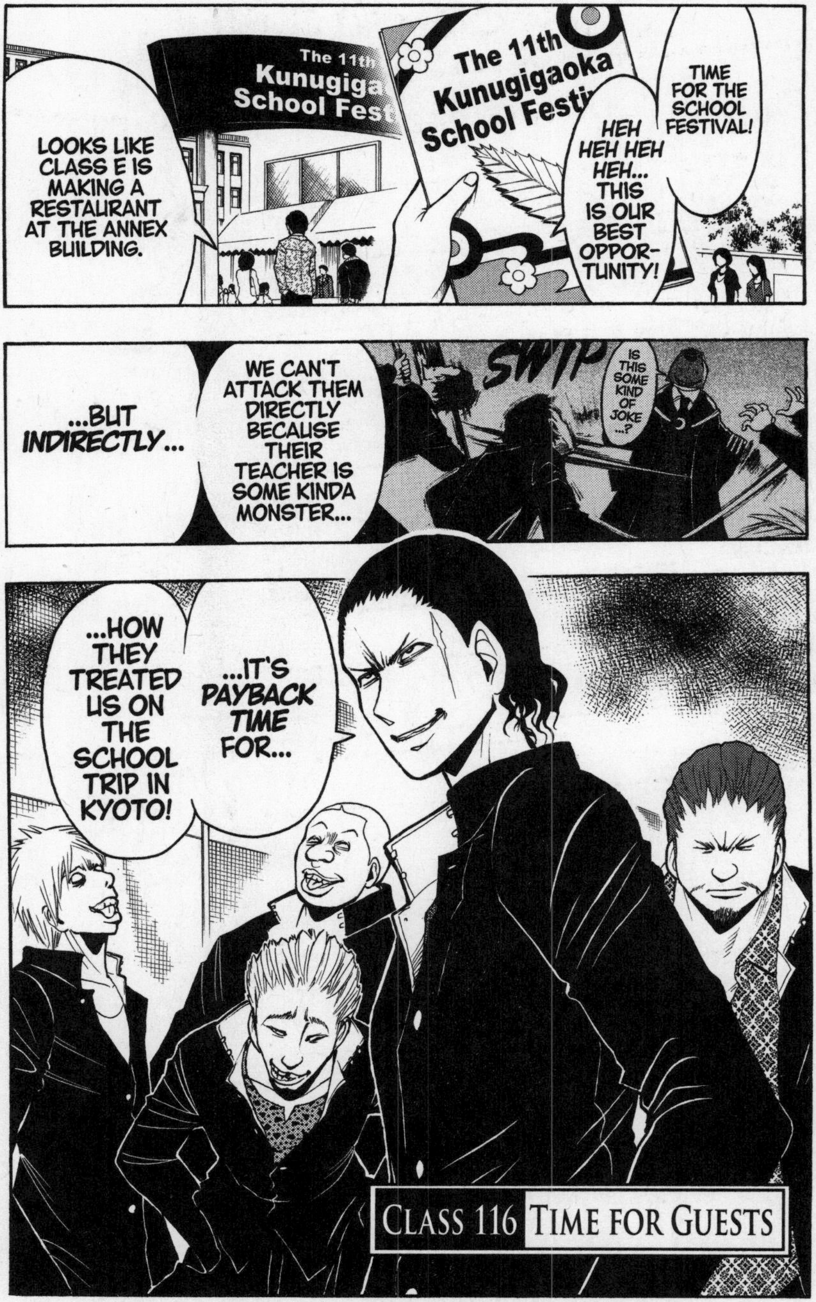
The 11th Kunugigaoka School Festi
The 11th Kunugiga School Fest
TIME FOR THE SCHOOL FESTIVAL!
HEH HEH HEH HEH... THIS IS OUR BEST OPPORTUNITY!
LOOKS LIKE CLASS E IS MAKING A RESTAURANT AT THE ANNEX BUILDING.
SWIP
IS THIS SOME KIND OF JOKE ...?
WE CAN'T ATTACK THEM DIRECTLY BECAUSE THEIR TEACHER IS SOME KINDA MONSTER...
...BUT INDIRECTLY...
...IT'S PAYBACK TIME FOR...
...HOW THEY TREATED US ON THE SCHOOL TRIP IN KYOTO!
CLASS 116 TIME FOR GUESTS

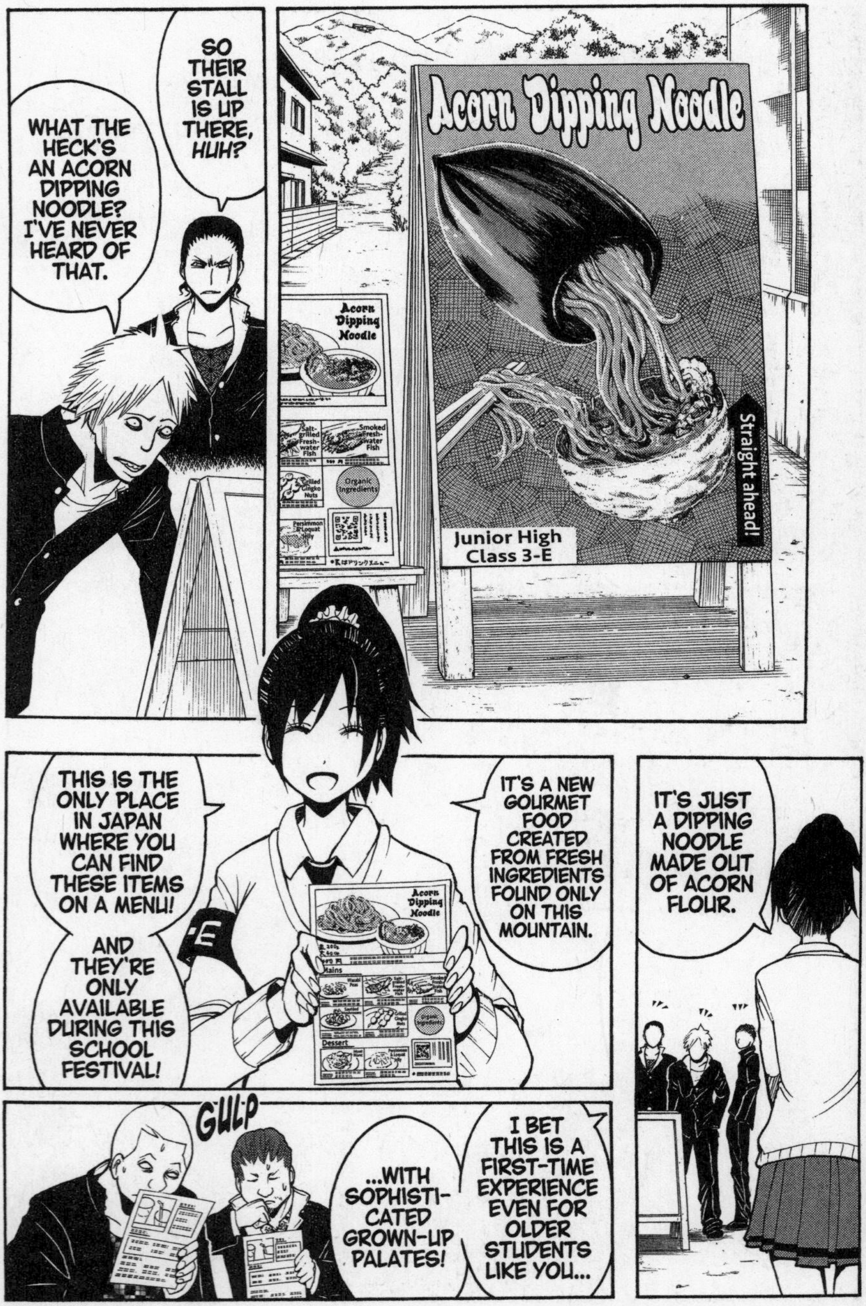
Acorn Dipping Noodle
Acorn Dipping Noodle
Salt-grilled Fresh-water Fish
Smoked Fresh-water Fish
Grilled Gingko Nuts
Organic Ingredients
Persimmon & Loquat Jelly
Junior High Class 3-E
Straight ahead!
SO THEIR STALL IS UP THERE, HUH?
WHAT THE HECK'S AN ACORN DIPPING NOODLE? I'VE NEVER HEARD OF THAT.
IT'S JUST A DIPPING NOODLE MADE OUT OF ACORN FLOUR.
IT'S A NEW GOURMET FOOD CREATED FROM FRESH INGREDIENTS FOUND ONLY ON THIS MOUNTAIN.
THIS IS THE ONLY PLACE IN JAPAN WHERE YOU CAN FIND THESE ITEMS ON A MENU!
AND THEY'RE ONLY AVAILABLE DURING THIS SCHOOL FESTIVAL!
Acorn Dipping Noodle
I BET THIS IS A FIRST-TIME EXPERIENCE EVEN FOR OLDER STUDENTS LIKE YOU...
...WITH SOPHISTI-CATED GROWN-UP PALATES!
GULP

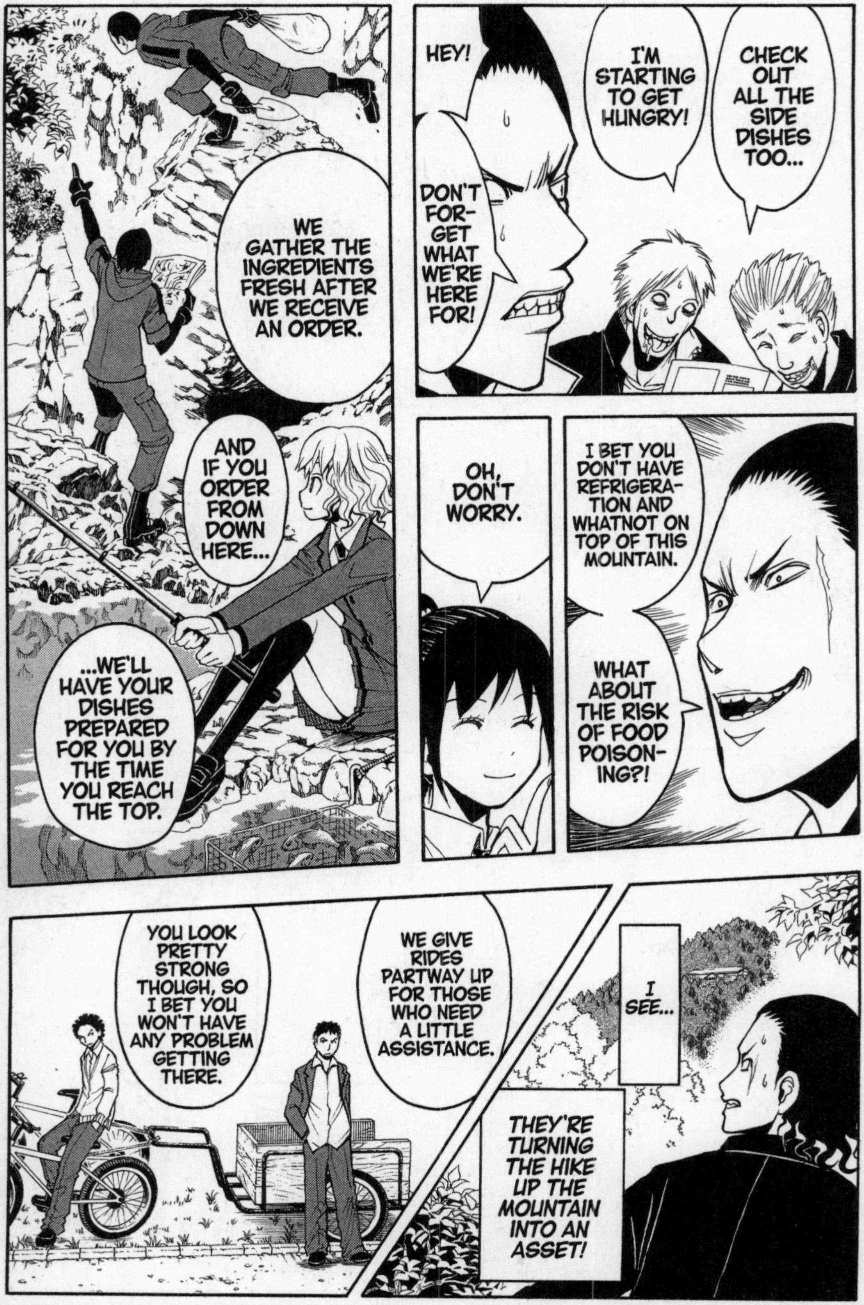
CHECK OUT ALL THE SIDE DISHES TOO...
I'M STARTING TO GET HUNGRY!
HEY!
DON'T FOR-GET WHAT WE'RE HERE FOR!
I BET YOU DON'T HAVE REFRIGERA-TION AND WHATNOT ON TOP OF THIS MOUNTAIN.
WHAT ABOUT THE RISK OF FOOD POISON-ING?!
OH, DON'T WORRY.
WE GATHER THE INGREDIENTS FRESH AFTER WE RECEIVE AN ORDER.
AND IF YOU ORDER FROM DOWN HERE...
...WE'LL HAVE YOUR DISHES PREPARED FOR YOU BY THE TIME YOU REACH THE TOP.
I SEE...
THEY'RE TURNING THE HIKE UP THE MOUNTAIN INTO AN ASSET!
WE GIVE RIDES PARTWAY UP FOR THOSE WHO NEED A LITTLE ASSISTANCE.
YOU LOOK PRETTY STRONG THOUGH, SO I BET YOU WON'T HAVE ANY PROBLEM GETTING THERE.

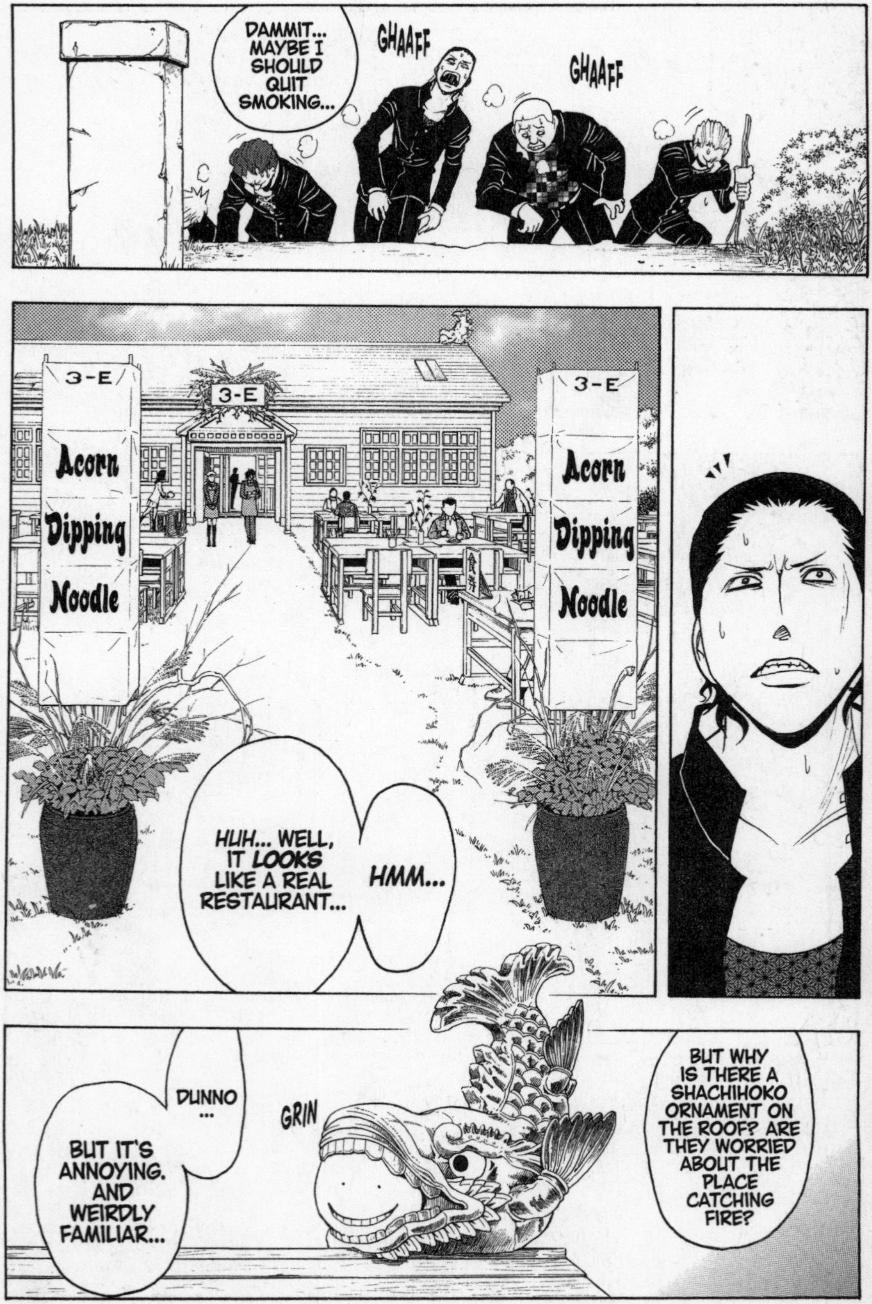
GHAAFF
GHAAFF
DAMMIT... MAYBE I SHOULD QUIT SMOKING...
HMM...
HUH... WELL, IT LOOKS LIKE A REAL RESTAURANT...
3-E
3-E Acorn Dipping Noodle
3-E Acorn Dipping Noodle
BUT WHY IS THERE A SHACHIHOKO ORNAMENT ON THE ROOF? ARE THEY WORRIED ABOUT THE PLACE CATCHING FIRE?
GRIN
DUNNO...
BUT IT'S ANNOYING. AND WEIRDLY FAMILIAR...

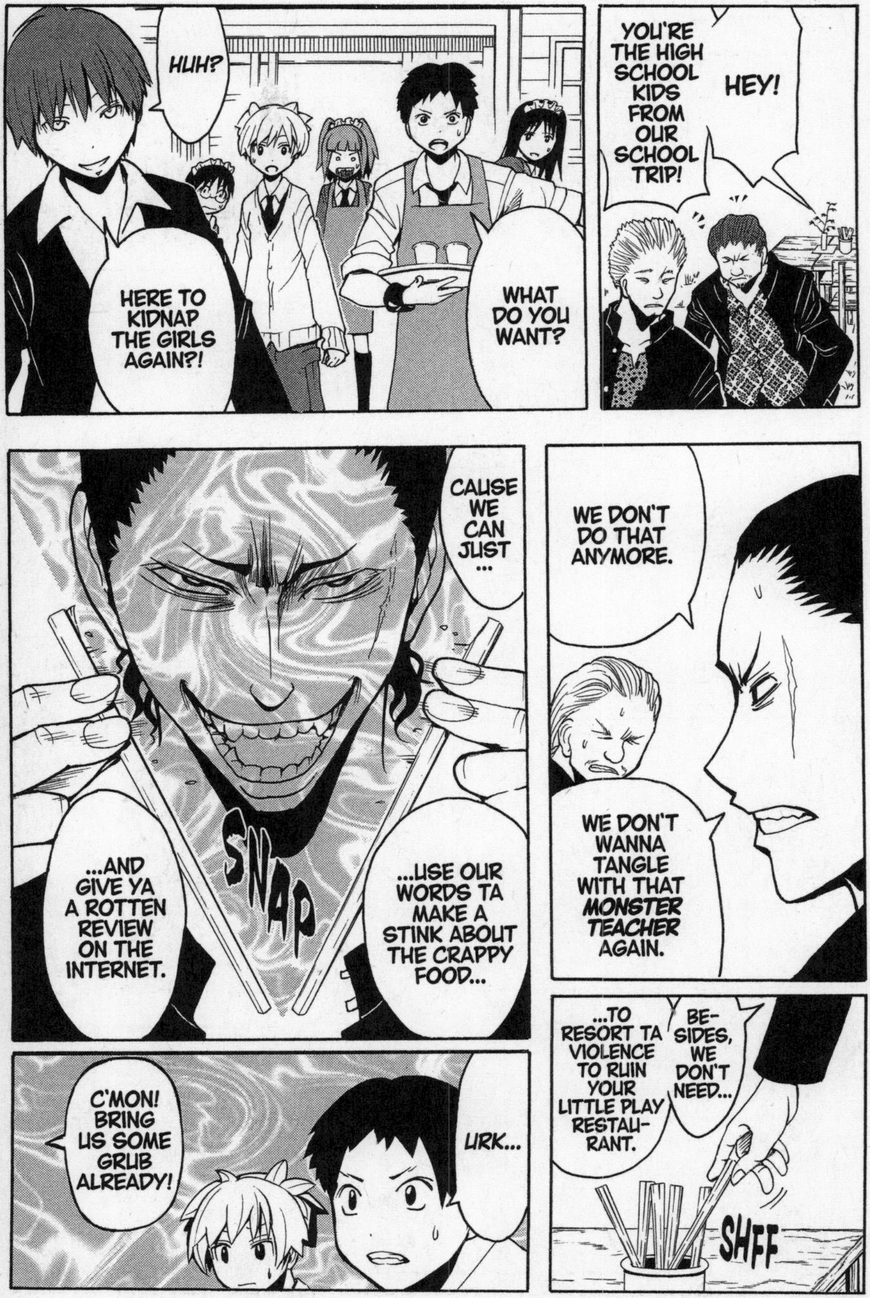
HEY!
YOU'RE THE HIGH SCHOOL KIDS FROM OUR SCHOOL TRIP!
WHAT DO YOU WANT?
HERE TO KIDNAP THE GIRLS AGAIN?!
HUH?
WE DON'T DO THAT ANYMORE.
WE DON'T WANNA TANGLE WITH THAT *MONSTER TEACHER* AGAIN.
BE-SIDES, WE DON'T NEED...
...TO RESORT TA VIOLENCE TO RUIN YOUR LITTLE PLAY RESTAU-RANT.
SHFF
CAUSE WE CAN JUST...
...USE OUR WORDS TA MAKE A STINK ABOUT THE CRAPPY FOOD...
...AND GIVE YA A ROTTEN REVIEW ON THE INTERNET.
SNAP
URK...
C'MON! BRING US SOME GRUB ALREADY!

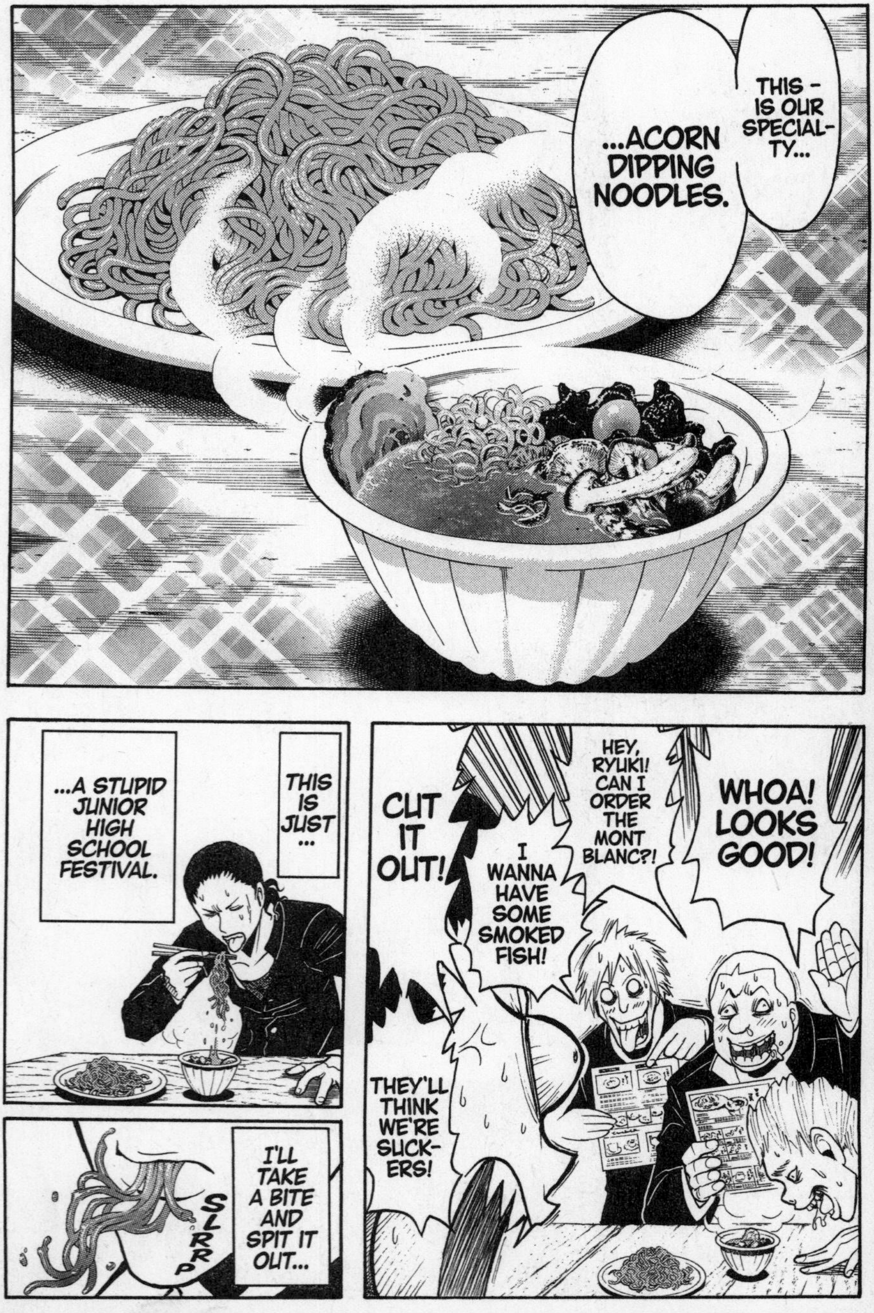
THIS - IS OUR SPECIAL-TY...
...ACORN DIPPING NOODLES.
WHOA! LOOKS GOOD!
HEY, RYUKI! CAN I ORDER THE MONT BLANC?!
I WANNA HAVE SOME SMOKED FISH!
CUT IT OUT!
THEY'LL THINK WE'RE SUCK-ERS!
THIS IS JUST ...
...A STUPID JUNIOR HIGH SCHOOL FESTIVAL.
I'LL TAKE A BITE AND SPIT IT OUT...
SLRRP

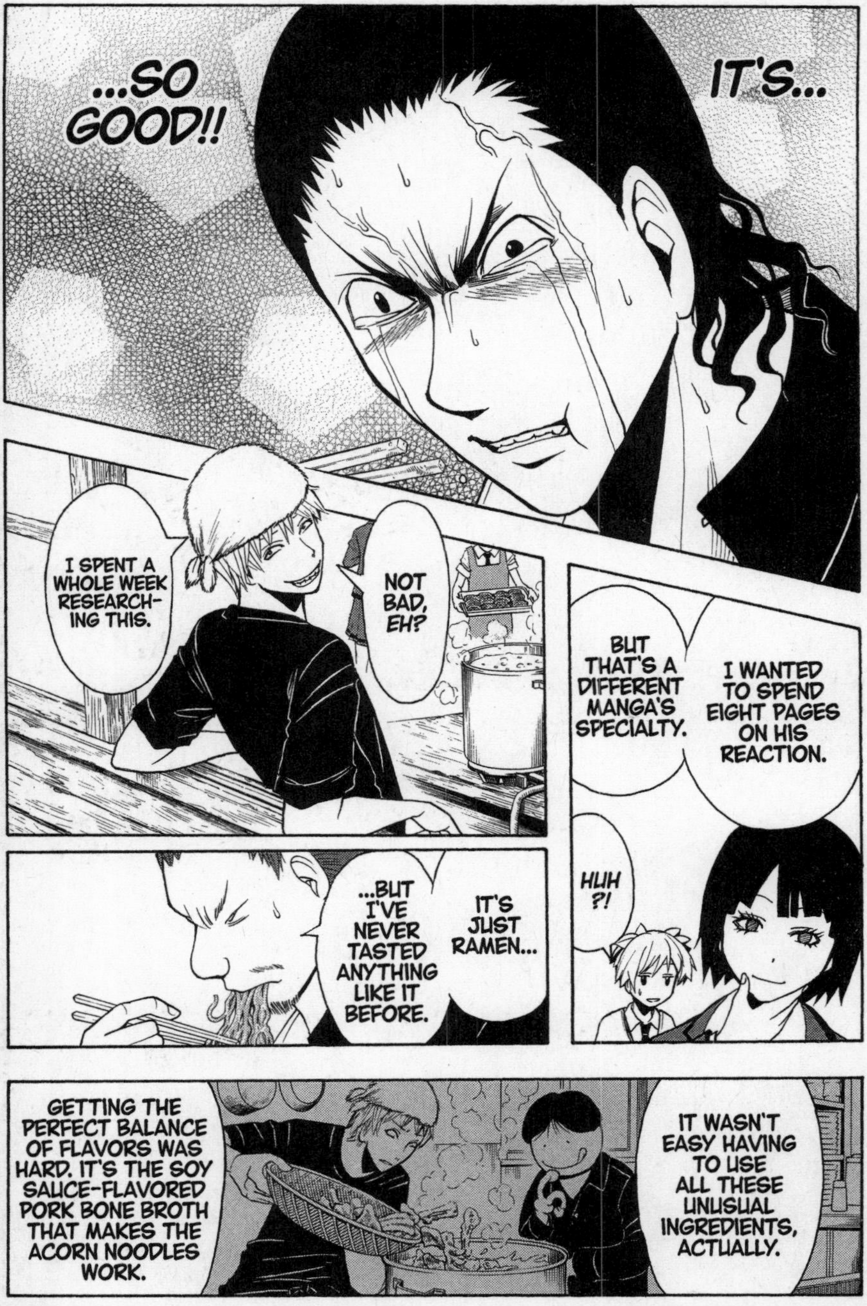
IT'S...
...SO GOOD!!
I WANTED TO SPEND EIGHT PAGES ON HIS REACTION.
BUT THAT'S A DIFFERENT MANGA'S SPECIALTY.
HUH?!
NOT BAD, EH?
I SPENT A WHOLE WEEK RESEARCHING THIS.
IT'S JUST RAMEN...
...BUT I'VE NEVER TASTED ANYTHING LIKE IT BEFORE.
IT WASN'T EASY HAVING TO USE ALL THESE UNUSUAL INGREDIENTS, ACTUALLY.
GETTING THE PERFECT BALANCE OF FLAVORS WAS HARD. IT'S THE SOY SAUCE-FLAVORED PORK BONE BROTH THAT MAKES THE ACORN NOODLES WORK.

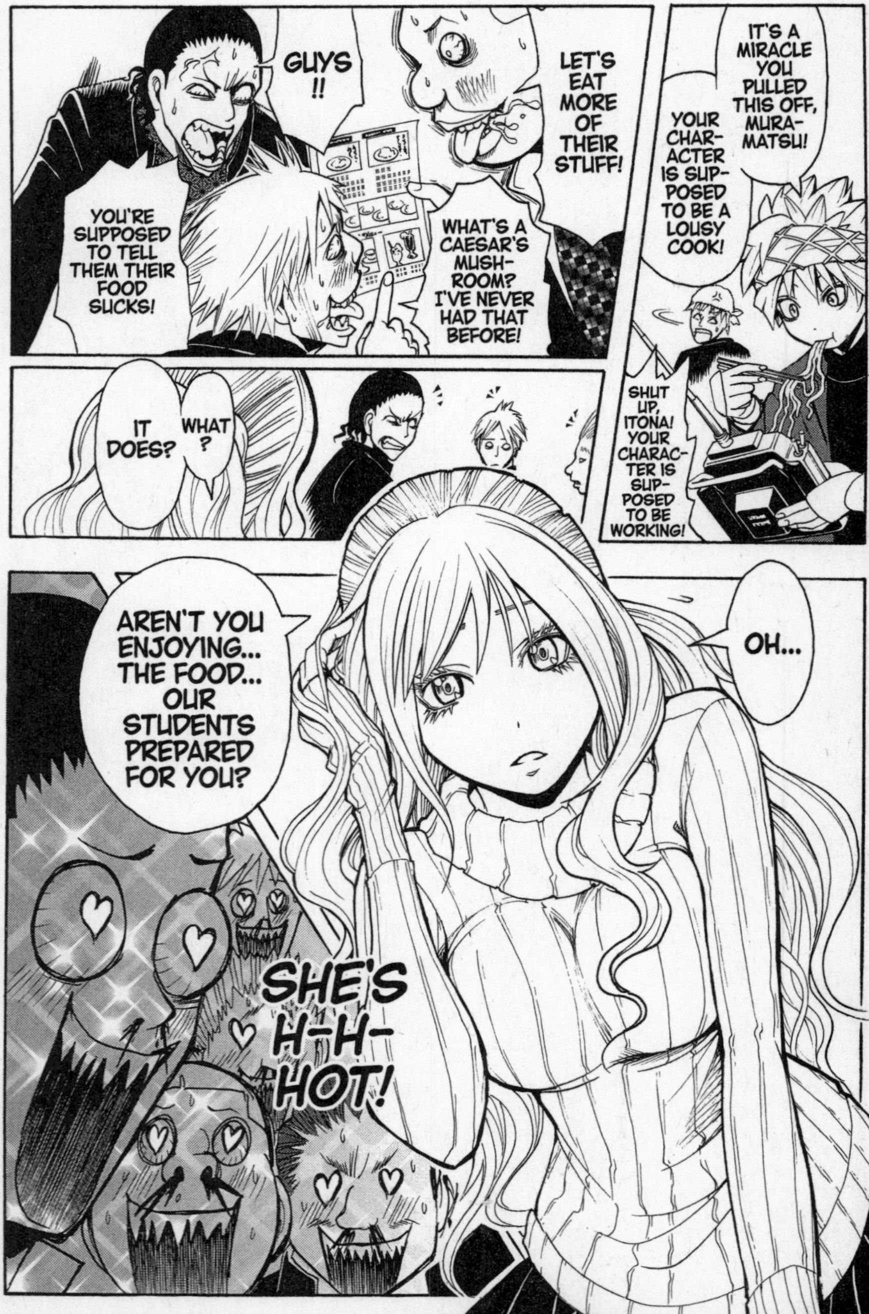
IT'S A MIRACLE YOU PULLED THIS OFF, MURAMATSU!
YOUR CHARACTER IS SUPPOSED TO BE A LOUSY COOK!
SHUT UP, ITONA! YOUR CHARACTER IS SUPPOSED TO BE WORKING!
LET'S EAT MORE OF THEIR STUFF!
GUYS !!
WHAT'S A CAESAR'S MUSHROOM? I'VE NEVER HAD THAT BEFORE!
YOU'RE SUPPOSED TO TELL THEM THEIR FOOD SUCKS!
WHAT ?
IT DOES?
OH...
AREN'T YOU ENJOYING... THE FOOD... OUR STUDENTS PREPARED FOR YOU?
SHE'S H-H-HOT!

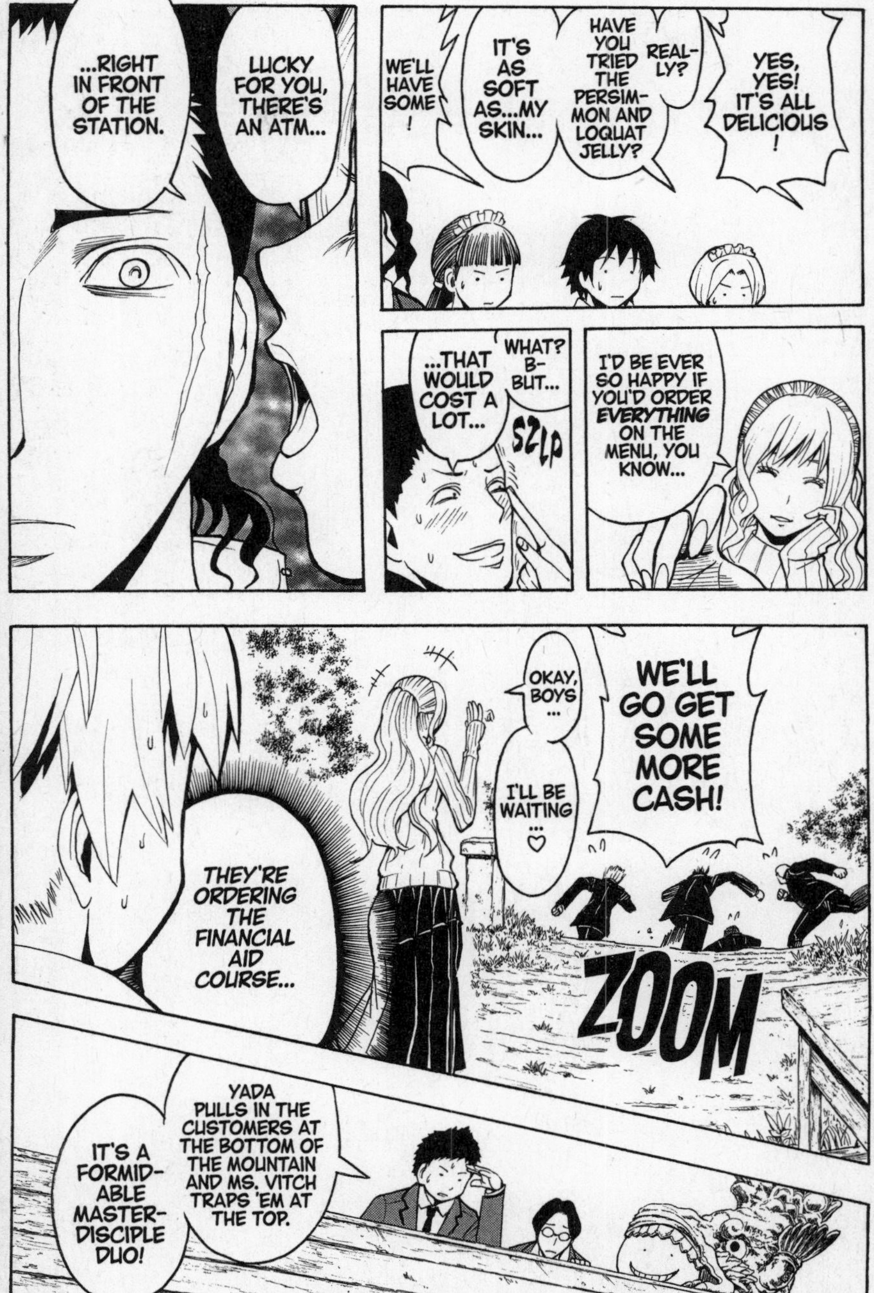
YES, YES! IT'S ALL DELICIOUS!
REALLY?
HAVE YOU TRIED THE PERSIMMON AND LOQUAT JELLY?
IT'S AS SOFT AS...MY SKIN...
WE'LL HAVE SOME!
I'D BE EVER SO HAPPY IF YOU'D ORDER *EVERYTHING* ON THE MENU, YOU KNOW...
WHAT? B-BUT...
...THAT WOULD COST A LOT...
SZLP
LUCKY FOR YOU, THERE'S AN ATM...
...RIGHT IN FRONT OF THE STATION.
WE'LL GO GET SOME MORE CASH!
OKAY, BOYS...
I'LL BE WAITING... ♡
ZOOM
THEY'RE ORDERING THE FINANCIAL AID COURSE...
YADA PULLS IN THE CUSTOMERS AT THE BOTTOM OF THE MOUNTAIN AND MS. VITCH TRAPS 'EM AT THE TOP.
IT'S A FORMIDABLE MASTER-DISCIPLE DUO!

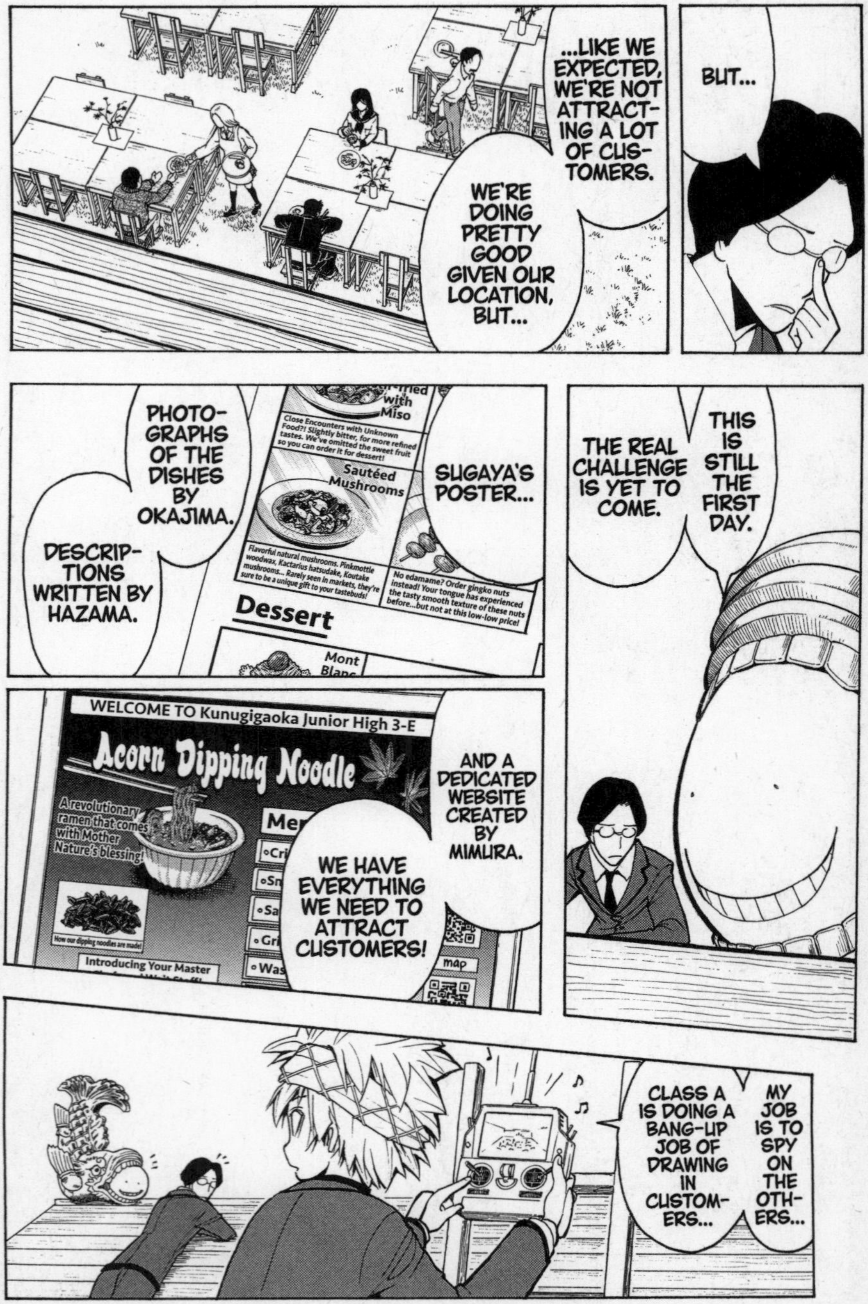
BUT...
...LIKE WE EXPECTED, WE'RE NOT ATTRACTING A LOT OF CUSTOMERS.
WE'RE DOING PRETTY GOOD GIVEN OUR LOCATION, BUT...
THIS IS STILL THE FIRST DAY.
THE REAL CHALLENGE IS YET TO COME.
SUGAYA'S POSTER...
PHOTOGRAPHS OF THE DISHES BY OKAJIMA.
DESCRIPTIONS WRITTEN BY HAZAMA.
Close Encounters with Unknown Food?! Slightly bitter, for more refined tastes. We've omitted the sweet fruit so you can order it for dessert!
Sautéed Mushrooms
Flavorful natural mushrooms. Pinkmottle woodwax, Kactarius hatsudake, Koutake mushrooms... Rarely seen in markets, they're sure to be a unique gift to your tastebuds!
No edamame? Order gingko nuts instead! Your tongue has experienced the tasty smooth texture of these nuts before...but not at this low-low price!
Dessert
WELCOME TO Kunugigaoka Junior High 3-E
Acorn Dipping Noodle
A revolutionary ramen that comes with Mother Nature's blessing!
How our dipping noodles are made!
map
AND A DEDICATED WEBSITE CREATED BY MIMURA.
WE HAVE EVERYTHING WE NEED TO ATTRACT CUSTOMERS!
MY JOB IS TO SPY ON THE OTHERS...
CLASS A IS DOING A BANG-UP JOB OF DRAWING IN CUSTOMERS...

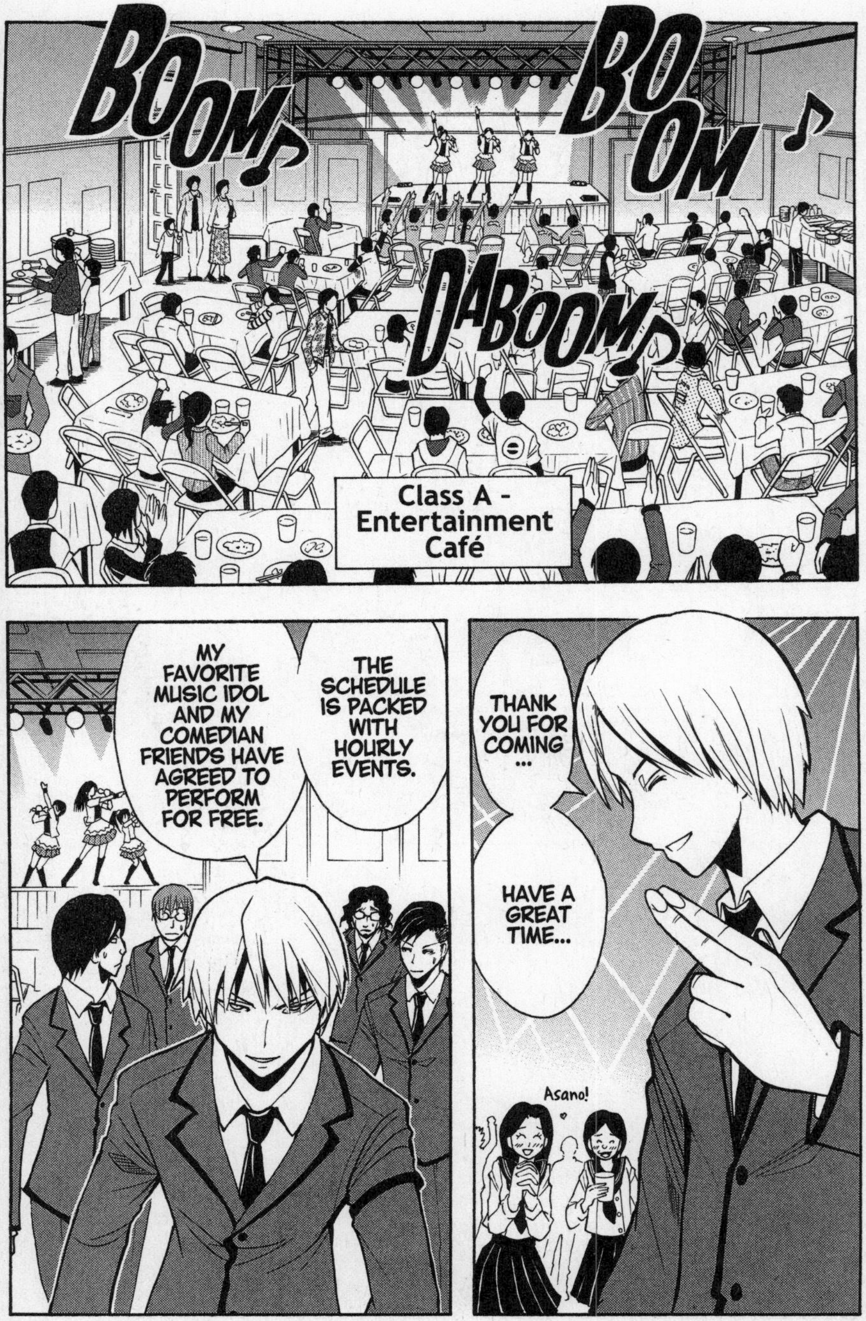
BOOM ♪
BOOM ♪
DABOOM ♪
Class A - Entertainment Café
THANK YOU FOR COMING...
HAVE A GREAT TIME...
Asano!
THE SCHEDULE IS PACKED WITH HOURLY EVENTS.
MY FAVORITE MUSIC IDOL AND MY COMEDIAN FRIENDS HAVE AGREED TO PERFORM FOR FREE.

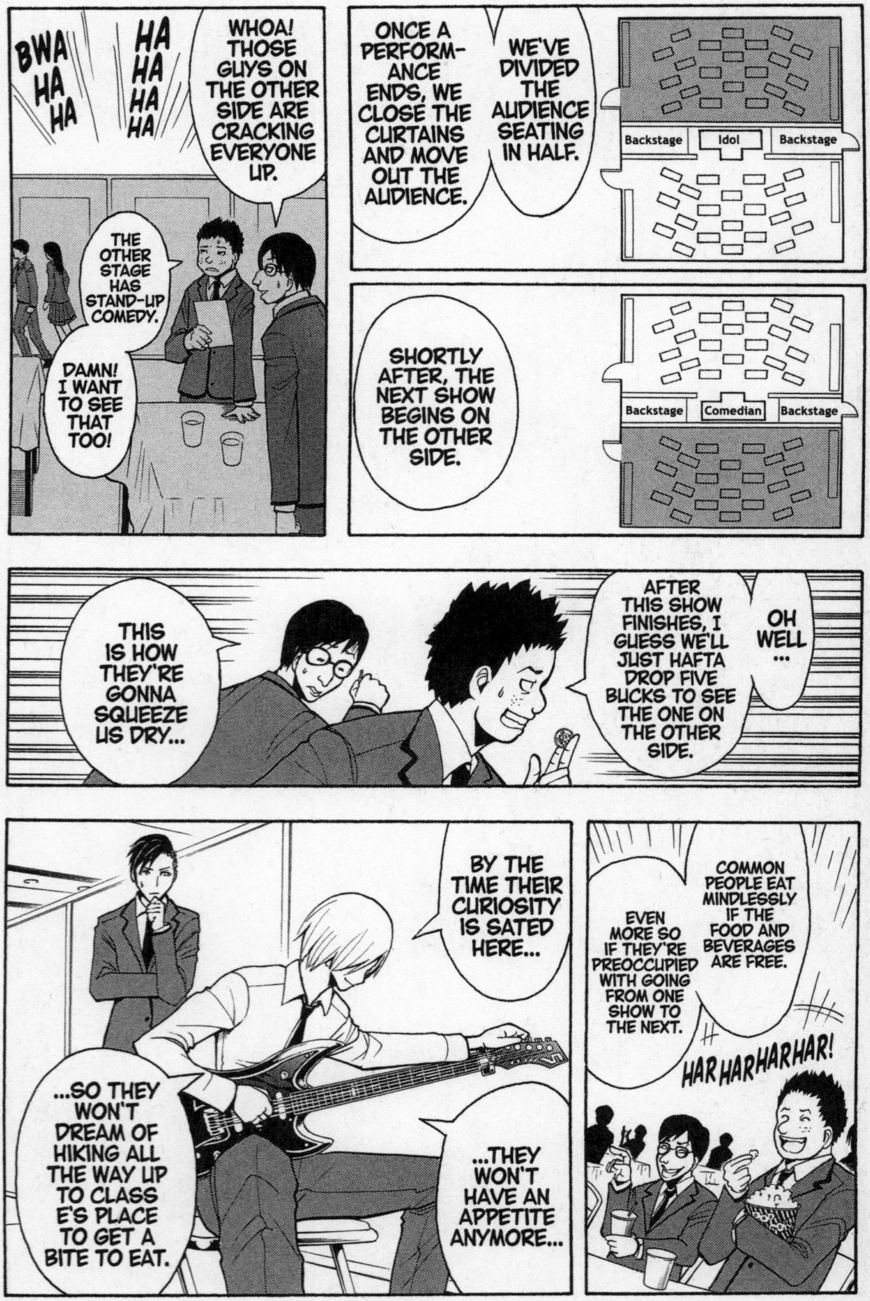
WE'VE DIVIDED THE AUDIENCE SEATING IN HALF.
ONCE A PERFORMANCE ENDS, WE CLOSE THE CURTAINS AND MOVE OUT THE AUDIENCE.
Backstage
Idol
Backstage
Backstage
Comedian
Backstage
SHORTLY AFTER, THE NEXT SHOW BEGINS ON THE OTHER SIDE.
WHOA! THOSE GUYS ON THE OTHER SIDE ARE CRACKING EVERYONE UP.
HA HA HA HA HA
BWA HA HA
THE OTHER STAGE HAS STAND-UP COMEDY.
DAMN! I WANT TO SEE THAT TOO!
OH WELL...
AFTER THIS SHOW FINISHES, I GUESS WE'LL JUST HAFTA DROP FIVE BUCKS TO SEE THE ONE ON THE OTHER SIDE.
THIS IS HOW THEY'RE GONNA SQUEEZE US DRY...
COMMON PEOPLE EAT MINDLESSLY IF THE FOOD AND BEVERAGES ARE FREE.
EVEN MORE SO IF THEY'RE PREOCCUPIED WITH GOING FROM ONE SHOW TO THE NEXT.
HAR HAR HAR HAR!
BY THE TIME THEIR CURIOSITY IS SATED HERE...
...THEY WON'T HAVE AN APPETITE ANYMORE...
...SO THEY WON'T DREAM OF HIKING ALL THE WAY UP TO CLASS E'S PLACE TO GET A BITE TO EAT.

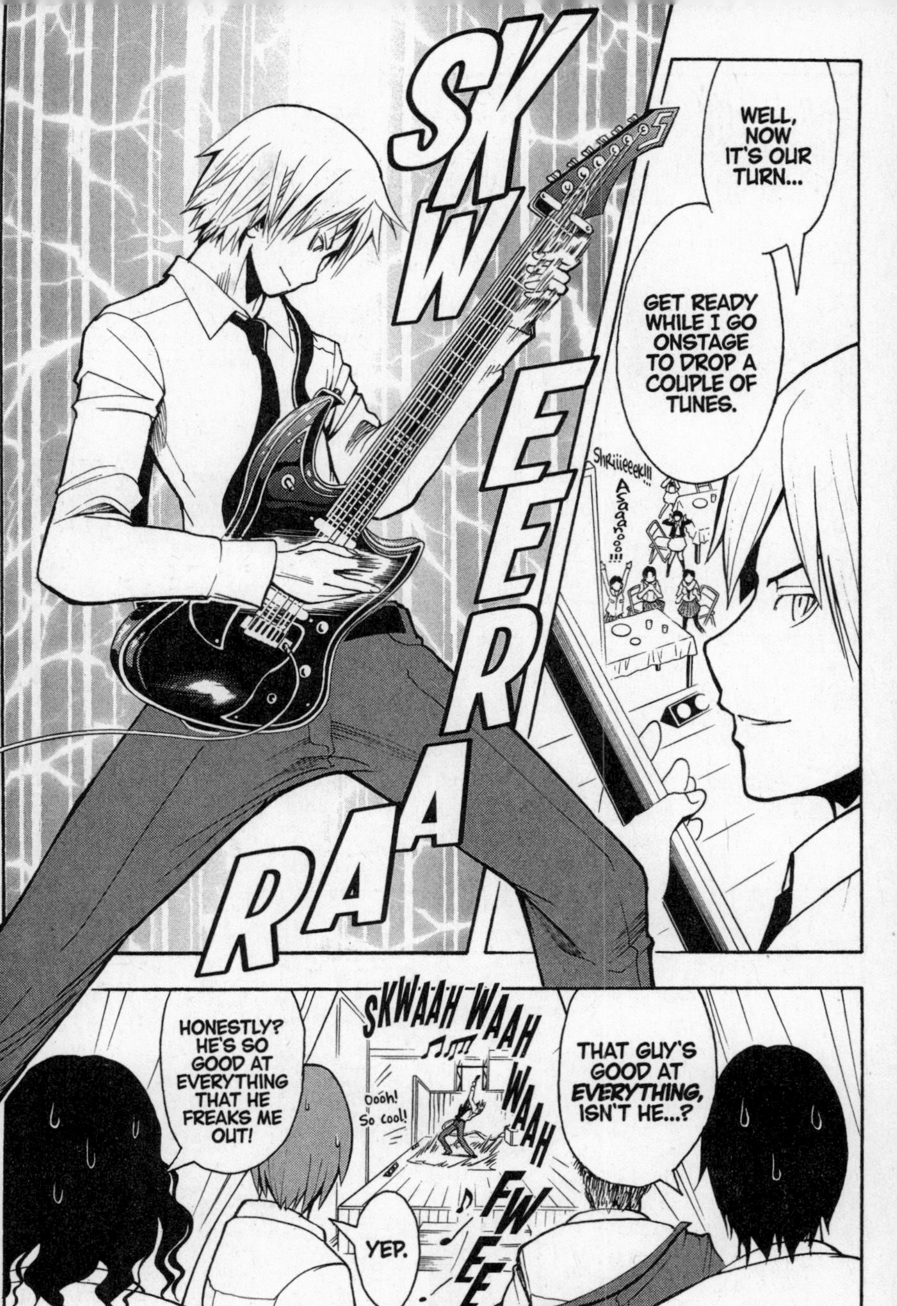
WELL, NOW IT'S OUR TURN...
GET READY WHILE I GO ONSTAGE TO DROP A COUPLE OF TUNES.
Shriiiieeek!!!
Asaaanooo!!!
SKWEERRAARAA
THAT GUY'S GOOD AT EVERYTHING, ISN'T HE...?
SKWAAH WAAH WAAH WAAH
Oooh! So cool!
HONESTLY? HE'S SO GOOD AT EVERYTHING THAT HE FREAKS ME OUT!
FWEEEE
YEP.

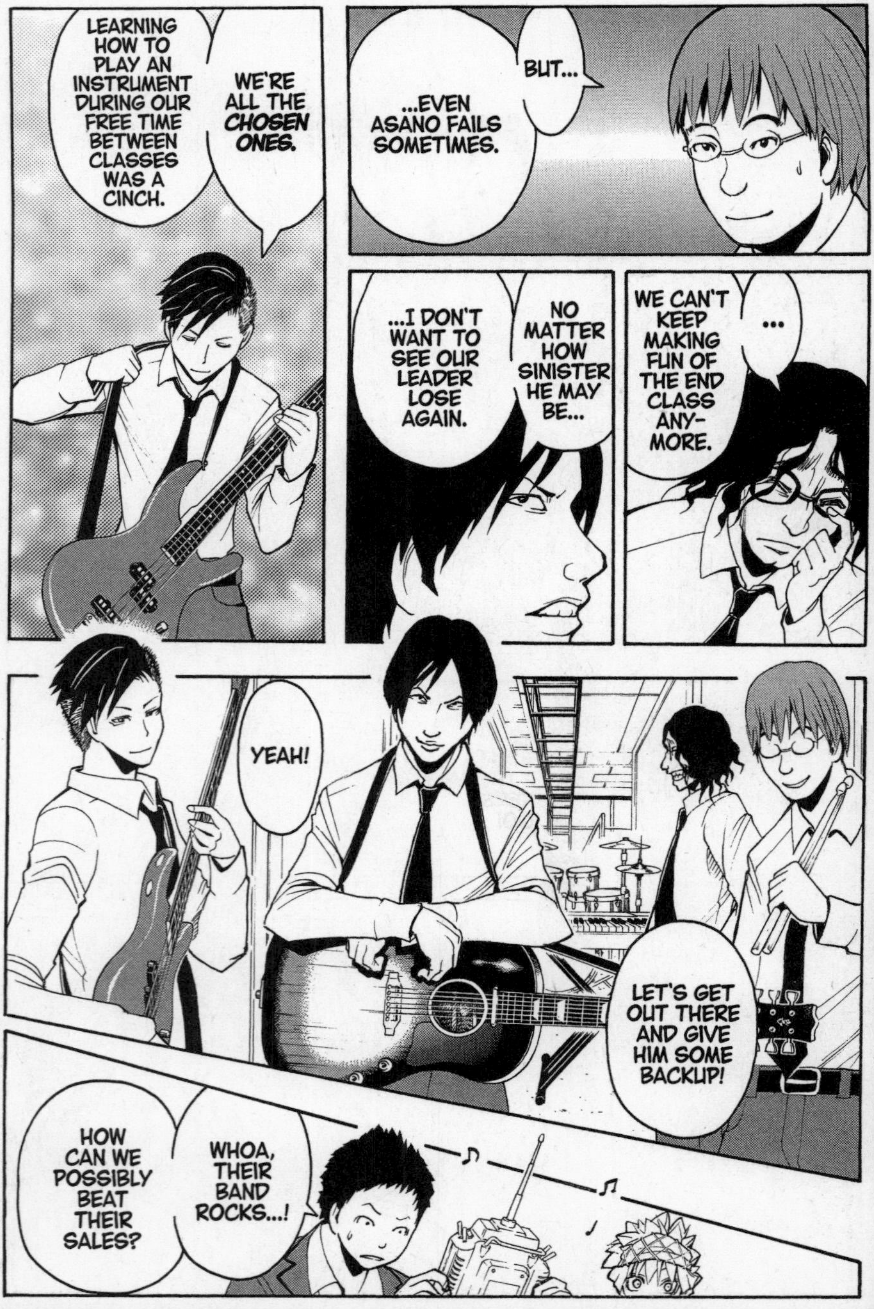
BUT...
...EVEN ASANO FAILS SOMETIMES.
...
WE CAN'T KEEP MAKING FUN OF THE END CLASS ANY-MORE.
NO MATTER HOW SINISTER HE MAY BE...
...I DON'T WANT TO SEE OUR LEADER LOSE AGAIN.
WE'RE ALL THE *CHOSEN ONES.*
LEARNING HOW TO PLAY AN INSTRUMENT DURING OUR FREE TIME BETWEEN CLASSES WAS A CINCH.
LET'S GET OUT THERE AND GIVE HIM SOME BACKUP!
YEAH!
WHOA, THEIR BAND ROCKS...!
HOW CAN WE POSSIBLY BEAT THEIR SALES?

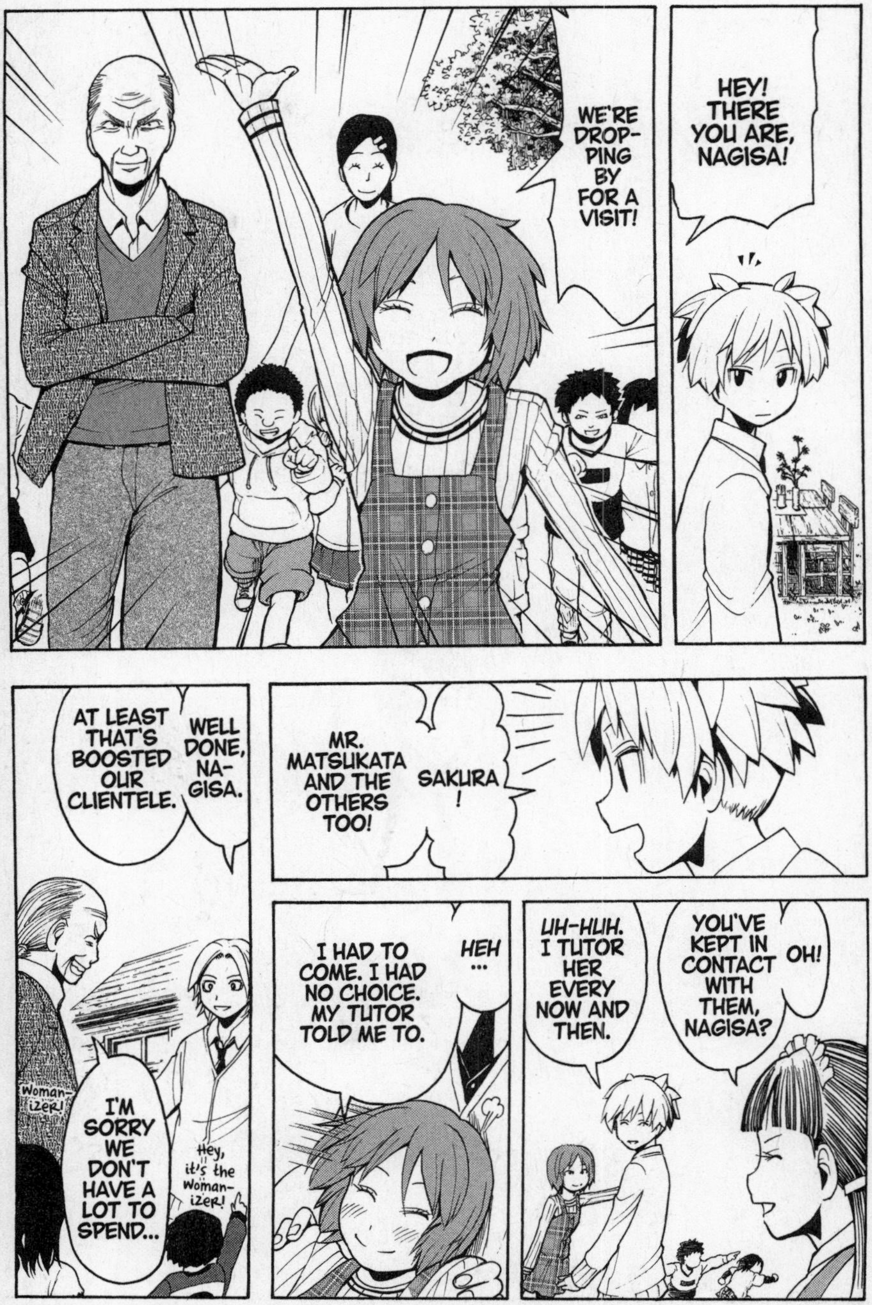
HEY! THERE YOU ARE, NAGISA!
WE'RE DROPPING BY FOR A VISIT!
SAKURA!
MR. MATSUKATA AND THE OTHERS TOO!
WELL DONE, NAGISA.
AT LEAST THAT'S BOOSTED OUR CLIENTELE.
OH!
YOU'VE KEPT IN CONTACT WITH THEM, NAGISA?
UH-HUH. I TUTOR HER EVERY NOW AND THEN.
HEH...
I HAD TO COME. I HAD NO CHOICE. MY TUTOR TOLD ME TO.
Hey, it's the Womanizer!
Womanizer!
I'M SORRY WE DON'T HAVE A LOT TO SPEND...

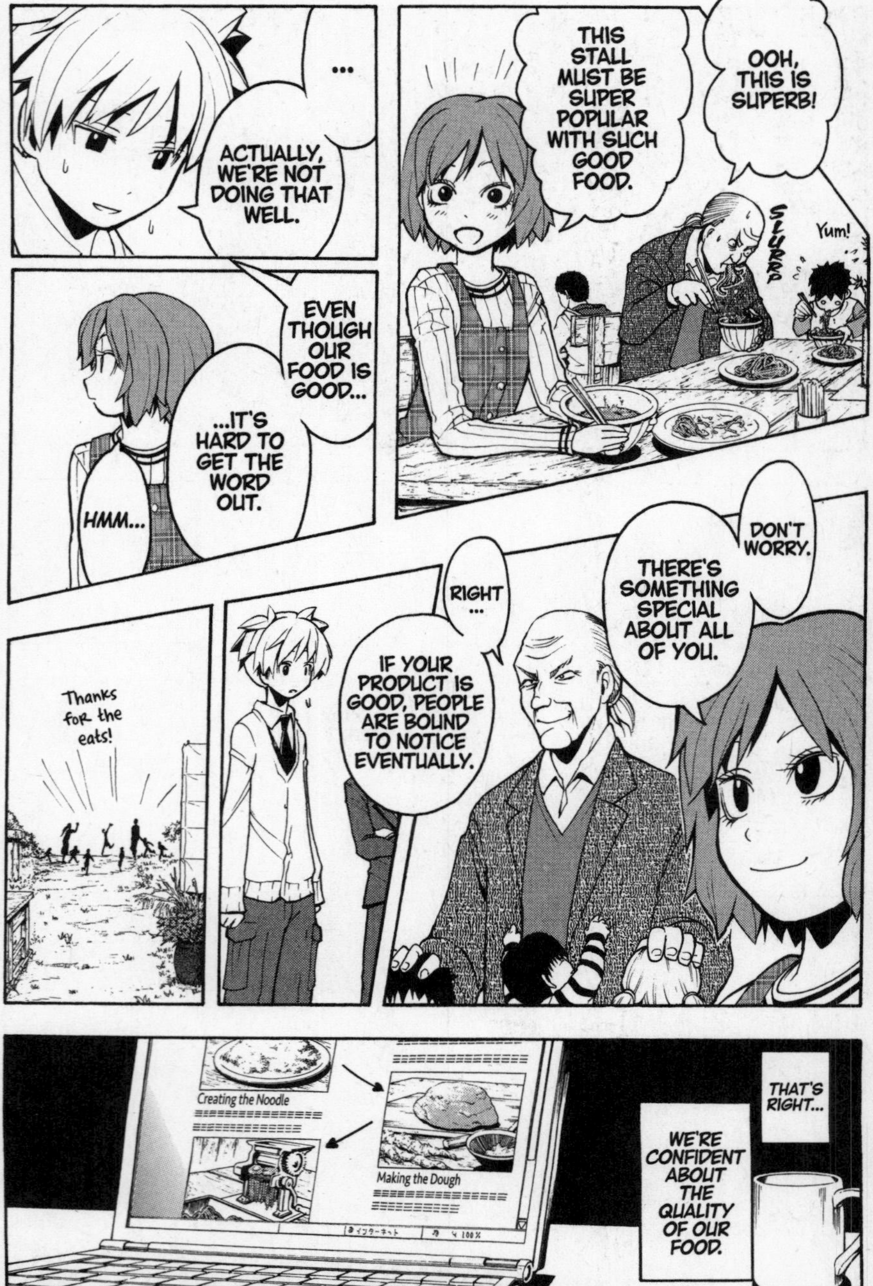
OOH, THIS IS SUPERB!
THIS STALL MUST BE SUPER POPULAR WITH SUCH GOOD FOOD.
SLURRP
Yum!
...
ACTUALLY, WE'RE NOT DOING THAT WELL.
EVEN THOUGH OUR FOOD IS GOOD...
...IT'S HARD TO GET THE WORD OUT.
HMM...
DON'T WORRY.
THERE'S SOMETHING SPECIAL ABOUT ALL OF YOU.
IF YOUR PRODUCT IS GOOD, PEOPLE ARE BOUND TO NOTICE EVENTUALLY.
RIGHT...
Thanks for the eats!
THAT'S RIGHT...
WE'RE CONFIDENT ABOUT THE QUALITY OF OUR FOOD.
Creating the Noodle
Making the Dough

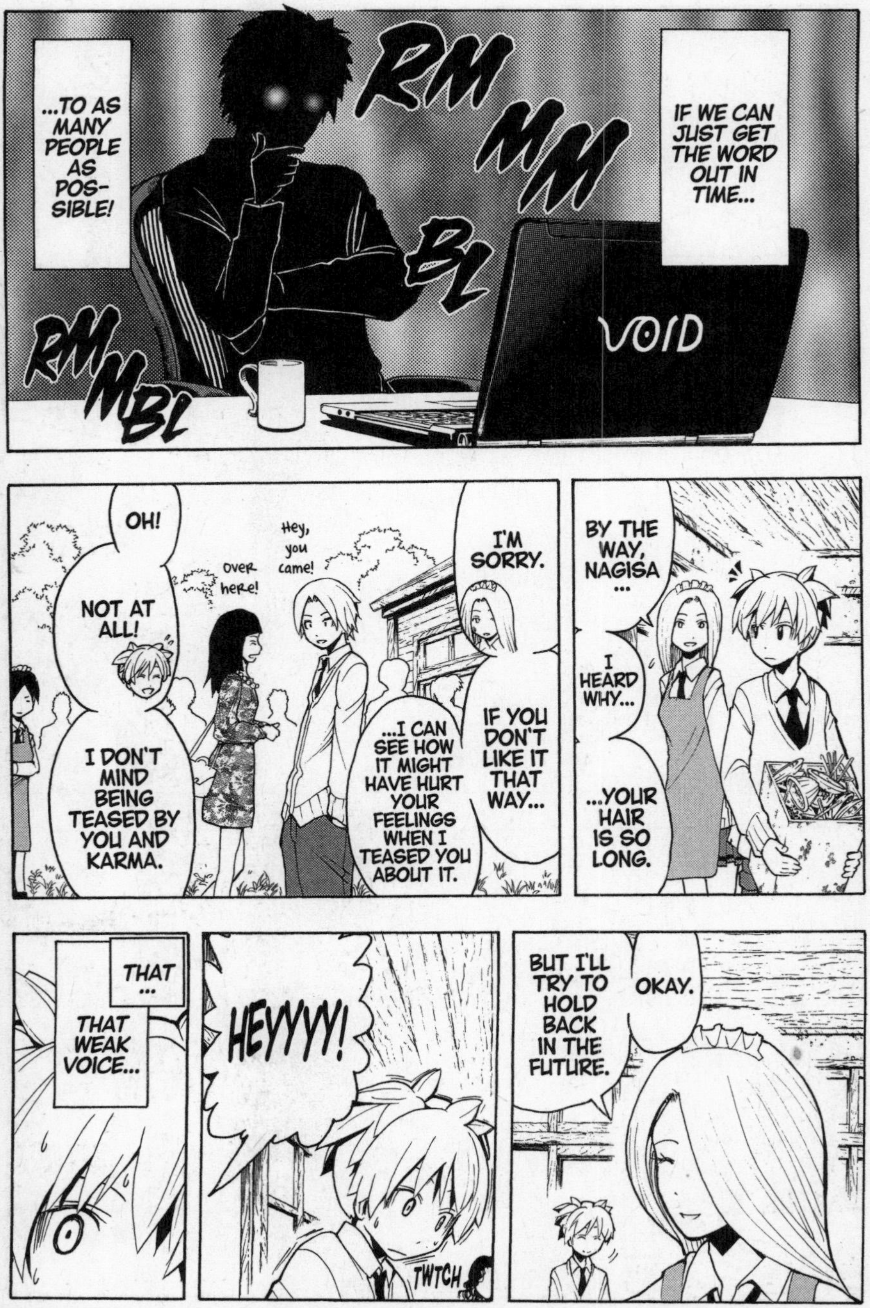
IF WE CAN JUST GET THE WORD OUT IN TIME...
RMMMM
BL
...TO AS MANY PEOPLE AS POS-SIBLE!
RMMMBL
VOID
BY THE WAY, NAGISA...
I HEARD WHY...
...YOUR HAIR IS SO LONG.
I'M SORRY.
IF YOU DON'T LIKE IT THAT WAY...
...I CAN SEE HOW IT MIGHT HAVE HURT YOUR FEELINGS WHEN I TEASED YOU ABOUT IT.
Hey, you came!
Over here!
OH!
NOT AT ALL!
I DON'T MIND BEING TEASED BY YOU AND KARMA.
OKAY.
BUT I'LL TRY TO HOLD BACK IN THE FUTURE.
HEYYYY!
TWTCH
THAT...
THAT WEAK VOICE...

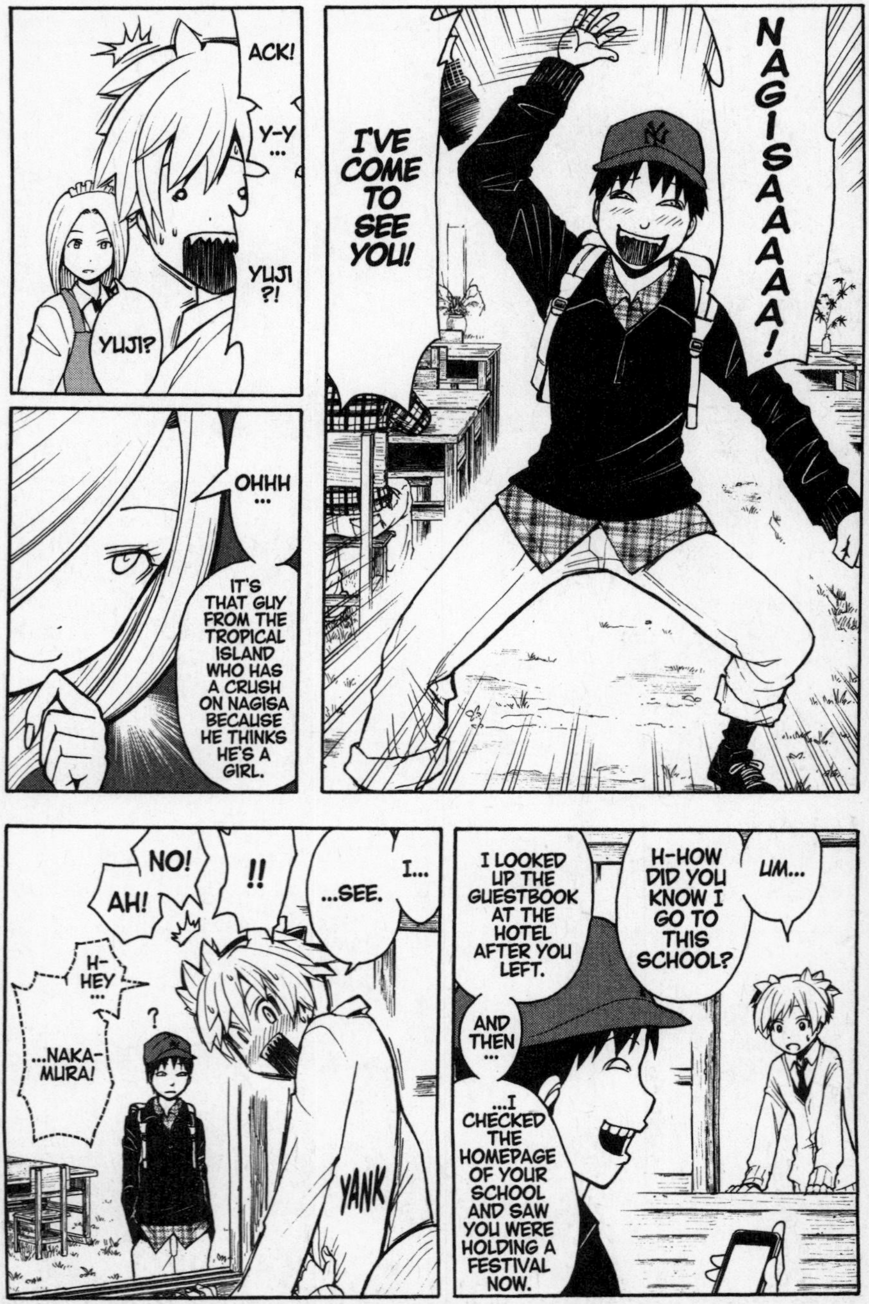
NAGISAAAAAA!
I'VE COME TO SEE YOU!
ACK!
Y-Y...
YUJI?!
YUJI?
OHHH...
IT'S THAT GUY FROM THE TROPICAL ISLAND WHO HAS A CRUSH ON NAGISA BECAUSE HE THINKS HE'S A GIRL.
UM...
H-HOW DID YOU KNOW I GO TO THIS SCHOOL?
I LOOKED UP THE GUESTBOOK AT THE HOTEL AFTER YOU LEFT.
AND THEN...
...I CHECKED THE HOMEPAGE OF YOUR SCHOOL AND SAW YOU WERE HOLDING A FESTIVAL NOW.
I...
...SEE.
!!
NO!
AH!
H-HEY...
...NAKAMURA!
?
YANK

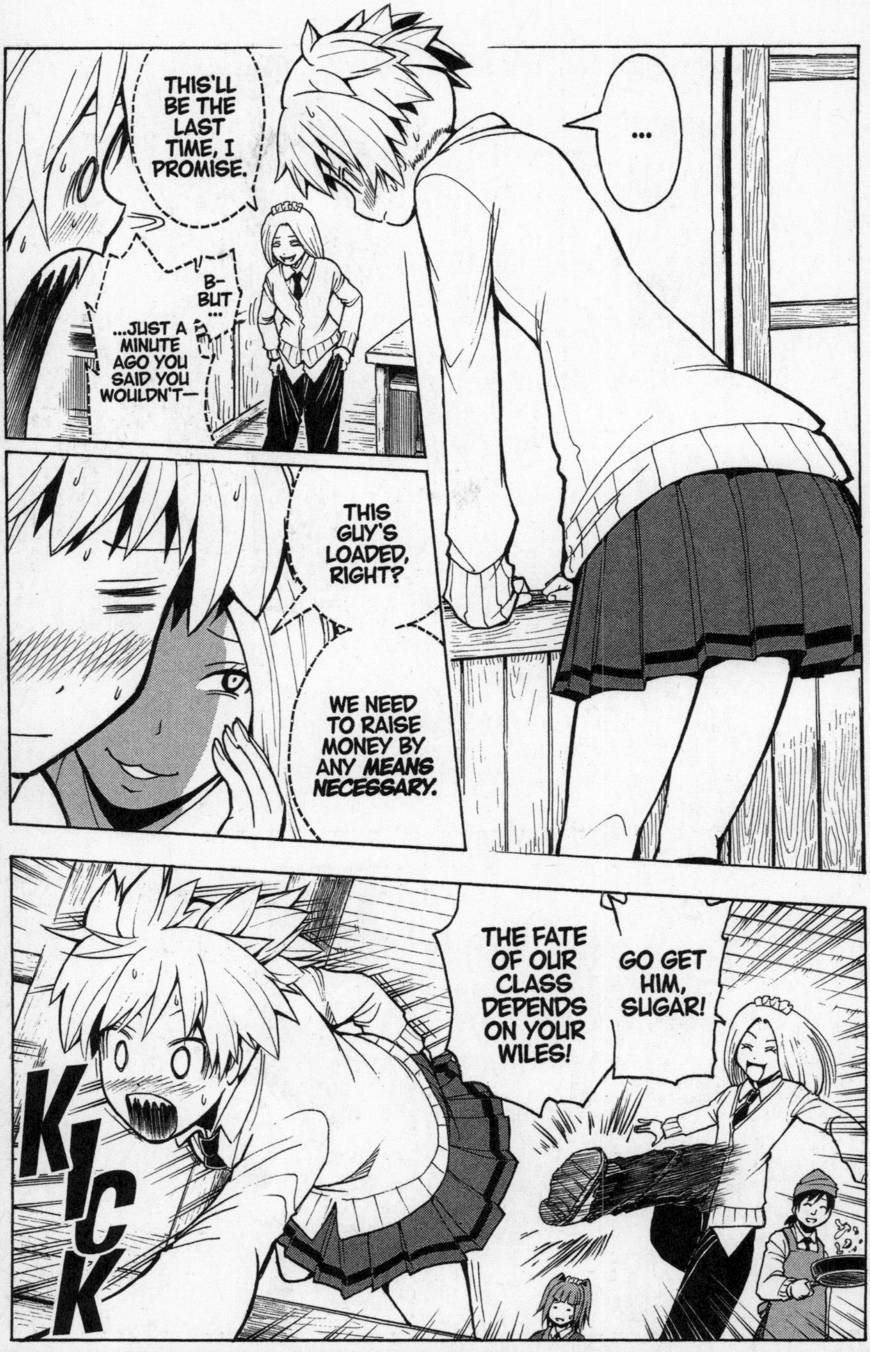
...
THIS'LL BE THE LAST TIME, I PROMISE.
B-BUT...
...JUST A MINUTE AGO YOU SAID YOU WOULDN'T—
THIS GUY'S LOADED, RIGHT?
WE NEED TO RAISE MONEY BY ANY *MEANS NECESSARY.*
GO GET HIM, SUGAR!
THE FATE OF OUR CLASS DEPENDS ON YOUR WILES!
KICK

The Wakaba Park children's nicknames for Class E students

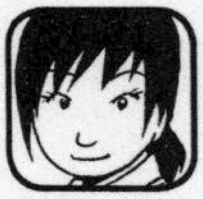
Sumire Hara: Mommy

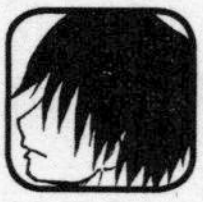
Ryunosuke Chiba: Mr. Carpenter

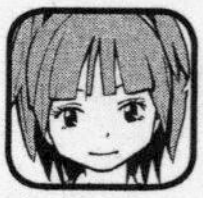
Kaede Kayano: Princess

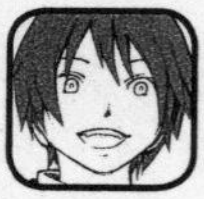
Karma Akabane: Knight

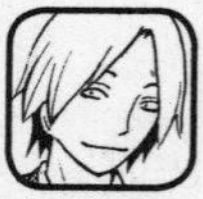
Sosuke Sugaya: Picasso

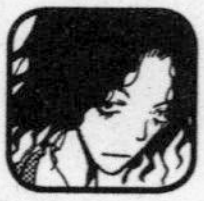
Kirara Hazama: Witch

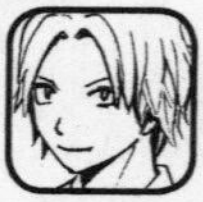
Hiroto Maehara: Womanizer

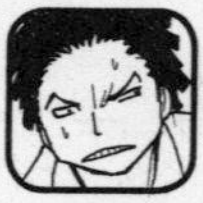
Taisei Yoshida: Black Noodles

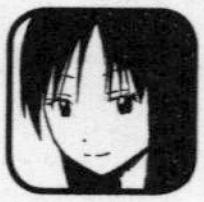
Yukiko Kanzaki: Wife

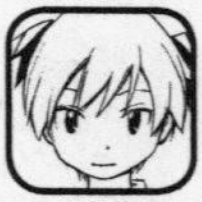
Nagisa Shiota: Sakura's Wife

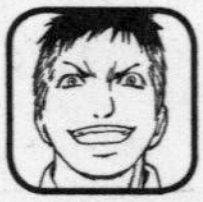
Ryoma Terasaka: Big G and Gorilla

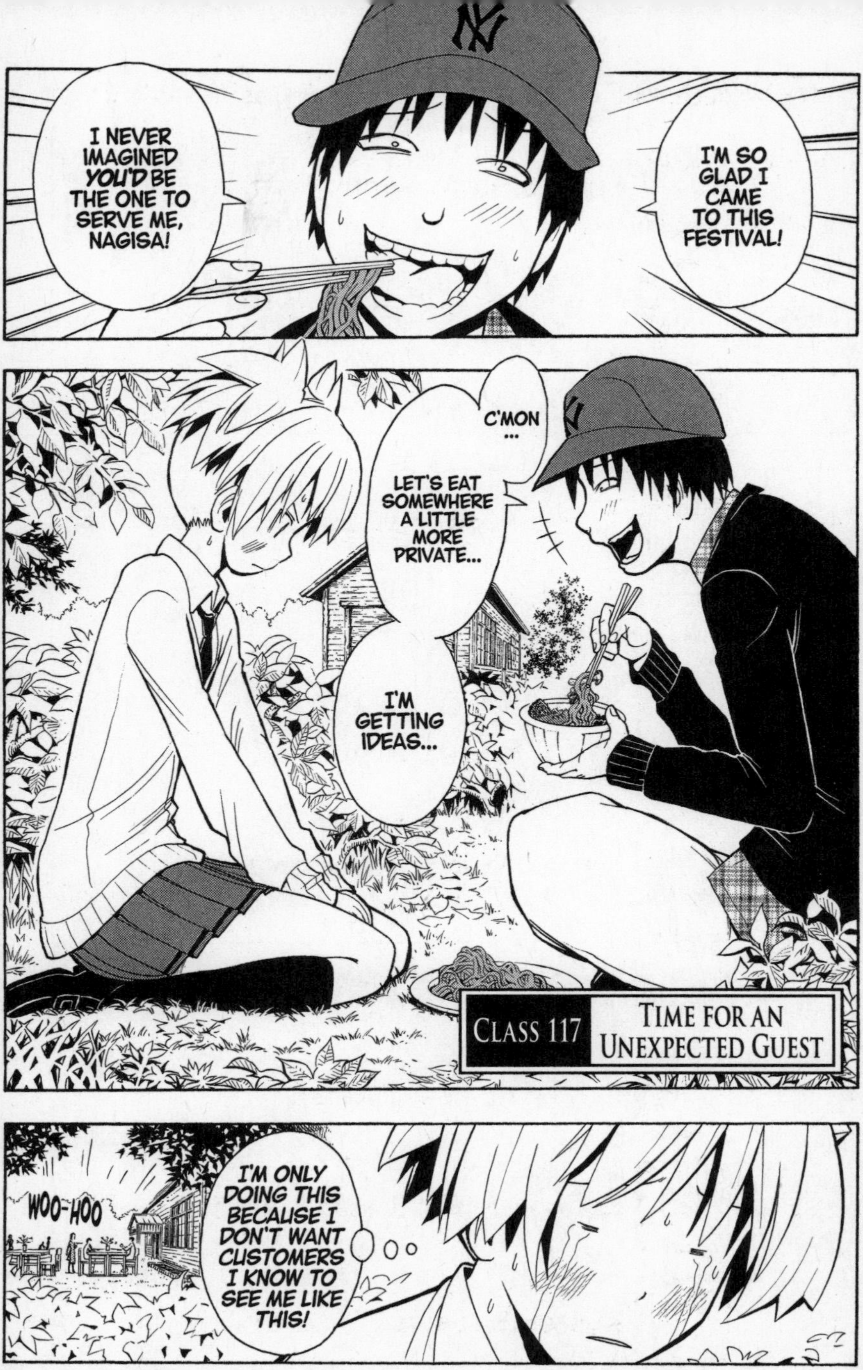
I'M SO GLAD I CAME TO THIS FESTIVAL!
I NEVER IMAGINED *YOU'D* BE THE ONE TO SERVE ME, NAGISA!
C'MON ...
LET'S EAT SOMEWHERE A LITTLE MORE PRIVATE...
I'M GETTING IDEAS...
CLASS 117
TIME FOR AN UNEXPECTED GUEST
I'M ONLY DOING THIS BECAUSE I DON'T WANT CUSTOMERS I KNOW TO SEE ME LIKE THIS!
WOO-HOO

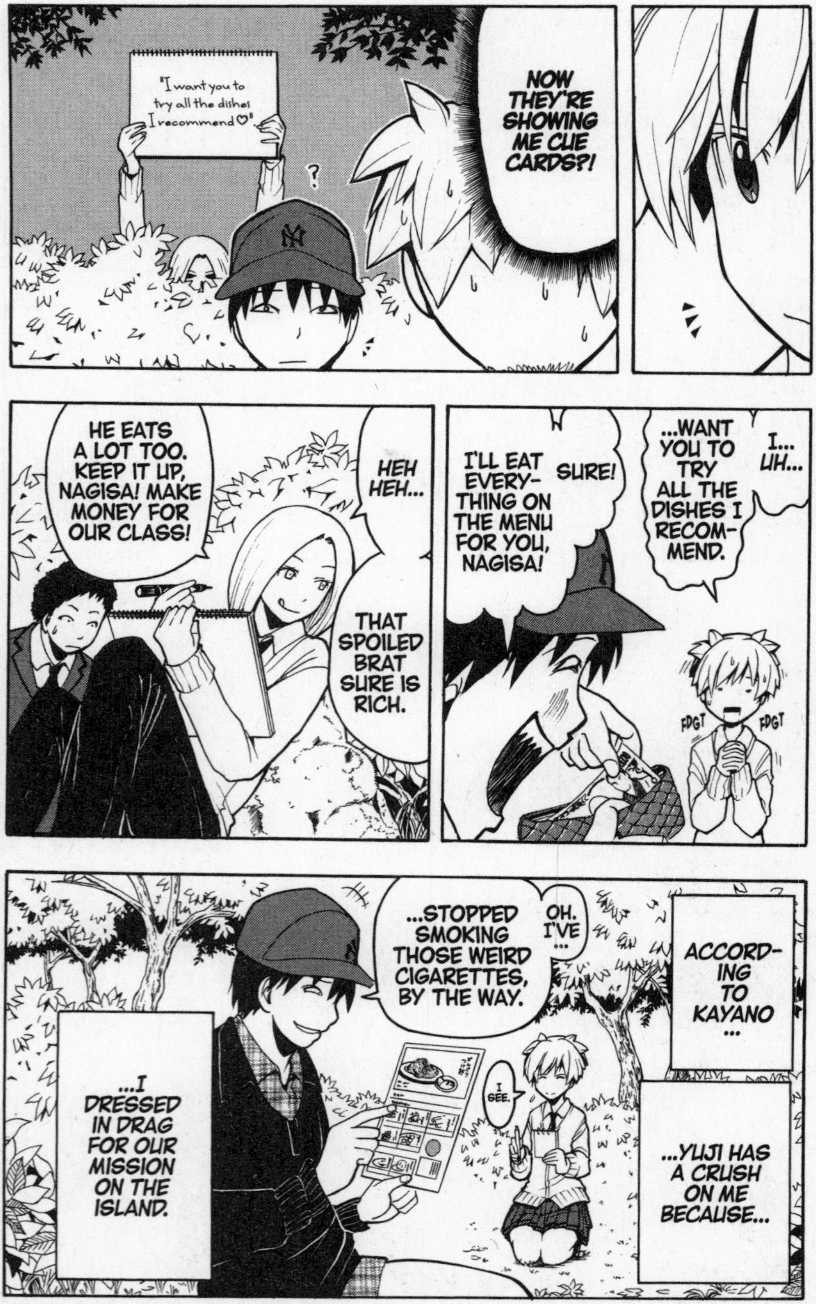
NOW THEY'RE SHOWING ME CUE CARDS?!
"I want you to try all the dishes I recommend♡".
?
I... UH...
...WANT YOU TO TRY ALL THE DISHES I RECOMMEND.
SURE!
I'LL EAT EVERY-THING ON THE MENU FOR YOU, NAGISA!
FDGT
FDGT
HEH HEH...
HE EATS A LOT TOO. KEEP IT UP, NAGISA! MAKE MONEY FOR OUR CLASS!
THAT SPOILED BRAT SURE IS RICH.
ACCORD-ING TO KAYANO...
OH. I'VE...
...STOPPED SMOKING THOSE WEIRD CIGARETTES, BY THE WAY.
...YUJI HAS A CRUSH ON ME BECAUSE...
I SEE.
...I DRESSED IN DRAG FOR OUR MISSION ON THE ISLAND.

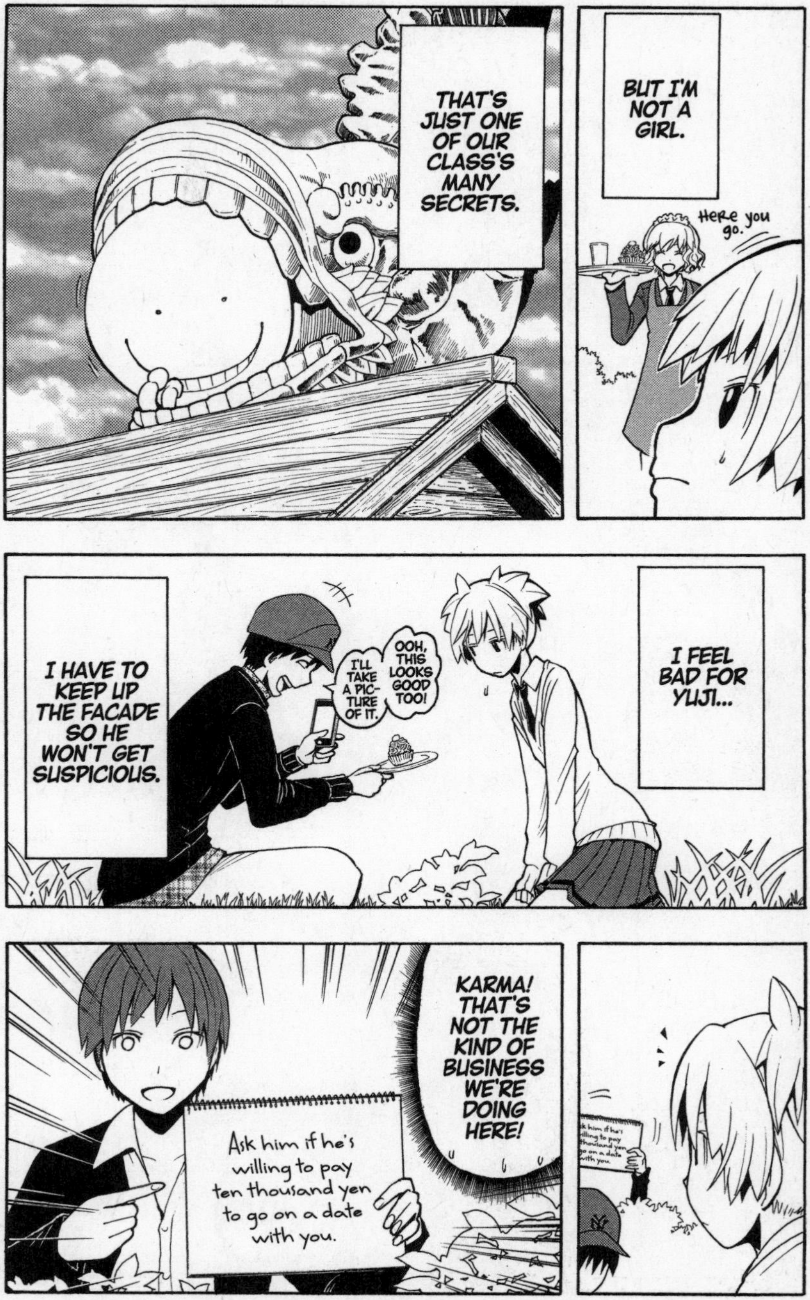
BUT I'M NOT A GIRL.
Here you go.
THAT'S JUST ONE OF OUR CLASS'S MANY SECRETS.
I FEEL BAD FOR YUJI...
OOH, THIS LOOKS GOOD TOO!
I'LL TAKE A PIC-TURE OF IT.
I HAVE TO KEEP UP THE FACADE SO HE WON'T GET SUSPICIOUS.
KARMA! THAT'S NOT THE KIND OF BUSINESS WE'RE DOING HERE!
Ask him if he's willing to pay ten thousand yen to go on a date with you.

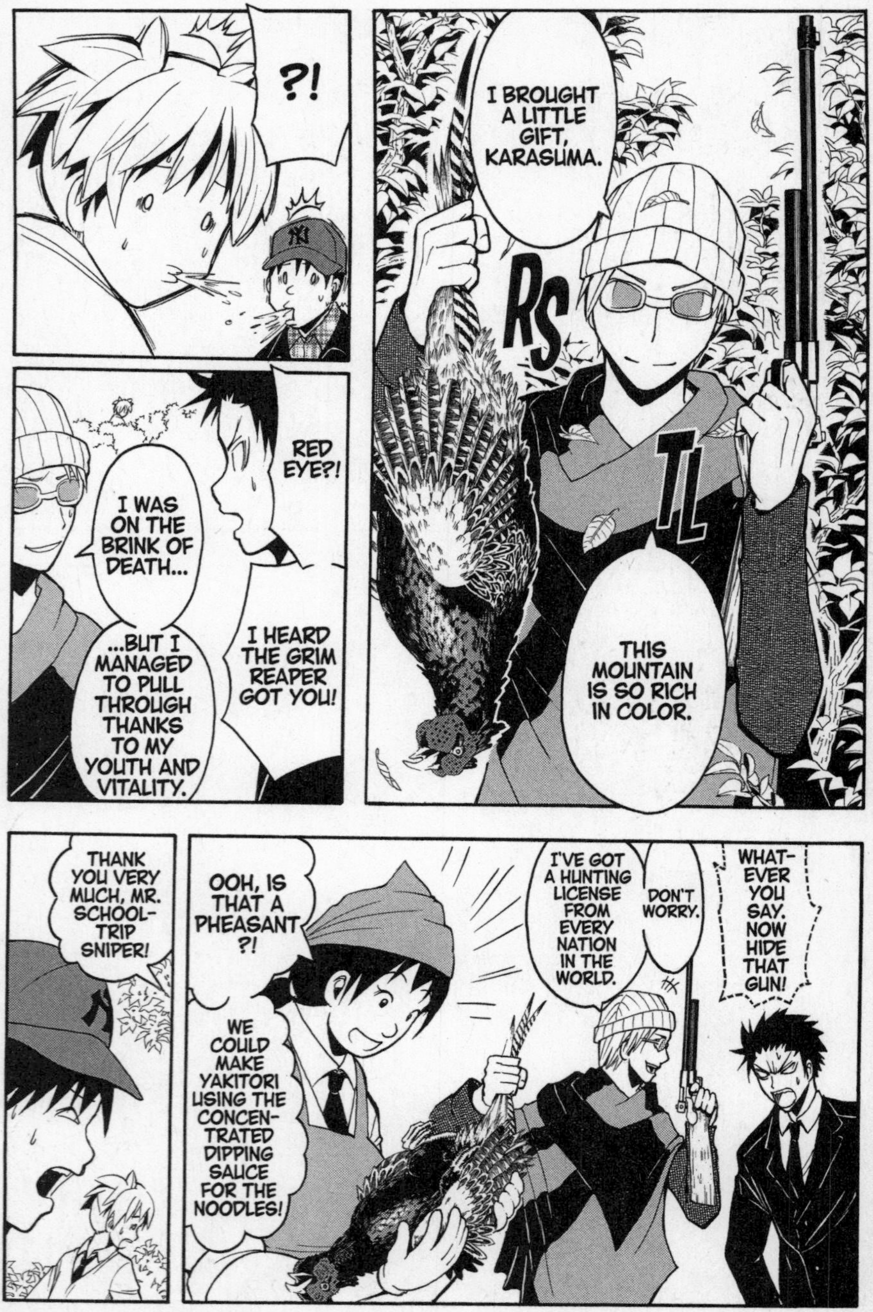
I BROUGHT A LITTLE GIFT, KARASUMA.
RS
TL
THIS MOUNTAIN IS SO RICH IN COLOR.
?!
RED EYE?!
I WAS ON THE BRINK OF DEATH...
I HEARD THE GRIM REAPER GOT YOU!
...BUT I MANAGED TO PULL THROUGH THANKS TO MY YOUTH AND VITALITY.
WHAT-EVER YOU SAY. NOW HIDE THAT GUN!
DON'T WORRY.
I'VE GOT A HUNTING LICENSE FROM EVERY NATION IN THE WORLD.
OOH, IS THAT A PHEASANT?!
WE COULD MAKE YAKITORI USING THE CONCEN-TRATED DIPPING SAUCE FOR THE NOODLES!
THANK YOU VERY MUCH, MR. SCHOOL-TRIP SNIPER!

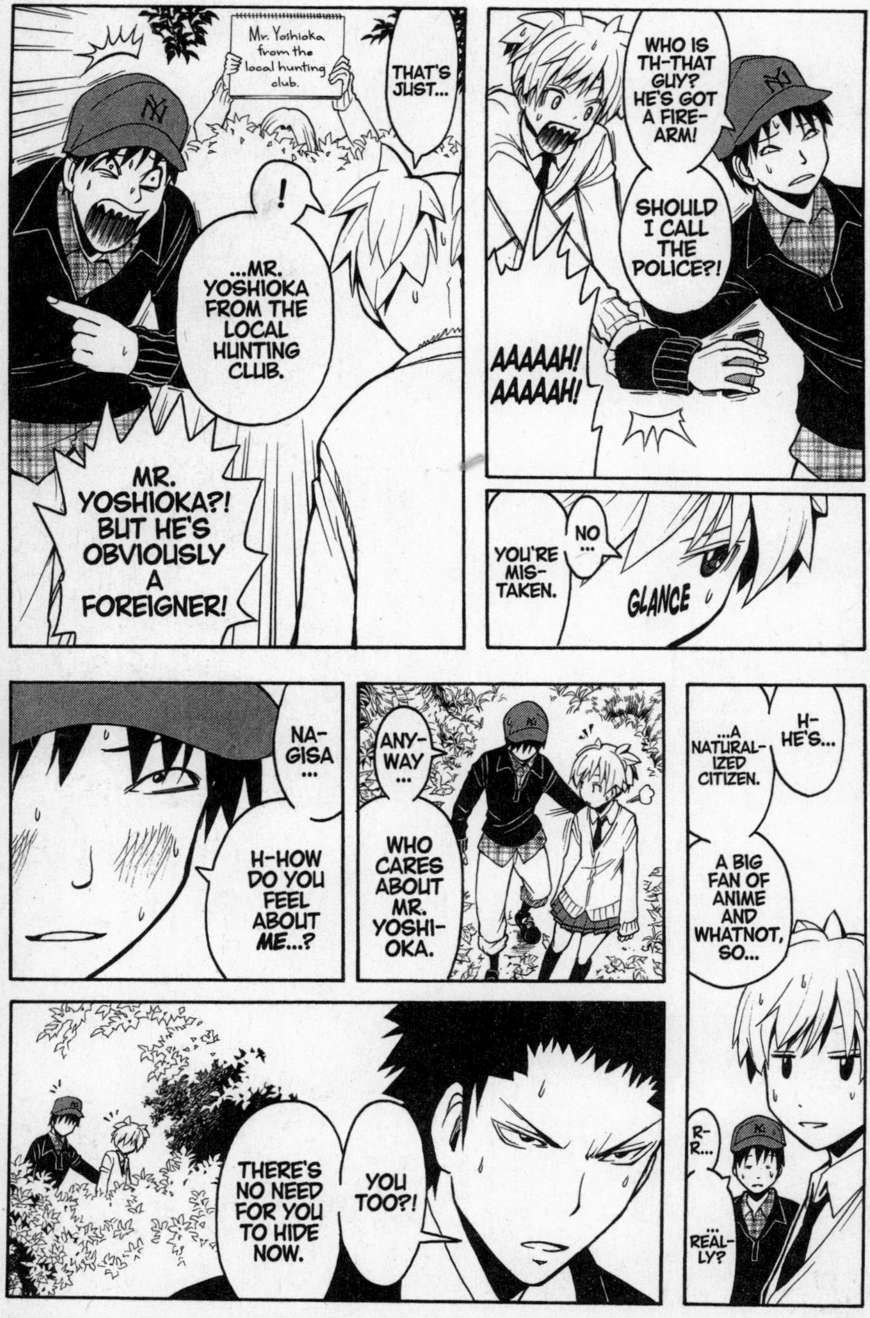
WHO IS TH-THAT GUY? HE'S GOT A FIRE-ARM!
SHOULD I CALL THE POLICE?!
AAAAAH! AAAAAH!
NO...
YOU'RE MIS-TAKEN.
GLANCE
THAT'S JUST...
Mr. Yoshioka from the local hunting club.
!
...MR. YOSHIOKA FROM THE LOCAL HUNTING CLUB.
MR. YOSHIOKA?! BUT HE'S OBVIOUSLY A FOREIGNER!
H-HE'S...
...A NATURAL-IZED CITIZEN.
A BIG FAN OF ANIME AND WHATNOT, SO...
R-R...
...REAL-LY?
ANY-WAY...
WHO CARES ABOUT MR. YOSHI-OKA.
NA-GISA...
H-HOW DO YOU FEEL ABOUT ME...?
YOU TOO?!
THERE'S NO NEED FOR YOU TO HIDE NOW.

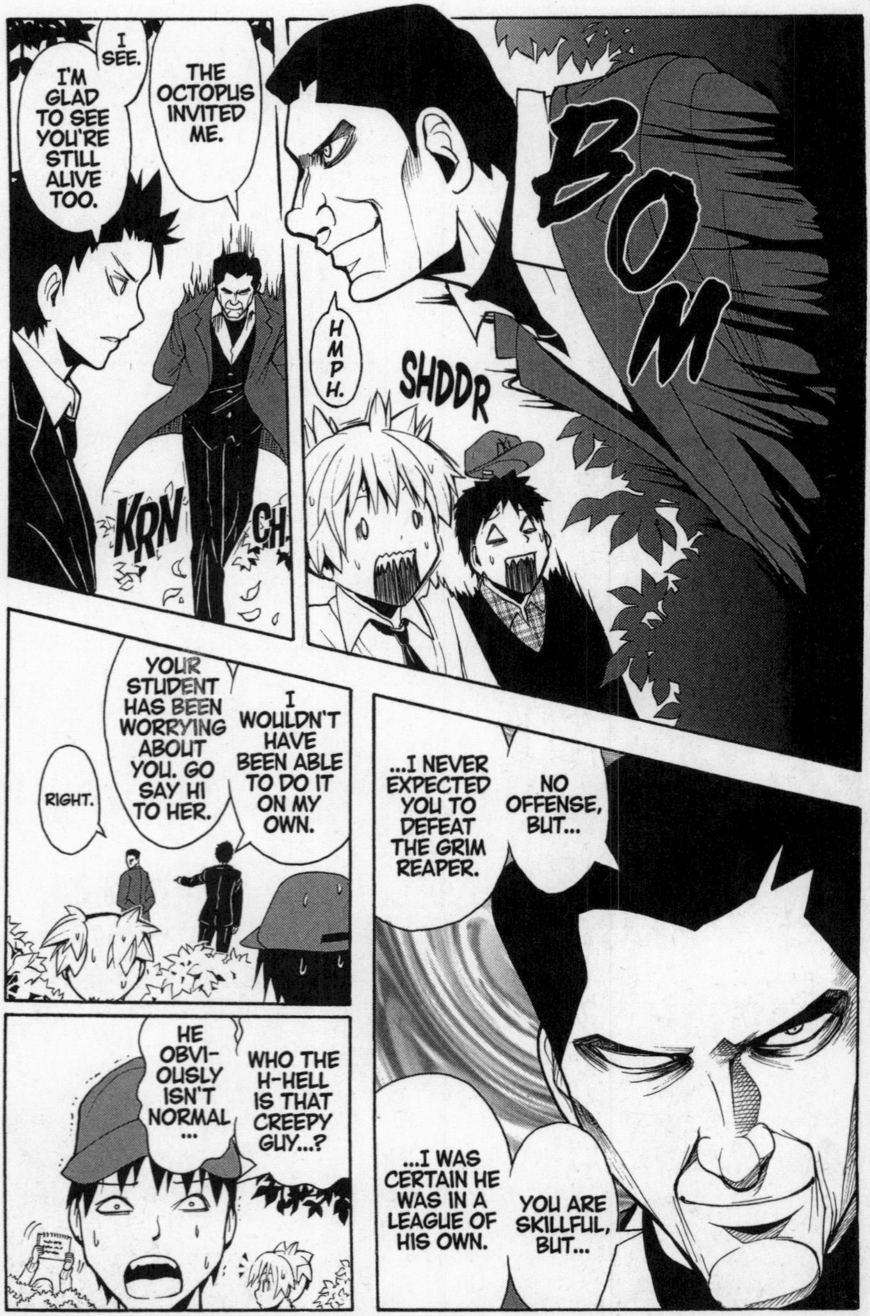
BOM
HMPH.
SHDDR
THE OCTOPUS INVITED ME.
I SEE.
I'M GLAD TO SEE YOU'RE STILL ALIVE TOO.
KRNCH
NO OFFENSE, BUT...
...I NEVER EXPECTED YOU TO DEFEAT THE GRIM REAPER.
YOU ARE SKILLFUL, BUT...
...I WAS CERTAIN HE WAS IN A LEAGUE OF HIS OWN.
I WOULDN'T HAVE BEEN ABLE TO DO IT ON MY OWN.
YOUR STUDENT HAS BEEN WORRYING ABOUT YOU. GO SAY HI TO HER.
RIGHT.
WHO THE H-HELL IS THAT CREEPY GUY...?
HE OBVIOUSLY ISN'T NORMAL...

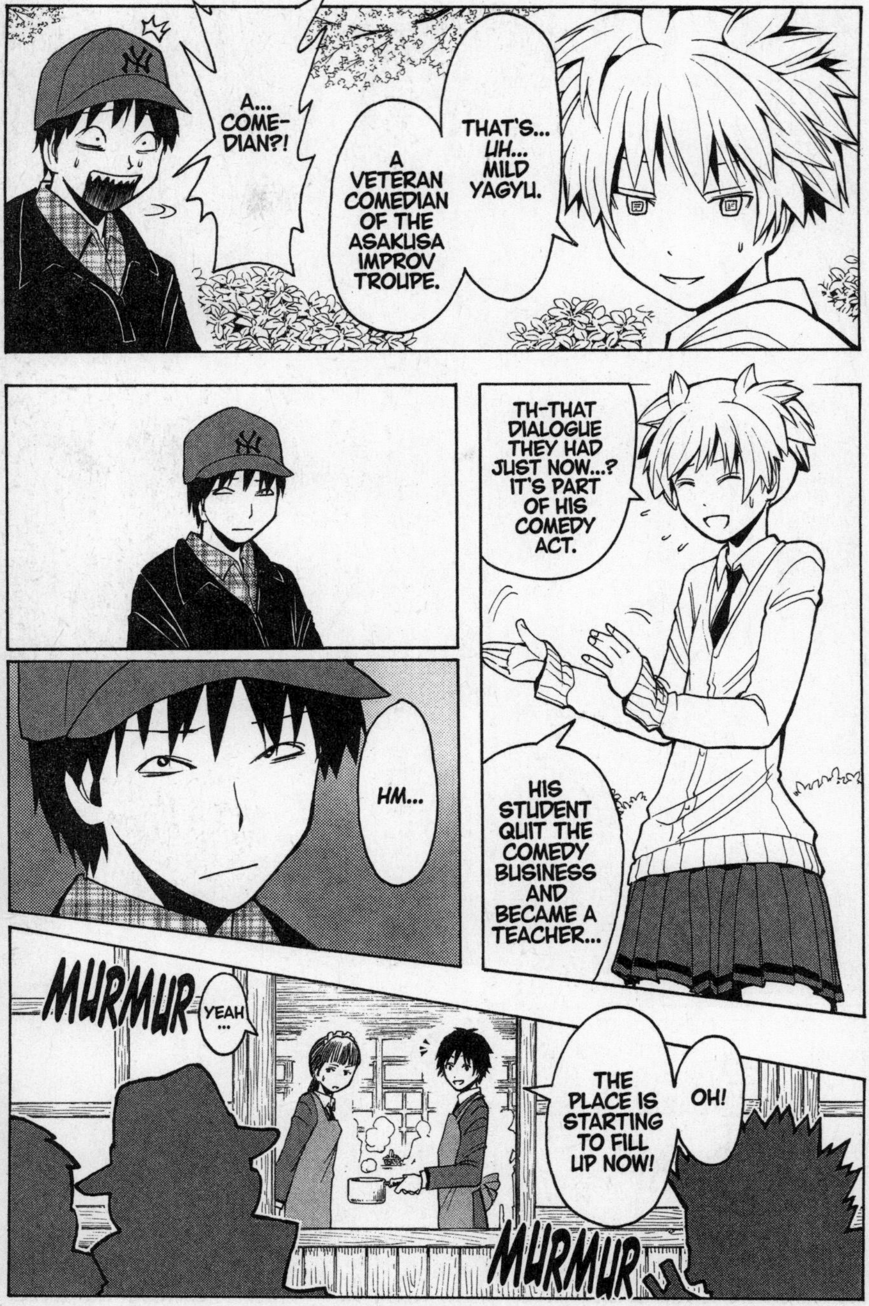
THAT'S... UH... MILD YAGYU.
A VETERAN COMEDIAN OF THE ASAKUSA IMPROV TROUPE.
A... COME-DIAN?!
TH-THAT DIALOGUE THEY HAD JUST NOW...? IT'S PART OF HIS COMEDY ACT.
HIS STUDENT QUIT THE COMEDY BUSINESS AND BECAME A TEACHER...
HM...
OH!
THE PLACE IS STARTING TO FILL UP NOW!
YEAH...
MURMUR
MURMUR

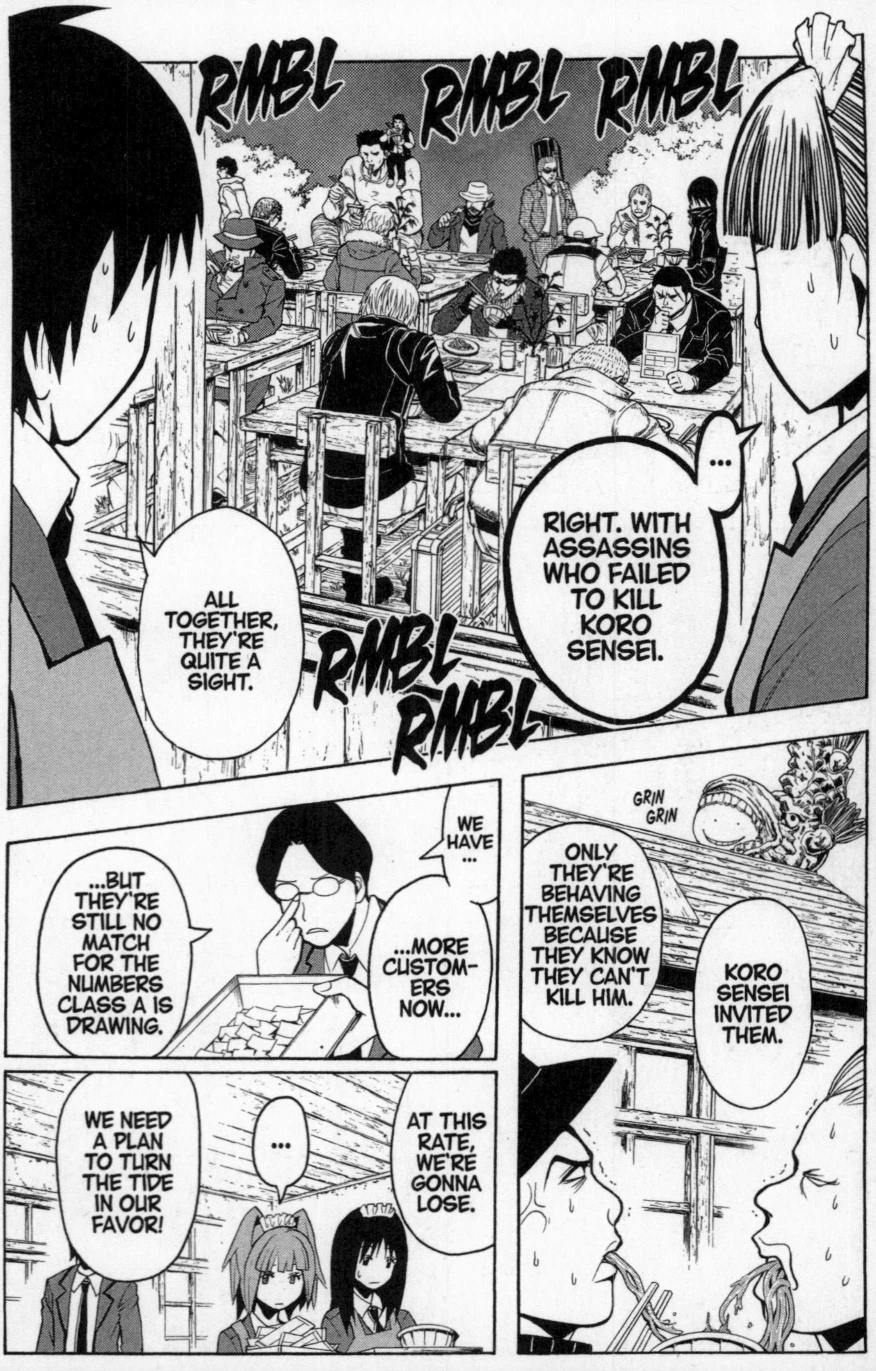
RMBL RMBL RMBL
...
RIGHT. WITH ASSASSINS WHO FAILED TO KILL KORO SENSEI.
ALL TOGETHER, THEY'RE QUITE A SIGHT.
RMBL RMBL
RMBL
GRIN GRIN
KORO SENSEI INVITED THEM.
ONLY THEY'RE BEHAVING THEMSELVES BECAUSE THEY KNOW THEY CAN'T KILL HIM.
WE HAVE...
...MORE CUSTOM-ERS NOW...
...BUT THEY'RE STILL NO MATCH FOR THE NUMBERS CLASS A IS DRAWING.
AT THIS RATE, WE'RE GONNA LOSE.
...
WE NEED A PLAN TO TURN THE TIDE IN OUR FAVOR!

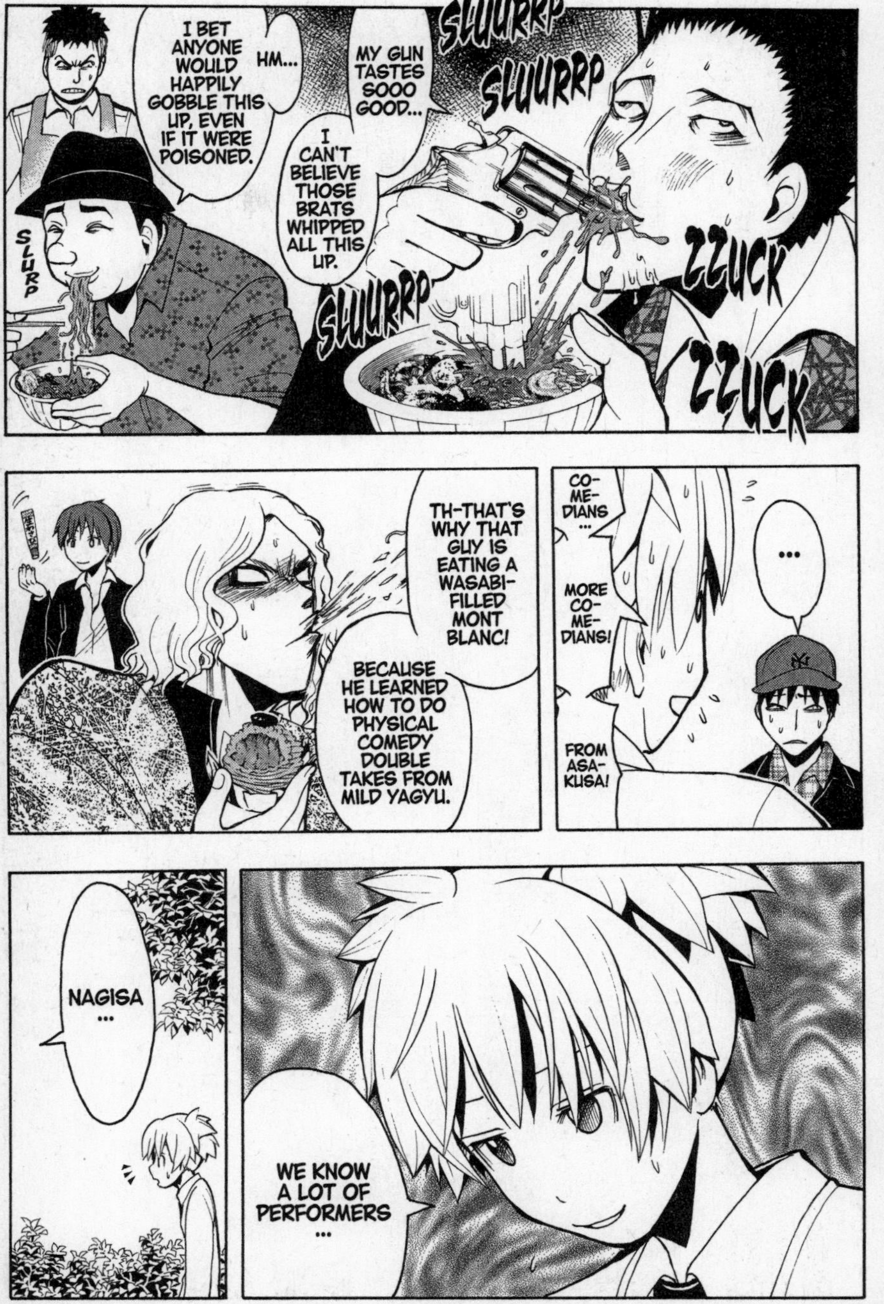
SLUURRP
SLUURRP
MY GUN TASTES SOOO GOOD...
HM...
I BET ANYONE WOULD HAPPILY GOBBLE THIS UP, EVEN IF IT WERE POISONED.
I CAN'T BELIEVE THOSE BRATS WHIPPED ALL THIS UP.
ZZUCK
ZZUCK
SLUURRP
SLURP
...
COMEDIANS...
MORE COMEDIANS!
FROM ASAKUSA!
TH-THAT'S WHY THAT GUY IS EATING A WASABI-FILLED MONT BLANC!
BECAUSE HE LEARNED HOW TO DO PHYSICAL COMEDY DOUBLE TAKES FROM MILD YAGYU.
WE KNOW A LOT OF PERFORMERS...
NAGISA...

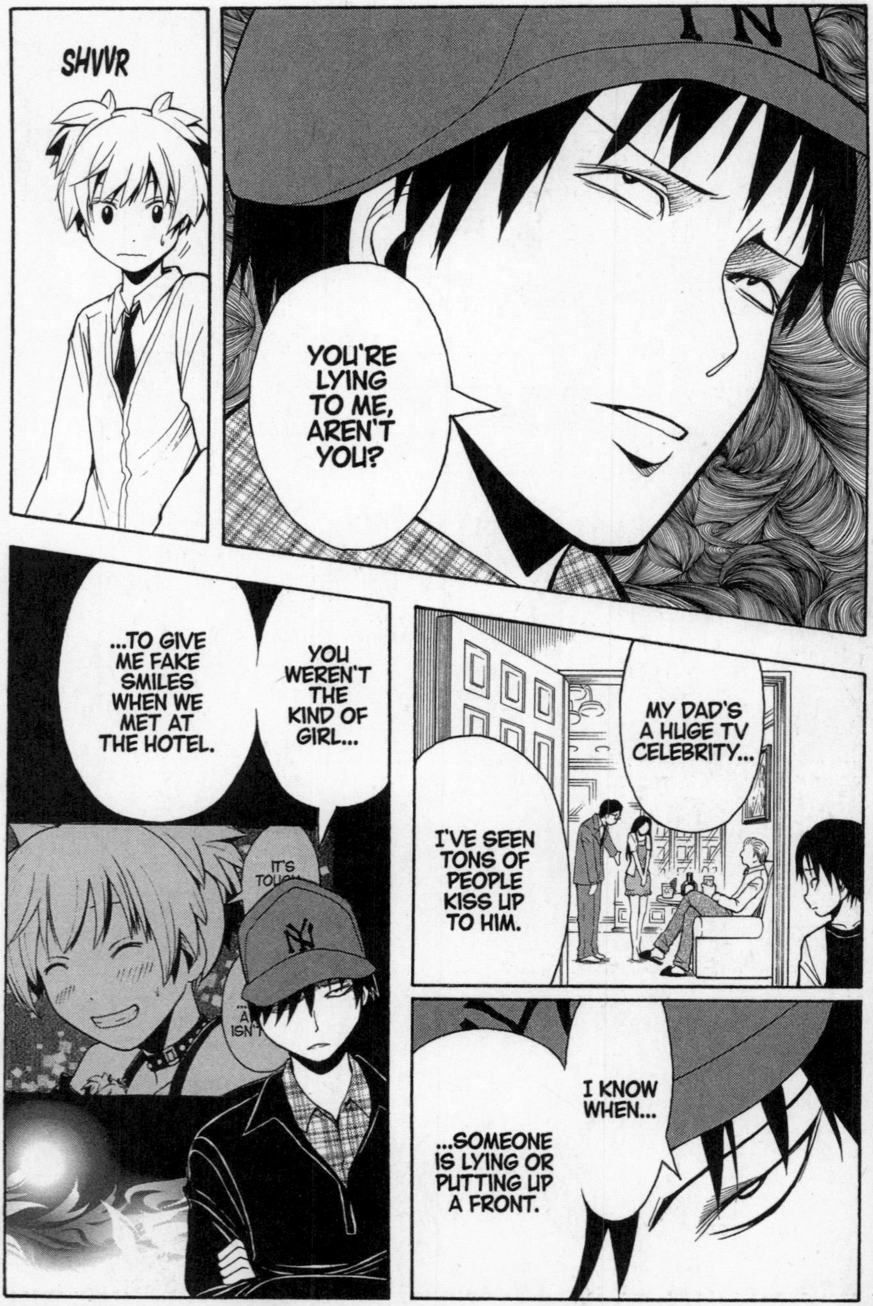
YOU'RE LYING TO ME, AREN'T YOU?
SHVVR
MY DAD'S A HUGE TV CELEBRITY...
I'VE SEEN TONS OF PEOPLE KISS UP TO HIM.
I KNOW WHEN...
...SOMEONE IS LYING OR PUTTING UP A FRONT.
YOU WEREN'T THE KIND OF GIRL...
...TO GIVE ME FAKE SMILES WHEN WE MET AT THE HOTEL.

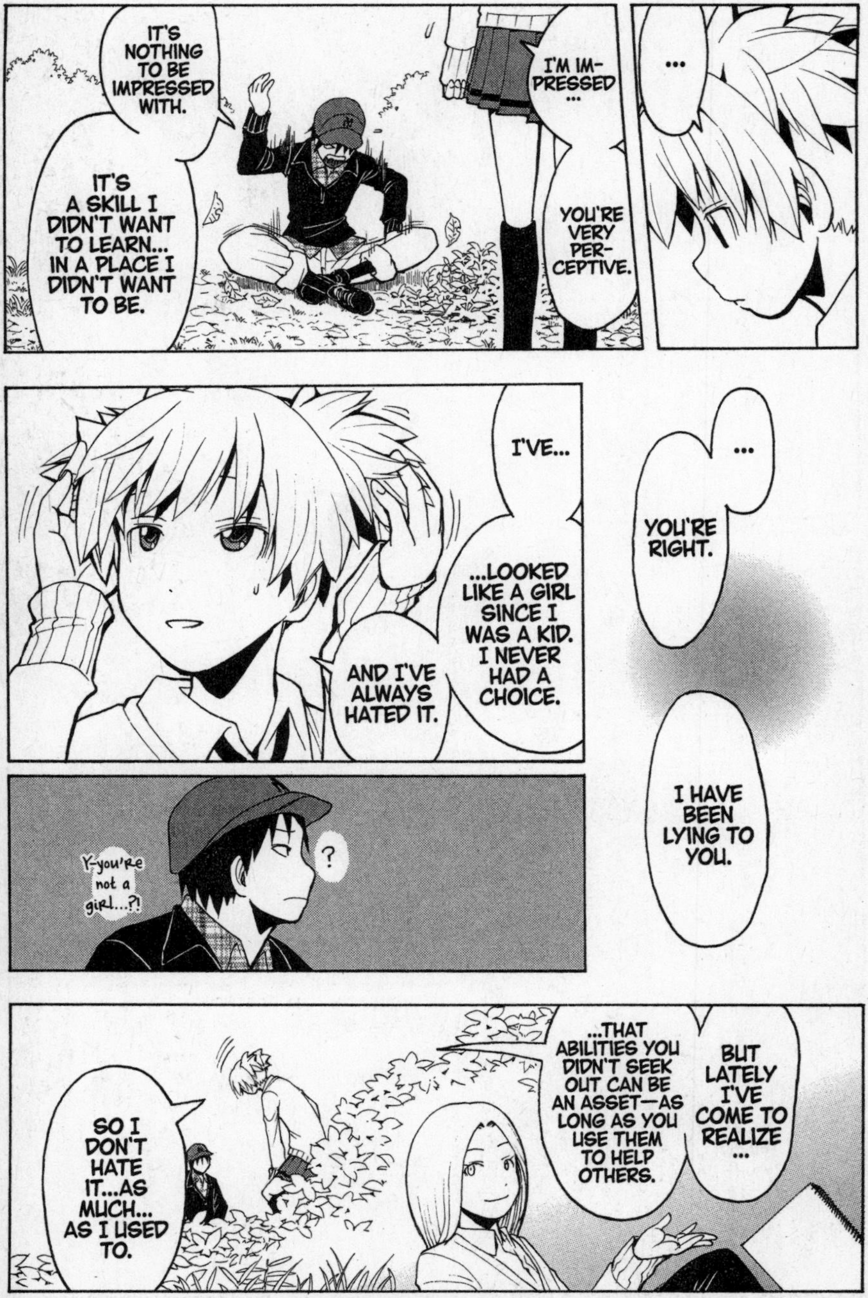
...
I'M IMPRESSED...
YOU'RE VERY PERCEPTIVE.
IT'S NOTHING TO BE IMPRESSED WITH.
IT'S A SKILL I DIDN'T WANT TO LEARN... IN A PLACE I DIDN'T WANT TO BE.
...
YOU'RE RIGHT.
I HAVE BEEN LYING TO YOU.
I'VE...
...LOOKED LIKE A GIRL SINCE I WAS A KID. I NEVER HAD A CHOICE.
AND I'VE ALWAYS HATED IT.
?
Y-you're not a girl...?!
BUT LATELY I'VE COME TO REALIZE...
...THAT ABILITIES YOU DIDN'T SEEK OUT CAN BE AN ASSET—AS LONG AS YOU USE THEM TO HELP OTHERS.
SO I DON'T HATE IT...AS MUCH... AS I USED TO.

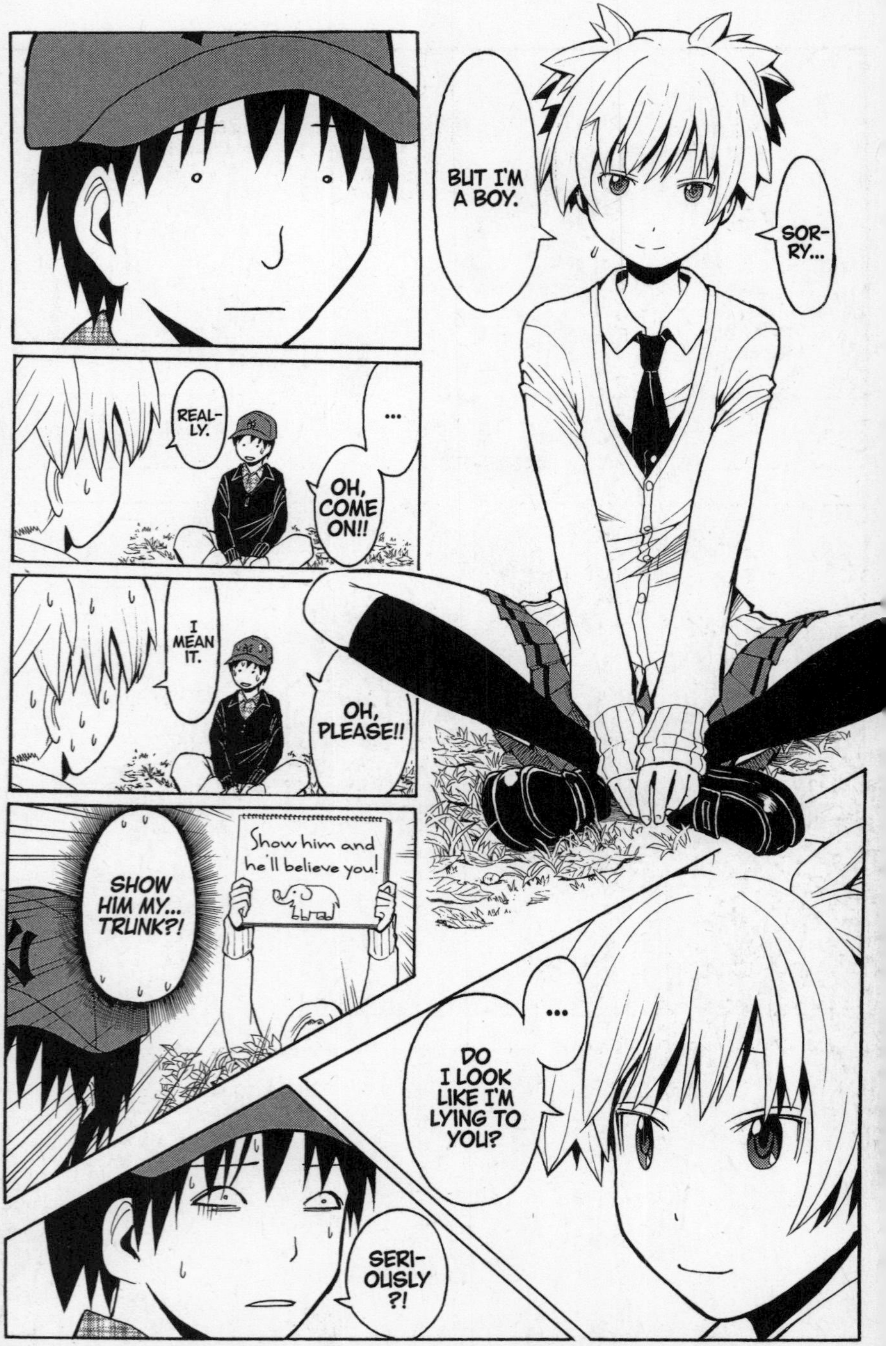
SORRY...
BUT I'M A BOY.
...
OH, COME ON!!
REALLY.
OH, PLEASE!!
I MEAN IT.
Show him and he'll believe you!
SHOW HIM MY... TRUNK?!
...
DO I LOOK LIKE I'M LYING TO YOU?
SERIOUSLY?!

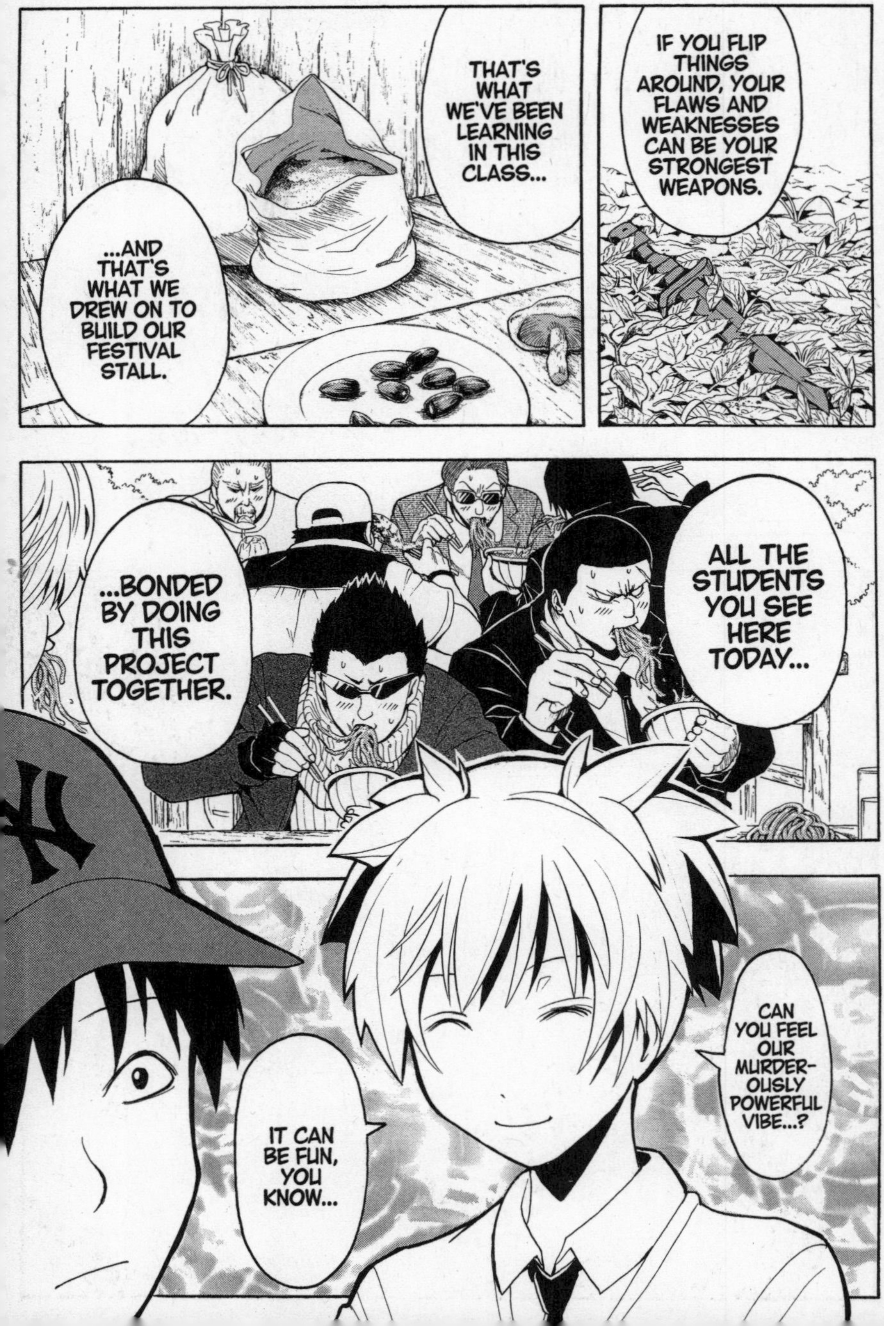
IF YOU FLIP THINGS AROUND, YOUR FLAWS AND WEAKNESSES CAN BE YOUR STRONGEST WEAPONS.
THAT'S WHAT WE'VE BEEN LEARNING IN THIS CLASS...
...AND THAT'S WHAT WE DREW ON TO BUILD OUR FESTIVAL STALL.
ALL THE STUDENTS YOU SEE HERE TODAY...
...BONDED BY DOING THIS PROJECT TOGETHER.
CAN YOU FEEL OUR MURDER-OUSLY POWERFUL VIBE...?
IT CAN BE FUN, YOU KNOW...

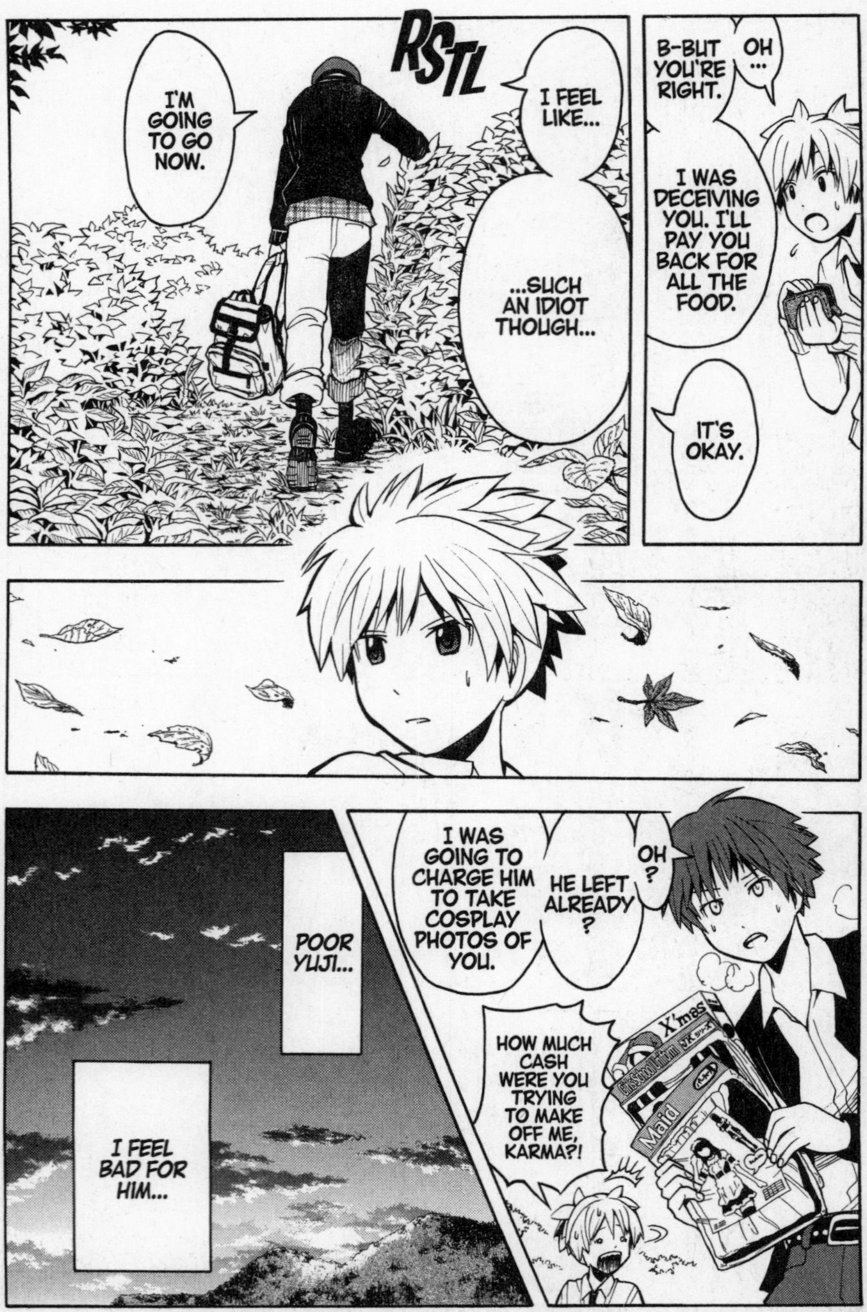
OH ...
B-BUT YOU'RE RIGHT.
I WAS DECEIVING YOU. I'LL PAY YOU BACK FOR ALL THE FOOD.
IT'S OKAY.
RSTL
I FEEL LIKE...
...SUCH AN IDIOT THOUGH...
I'M GOING TO GO NOW.
OH ?
HE LEFT ALREADY ?
I WAS GOING TO CHARGE HIM TO TAKE COSPLAY PHOTOS OF YOU.
HOW MUCH CASH WERE YOU TRYING TO MAKE OFF ME, KARMA?!
X'mas
Maid
POOR YUJI...
I FEEL BAD FOR HIM...

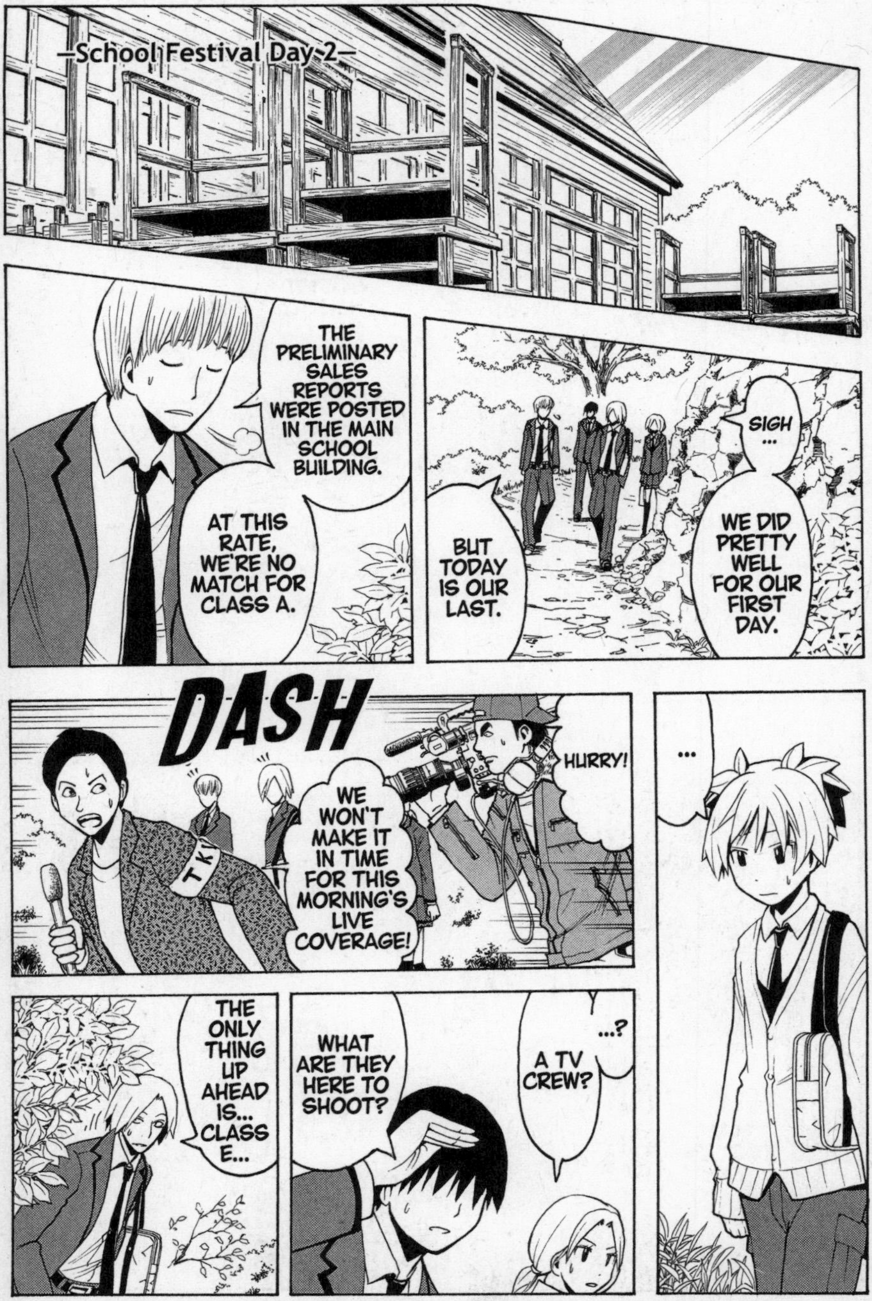
—School Festival Day 2—
SIGH...
WE DID PRETTY WELL FOR OUR FIRST DAY.
BUT TODAY IS OUR LAST.
THE PRELIMINARY SALES REPORTS WERE POSTED IN THE MAIN SCHOOL BUILDING.
AT THIS RATE, WE'RE NO MATCH FOR CLASS A.
...
DASH
HURRY!
WE WON'T MAKE IT IN TIME FOR THIS MORNING'S LIVE COVERAGE!
TKY
...?
A TV CREW?
WHAT ARE THEY HERE TO SHOOT?
THE ONLY THING UP AHEAD IS... CLASS E...

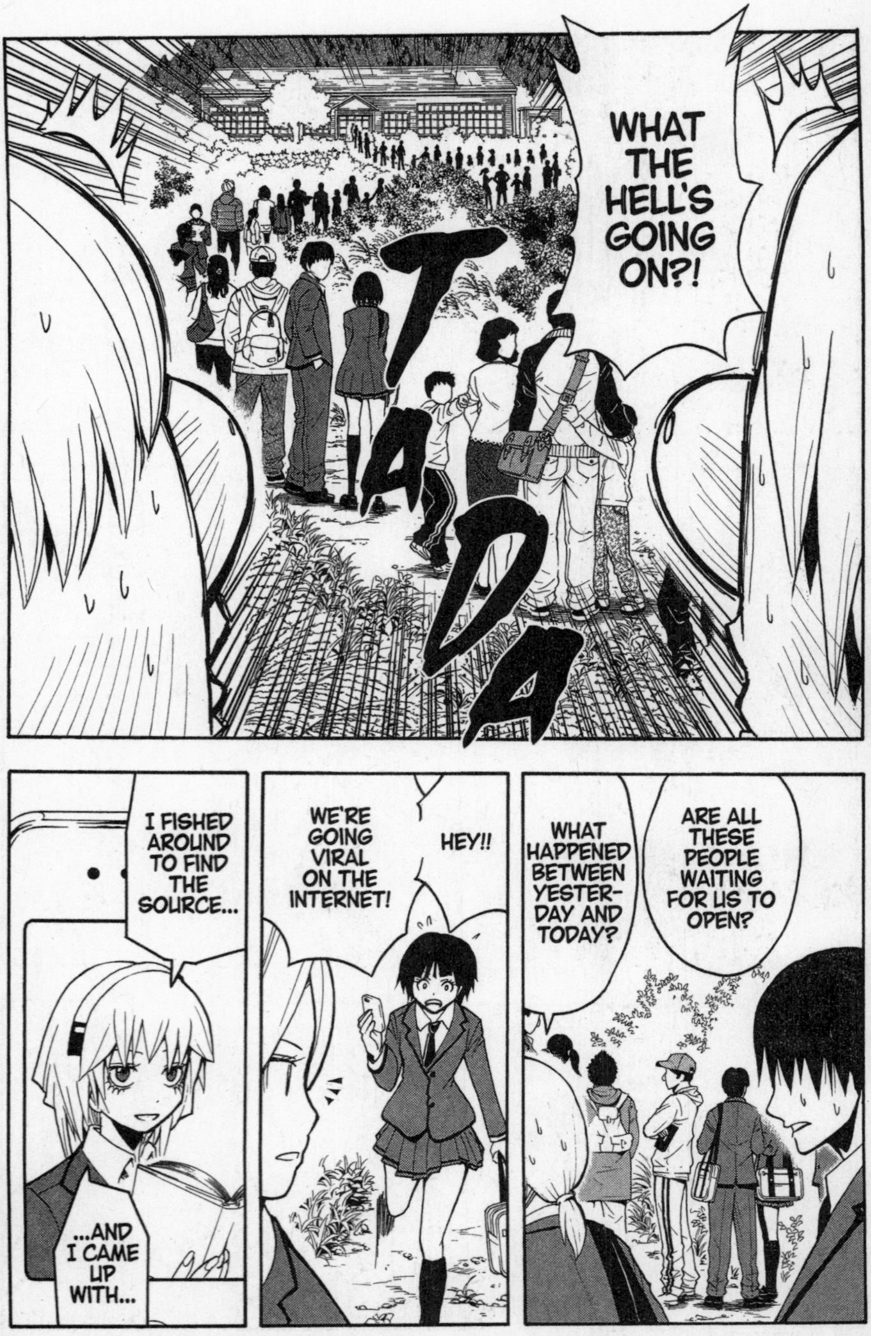
WHAT THE HELL'S GOING ON?!
ARE ALL THESE PEOPLE WAITING FOR US TO OPEN?
WHAT HAPPENED BETWEEN YESTER-DAY AND TODAY?
HEY!!
WE'RE GOING VIRAL ON THE INTERNET!
I FISHED AROUND TO FIND THE SOURCE...
...AND I CAME UP WITH...

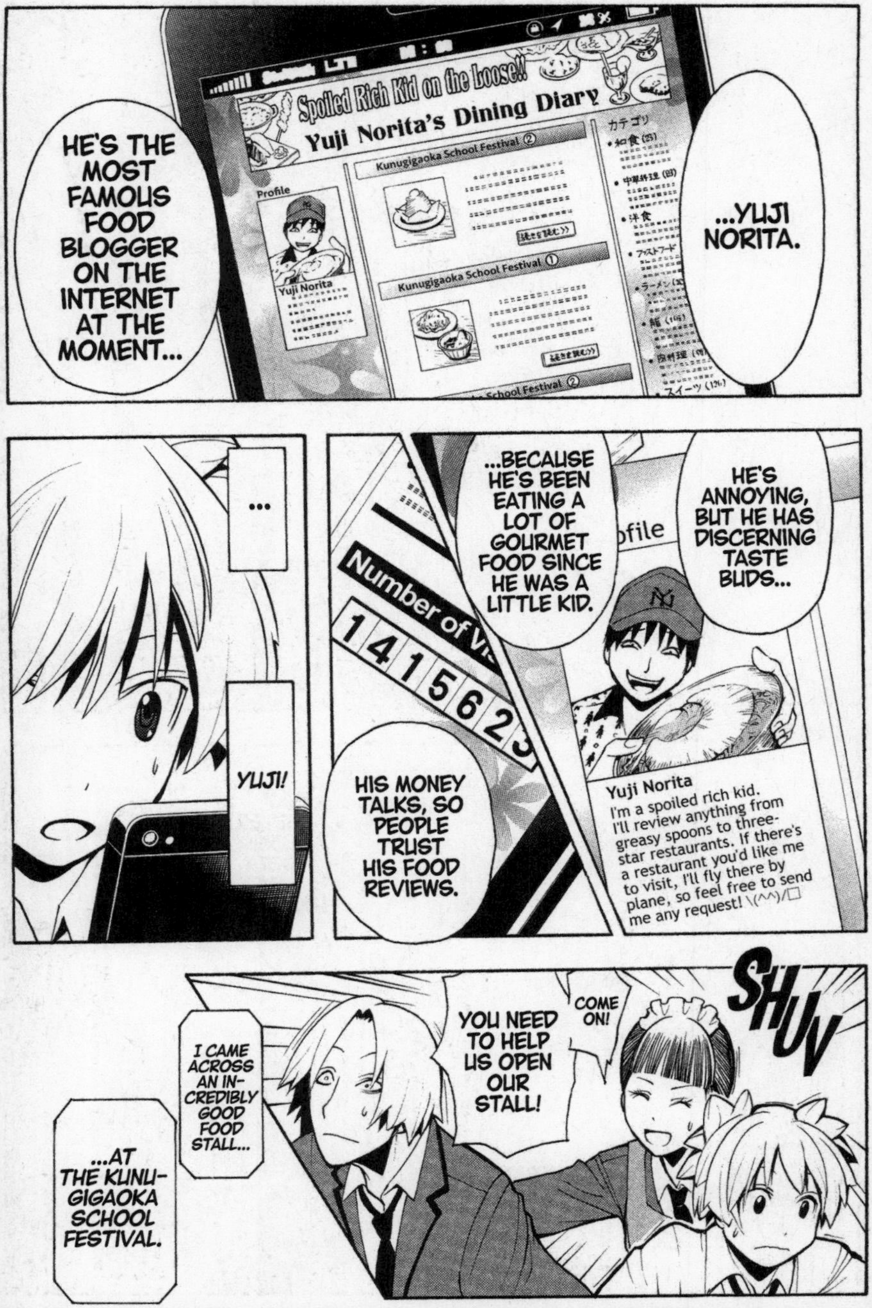
...YUJI NORITA.
Spoiled Rich Kid on the Loose!!
Yuji Norita's Dining Diary
Kunugigaoka School Festival ②
Kunugigaoka School Festival ②
Profile
Yuji Norita
Kunugigaoka School Festival ①
カテゴリ
HE'S THE MOST FAMOUS FOOD BLOGGER ON THE INTERNET AT THE MOMENT...
HE'S ANNOYING, BUT HE HAS DISCERNING TASTE BUDS...
...BECAUSE HE'S BEEN EATING A LOT OF GOURMET FOOD SINCE HE WAS A LITTLE KID.
ofile
Number of Vi
1415623
Yuji Norita
I'm a spoiled rich kid.
I'll review anything from
greasy spoons to three-
star restaurants. If there's
a restaurant you'd like me
to visit, I'll fly there by
plane, so feel free to send
me any request! \(^^)/□
HIS MONEY TALKS, SO PEOPLE TRUST HIS FOOD REVIEWS.
...
YUJI!
SHUV
COME ON!
YOU NEED TO HELP US OPEN OUR STALL!
I CAME ACROSS AN INCREDIBLY GOOD FOOD STALL...
...AT THE KUNUGIGAOKA SCHOOL FESTIVAL.

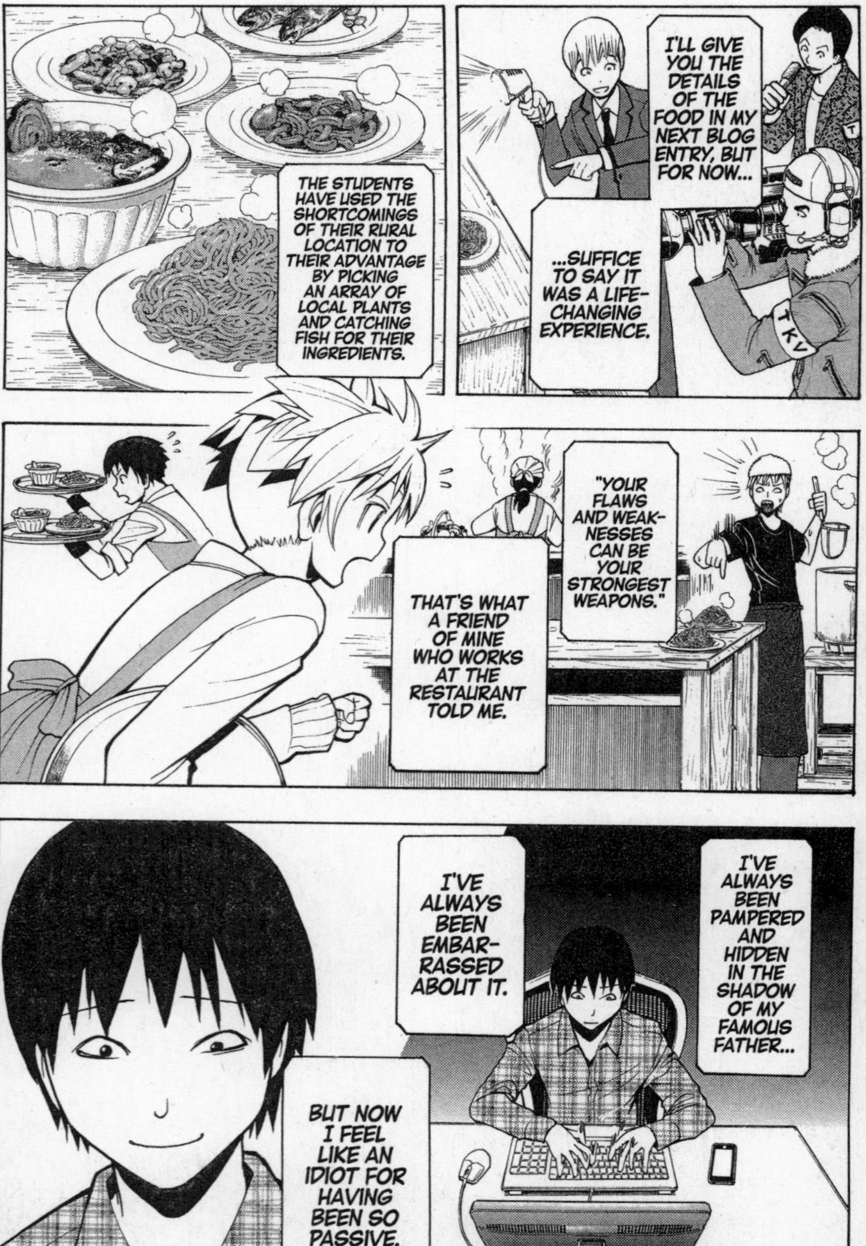
I'LL GIVE YOU THE DETAILS OF THE FOOD IN MY NEXT BLOG ENTRY, BUT FOR NOW...
TKV
...SUFFICE TO SAY IT WAS A LIFE-CHANGING EXPERIENCE.
THE STUDENTS HAVE USED THE SHORTCOMINGS OF THEIR RURAL LOCATION TO THEIR ADVANTAGE BY PICKING AN ARRAY OF LOCAL PLANTS AND CATCHING FISH FOR THEIR INGREDIENTS.
"YOUR FLAWS AND WEAKNESSES CAN BE YOUR STRONGEST WEAPONS."
THAT'S WHAT A FRIEND OF MINE WHO WORKS AT THE RESTAURANT TOLD ME.
I'VE ALWAYS BEEN PAMPERED AND HIDDEN IN THE SHADOW OF MY FAMOUS FATHER...
I'VE ALWAYS BEEN EMBARRASSED ABOUT IT.
BUT NOW I FEEL LIKE AN IDIOT FOR HAVING BEEN SO PASSIVE.

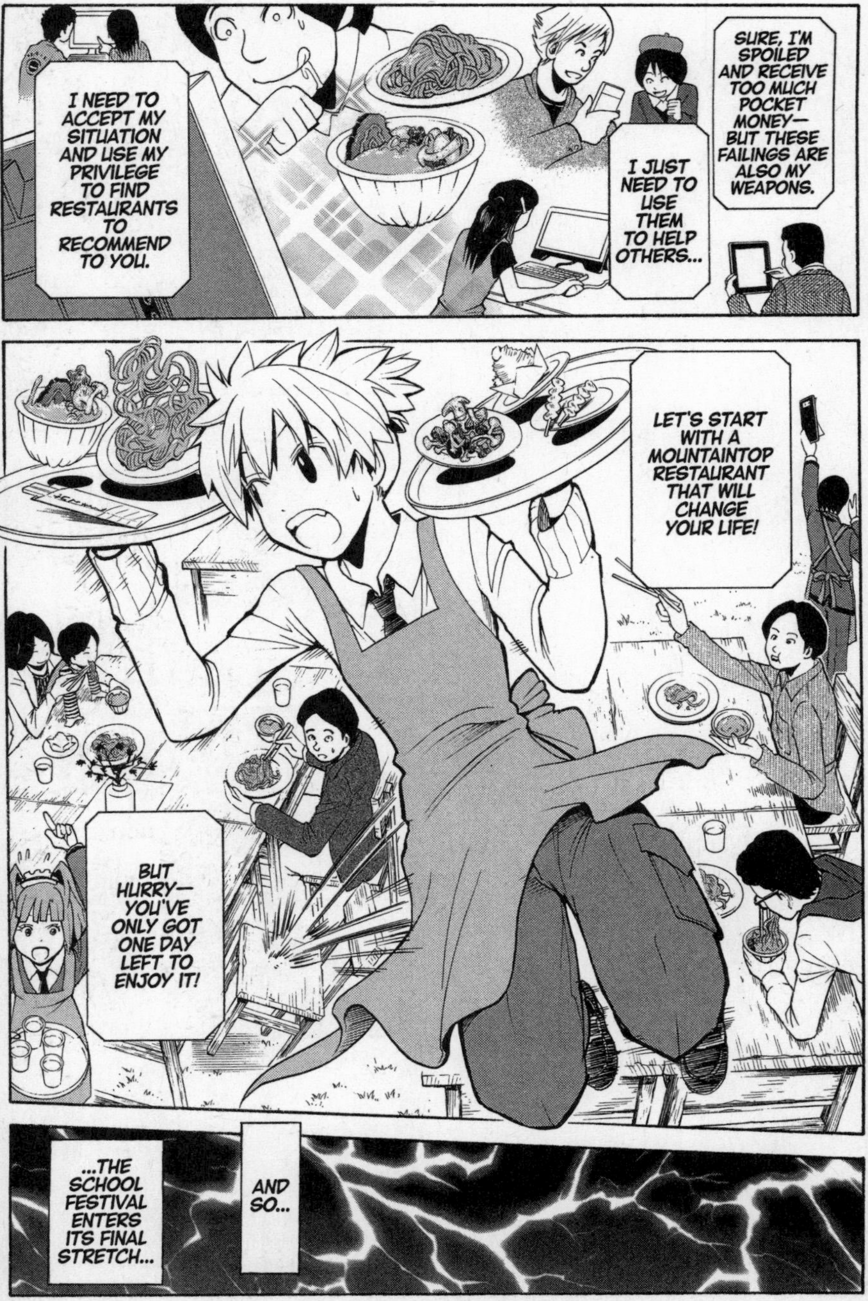
SURE, I'M SPOILED AND RECEIVE TOO MUCH POCKET MONEY—BUT THESE FAILINGS ARE ALSO MY WEAPONS.
I JUST NEED TO USE THEM TO HELP OTHERS...
I NEED TO ACCEPT MY SITUATION AND USE MY PRIVILEGE TO FIND RESTAURANTS TO RECOMMEND TO YOU.
LET'S START WITH A MOUNTAINTOP RESTAURANT THAT WILL CHANGE YOUR LIFE!
BUT HURRY—YOU'VE ONLY GOT ONE DAY LEFT TO ENJOY IT!
AND SO...
...THE SCHOOL FESTIVAL ENTERS ITS FINAL STRETCH...

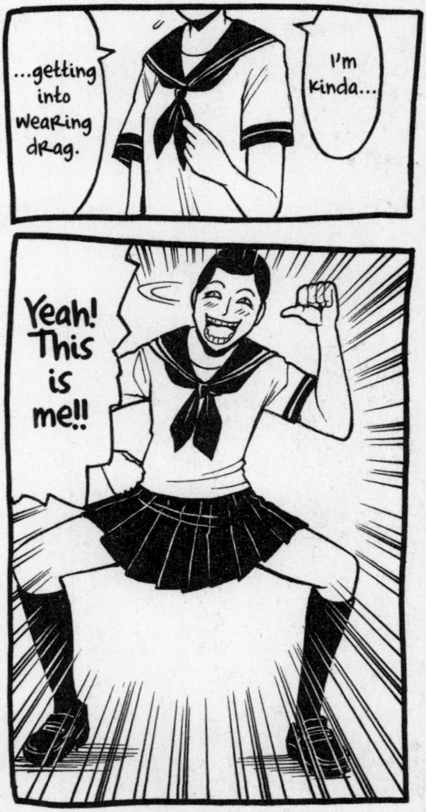
I'm kinda...
...getting into wearing drag.
Yeah! This is me!!

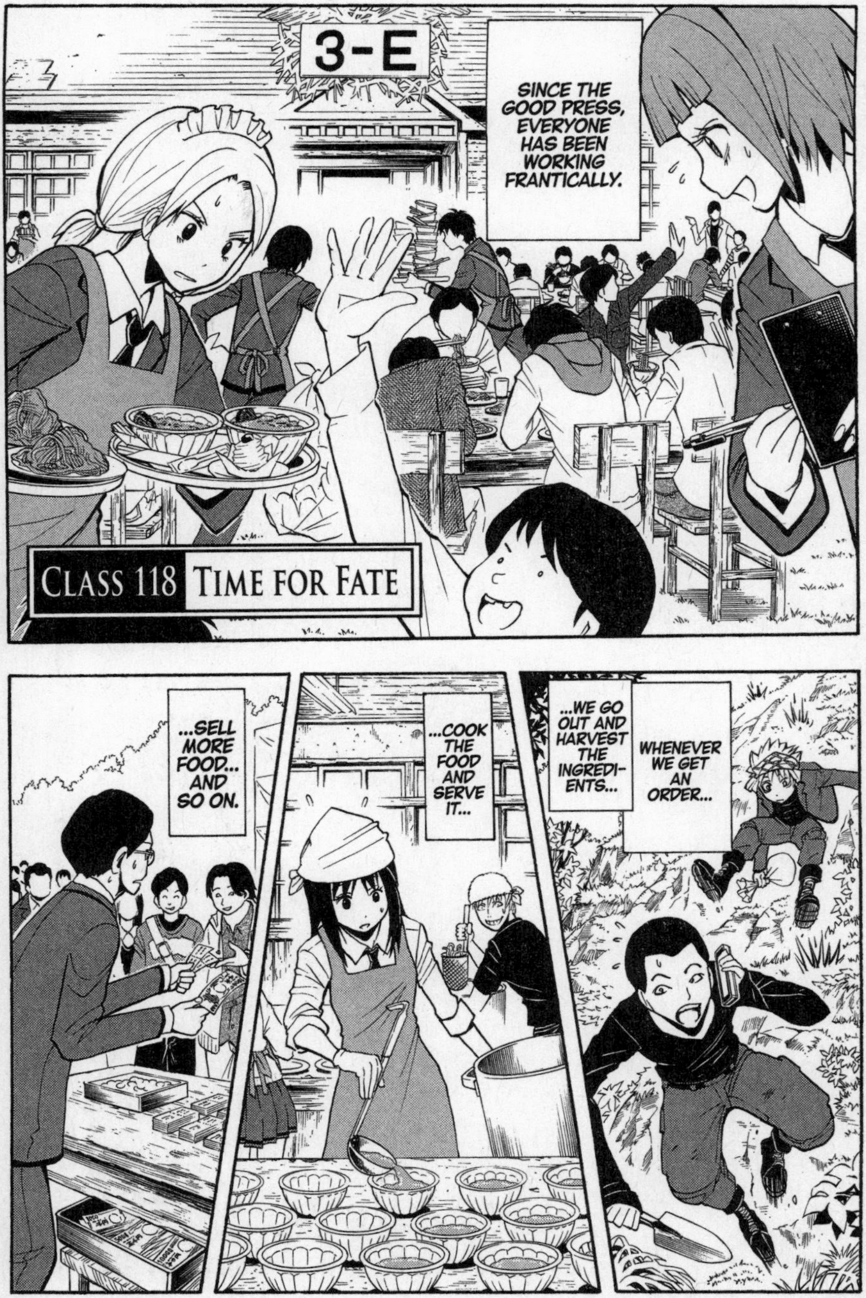
3-E
SINCE THE GOOD PRESS, EVERYONE HAS BEEN WORKING FRANTICALLY.
CLASS 118 TIME FOR FATE
WHENEVER WE GET AN ORDER...
...WE GO OUT AND HARVEST THE INGREDI-ENTS...
...COOK THE FOOD AND SERVE IT...
...SELL MORE FOOD... AND SO ON.

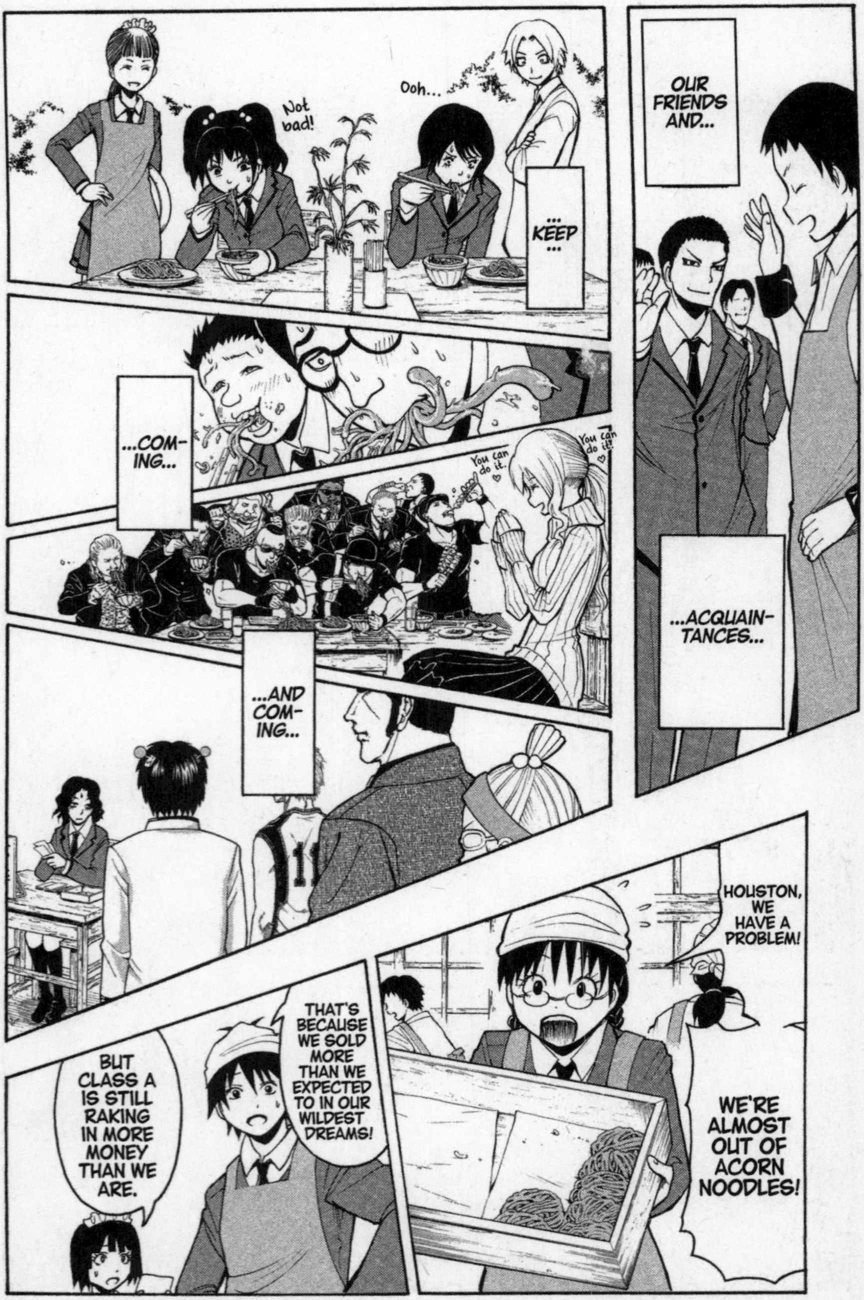
OUR FRIENDS AND...
...ACQUAIN-TANCES...
...KEEP...
Ooh...
Not bad!
...COM-ING...
You can do it!
You can do it.
...AND COM-ING...
HOUSTON, WE HAVE A PROBLEM!
WE'RE ALMOST OUT OF ACORN NOODLES!
THAT'S BECAUSE WE SOLD MORE THAN WE EXPECTED TO IN OUR WILDEST DREAMS!
BUT CLASS A IS STILL RAKING IN MORE MONEY THAN WE ARE.

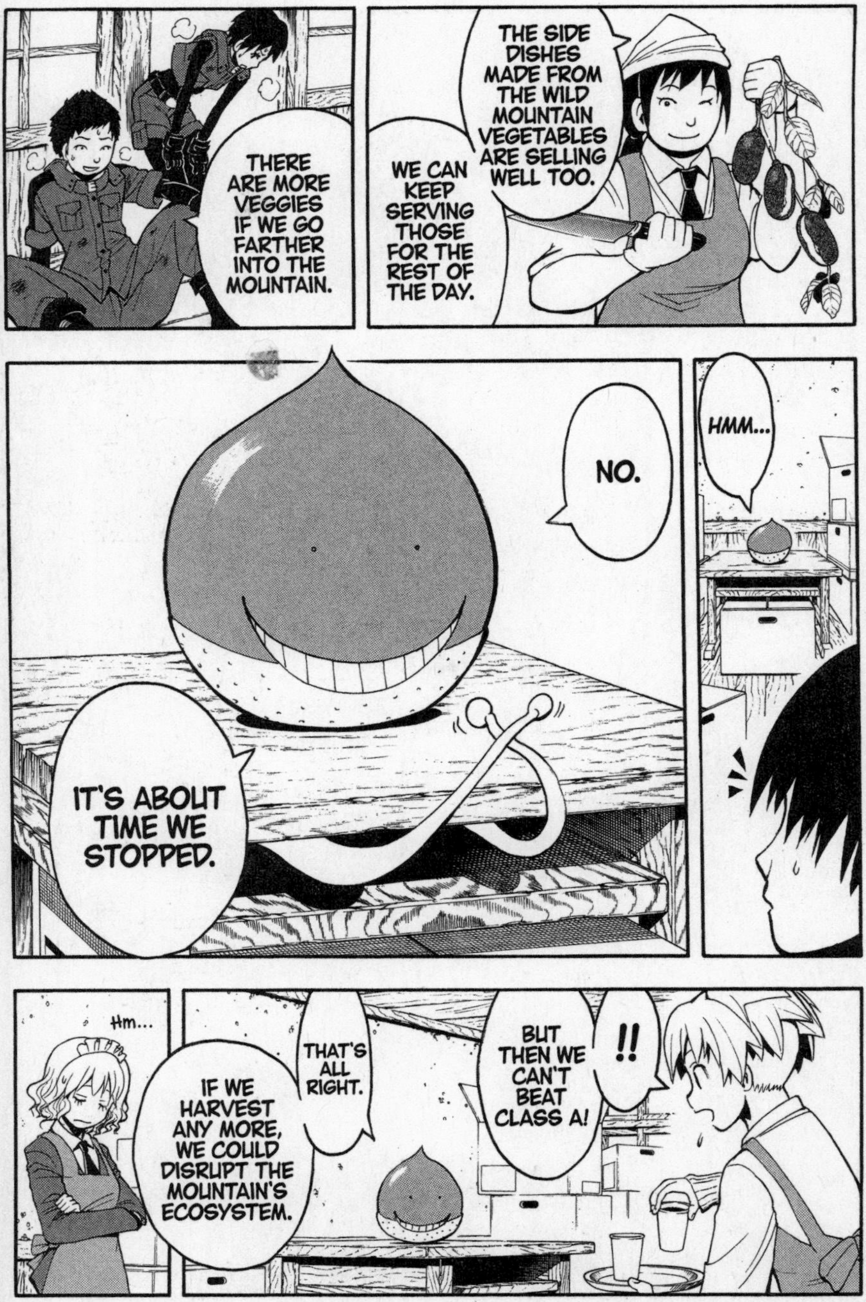
THE SIDE DISHES MADE FROM THE WILD MOUNTAIN VEGETABLES ARE SELLING WELL TOO.
WE CAN KEEP SERVING THOSE FOR THE REST OF THE DAY.
THERE ARE MORE VEGGIES IF WE GO FARTHER INTO THE MOUNTAIN.
HMM...
NO.
IT'S ABOUT TIME WE STOPPED.
!!
BUT THEN WE CAN'T BEAT CLASS A!
THAT'S ALL RIGHT.
IF WE HARVEST ANY MORE, WE COULD DISRUPT THE MOUNTAIN'S ECOSYSTEM.
Hm...

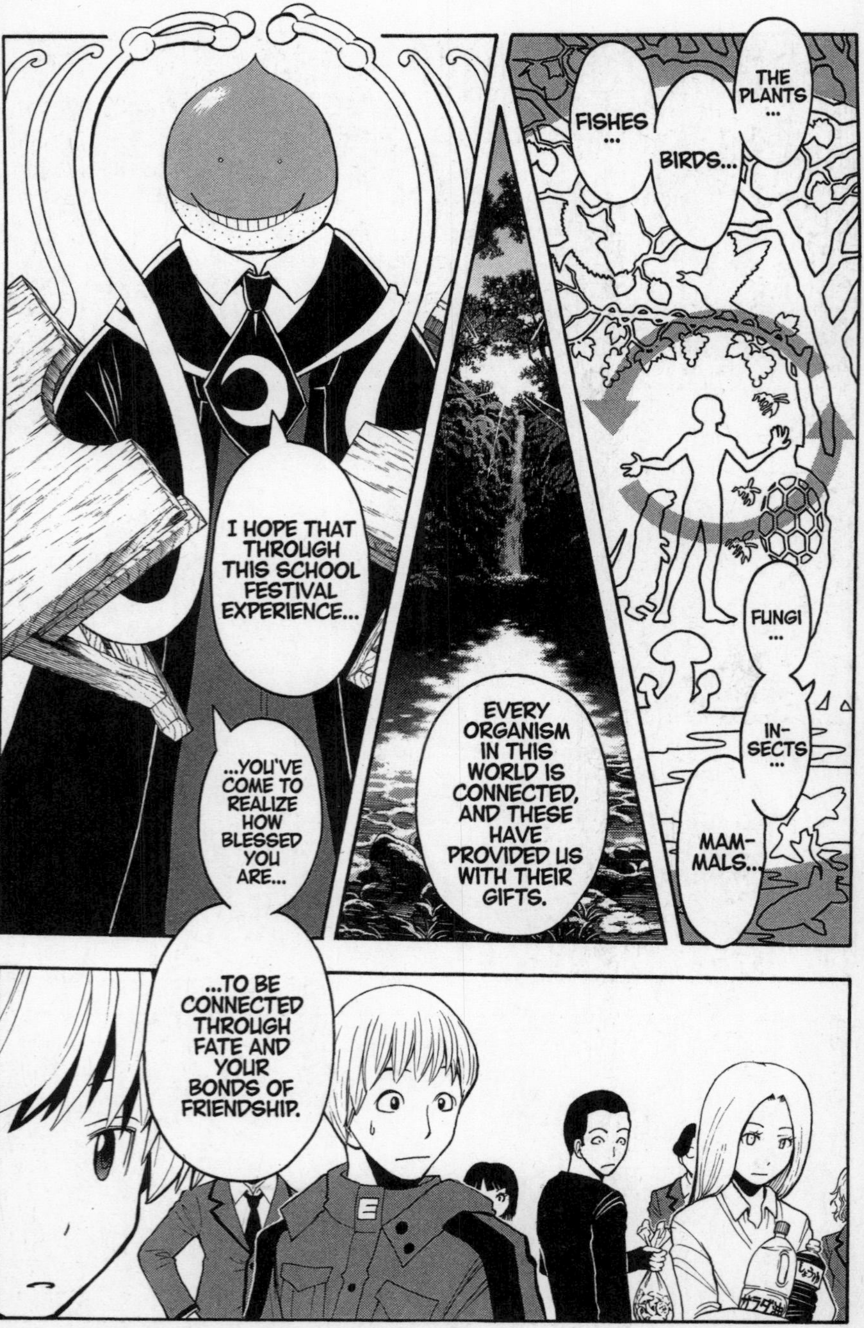
THE PLANTS...
BIRDS...
FISHES...
FUNGI...
IN-SECTS...
MAM-MALS...
EVERY ORGANISM IN THIS WORLD IS CONNECTED, AND THESE HAVE PROVIDED US WITH THEIR GIFTS.
I HOPE THAT THROUGH THIS SCHOOL FESTIVAL EXPERIENCE...
...YOU'VE COME TO REALIZE HOW BLESSED YOU ARE...
...TO BE CONNECTED THROUGH FATE AND YOUR BONDS OF FRIENDSHIP.

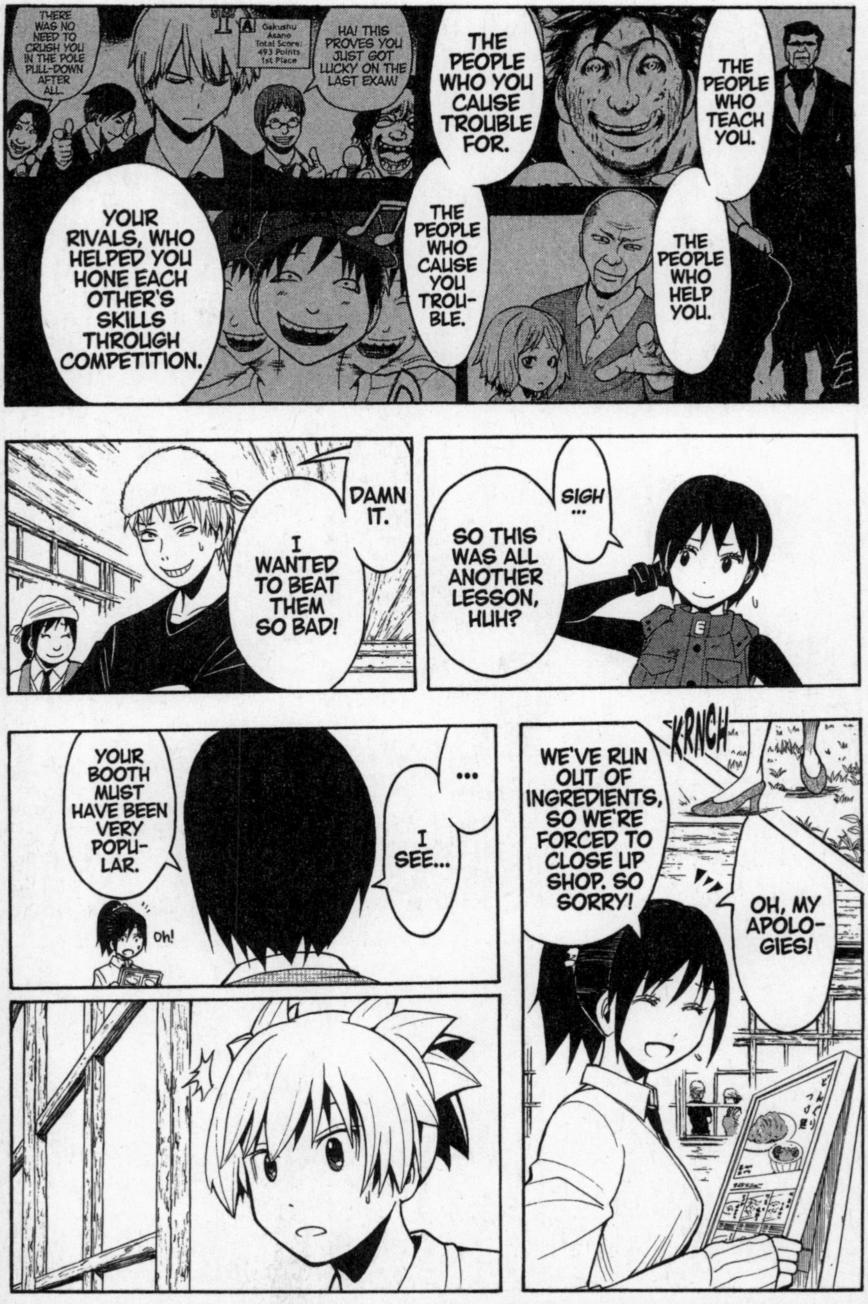
THE PEOPLE WHO TEACH YOU.
THE PEOPLE WHO YOU CAUSE TROUBLE FOR.
HA! THIS PROVES YOU JUST GOT LUCKY ON THE LAST EXAM!
Gakushu Asano Total Score: 493 Points 1st Place
THERE WAS NO NEED TO CRUSH YOU IN THE POLE PULL-DOWN AFTER ALL...
THE PEOPLE WHO HELP YOU.
THE PEOPLE WHO CAUSE YOU TROU-BLE.
YOUR RIVALS, WHO HELPED YOU HONE EACH OTHER'S SKILLS THROUGH COMPETITION.
SIGH ...
SO THIS WAS ALL ANOTHER LESSON, HUH?
DAMN IT.
I WANTED TO BEAT THEM SO BAD!
K-RNCH
OH, MY APOLO-GIES!
WE'VE RUN OUT OF INGREDIENTS, SO WE'RE FORCED TO CLOSE UP SHOP. SO SORRY!
...
I SEE...
YOUR BOOTH MUST HAVE BEEN VERY POPU-LAR.
Oh!

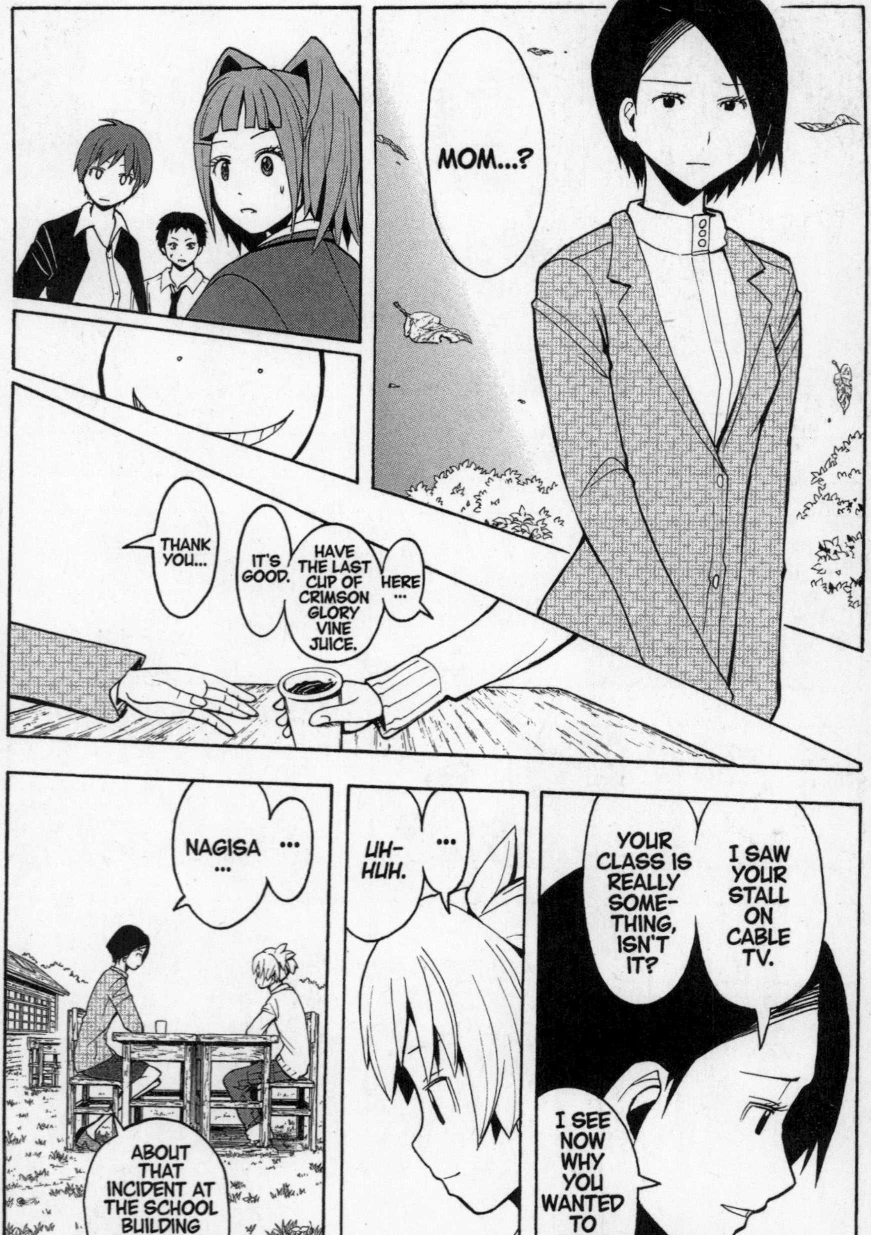
MOM...?
HERE...
HAVE THE LAST CUP OF CRIMSON GLORY VINE JUICE.
IT'S GOOD.
THANK YOU...
I SAW YOUR STALL ON CABLE TV.
YOUR CLASS IS REALLY SOME-THING, ISN'T IT?
I SEE NOW WHY YOU WANTED TO STAY HERE.
...
UH-HUH.
NAGISA... ...
ABOUT THAT INCIDENT AT THE SCHOOL BUILDING THE OTHER DAY...

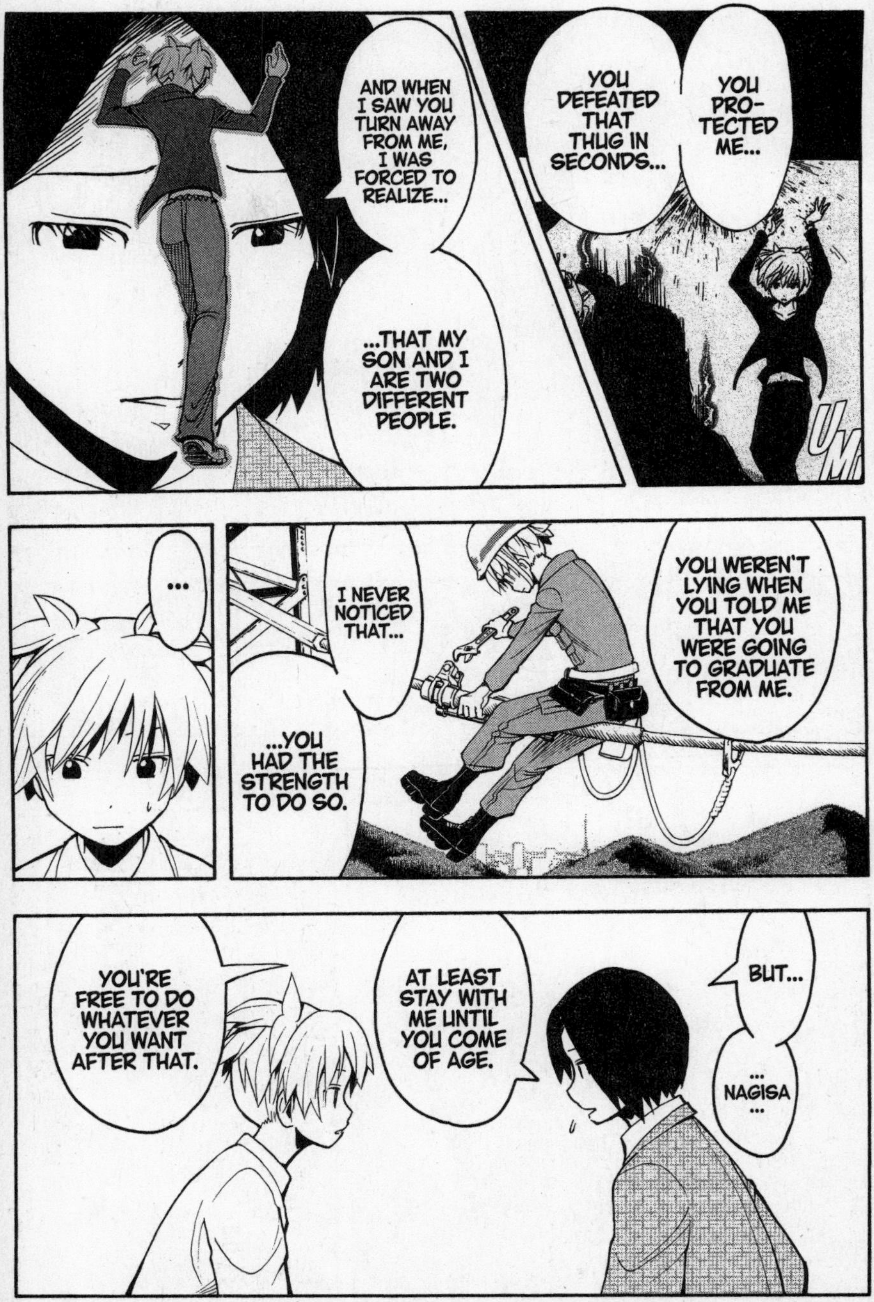
YOU PROTECTED ME...
YOU DEFEATED THAT THUG IN SECONDS...
UM
AND WHEN I SAW YOU TURN AWAY FROM ME, I WAS FORCED TO REALIZE...
...THAT MY SON AND I ARE TWO DIFFERENT PEOPLE.
YOU WEREN'T LYING WHEN YOU TOLD ME THAT YOU WERE GOING TO GRADUATE FROM ME.
I NEVER NOTICED THAT...
...YOU HAD THE STRENGTH TO DO SO.
...
BUT...
... NAGISA ...
AT LEAST STAY WITH ME UNTIL YOU COME OF AGE.
YOU'RE FREE TO DO WHATEVER YOU WANT AFTER THAT.

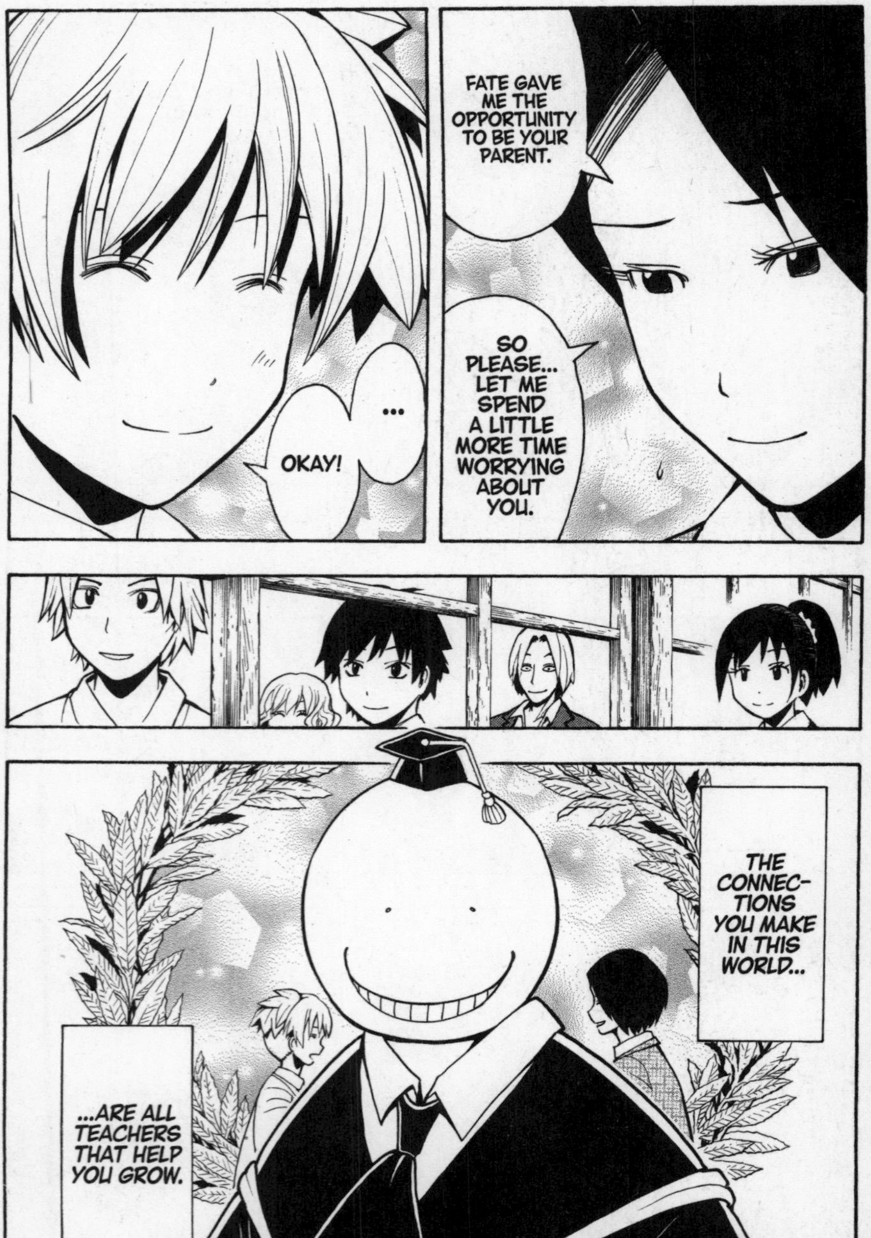
FATE GAVE ME THE OPPORTUNITY TO BE YOUR PARENT.
SO PLEASE... LET ME SPEND A LITTLE MORE TIME WORRYING ABOUT YOU.
...
OKAY!
THE CONNEC-TIONS YOU MAKE IN THIS WORLD...
...ARE ALL TEACHERS THAT HELP YOU GROW.

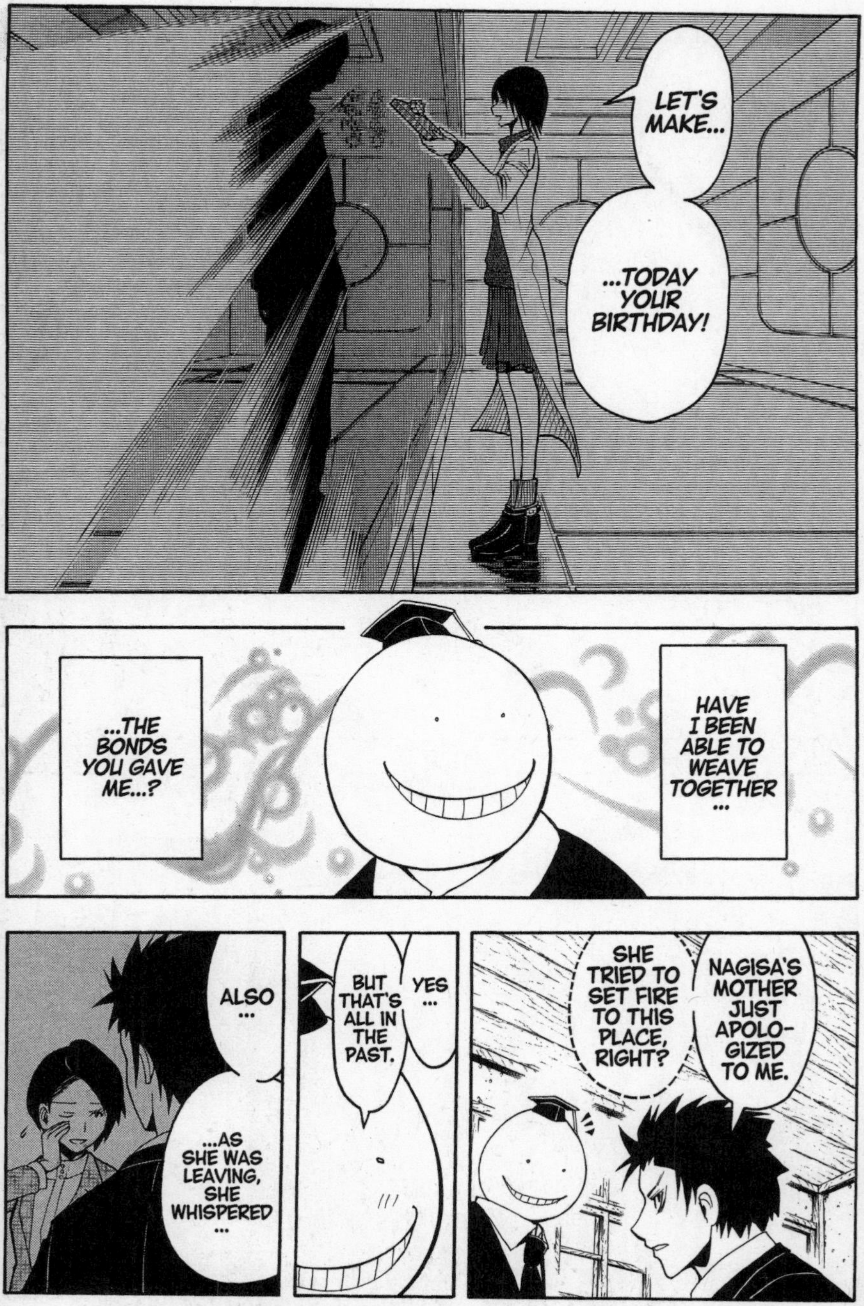
LET'S MAKE...
...TODAY YOUR BIRTHDAY!
HAVE I BEEN ABLE TO WEAVE TOGETHER...
...THE BONDS YOU GAVE ME...?
NAGISA'S MOTHER JUST APOLOGIZED TO ME.
SHE TRIED TO SET FIRE TO THIS PLACE, RIGHT?
YES...
BUT THAT'S ALL IN THE PAST.
ALSO...
...AS SHE WAS LEAVING, SHE WHISPERED...

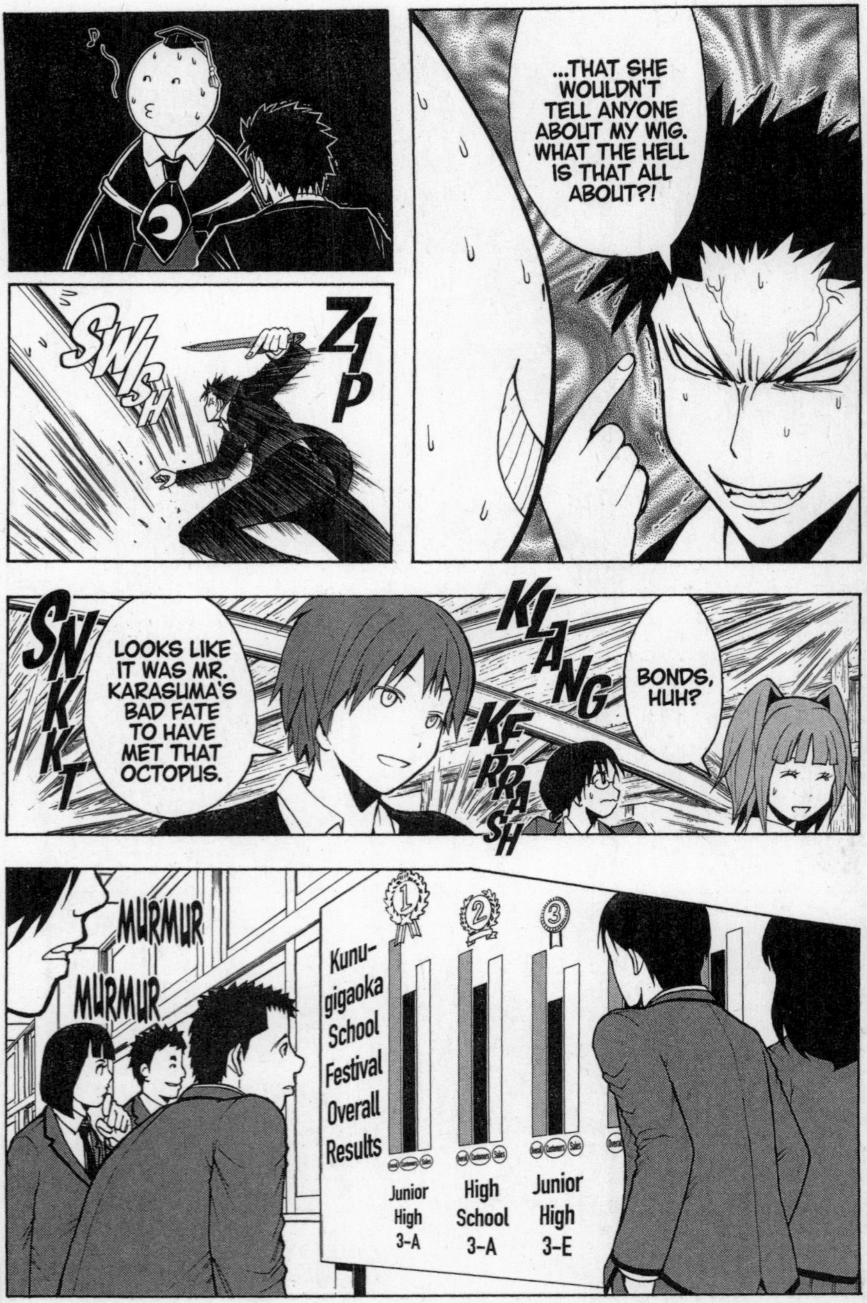
...THAT SHE WOULDN'T TELL ANYONE ABOUT MY WIG. WHAT THE HELL IS THAT ALL ABOUT?!
ZIP
SWISH
BONDS, HUH?
KLANG
KERRASH
LOOKS LIKE IT WAS MR. KARASUMA'S BAD FATE TO HAVE MET THAT OCTOPUS.
SNKKT
Kunugigaoka School Festival Overall Results
Junior High 3-A
High School 3-A
Junior High 3-E
MURMUR
MURMUR

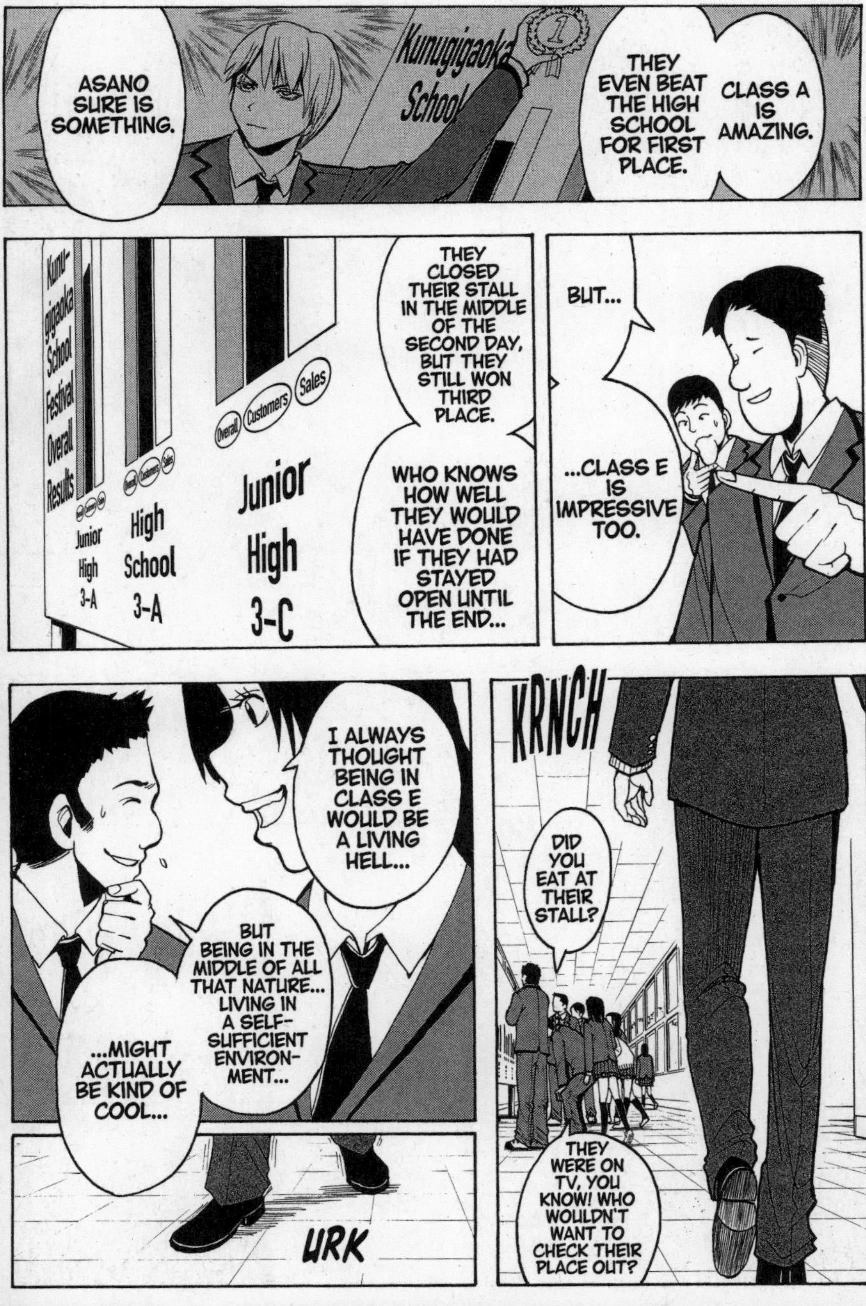
CLASS A IS AMAZING.
THEY EVEN BEAT THE HIGH SCHOOL FOR FIRST PLACE.
Kunugigaoka School
ASANO SURE IS SOMETHING.
BUT...
...CLASS E IS IMPRESSIVE TOO.
THEY CLOSED THEIR STALL IN THE MIDDLE OF THE SECOND DAY, BUT THEY STILL WON THIRD PLACE.
WHO KNOWS HOW WELL THEY WOULD HAVE DONE IF THEY HAD STAYED OPEN UNTIL THE END...
Kunugigaoka School Festival Overall Results
Junior High 3-A
High School 3-A
Junior High 3-C
Overall
Customers
Sales
KRNCH
DID YOU EAT AT THEIR STALL?
THEY WERE ON TV, YOU KNOW! WHO WOULDN'T WANT TO CHECK THEIR PLACE OUT?
I ALWAYS THOUGHT BEING IN CLASS E WOULD BE A LIVING HELL...
BUT BEING IN THE MIDDLE OF ALL THAT NATURE... LIVING IN A SELF-SUFFICIENT ENVIRONMENT...
...MIGHT ACTUALLY BE KIND OF COOL...
URK

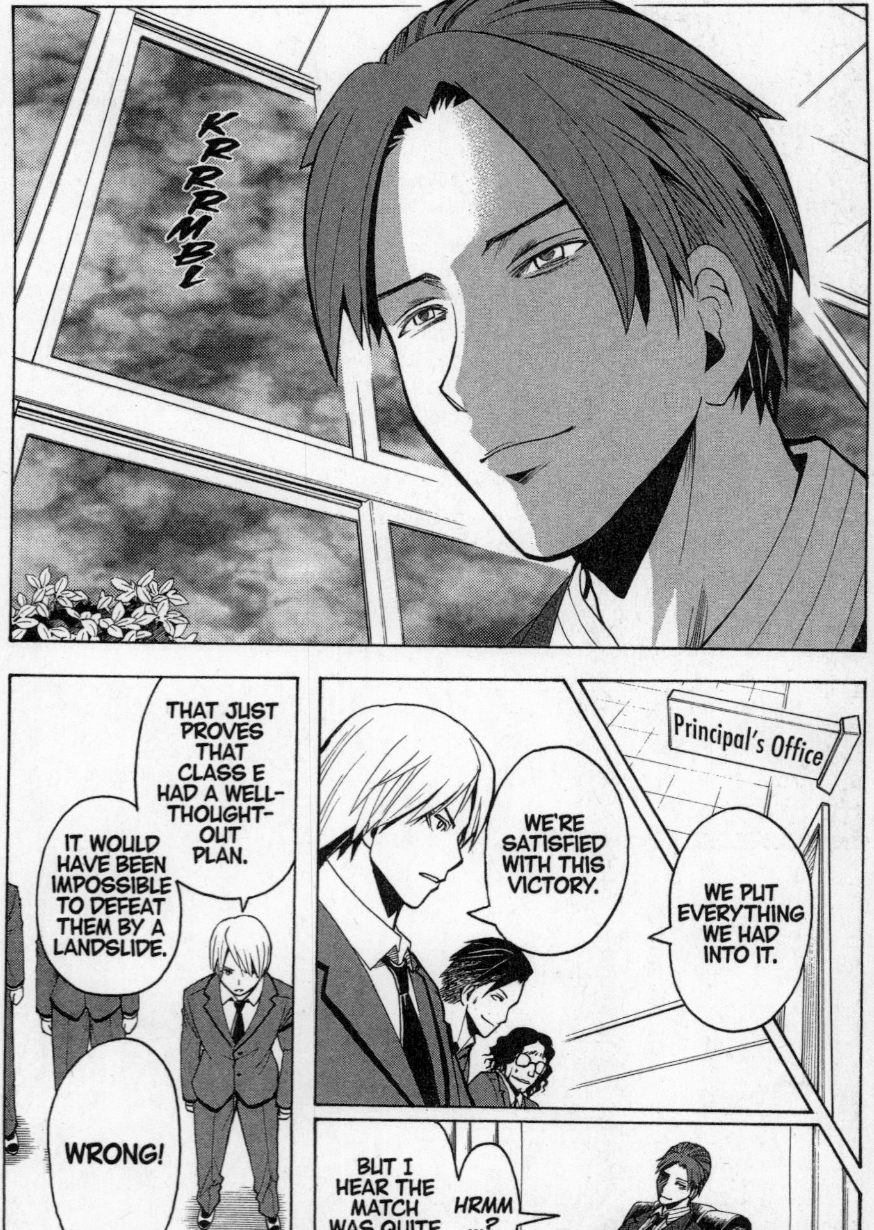
KRRRMBL
Principal's Office
WE PUT EVERYTHING WE HAD INTO IT.
WE'RE SATISFIED WITH THIS VICTORY.
HRMM ...?
BUT I HEAR THE MATCH WAS QUITE CLOSE.
THAT JUST PROVES THAT CLASS E HAD A WELL-THOUGHT-OUT PLAN.
IT WOULD HAVE BEEN IMPOSSIBLE TO DEFEAT THEM BY A LANDSLIDE.
WRONG!

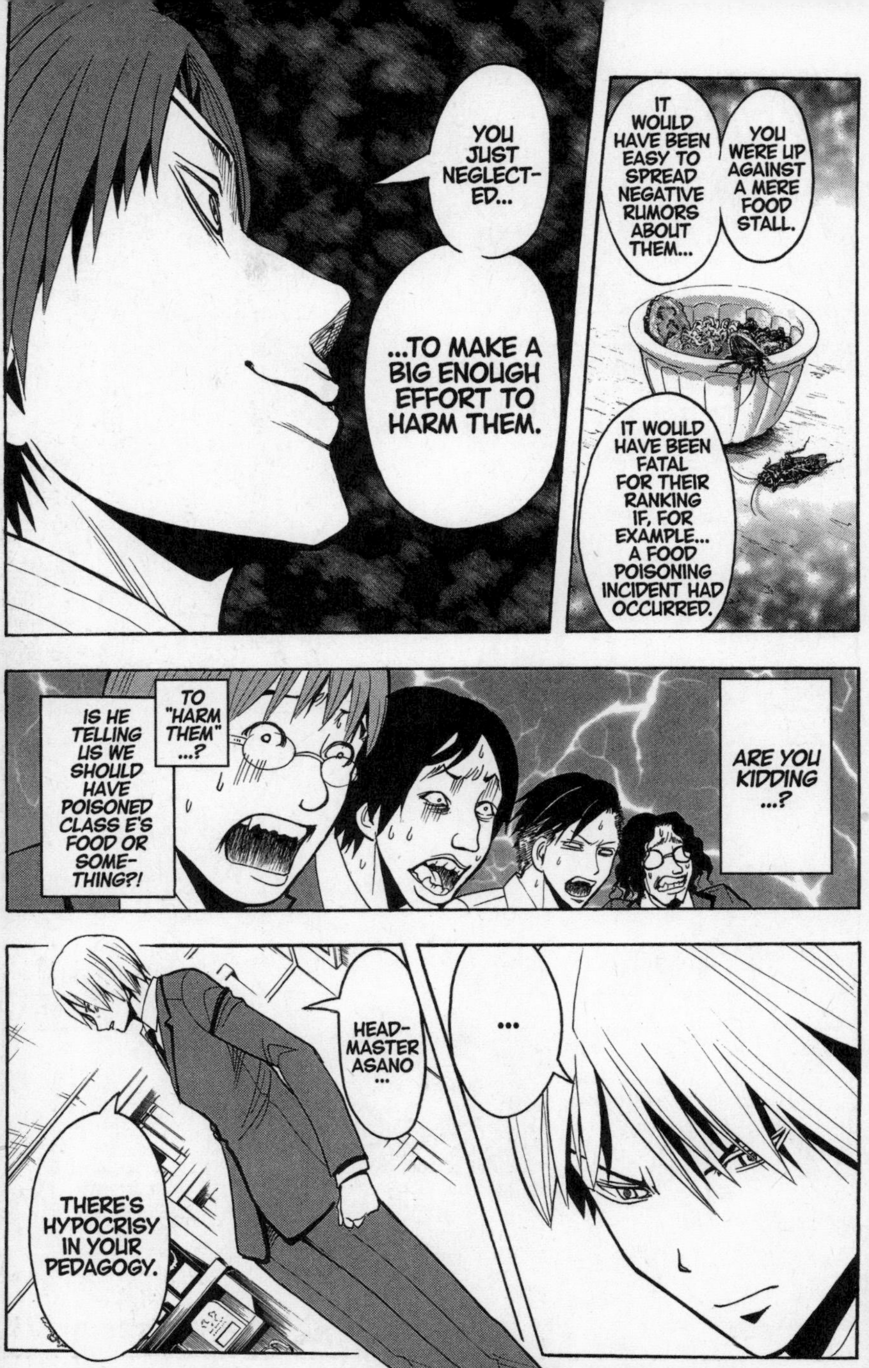
YOU WERE UP AGAINST A MERE FOOD STALL.
IT WOULD HAVE BEEN EASY TO SPREAD NEGATIVE RUMORS ABOUT THEM...
IT WOULD HAVE BEEN FATAL FOR THEIR RANKING IF, FOR EXAMPLE... A FOOD POISONING INCIDENT HAD OCCURRED.
YOU JUST NEGLECTED...
...TO MAKE A BIG ENOUGH EFFORT TO HARM THEM.
ARE YOU KIDDING ...?
TO "HARM THEM" ...?
IS HE TELLING US WE SHOULD HAVE POISONED CLASS E'S FOOD OR SOMETHING?!
...
HEADMASTER ASANO ...
THERE'S HYPOCRISY IN YOUR PEDAGOGY.

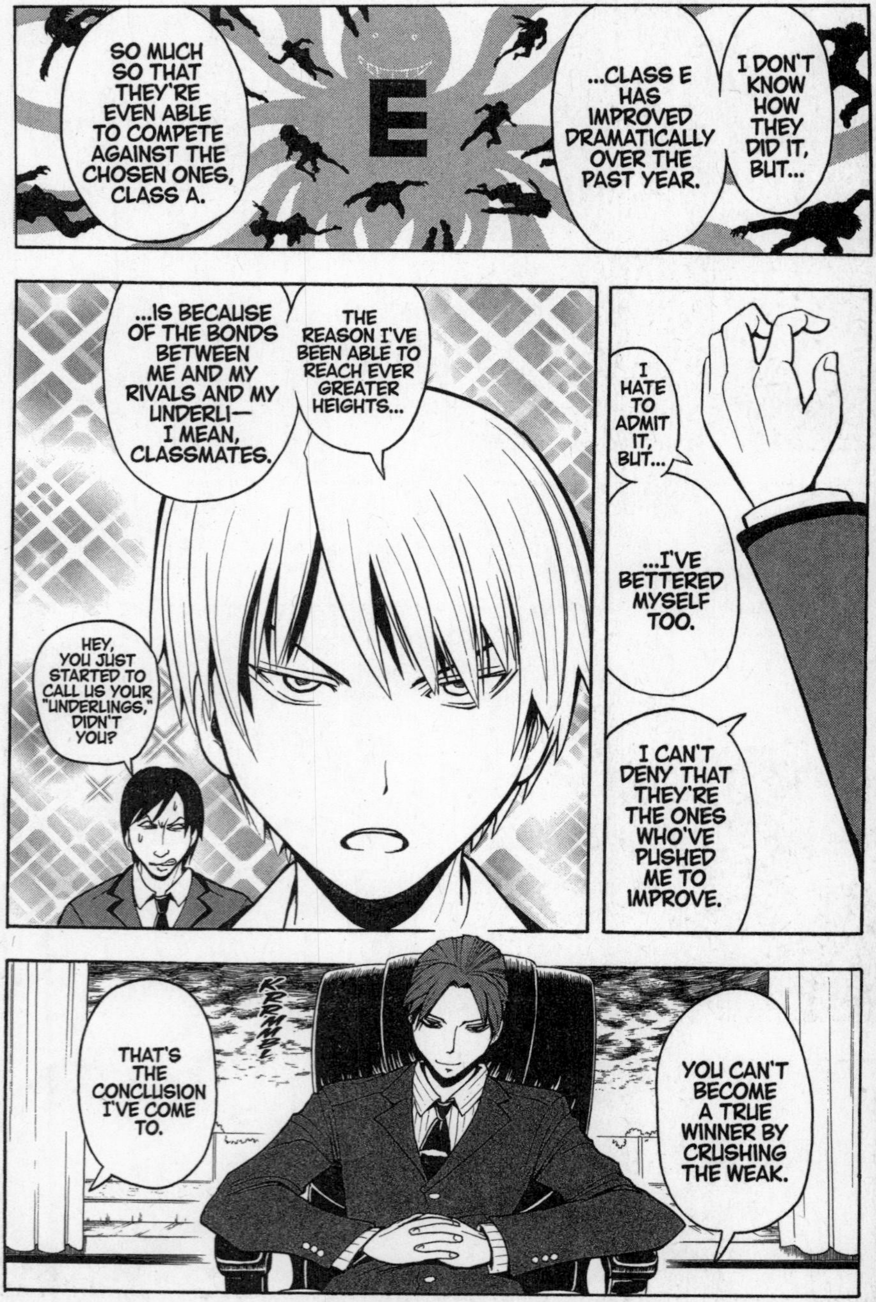
I DON'T KNOW HOW THEY DID IT, BUT...
...CLASS E HAS IMPROVED DRAMATICALLY OVER THE PAST YEAR.
SO MUCH SO THAT THEY'RE EVEN ABLE TO COMPETE AGAINST THE CHOSEN ONES, CLASS A.
I HATE TO ADMIT IT, BUT...
...I'VE BETTERED MYSELF TOO.
I CAN'T DENY THAT THEY'RE THE ONES WHO'VE PUSHED ME TO IMPROVE.
THE REASON I'VE BEEN ABLE TO REACH EVER GREATER HEIGHTS...
...IS BECAUSE OF THE BONDS BETWEEN ME AND MY RIVALS AND MY UNDERLI— I MEAN, CLASSMATES.
HEY, YOU JUST STARTED TO CALL US YOUR "UNDERLINGS," DIDN'T YOU?
YOU CAN'T BECOME A TRUE WINNER BY CRUSHING THE WEAK.
KRRMMBL
THAT'S THE CONCLUSION I'VE COME TO.

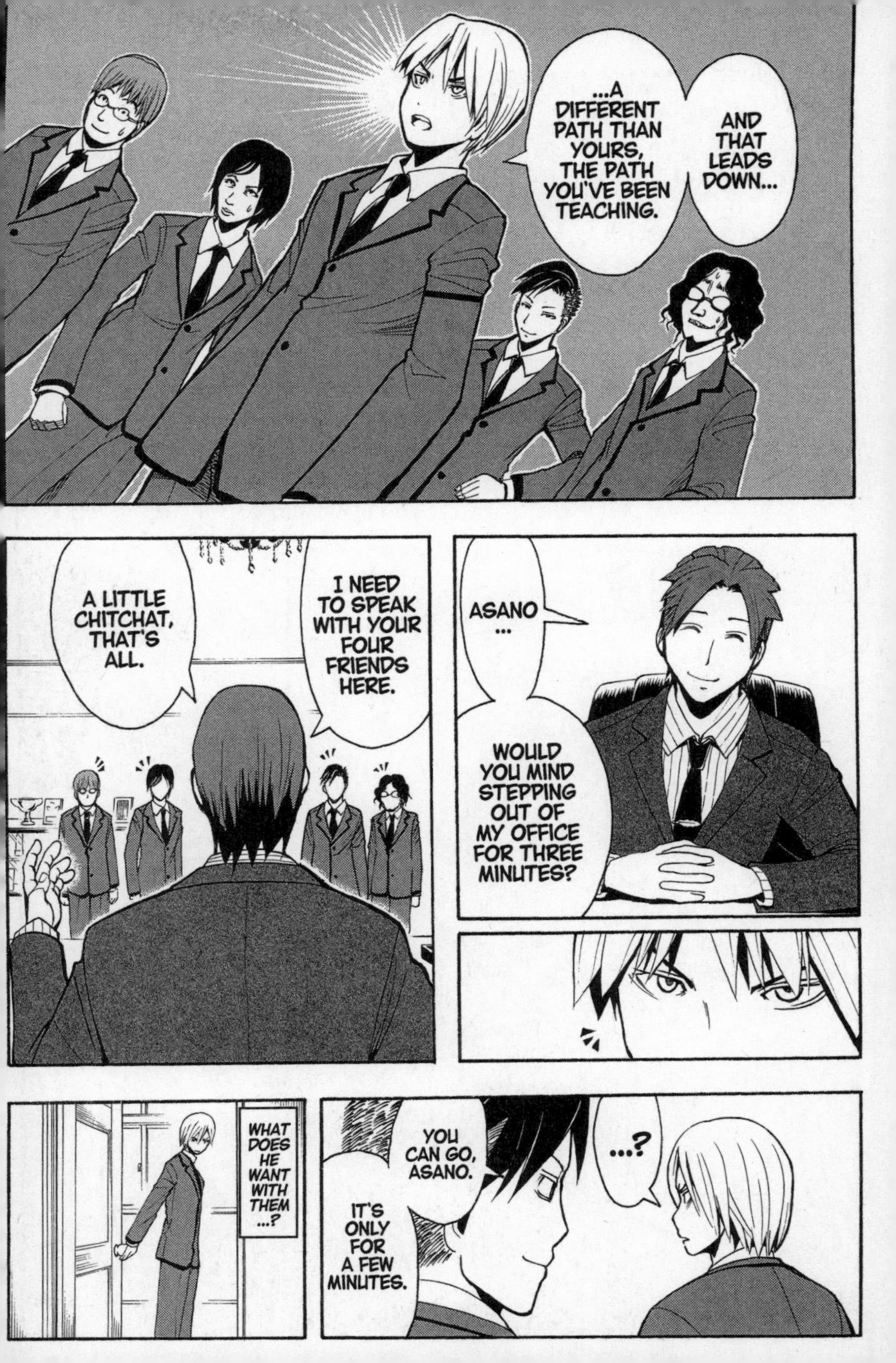
...A DIFFERENT PATH THAN YOURS, THE PATH YOU'VE BEEN TEACHING.
AND THAT LEADS DOWN...
ASANO...
WOULD YOU MIND STEPPING OUT OF MY OFFICE FOR THREE MINUTES?
I NEED TO SPEAK WITH YOUR FOUR FRIENDS HERE.
A LITTLE CHITCHAT, THAT'S ALL.
...?
YOU CAN GO, ASANO.
IT'S ONLY FOR A FEW MINUTES.
WHAT DOES HE WANT WITH THEM ...?

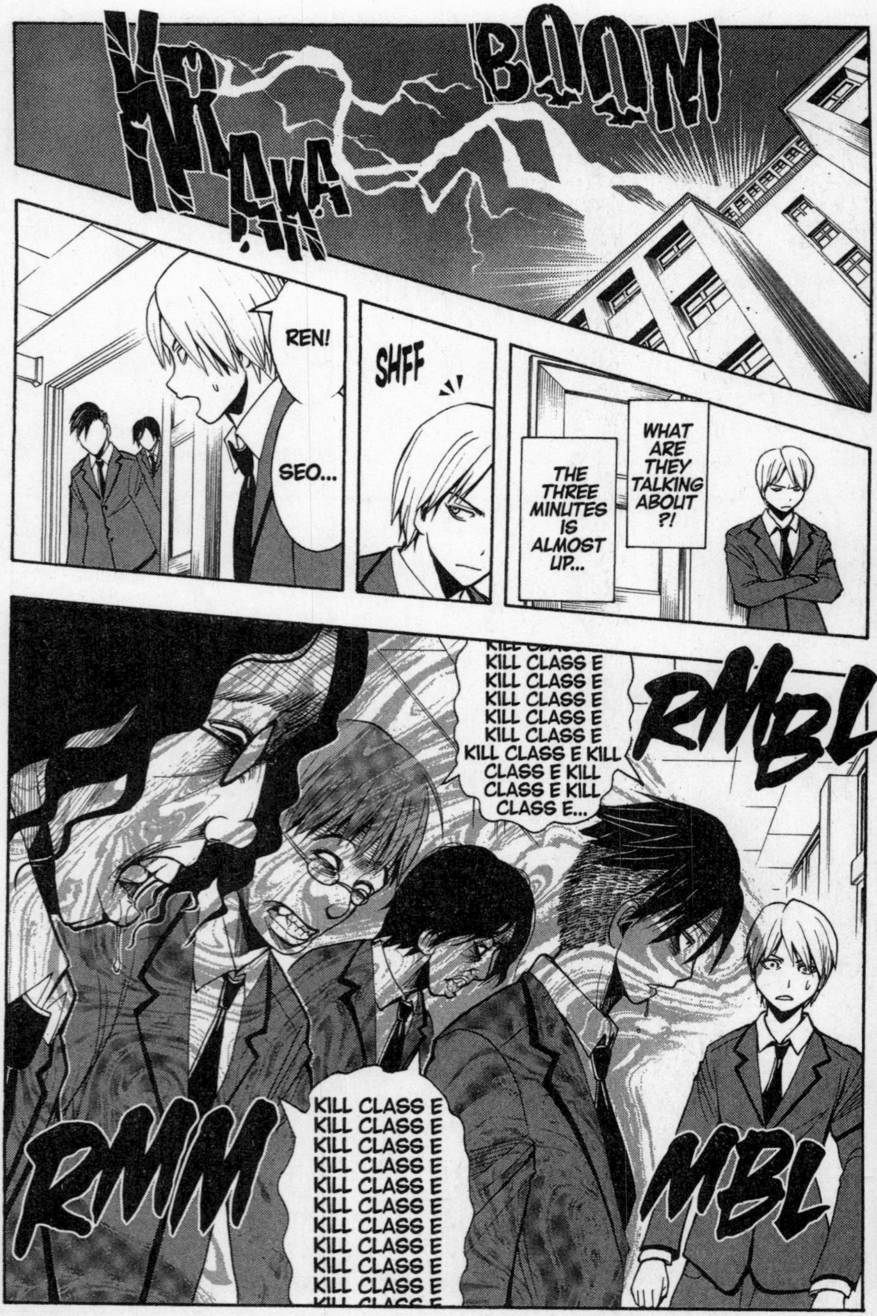
BOOM
KRAKA
WHAT ARE THEY TALKING ABOUT?!
THE THREE MINUTES IS ALMOST UP...
SHFF
REN!
SEO...
RMBL
KILL CLASS E KILL CLASS E KILL CLASS E KILL CLASS E KILL CLASS E KILL CLASS E KILL CLASS E KILL CLASS E KILL CLASS E...
MBL
KILL CLASS E KILL CLASS E KILL CLASS E KILL CLASS E KILL CLASS E KILL CLASS E KILL CLASS E KILL CLASS E KILL CLASS E KILL CLASS E KILL CLASS E KILL CLASS E
RMM

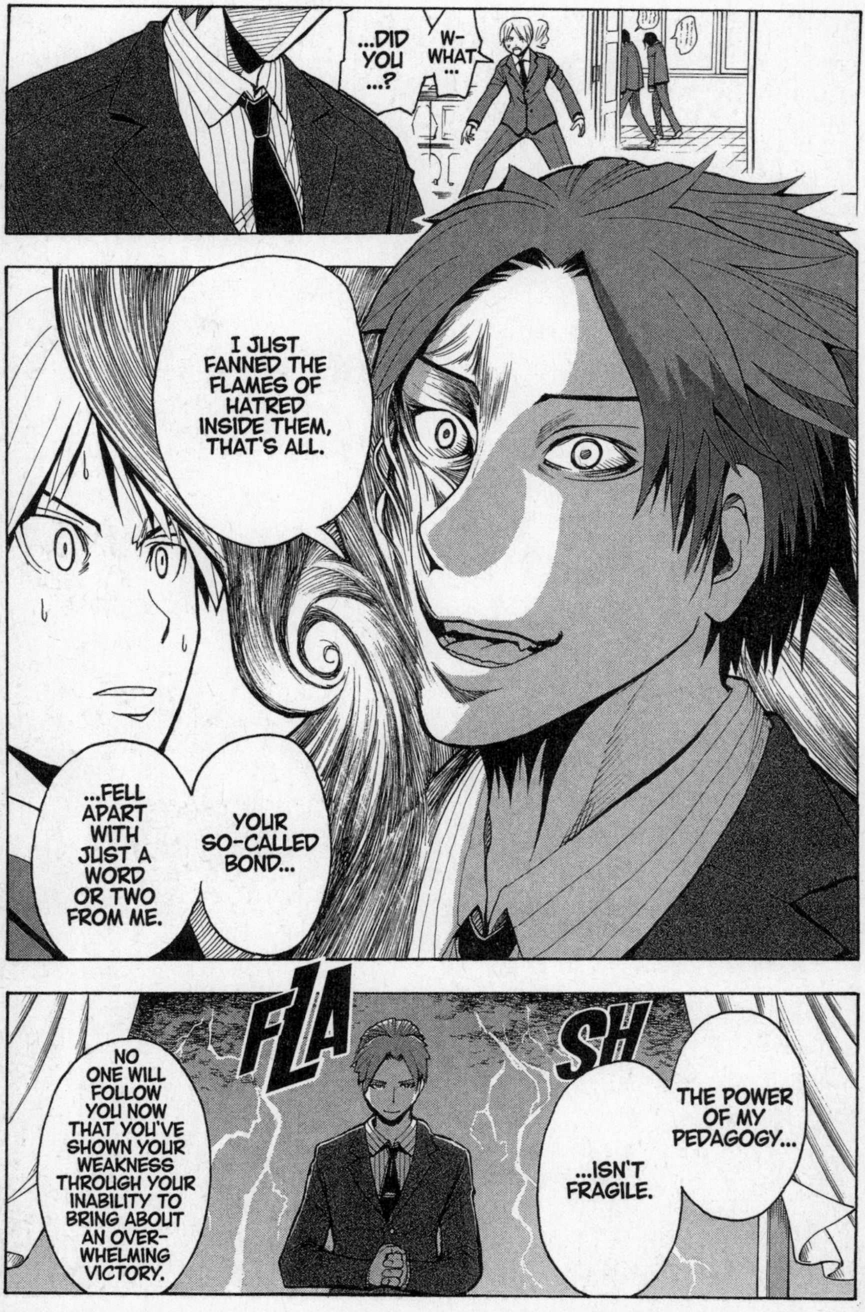
W-WHAT...
...DID YOU ...?
I JUST FANNED THE FLAMES OF HATRED INSIDE THEM, THAT'S ALL.
YOUR SO-CALLED BOND...
...FELL APART WITH JUST A WORD OR TWO FROM ME.
THE POWER OF MY PEDAGOGY...
FLASH
...ISN'T FRAGILE.
NO ONE WILL FOLLOW YOU NOW THAT YOU'VE SHOWN YOUR WEAKNESS THROUGH YOUR INABILITY TO BRING ABOUT AN OVER-WHELMING VICTORY.

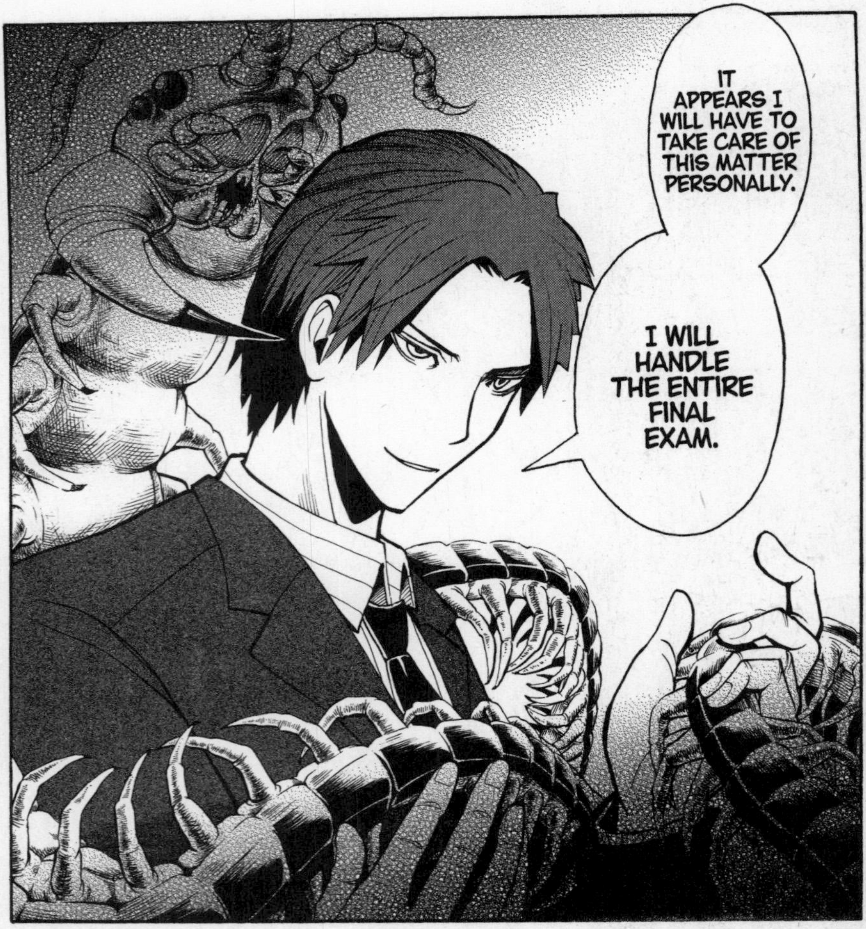
IT APPEARS I WILL HAVE TO TAKE CARE OF THIS MATTER PERSONALLY.
I WILL HANDLE THE ENTIRE FINAL EXAM.
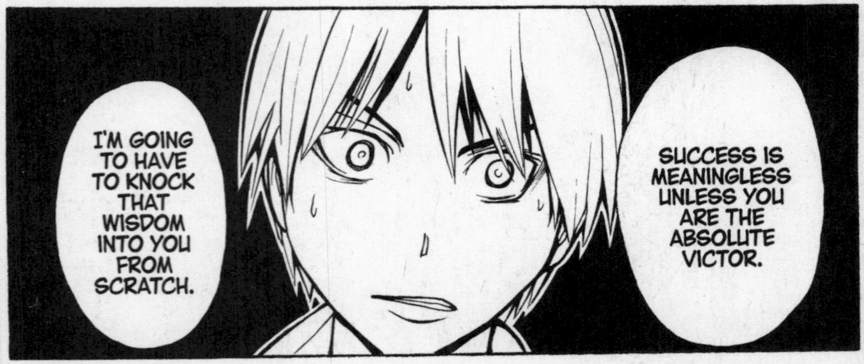
SUCCESS IS MEANINGLESS UNLESS YOU ARE THE ABSOLUTE VICTOR.
I'M GOING TO HAVE TO KNOCK THAT WISDOM INTO YOU FROM SCRATCH.

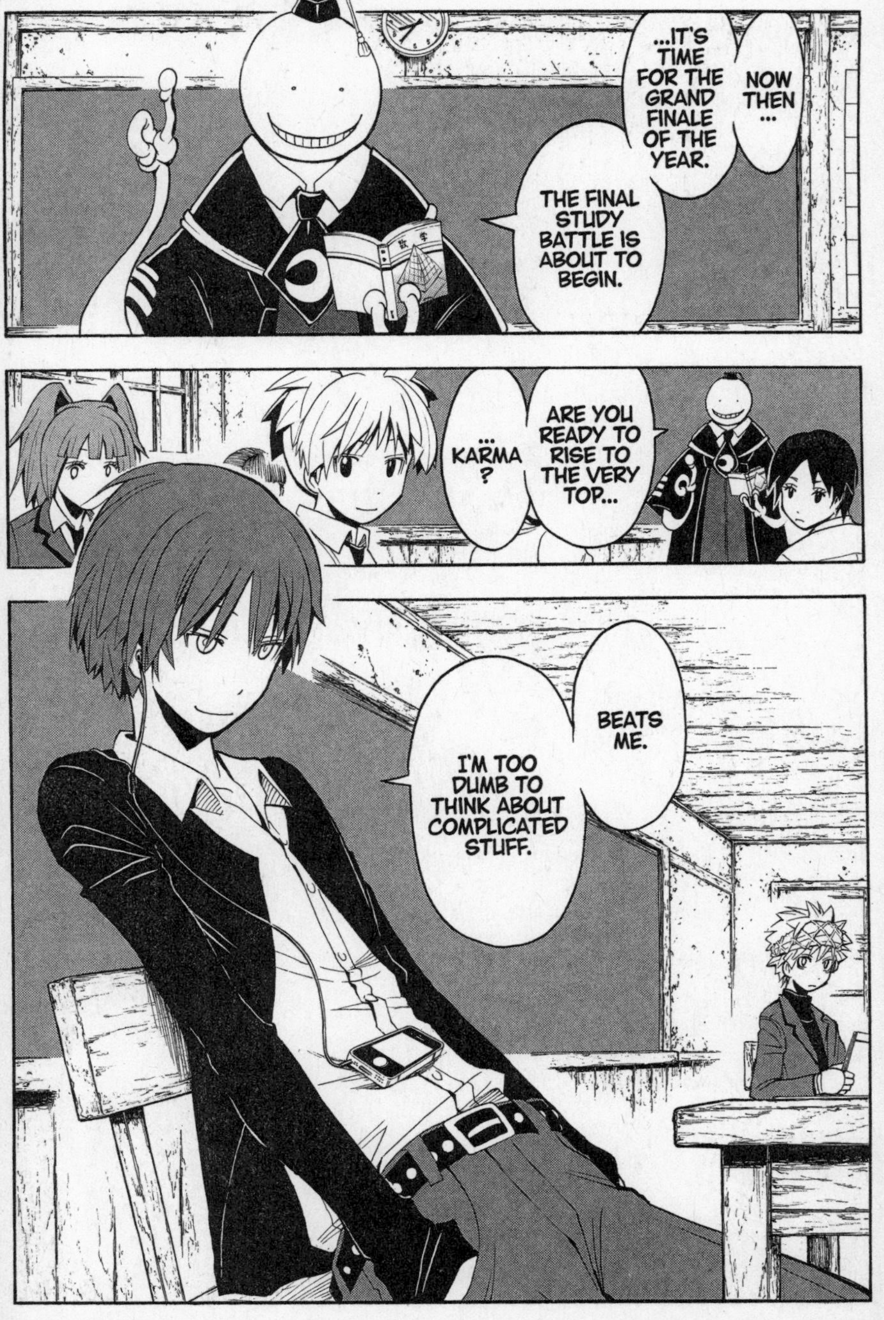
NOW THEN ...
...IT'S TIME FOR THE GRAND FINALE OF THE YEAR.
THE FINAL STUDY BATTLE IS ABOUT TO BEGIN.
ARE YOU READY TO RISE TO THE VERY TOP...
... KARMA ?
BEATS ME.
I'M TOO DUMB TO THINK ABOUT COMPLICATED STUFF.

E-22 HIROTO MAEHARA

- ☺ BIRTHDAY: DECEMBER 6
- ☺ HEIGHT: 5' 9"
- ☺ WEIGHT: 148 LBS.
- ☺ FAVORITE SUBJECT: MATHEMATICS
- ☺ LEAST FAVORITE SUBJECT: CIVICS
- ☺ HOBBY/SKILLS: HITTING ON GIRLS, SOCCER
- ☺ FUTURE GOAL: ANY JOB, AS LONG AS IT'S POPULAR WITH THE LADIES.
- ☺ GIRLS HE HIT ON IN CLASS E: PRETTY MUCH EVERYBODY EXCEPT KATAOKA. (AND HE CRASHED AND BURNED WITH ALL OF THEM.)
- ☺ REASON HE DIDN'T HIT ON KATAOKA: LOYALTY TO A FRIEND.

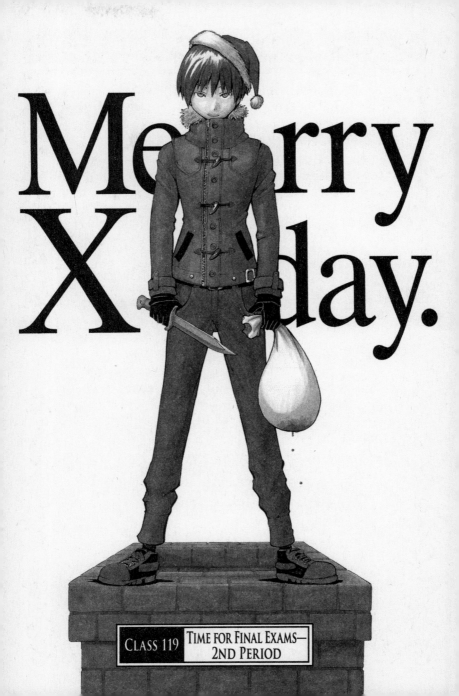

Merry X day.

CLASS 119 | TIME FOR FINAL EXAMS—2ND PERIOD

• Kunugigaoka Junior High Bulletin Board •

Kunugigaoka Junior High
Special Placement Class School Policies

Supplementary Note

○ Class E students must return to the main school building by the end of the second semester. Students unable to do so or who neglect to apply to return will be expelled.

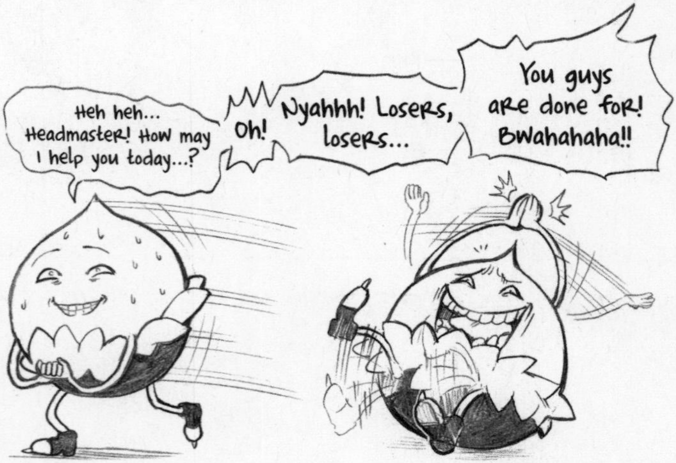
You guys are done for! Bwahahaha!!
Nyahhh! Losers, losers...
Oh!
Heh heh... Headmaster! How may I help you today...?

**Kunugigaoka
School Mascot
Kunudon**

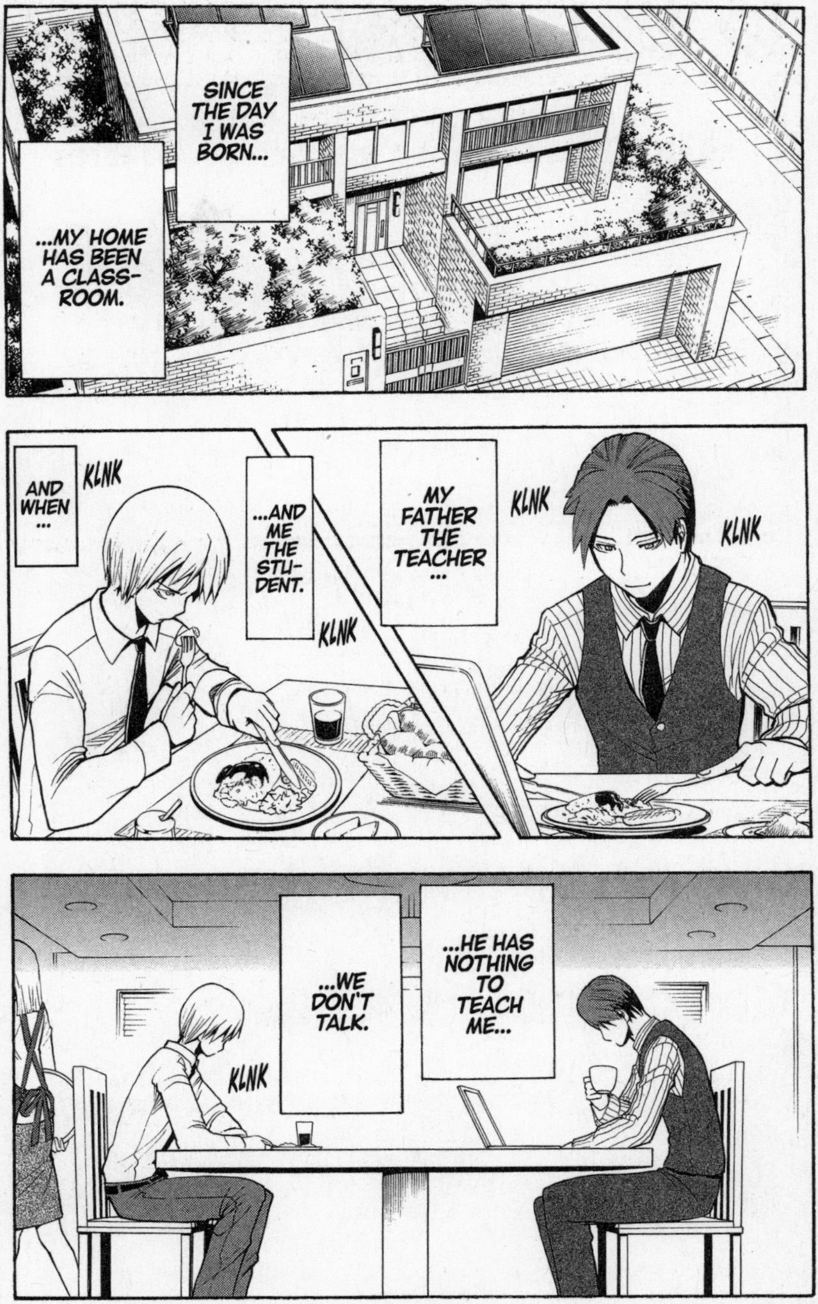
SINCE THE DAY I WAS BORN...
...MY HOME HAS BEEN A CLASS-ROOM.
KLNK
MY FATHER THE TEACHER ...
KLNK
...AND ME THE STU-DENT.
KLNK
KLNK
AND WHEN ...
...HE HAS NOTHING TO TEACH ME...
...WE DON'T TALK.
KLNK

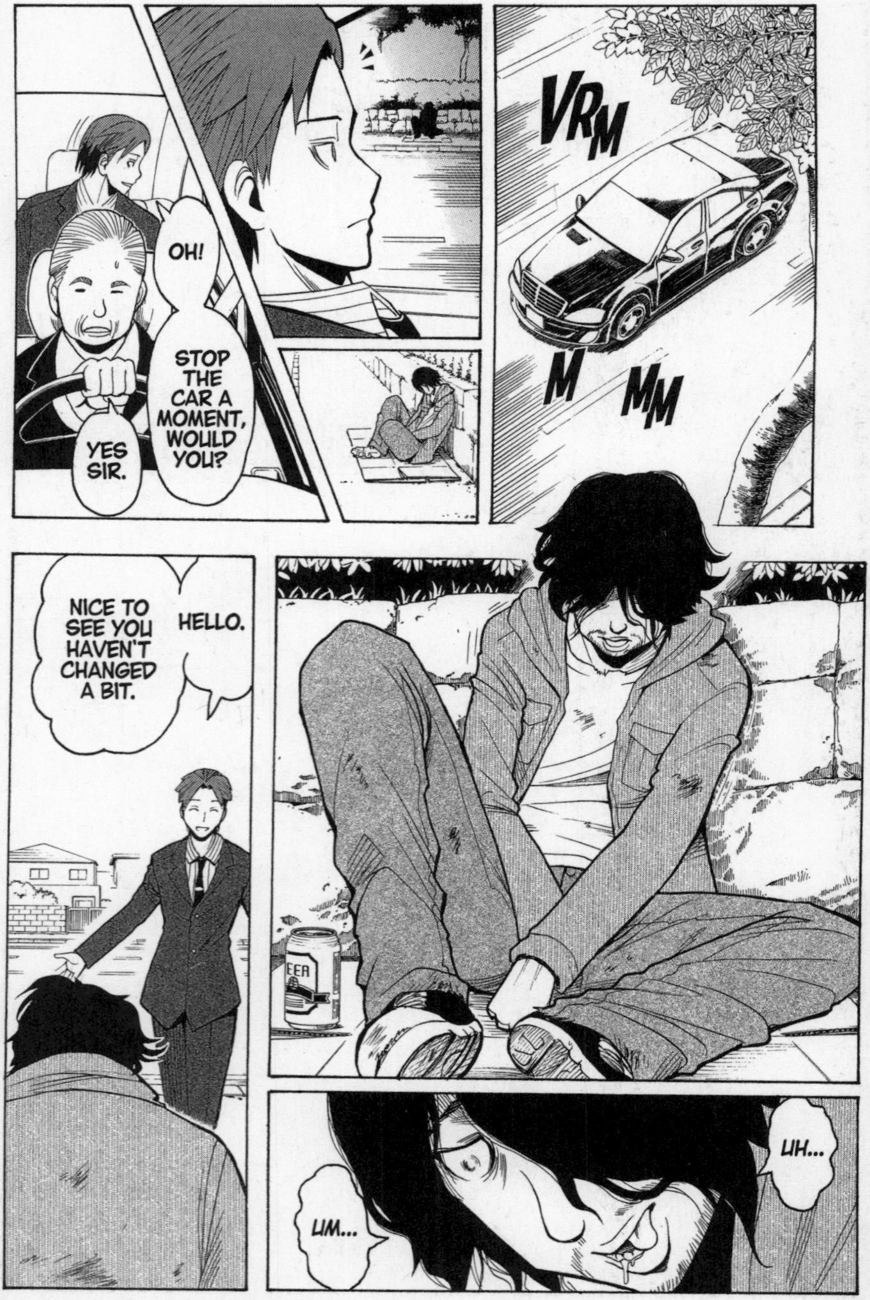
VRM
M MM
OH!
STOP THE CAR A MOMENT, WOULD YOU?
YES SIR.
UH...
UM...
HELLO.
NICE TO SEE YOU HAVEN'T CHANGED A BIT.

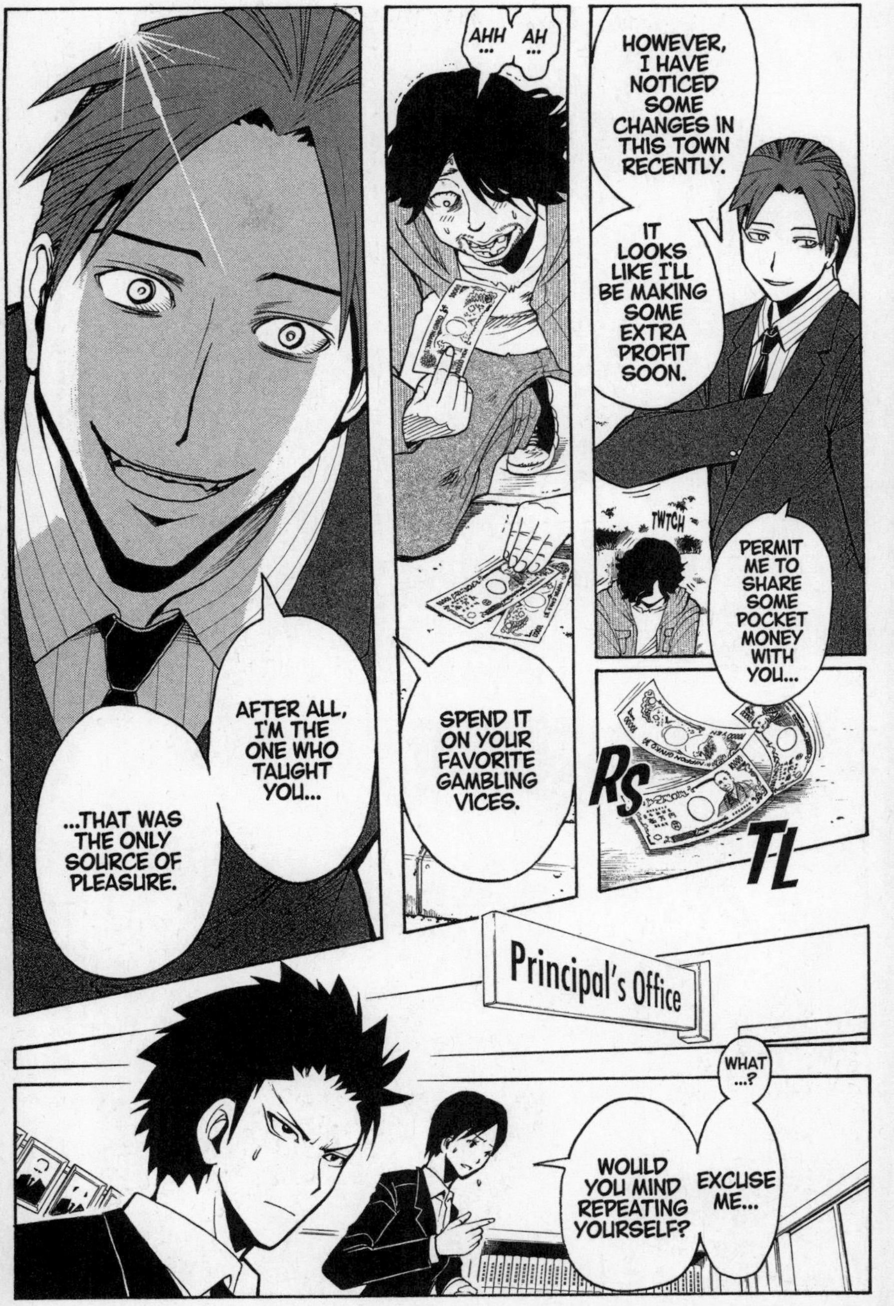
HOWEVER, I HAVE NOTICED SOME CHANGES IN THIS TOWN RECENTLY.
IT LOOKS LIKE I'LL BE MAKING SOME EXTRA PROFIT SOON.
TWTCH
PERMIT ME TO SHARE SOME POCKET MONEY WITH YOU...
RS
T-L
AHH...
AH...
SPEND IT ON YOUR FAVORITE GAMBLING VICES.
AFTER ALL, I'M THE ONE WHO TAUGHT YOU...
...THAT WAS THE ONLY SOURCE OF PLEASURE.
Principal's Office
WHAT...?
EXCUSE ME...
WOULD YOU MIND REPEATING YOURSELF?

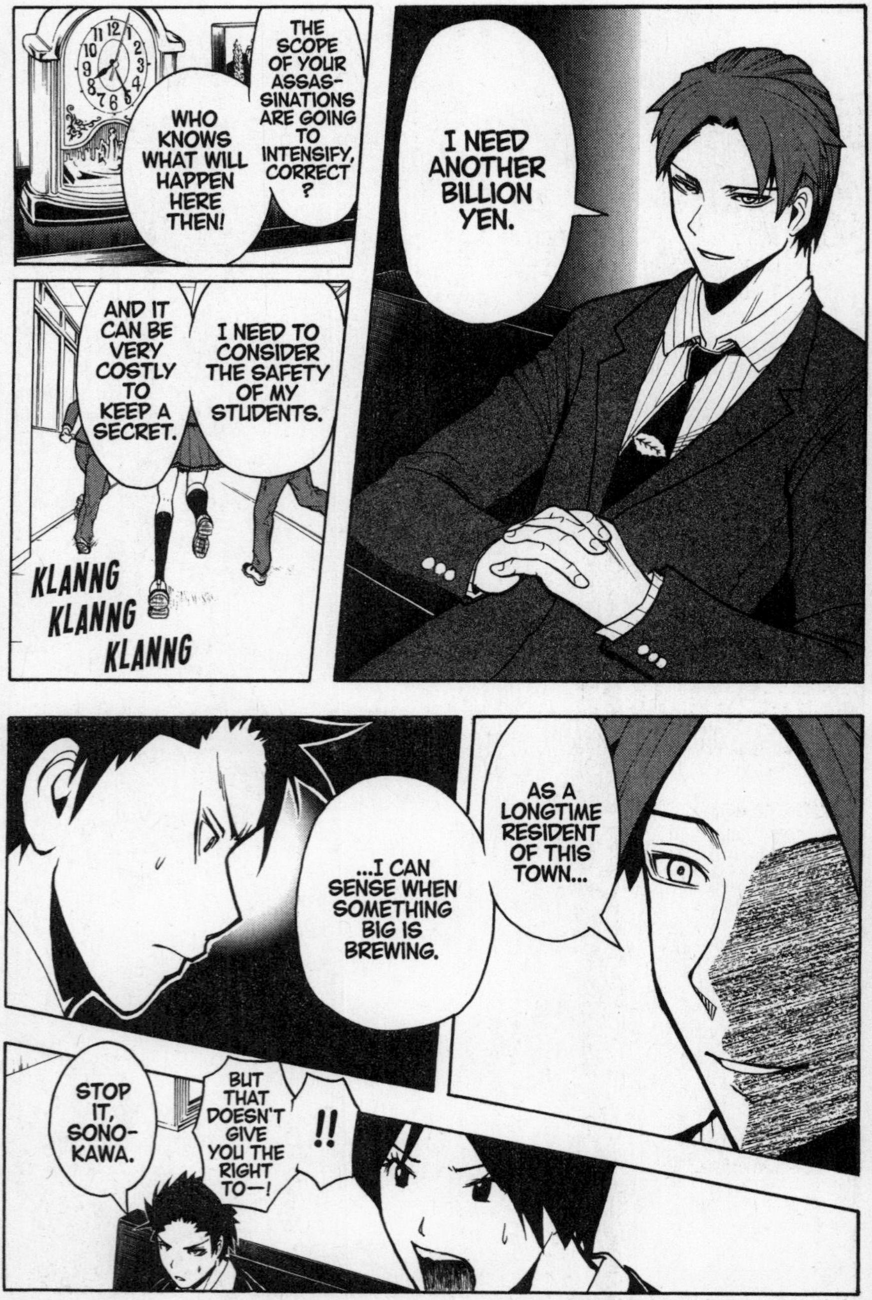
I NEED ANOTHER BILLION YEN.
THE SCOPE OF YOUR ASSAS-SINATIONS ARE GOING TO INTENSIFY, CORRECT?
WHO KNOWS WHAT WILL HAPPEN HERE THEN!
I NEED TO CONSIDER THE SAFETY OF MY STUDENTS.
AND IT CAN BE VERY COSTLY TO KEEP A SECRET.
KLANNG
KLANNG
KLANNG
AS A LONGTIME RESIDENT OF THIS TOWN...
...I CAN SENSE WHEN SOMETHING BIG IS BREWING.
!!
BUT THAT DOESN'T GIVE YOU THE RIGHT TO—!
STOP IT, SONO-KAWA.

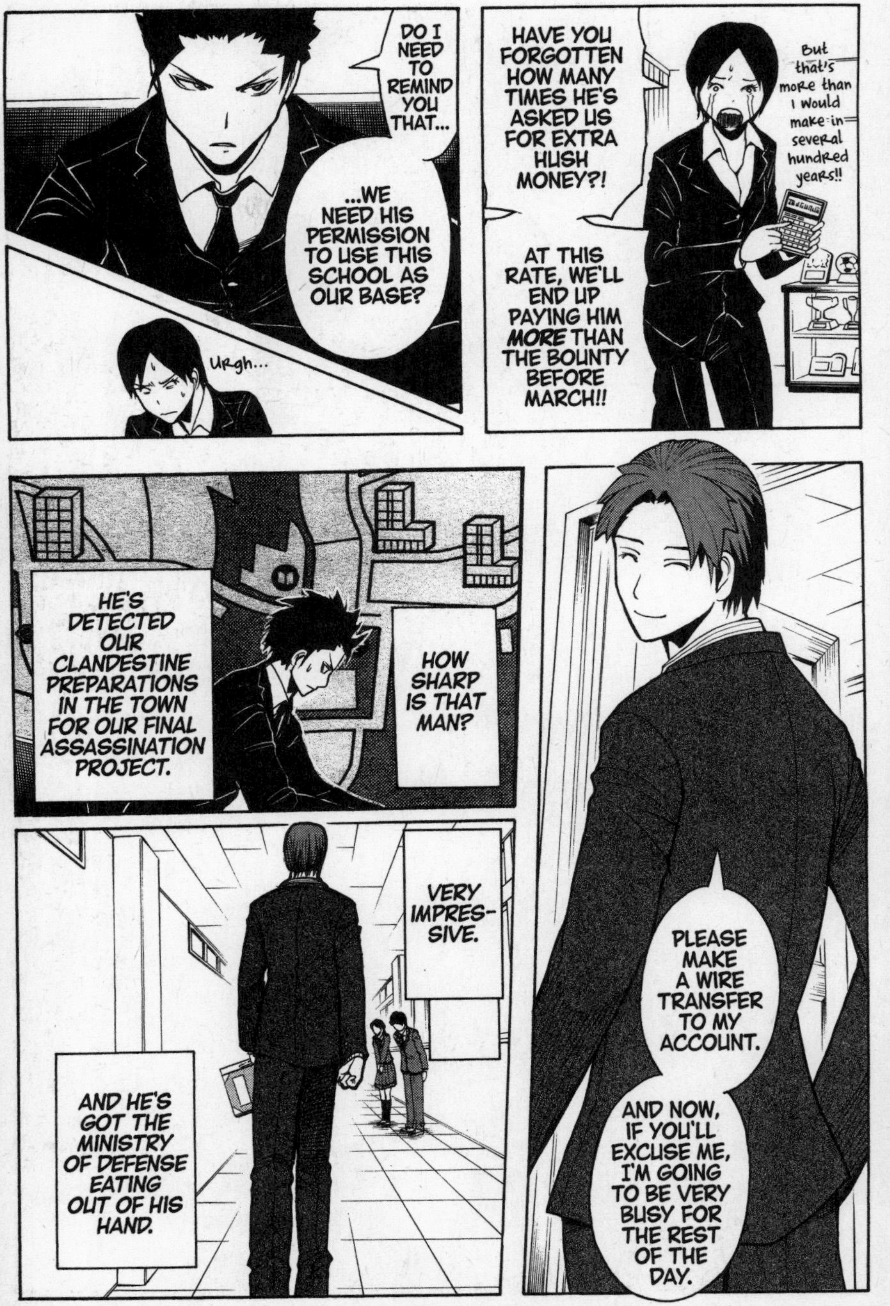
HAVE YOU FORGOTTEN HOW MANY TIMES HE'S ASKED US FOR EXTRA HUSH MONEY?!
But that's more than I would make in several hundred years!!
AT THIS RATE, WE'LL END UP PAYING HIM MORE THAN THE BOUNTY BEFORE MARCH!!
DO I NEED TO REMIND YOU THAT...
...WE NEED HIS PERMISSION TO USE THIS SCHOOL AS OUR BASE?
Urgh...
PLEASE MAKE A WIRE TRANSFER TO MY ACCOUNT.
AND NOW, IF YOU'LL EXCUSE ME, I'M GOING TO BE VERY BUSY FOR THE REST OF THE DAY.
HE'S DETECTED OUR CLANDESTINE PREPARATIONS IN THE TOWN FOR OUR FINAL ASSASSINATION PROJECT.
HOW SHARP IS THAT MAN?
VERY IMPRES-SIVE.
AND HE'S GOT THE MINISTRY OF DEFENSE EATING OUT OF HIS HAND.

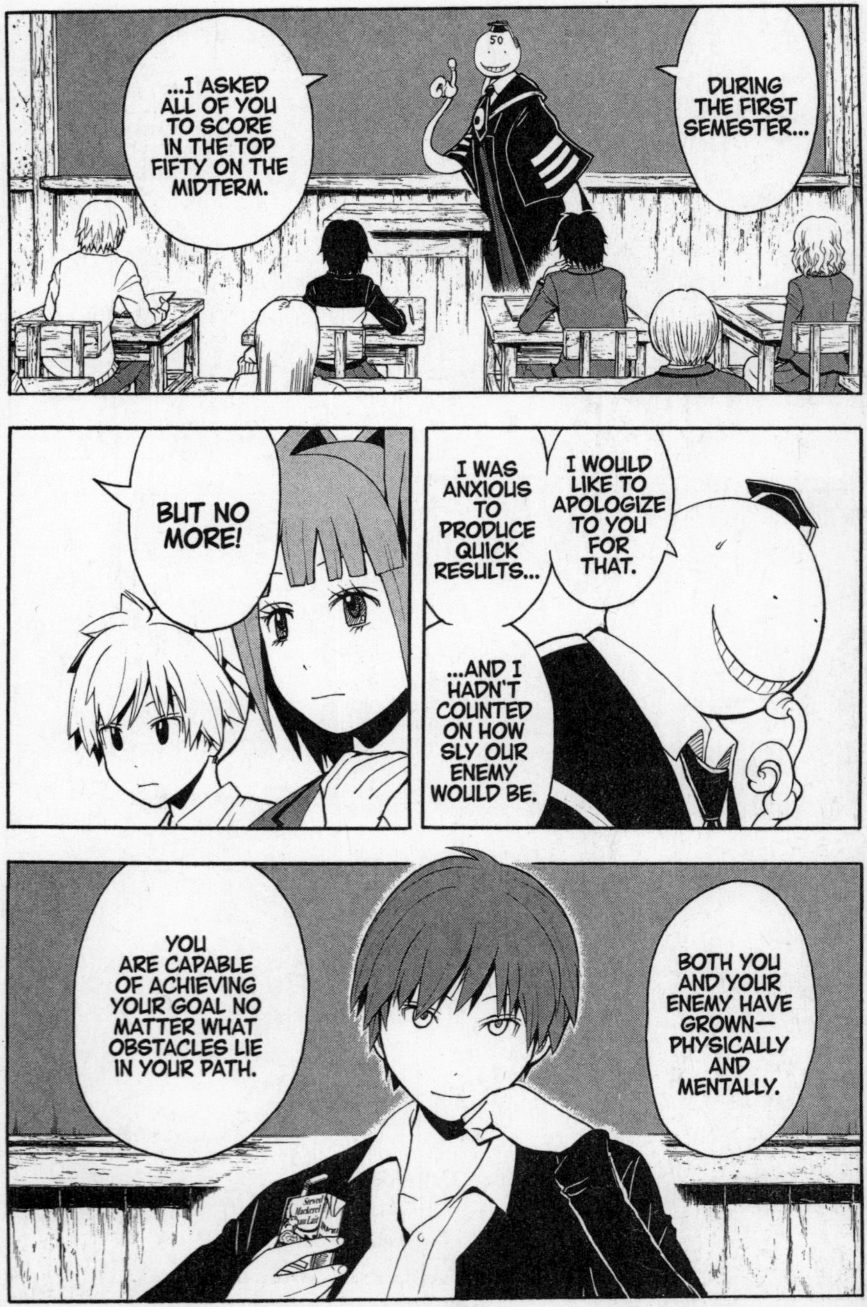
DURING THE FIRST SEMESTER...
...I ASKED ALL OF YOU TO SCORE IN THE TOP FIFTY ON THE MIDTERM.
I WOULD LIKE TO APOLOGIZE TO YOU FOR THAT.
I WAS ANXIOUS TO PRODUCE QUICK RESULTS...
...AND I HADN'T COUNTED ON HOW SLY OUR ENEMY WOULD BE.
BUT NO MORE!
BOTH YOU AND YOUR ENEMY HAVE GROWN—PHYSICALLY AND MENTALLY.
YOU ARE CAPABLE OF ACHIEVING YOUR GOAL NO MATTER WHAT OBSTACLES LIE IN YOUR PATH.

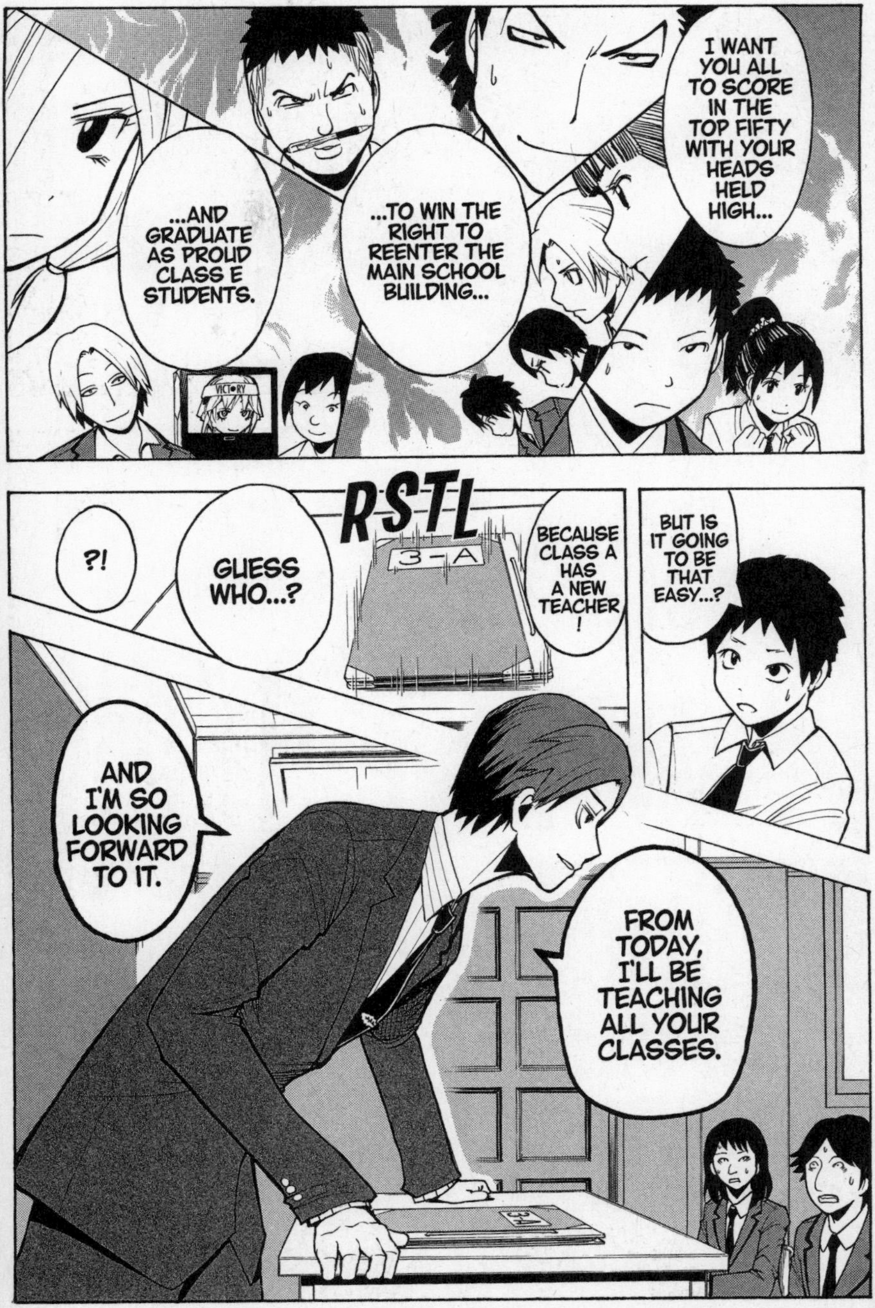
I WANT YOU ALL TO SCORE IN THE TOP FIFTY WITH YOUR HEADS HELD HIGH...
...TO WIN THE RIGHT TO REENTER THE MAIN SCHOOL BUILDING...
...AND GRADUATE AS PROUD CLASS E STUDENTS.
BUT IS IT GOING TO BE THAT EASY...?
BECAUSE CLASS A HAS A NEW TEACHER!
RSTL
3-A
GUESS WHO...?
?!
FROM TODAY, I'LL BE TEACHING ALL YOUR CLASSES.
AND I'M SO LOOKING FORWARD TO IT.

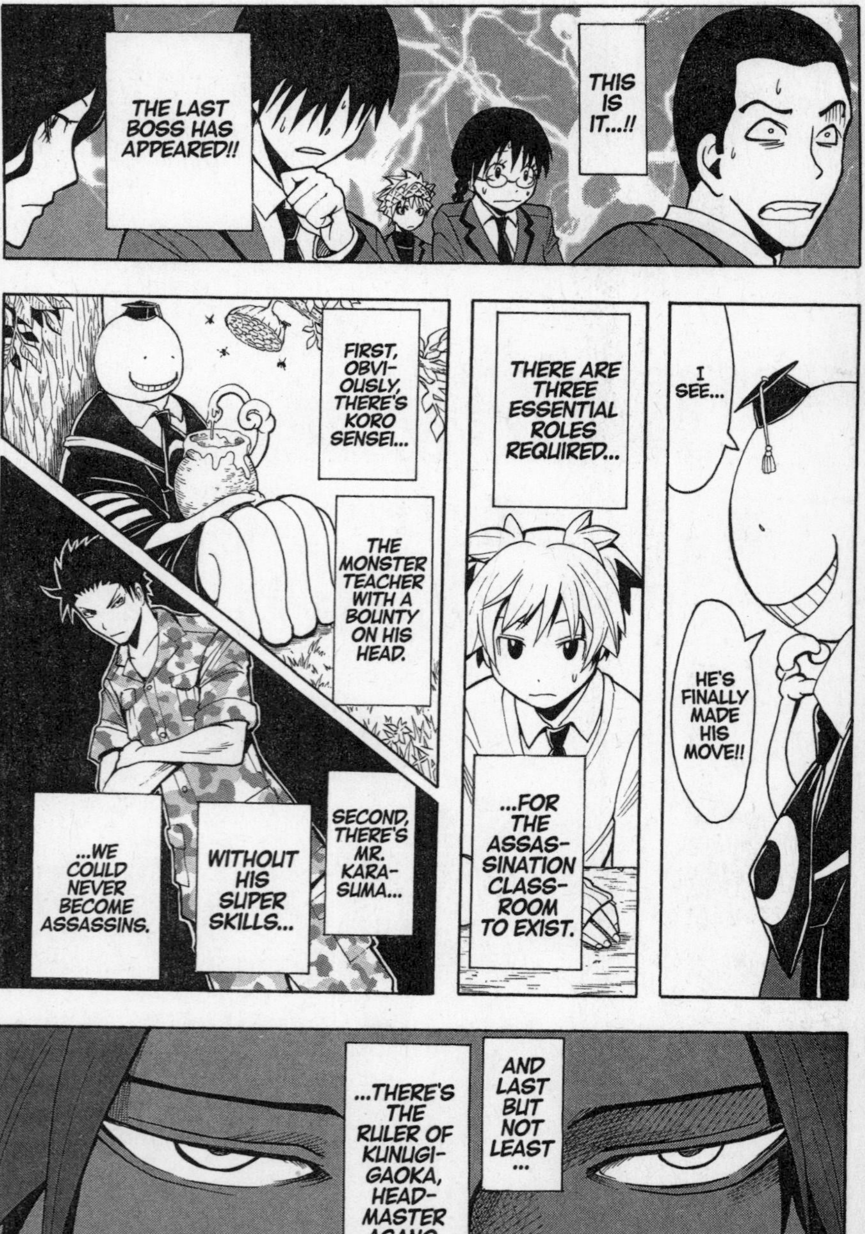
THIS IS IT...!!
THE LAST BOSS HAS APPEARED!!
I SEE...
HE'S FINALLY MADE HIS MOVE!!
THERE ARE THREE ESSENTIAL ROLES REQUIRED...
...FOR THE ASSASSINATION CLASSROOM TO EXIST.
FIRST, OBVIOUSLY, THERE'S KORO SENSEI...
THE MONSTER TEACHER WITH A BOUNTY ON HIS HEAD.
SECOND, THERE'S MR. KARASUMA...
WITHOUT HIS SUPER SKILLS...
...WE COULD NEVER BECOME ASSASSINS.
AND LAST BUT NOT LEAST...
...THERE'S THE RULER OF KUNUGIGAOKA, HEADMASTER ASANO.

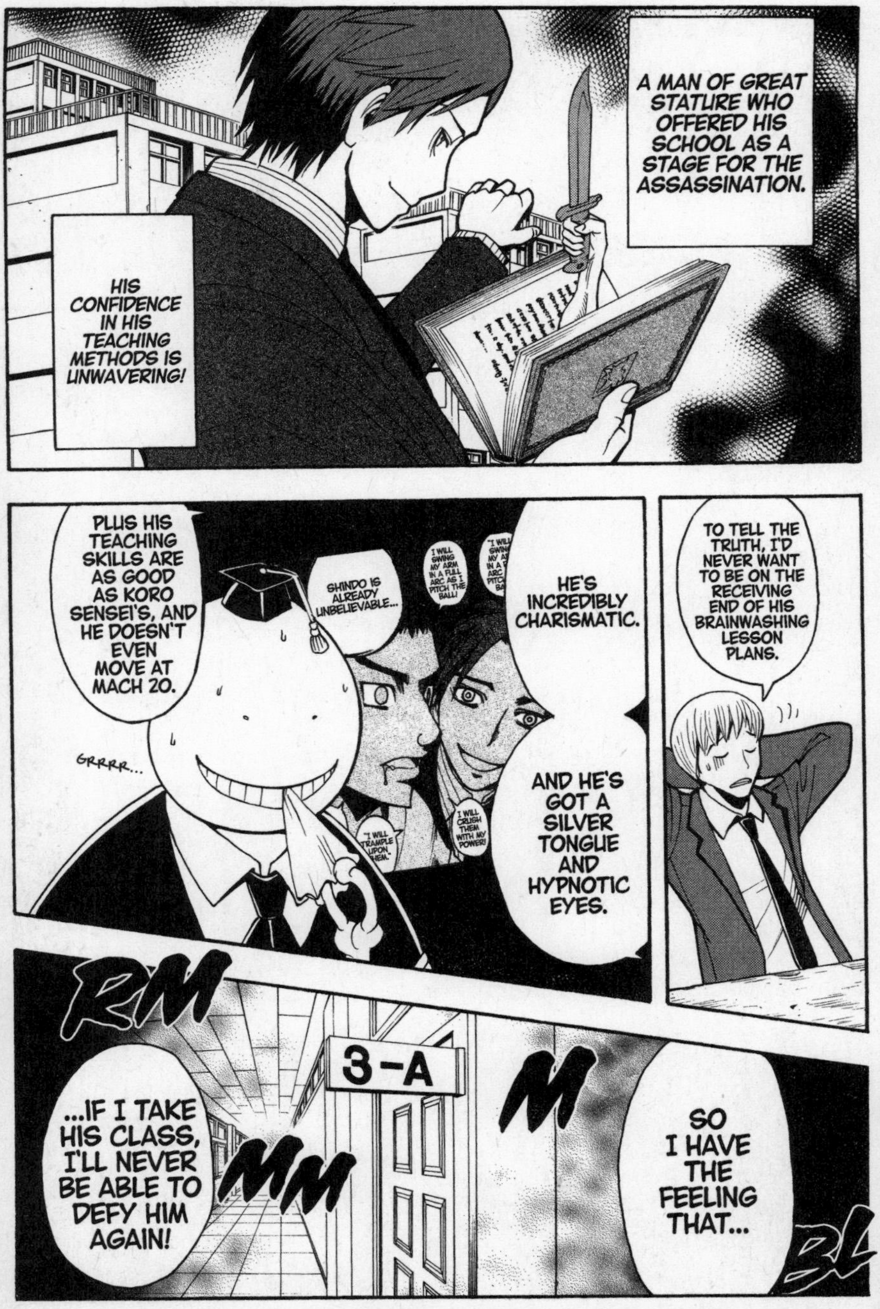
A MAN OF GREAT STATURE WHO OFFERED HIS SCHOOL AS A STAGE FOR THE ASSASSINATION.
HIS CONFIDENCE IN HIS TEACHING METHODS IS UNWAVERING!
TO TELL THE TRUTH, I'D NEVER WANT TO BE ON THE RECEIVING END OF HIS BRAINWASHING LESSON PLANS.
HE'S INCREDIBLY CHARISMATIC.
AND HE'S GOT A SILVER TONGUE AND HYPNOTIC EYES.
"I WILL SWING MY ARM IN A FULL ARC AS I PITCH THE BALL!"
"I WILL CRUSH THEM WITH MY POWER!"
"I WILL TRAMPLE UPON THEM."
SHINDO IS ALREADY UNBELIEVABLE...
PLUS HIS TEACHING SKILLS ARE AS GOOD AS KORO SENSEI'S, AND HE DOESN'T EVEN MOVE AT MACH 20.
GRRRR...
SO I HAVE THE FEELING THAT...
M
MM
3-A
...IF I TAKE HIS CLASS, I'LL NEVER BE ABLE TO DEFY HIM AGAIN!
RM

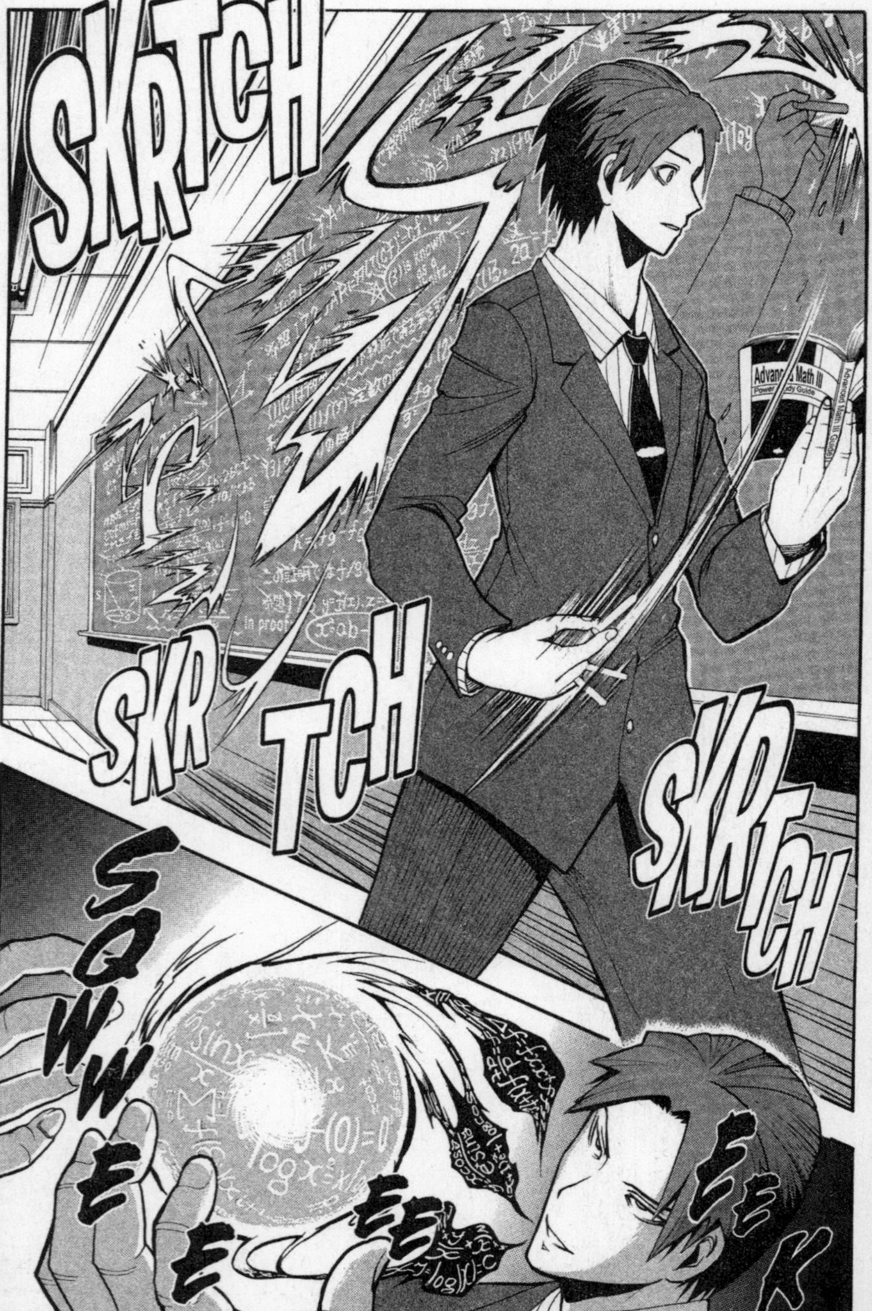
SKRTCH
SKR TCH
SKRTCH
SQWWEE
EE
EEK

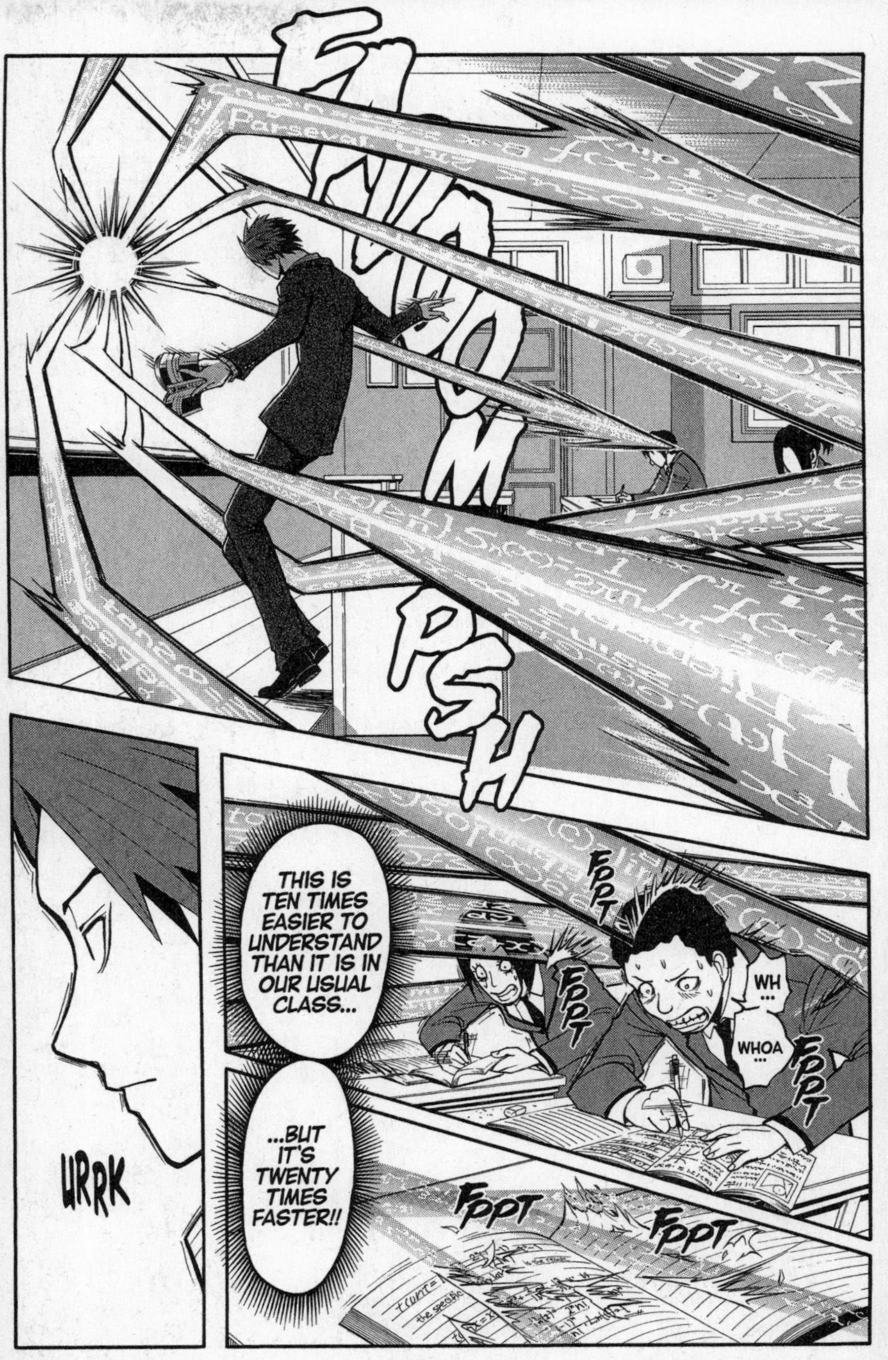
FWOOM
PSH
FPPT
WH...
WHOA...
FPPT
THIS IS TEN TIMES EASIER TO UNDERSTAND THAN IT IS IN OUR USUAL CLASS...
FPPT
...BUT IT'S TWENTY TIMES FASTER!!
FPPT
FPPT
URRK

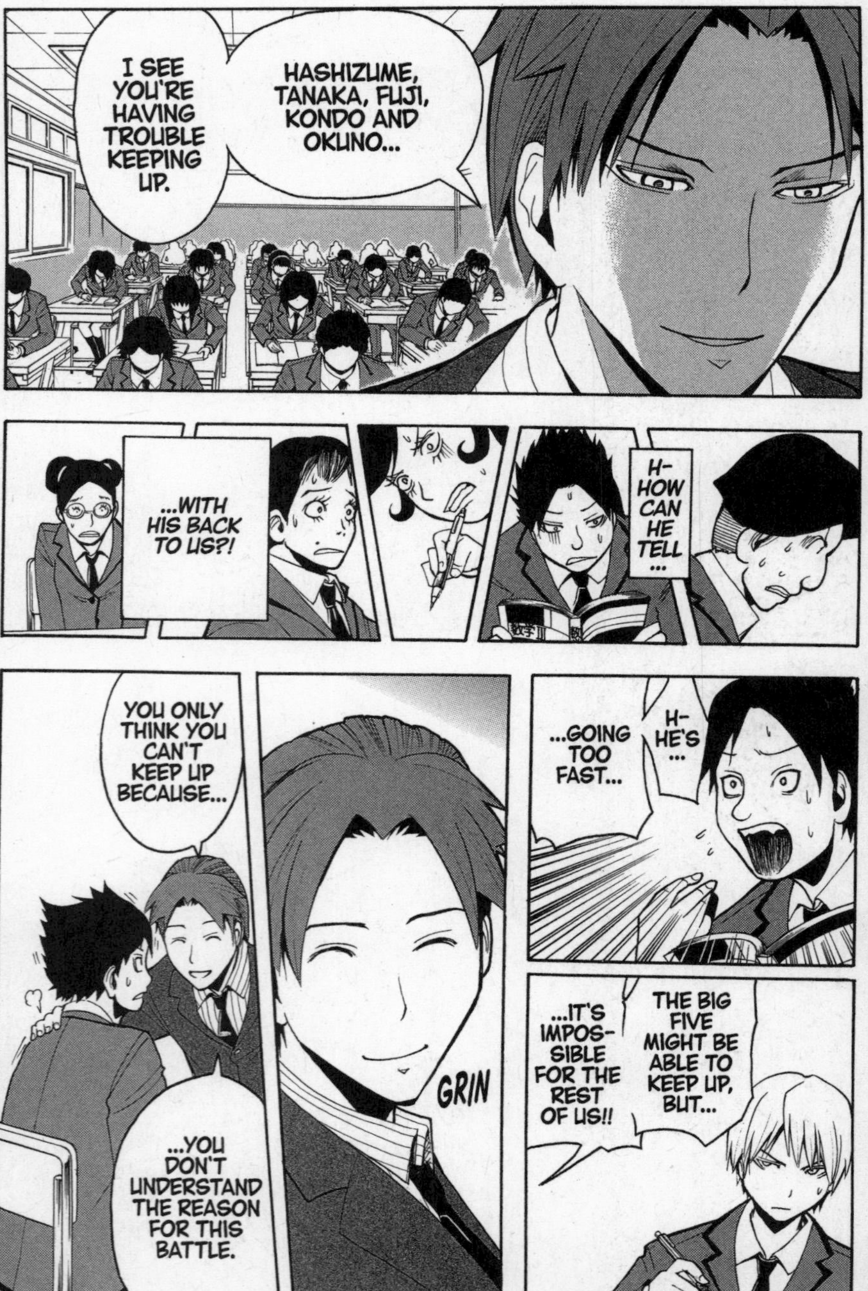
HASHIZUME, TANAKA, FUJI, KONDO AND OKUNO...
I SEE YOU'RE HAVING TROUBLE KEEPING UP.
H-HOW CAN HE TELL...
...WITH HIS BACK TO US?!
H-HE'S...
...GOING TOO FAST...
THE BIG FIVE MIGHT BE ABLE TO KEEP UP, BUT...
...IT'S IMPOS-SIBLE FOR THE REST OF US!!
GRIN
YOU ONLY THINK YOU CAN'T KEEP UP BECAUSE...
...YOU DON'T UNDERSTAND THE REASON FOR THIS BATTLE.

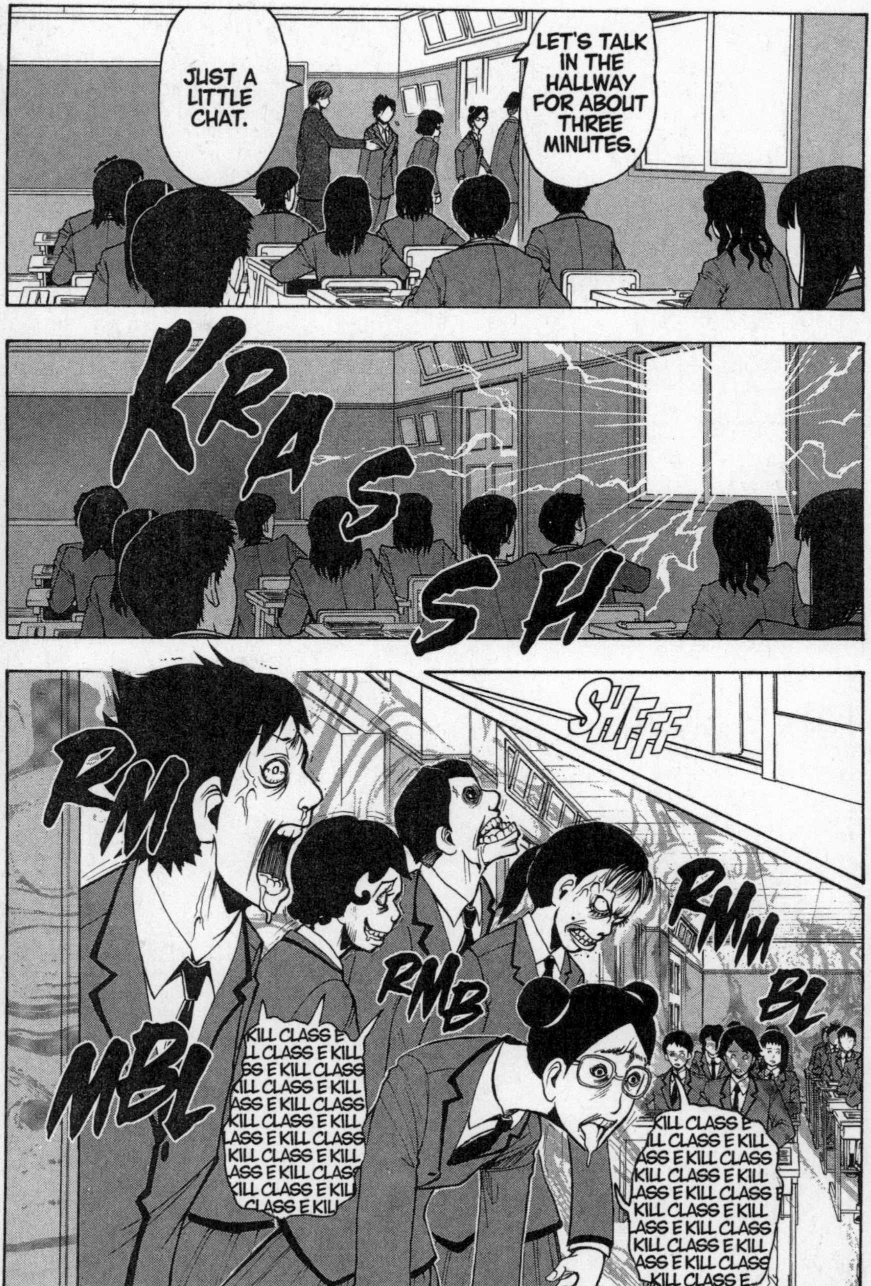
LET'S TALK IN THE HALLWAY FOR ABOUT THREE MINUTES.
JUST A LITTLE CHAT.
KRASSH
SHFFF
RMM
BL
KILL CLASS E KILL CLASS E KILL CLASS E KILL CLASS E KILL CLASS E KILL CLASS E KILL CLASS E KILL CLASS E KILL CLASS E KILL CLASS E KILL CLASS E
RMB
RM
MBL
KILL CLASS E KILL CLASS E KILL CLASS E KILL CLASS E KILL CLASS E KILL CLASS E KILL CLASS E KILL CLASS E KILL CLASS E KILL CLASS E KILL

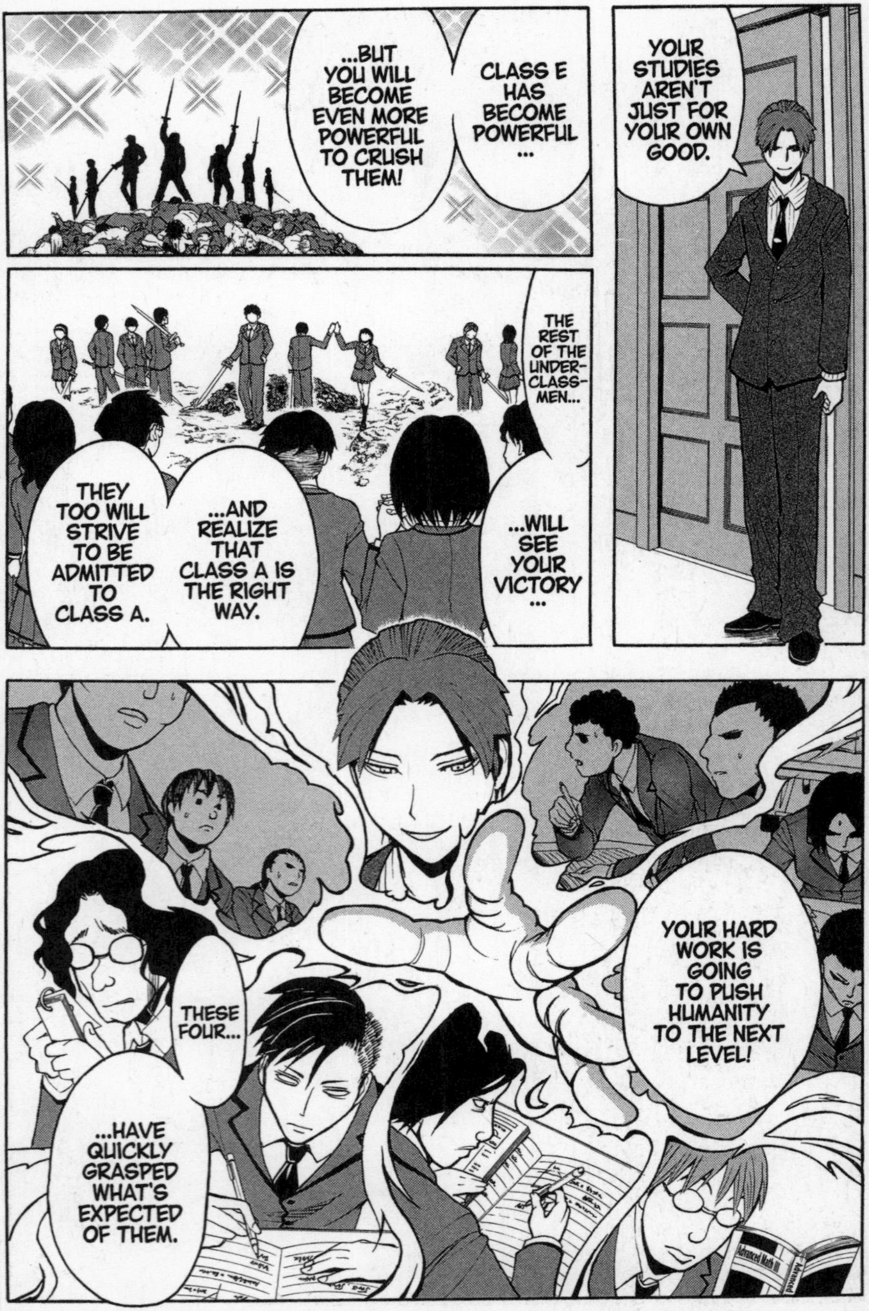
YOUR STUDIES AREN'T JUST FOR YOUR OWN GOOD.
CLASS E HAS BECOME POWERFUL...
...BUT YOU WILL BECOME EVEN MORE POWERFUL TO CRUSH THEM!
THE REST OF THE UNDER-CLASSMEN...
...WILL SEE YOUR VICTORY...
...AND REALIZE THAT CLASS A IS THE RIGHT WAY.
THEY TOO WILL STRIVE TO BE ADMITTED TO CLASS A.
YOUR HARD WORK IS GOING TO PUSH HUMANITY TO THE NEXT LEVEL!
THESE FOUR...
...HAVE QUICKLY GRASPED WHAT'S EXPECTED OF THEM.
Advanced Math III

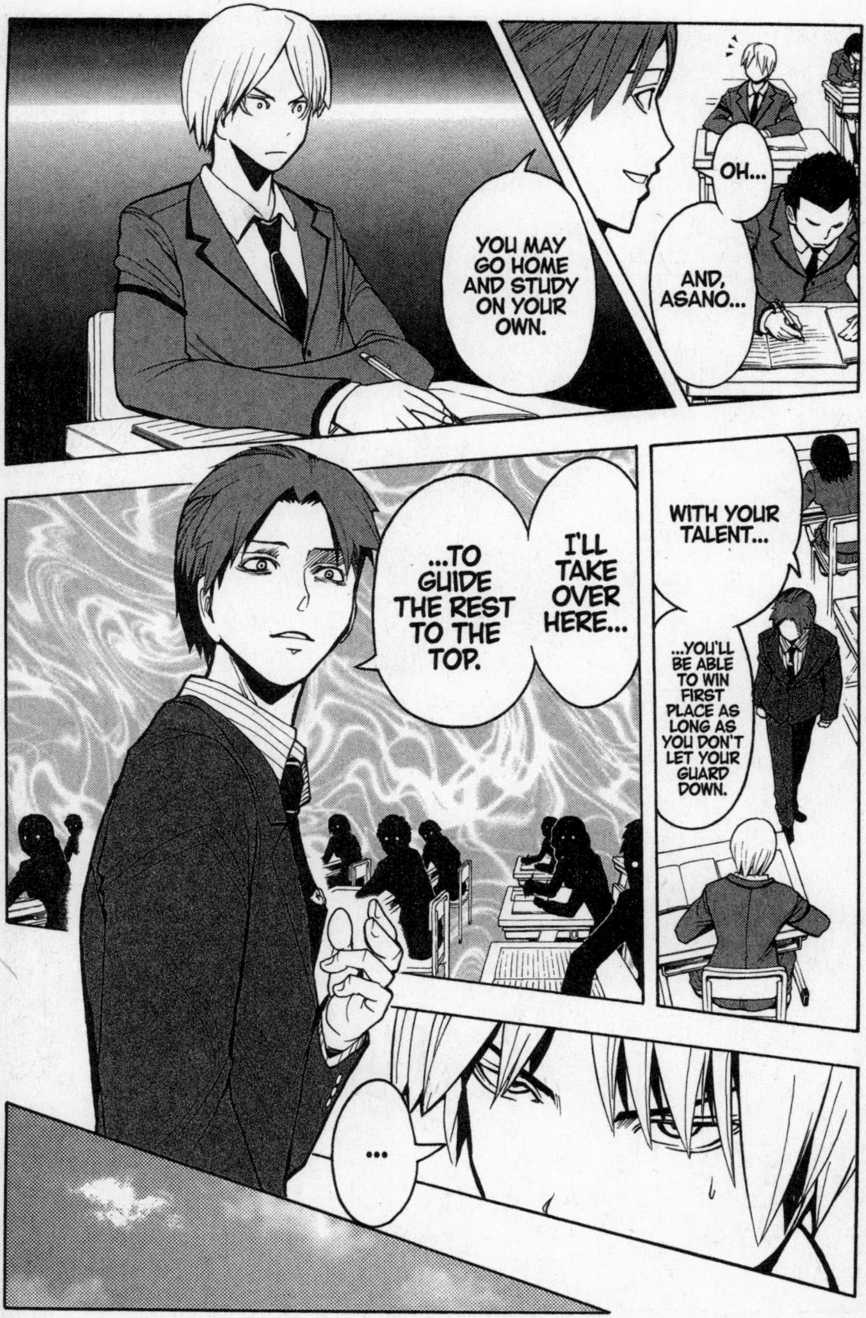
OH...
AND, ASANO...
YOU MAY GO HOME AND STUDY ON YOUR OWN.
WITH YOUR TALENT...
...YOU'LL BE ABLE TO WIN FIRST PLACE AS LONG AS YOU DON'T LET YOUR GUARD DOWN.
I'LL TAKE OVER HERE...
...TO GUIDE THE REST TO THE TOP.
...

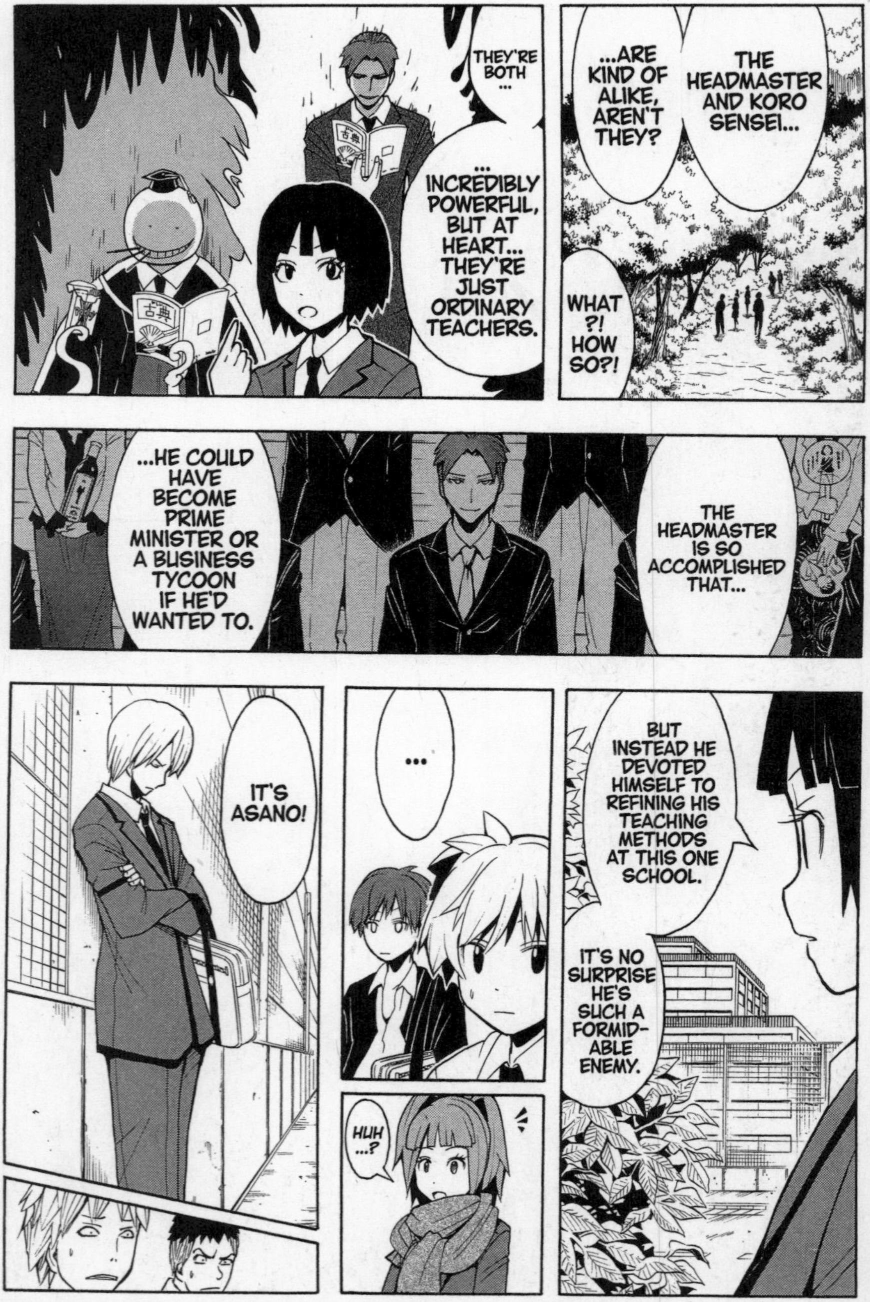
THE HEADMASTER AND KORO SENSEI...
...ARE KIND OF ALIKE, AREN'T THEY?
WHAT?! HOW SO?!
THEY'RE BOTH ...
... INCREDIBLY POWERFUL, BUT AT HEART... THEY'RE JUST ORDINARY TEACHERS.
THE HEADMASTER IS SO ACCOMPLISHED THAT...
...HE COULD HAVE BECOME PRIME MINISTER OR A BUSINESS TYCOON IF HE'D WANTED TO.
BUT INSTEAD HE DEVOTED HIMSELF TO REFINING HIS TEACHING METHODS AT THIS ONE SCHOOL.
IT'S NO SURPRISE HE'S SUCH A FORMIDABLE ENEMY.
...
HUH ...?
IT'S ASANO!

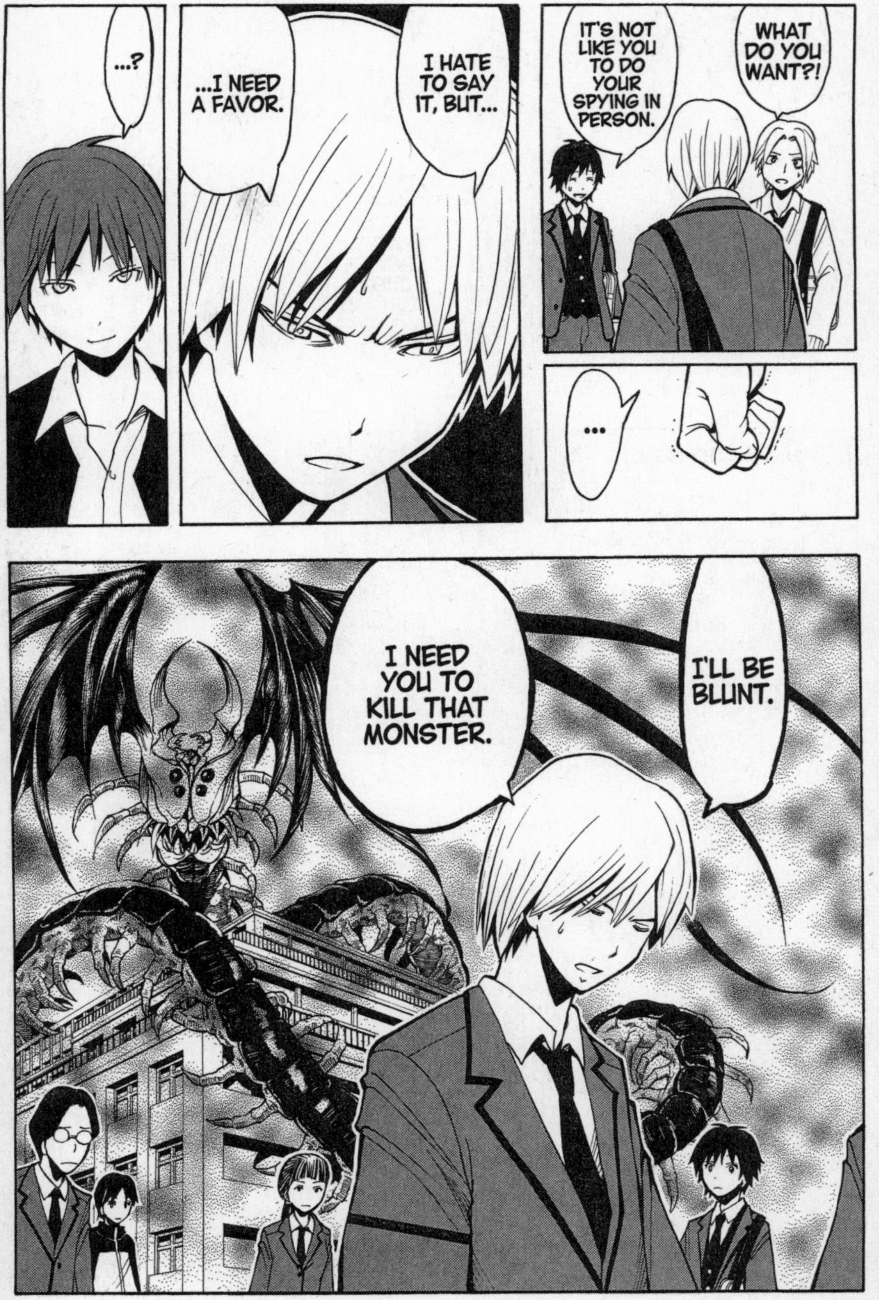
WHAT DO YOU WANT?!
IT'S NOT LIKE YOU TO DO YOUR SPYING IN PERSON.
...
I HATE TO SAY IT, BUT...
...I NEED A FAVOR.
...?
I'LL BE BLUNT.
I NEED YOU TO KILL THAT MONSTER.

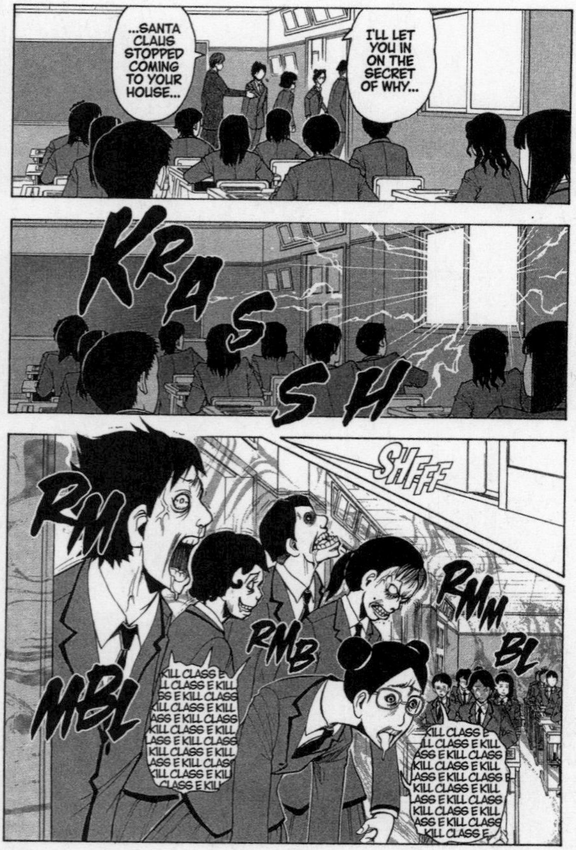
I'LL LET YOU IN ON THE SECRET OF WHY...
...SANTA CLAUS STOPPED COMING TO YOUR HOUSE...
KRASSH
SHFFF
RMM BL
RMB
RM MBL
KILL CLASS E KILL CLASS E KILL CLASS E KILL CLASS E KILL CLASS E KILL CLASS E KILL CLASS E KILL CLASS E KILL CLASS E KILL CLASS E
KILL CLASS E KILL CLASS E KILL CLASS E KILL CLASS E KILL CLASS E KILL CLASS E KILL CLASS E KILL CLASS E KILL CLASS E KILL CLASS E

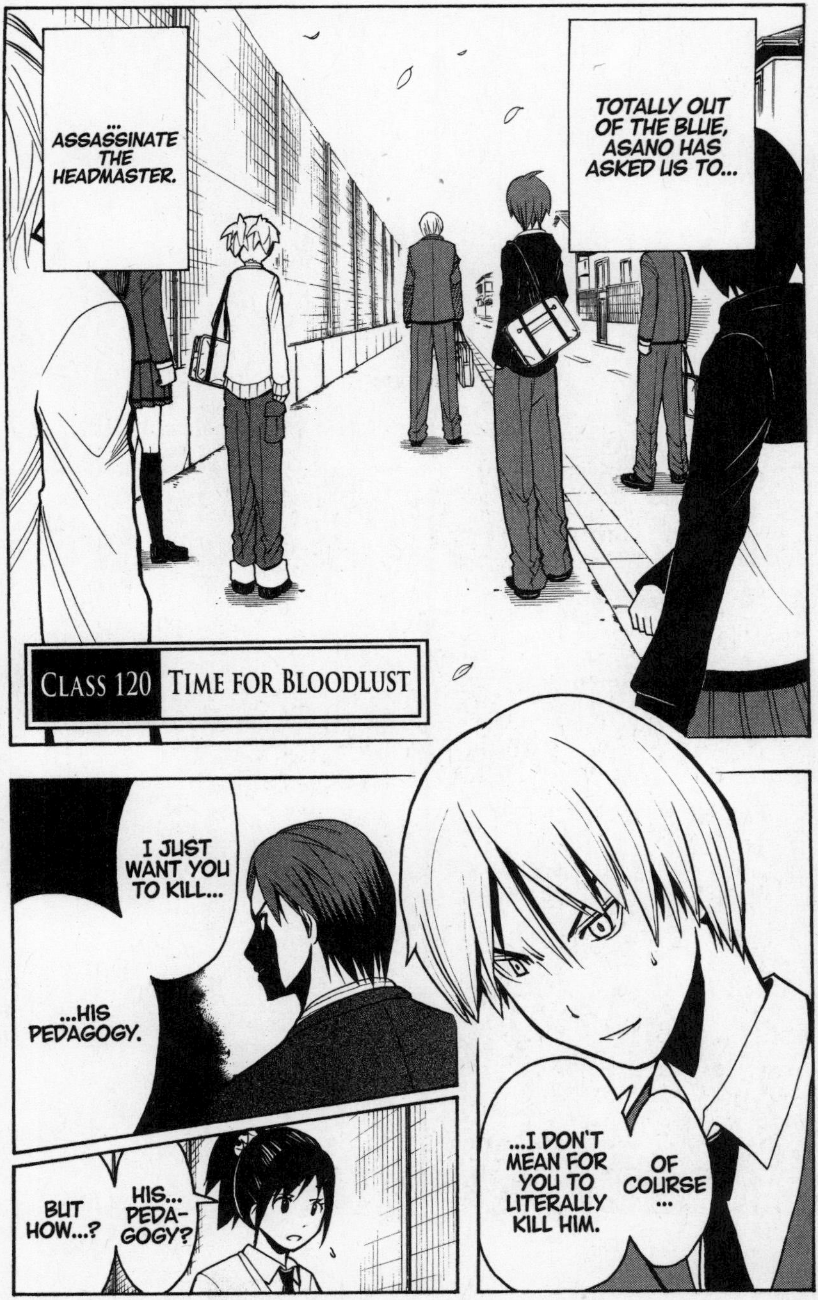
TOTALLY OUT OF THE BLUE, ASANO HAS ASKED US TO...
...ASSASSINATE THE HEADMASTER.
CLASS 120 TIME FOR BLOODLUST
OF COURSE...
...I DON'T MEAN FOR YOU TO LITERALLY KILL HIM.
I JUST WANT YOU TO KILL...
...HIS PEDAGOGY.
HIS... PEDA-GOGY?
BUT HOW...?

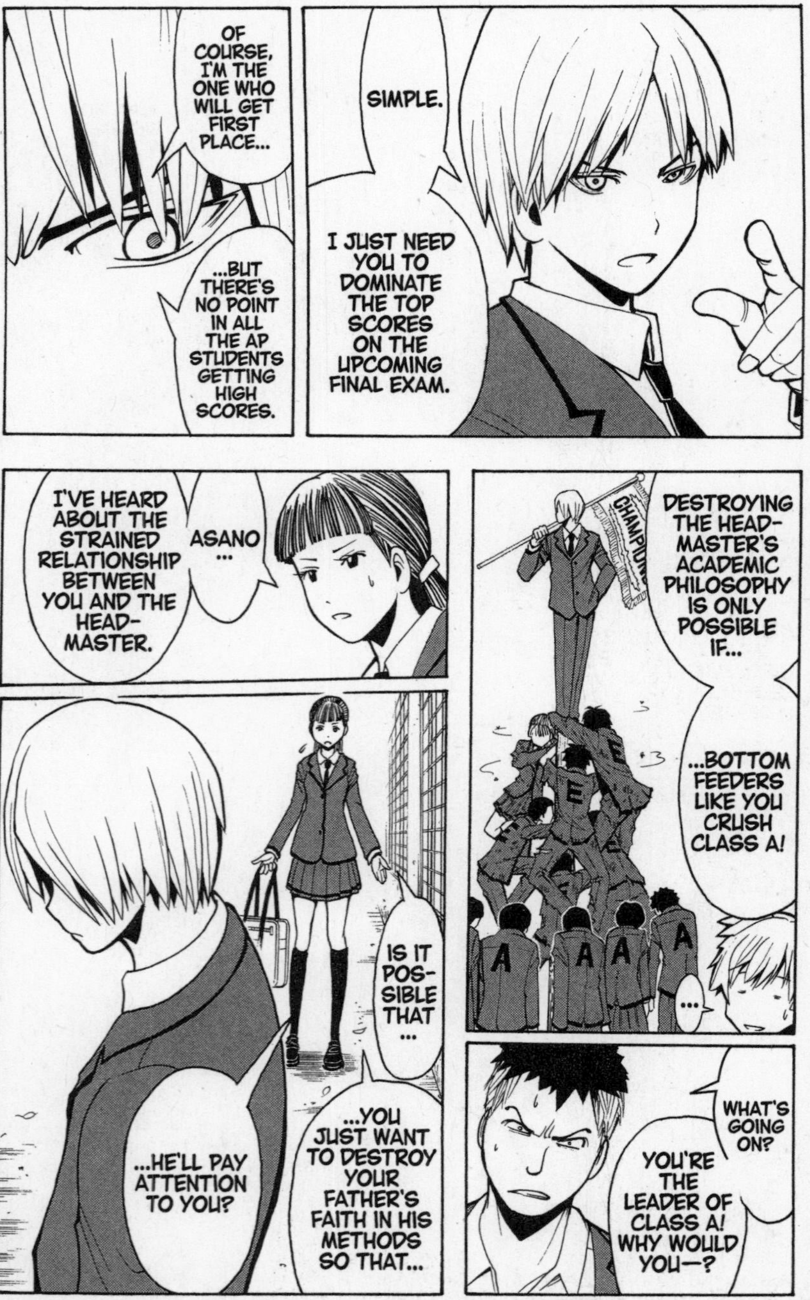
SIMPLE.
I JUST NEED YOU TO DOMINATE THE TOP SCORES ON THE UPCOMING FINAL EXAM.
OF COURSE, I'M THE ONE WHO WILL GET FIRST PLACE...
...BUT THERE'S NO POINT IN ALL THE AP STUDENTS GETTING HIGH SCORES.
DESTROYING THE HEAD-MASTER'S ACADEMIC PHILOSOPHY IS ONLY POSSIBLE IF...
...BOTTOM FEEDERS LIKE YOU CRUSH CLASS A!
...
WHAT'S GOING ON?
YOU'RE THE LEADER OF CLASS A! WHY WOULD YOU—?
ASANO...
I'VE HEARD ABOUT THE STRAINED RELATIONSHIP BETWEEN YOU AND THE HEAD-MASTER.
IS IT POSSIBLE THAT...
...YOU JUST WANT TO DESTROY YOUR FATHER'S FAITH IN HIS METHODS SO THAT...
...HE'LL PAY ATTENTION TO YOU?

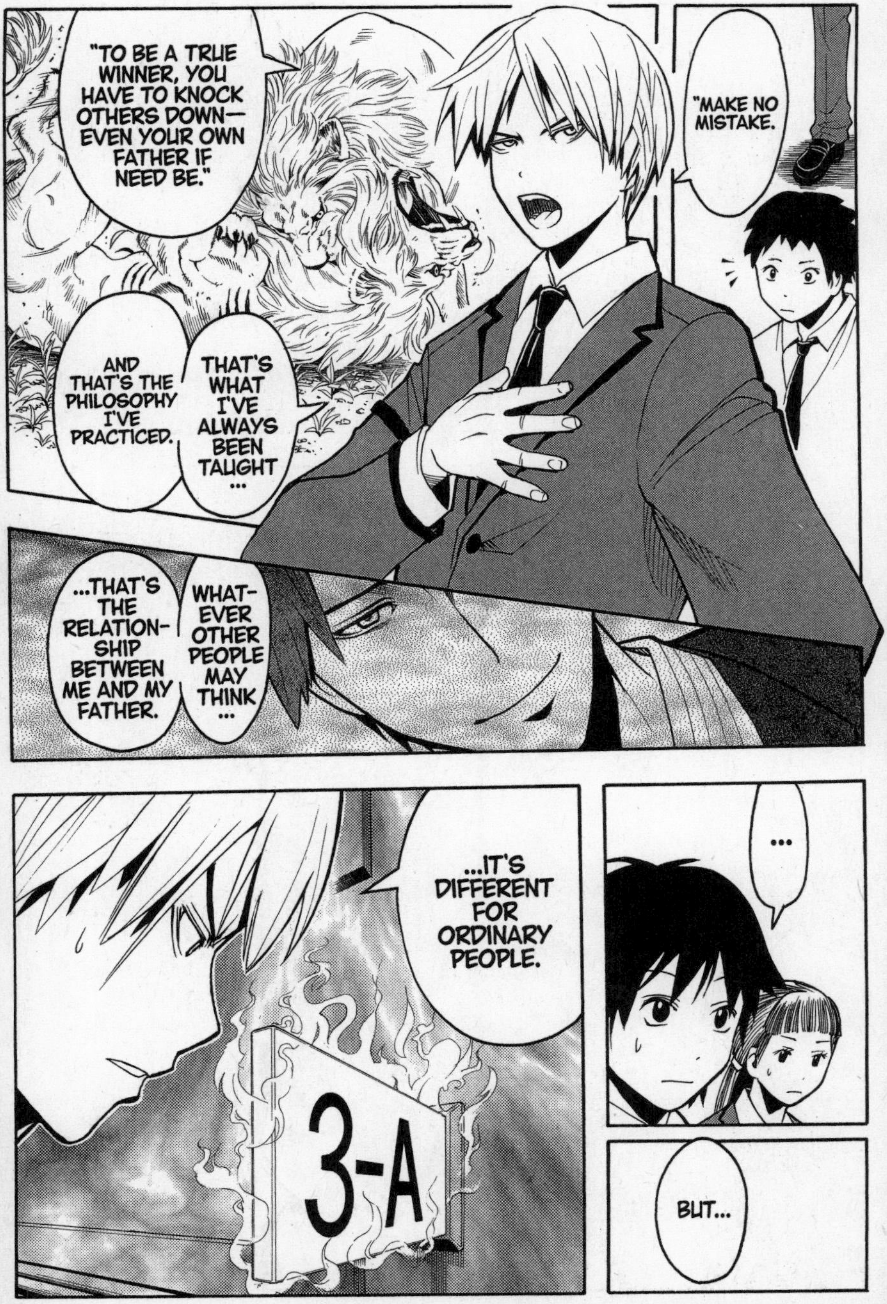
"MAKE NO MISTAKE.
"TO BE A TRUE WINNER, YOU HAVE TO KNOCK OTHERS DOWN—EVEN YOUR OWN FATHER IF NEED BE."
THAT'S WHAT I'VE ALWAYS BEEN TAUGHT...
AND THAT'S THE PHILOSOPHY I'VE PRACTICED.
WHAT-EVER OTHER PEOPLE MAY THINK...
...THAT'S THE RELATIONSHIP BETWEEN ME AND MY FATHER.
...
BUT...
...IT'S DIFFERENT FOR ORDINARY PEOPLE.
3-A

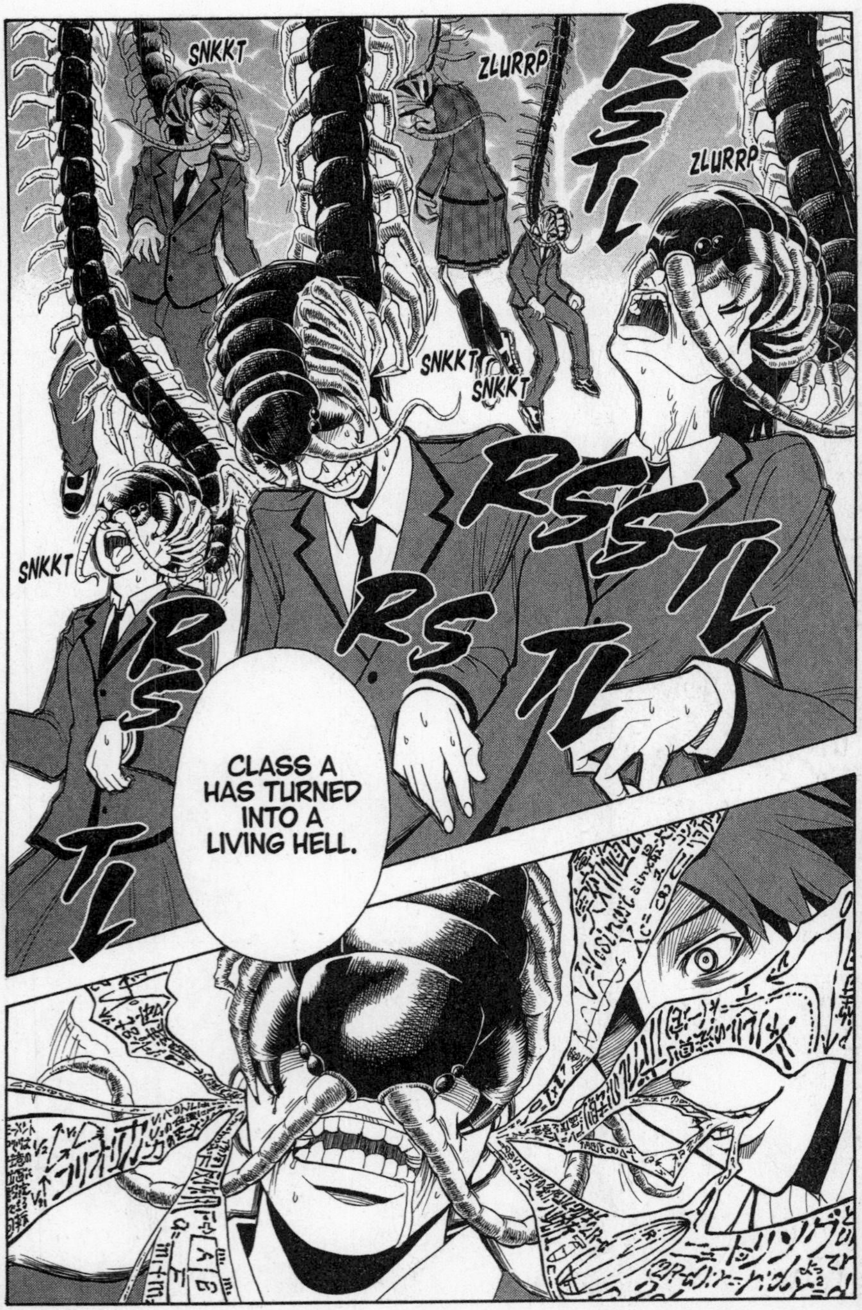
RSTL
ZLURRP
ZLURRP
SNKKT
RSSTL
SNKKT
SNKKT
RS TL
SNKKT
RSTL
CLASS A HAS TURNED INTO A LIVING HELL.

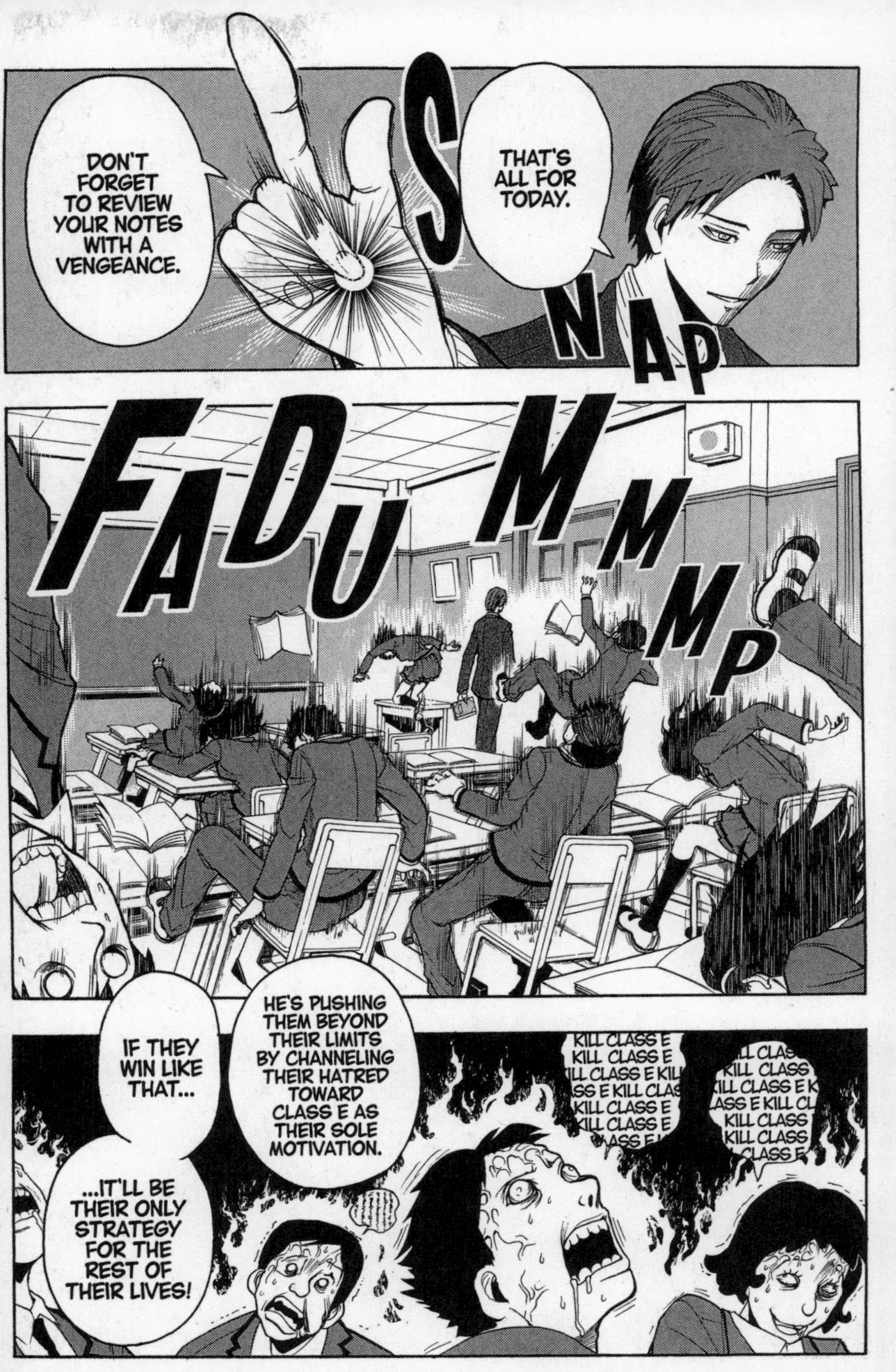
THAT'S ALL FOR TODAY.
SNAP
DON'T FORGET TO REVIEW YOUR NOTES WITH A VENGEANCE.
FADUMMMP
HE'S PUSHING THEM BEYOND THEIR LIMITS BY CHANNELING THEIR HATRED TOWARD CLASS E AS THEIR SOLE MOTIVATION.
IF THEY WIN LIKE THAT...
...IT'LL BE THEIR ONLY STRATEGY FOR THE REST OF THEIR LIVES!
KILL CLASS E KILL CLASS E KILL CLASS E KILL CLASS E KILL CLASS KILL CLASS E KILL CLASS E
KILL CLASS KILL CLASS E KILL CLASS E KILL CLASS KILL CLASS KILL CLASS E

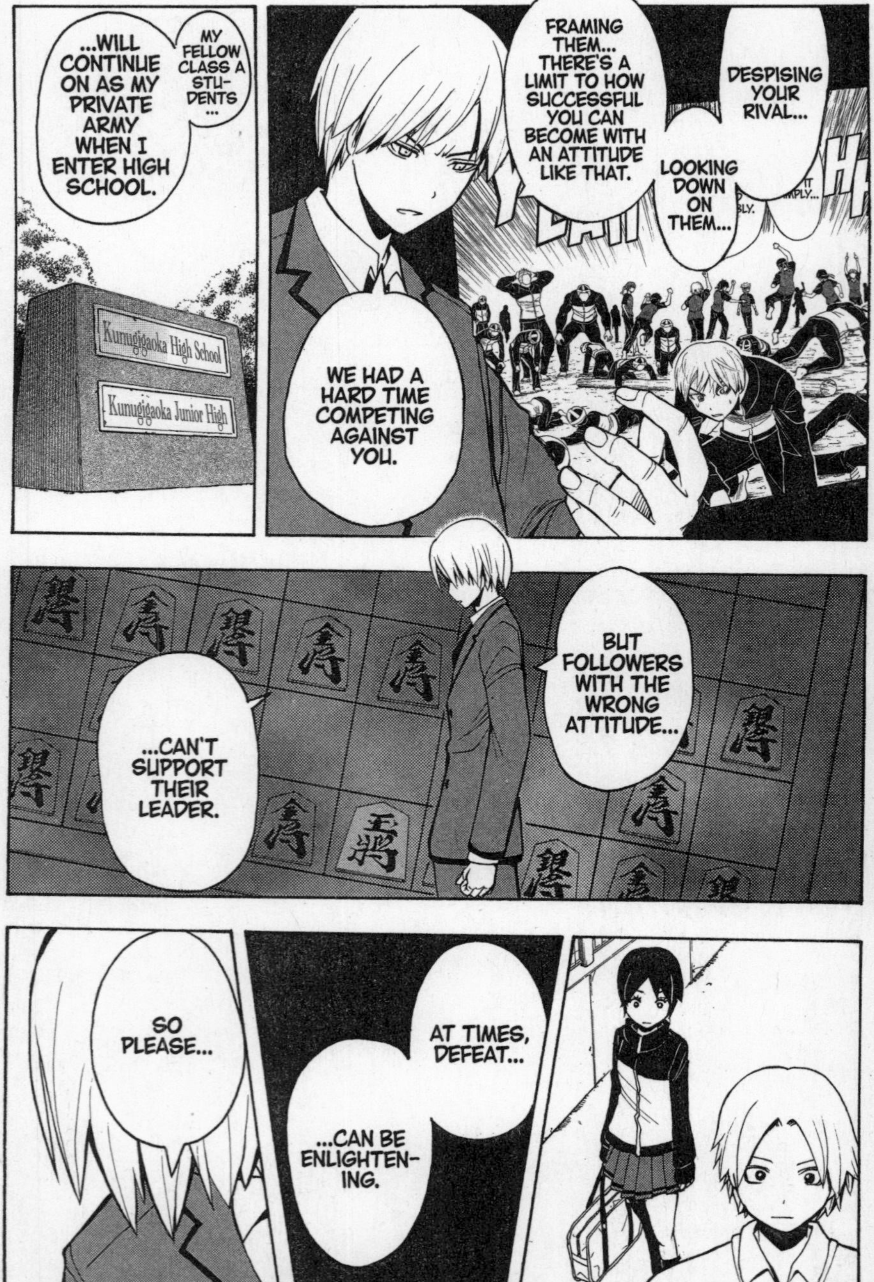
DESPISING YOUR RIVAL...
LOOKING DOWN ON THEM...
FRAMING THEM... THERE'S A LIMIT TO HOW SUCCESSFUL YOU CAN BECOME WITH AN ATTITUDE LIKE THAT.
WE HAD A HARD TIME COMPETING AGAINST YOU.
MY FELLOW CLASS A STU-DENTS...
...WILL CONTINUE ON AS MY PRIVATE ARMY WHEN I ENTER HIGH SCHOOL.
Kunugigaoka High School
Kunugigaoka Junior High
BUT FOLLOWERS WITH THE WRONG ATTITUDE...
...CAN'T SUPPORT THEIR LEADER.
AT TIMES, DEFEAT...
...CAN BE ENLIGHTEN-ING.
SO PLEASE...

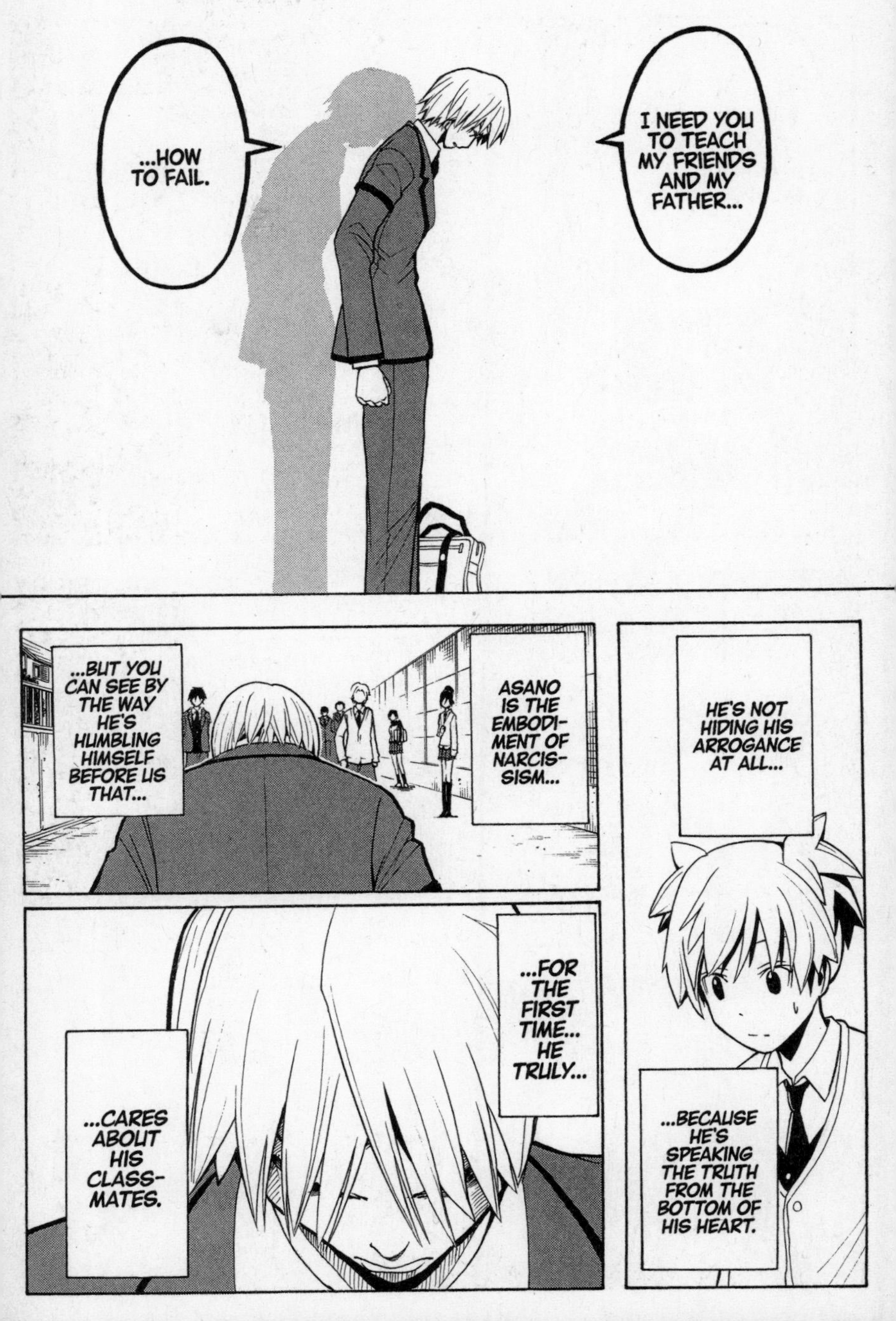
I NEED YOU TO TEACH MY FRIENDS AND MY FATHER...
...HOW TO FAIL.
HE'S NOT HIDING HIS ARROGANCE AT ALL...
...BECAUSE HE'S SPEAKING THE TRUTH FROM THE BOTTOM OF HIS HEART.
ASANO IS THE EMBODI-MENT OF NARCIS-SISM...
...BUT YOU CAN SEE BY THE WAY HE'S HUMBLING HIMSELF BEFORE US THAT...
...FOR THE FIRST TIME... HE TRULY...
...CARES ABOUT HIS CLASS-MATES.

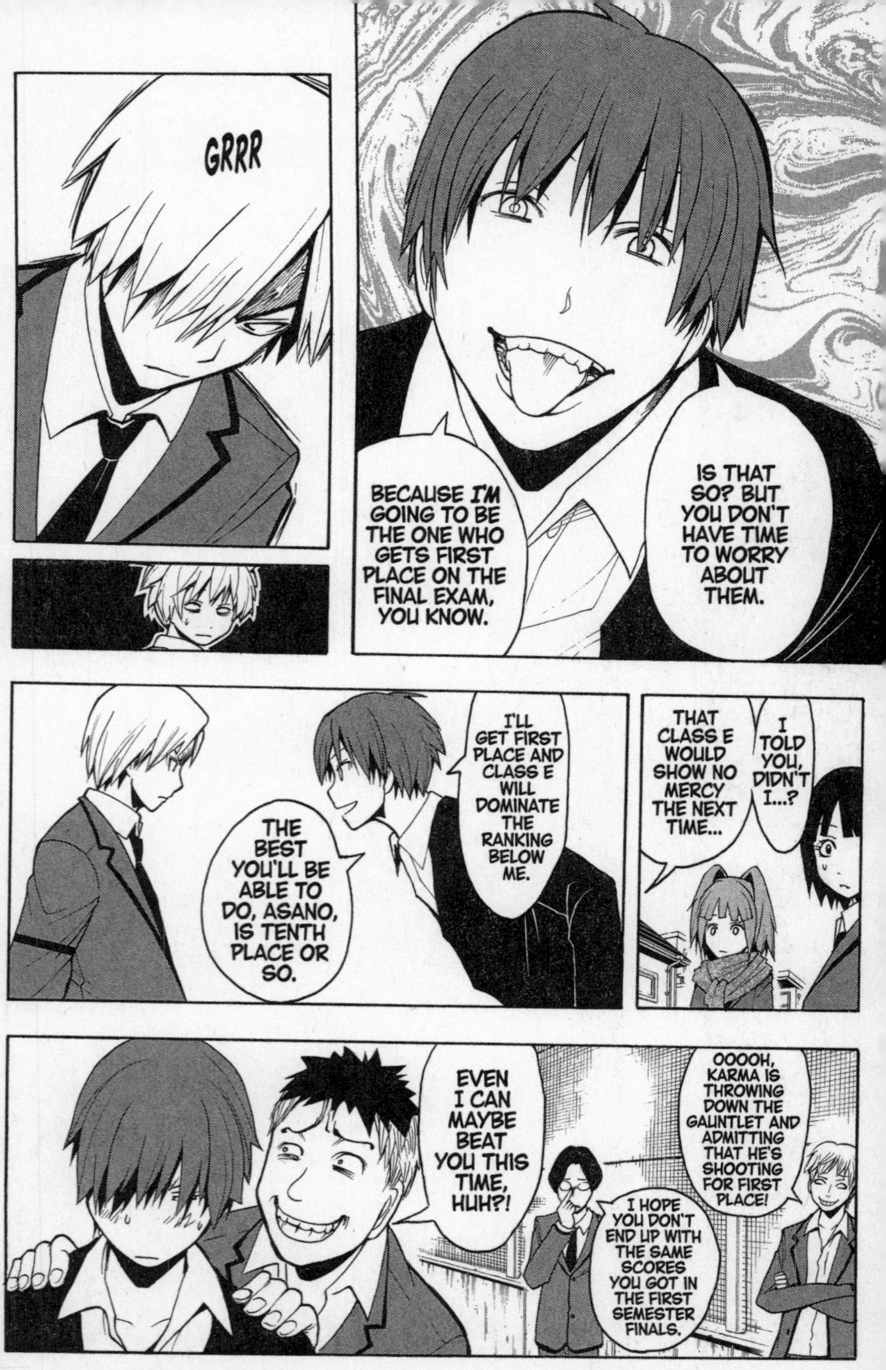
IS THAT SO? BUT YOU DON'T HAVE TIME TO WORRY ABOUT THEM.
BECAUSE *I'M* GOING TO BE THE ONE WHO GETS FIRST PLACE ON THE FINAL EXAM, YOU KNOW.
GRRR
I TOLD YOU, DIDN'T I...?
THAT CLASS E WOULD SHOW NO MERCY THE NEXT TIME...
I'LL GET FIRST PLACE AND CLASS E WILL DOMINATE THE RANKING BELOW ME.
THE BEST YOU'LL BE ABLE TO DO, ASANO, IS TENTH PLACE OR SO.
OOOOH, KARMA IS THROWING DOWN THE GAUNTLET AND ADMITTING THAT HE'S SHOOTING FOR FIRST PLACE!
I HOPE YOU DON'T END UP WITH THE SAME SCORES YOU GOT IN THE FIRST SEMESTER FINALS.
EVEN I CAN MAYBE BEAT YOU THIS TIME, HUH?!

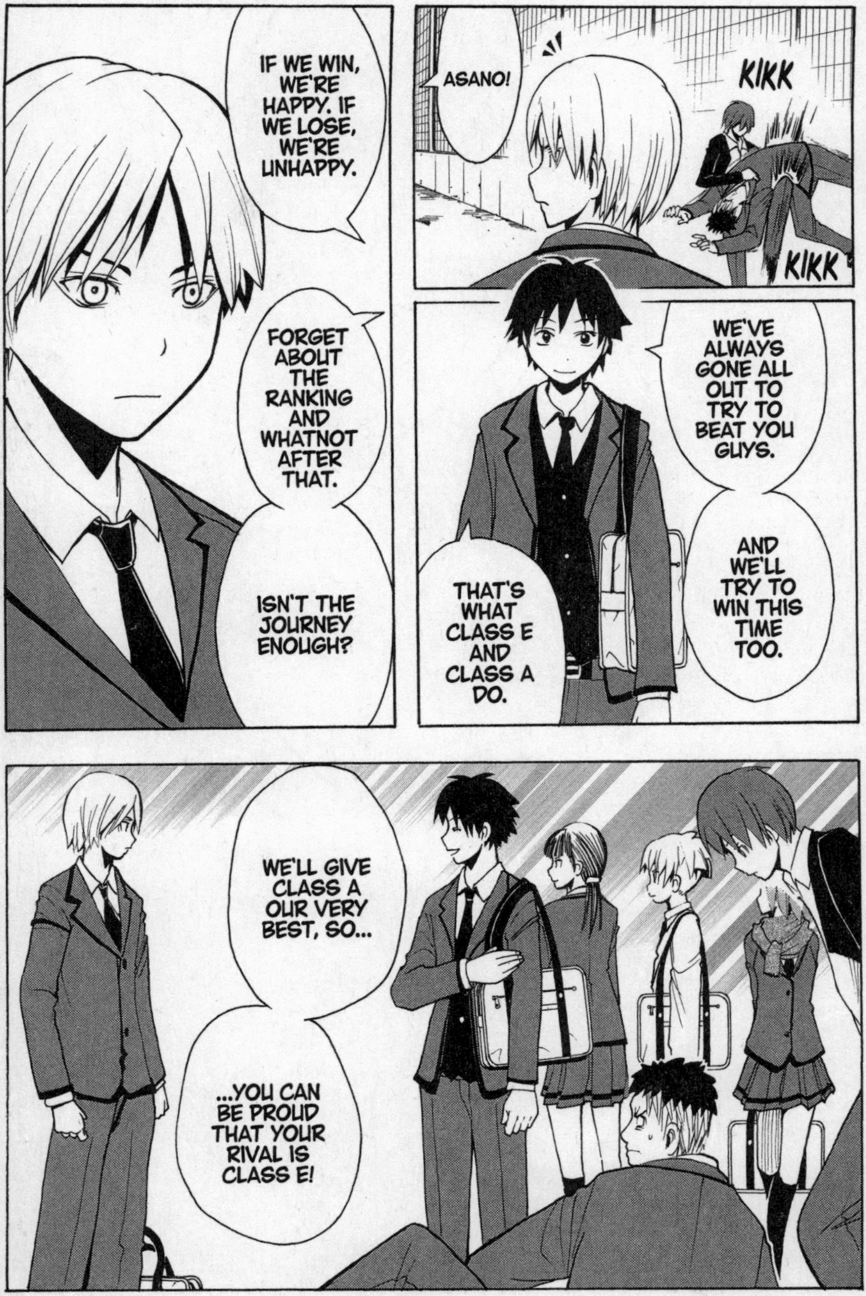
ASANO!
KIKK
KIKK
WE'VE ALWAYS GONE ALL OUT TO TRY TO BEAT YOU GUYS.
AND WE'LL TRY TO WIN THIS TIME TOO.
THAT'S WHAT CLASS E AND CLASS A DO.
IF WE WIN, WE'RE HAPPY. IF WE LOSE, WE'RE UNHAPPY.
FORGET ABOUT THE RANKING AND WHATNOT AFTER THAT.
ISN'T THE JOURNEY ENOUGH?
WE'LL GIVE CLASS A OUR VERY BEST, SO...
...YOU CAN BE PROUD THAT YOUR RIVAL IS CLASS E!

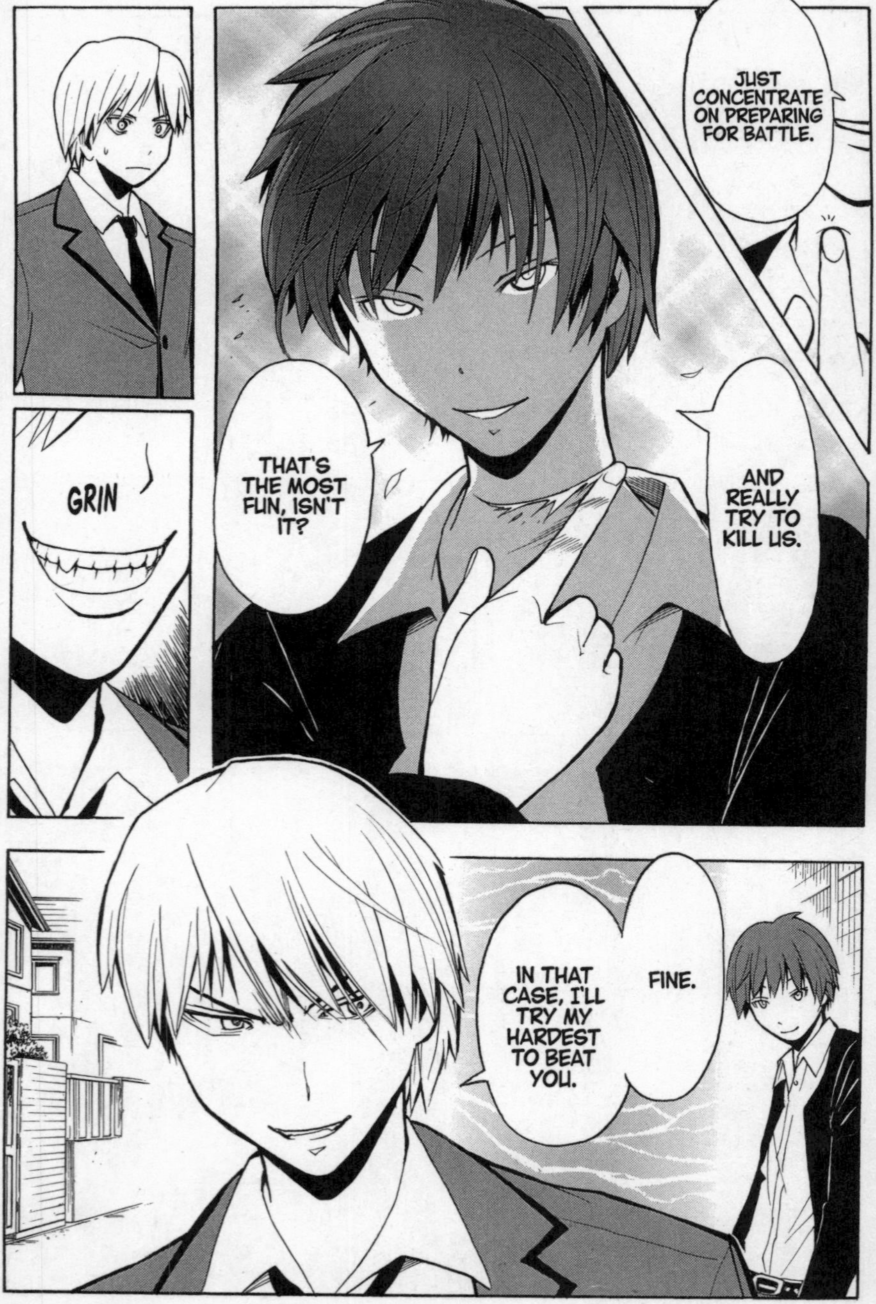
JUST CONCENTRATE ON PREPARING FOR BATTLE.
AND REALLY TRY TO KILL US.
THAT'S THE MOST FUN, ISN'T IT?
GRIN
FINE.
IN THAT CASE, I'LL TRY MY HARDEST TO BEAT YOU.

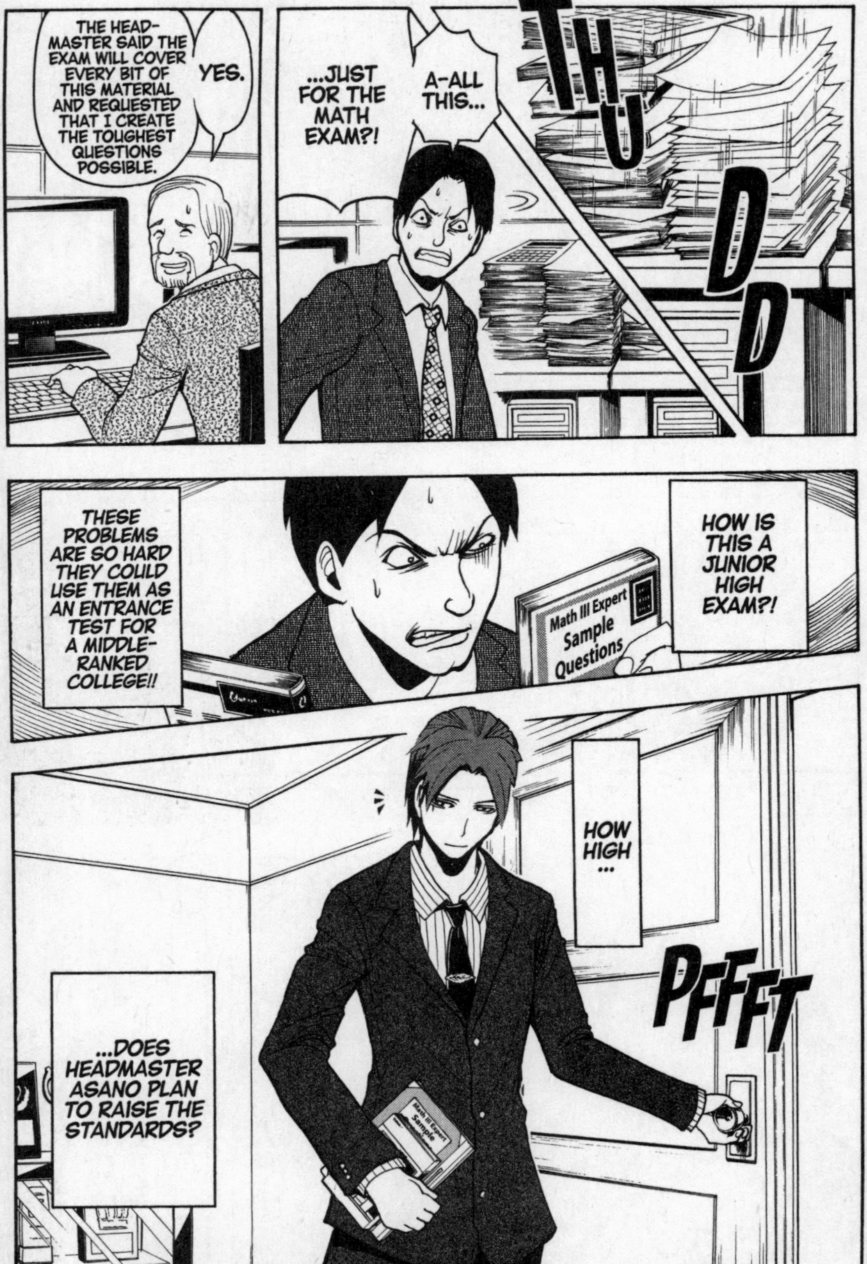
THUDD
A-ALL THIS...
...JUST FOR THE MATH EXAM?!
YES.
THE HEAD-MASTER SAID THE EXAM WILL COVER EVERY BIT OF THIS MATERIAL AND REQUESTED THAT I CREATE THE TOUGHEST QUESTIONS POSSIBLE.
HOW IS THIS A JUNIOR HIGH EXAM?!
Math III Expert Sample Questions
THESE PROBLEMS ARE SO HARD THEY COULD USE THEM AS AN ENTRANCE TEST FOR A MIDDLE-RANKED COLLEGE!!
HOW HIGH ...
PFFFT
Math III Expert Sample
...DOES HEADMASTER ASANO PLAN TO RAISE THE STANDARDS?

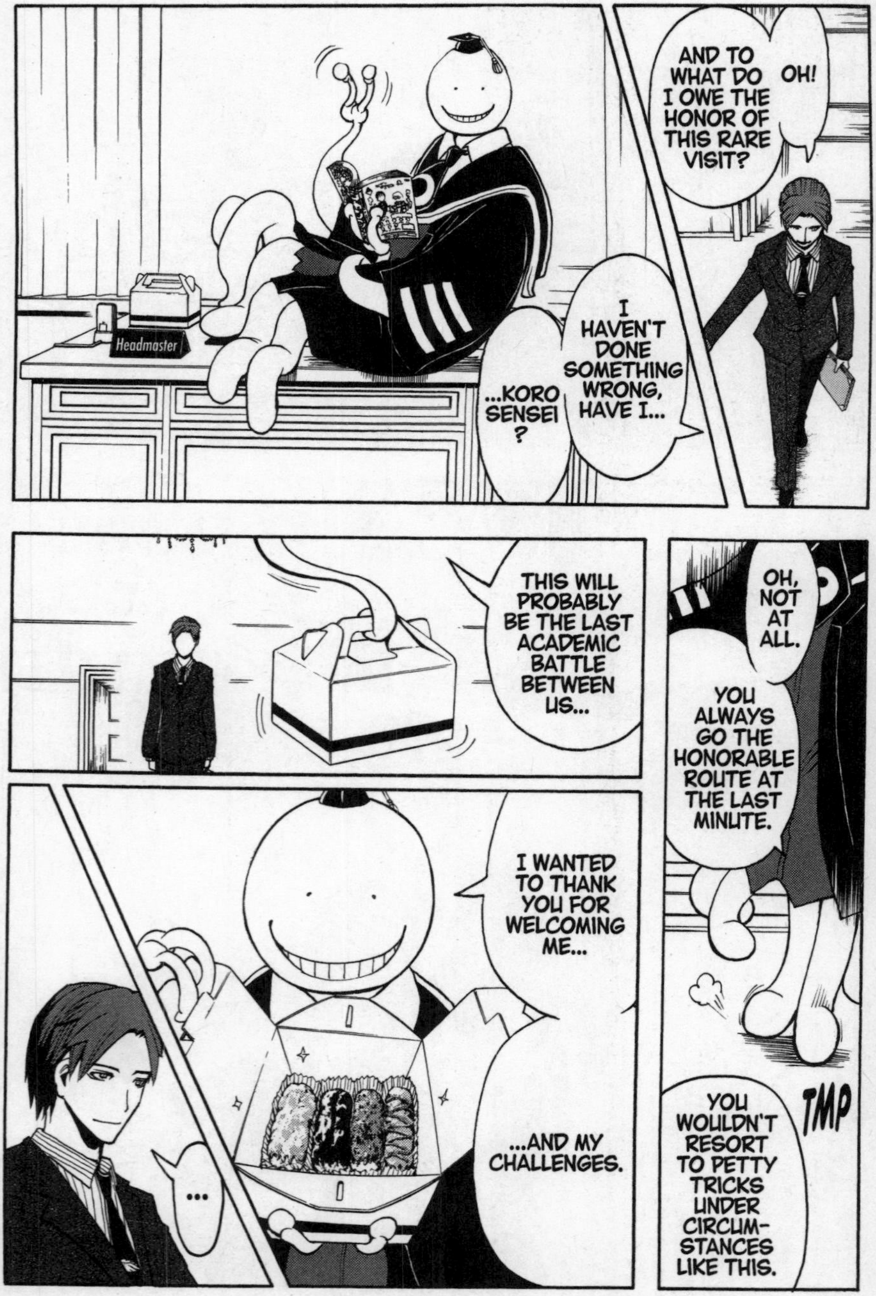
OH!
AND TO WHAT DO I OWE THE HONOR OF THIS RARE VISIT?
I HAVEN'T DONE SOMETHING WRONG, HAVE I...
...KORO SENSEI?
Headmaster
OH, NOT AT ALL.
YOU ALWAYS GO THE HONORABLE ROUTE AT THE LAST MINUTE.
TMP
YOU WOULDN'T RESORT TO PETTY TRICKS UNDER CIRCUM-STANCES LIKE THIS.
THIS WILL PROBABLY BE THE LAST ACADEMIC BATTLE BETWEEN US...
I WANTED TO THANK YOU FOR WELCOMING ME...
...AND MY CHALLENGES.
...

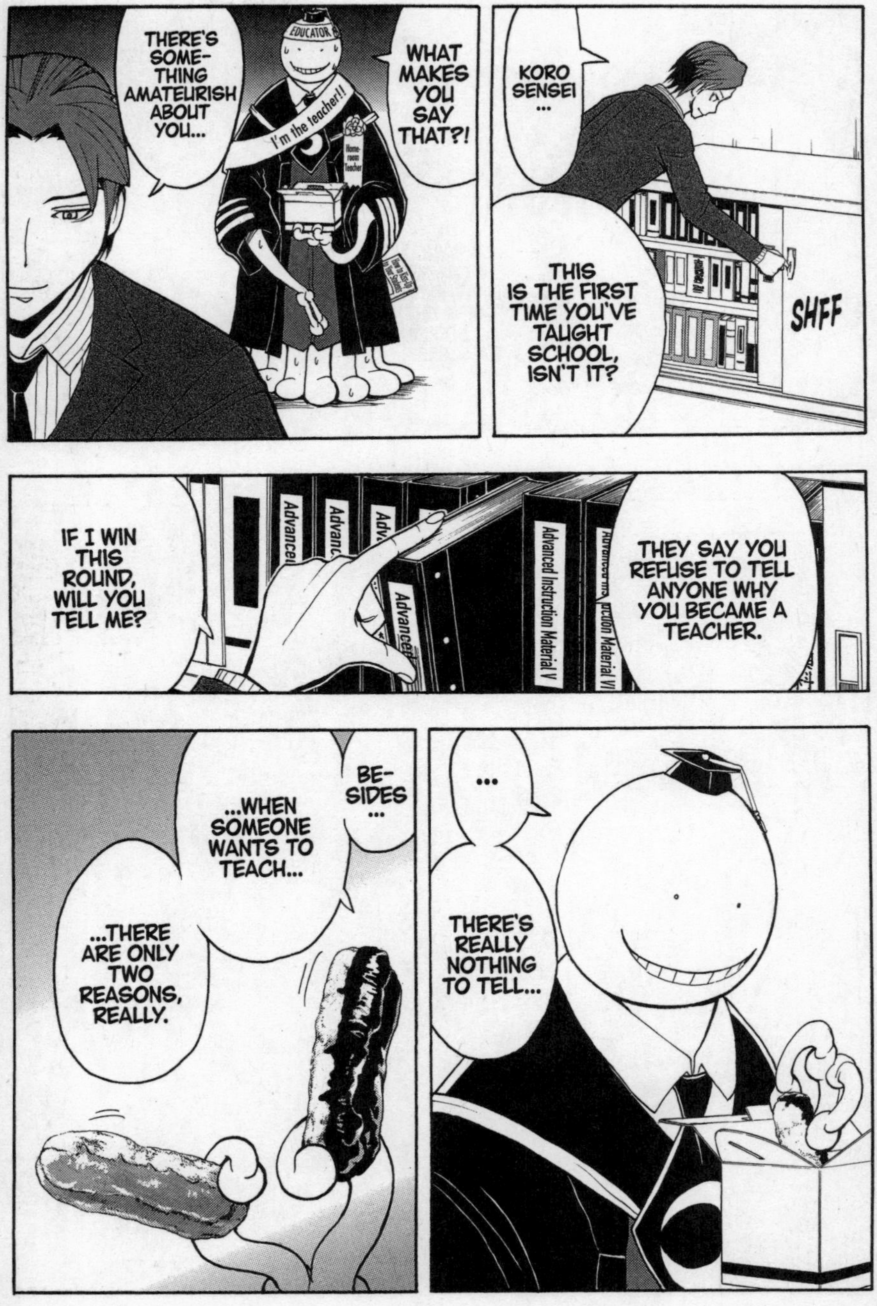

KORO SENSEI ...
THIS IS THE FIRST TIME YOU'VE TAUGHT SCHOOL, ISN'T IT?
SHFF
WHAT MAKES YOU SAY THAT?!
THERE'S SOME-THING AMATEURISH ABOUT YOU...
EDUCATOR
I'm the teacher!!
Home-room Teacher
THEY SAY YOU REFUSE TO TELL ANYONE WHY YOU BECAME A TEACHER.
Advanced Instruction Material V
IF I WIN THIS ROUND, WILL YOU TELL ME?
...
THERE'S REALLY NOTHING TO TELL...
BE-SIDES ...
...WHEN SOMEONE WANTS TO TEACH...
...THERE ARE ONLY TWO REASONS, REALLY.

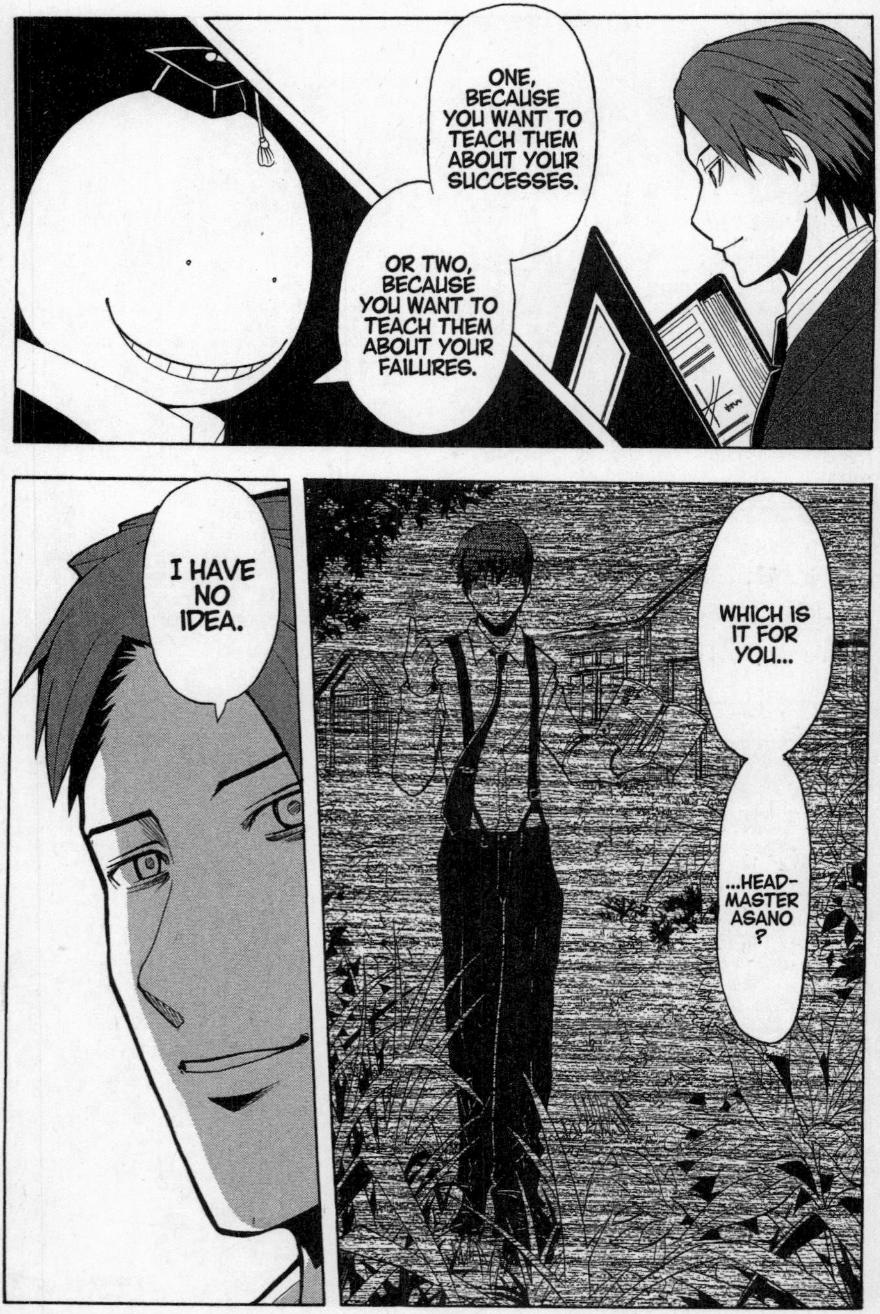
ONE, BECAUSE YOU WANT TO TEACH THEM ABOUT YOUR SUCCESSES.
OR TWO, BECAUSE YOU WANT TO TEACH THEM ABOUT YOUR FAILURES.
WHICH IS IT FOR YOU...
...HEAD-MASTER ASANO?
I HAVE NO IDEA.

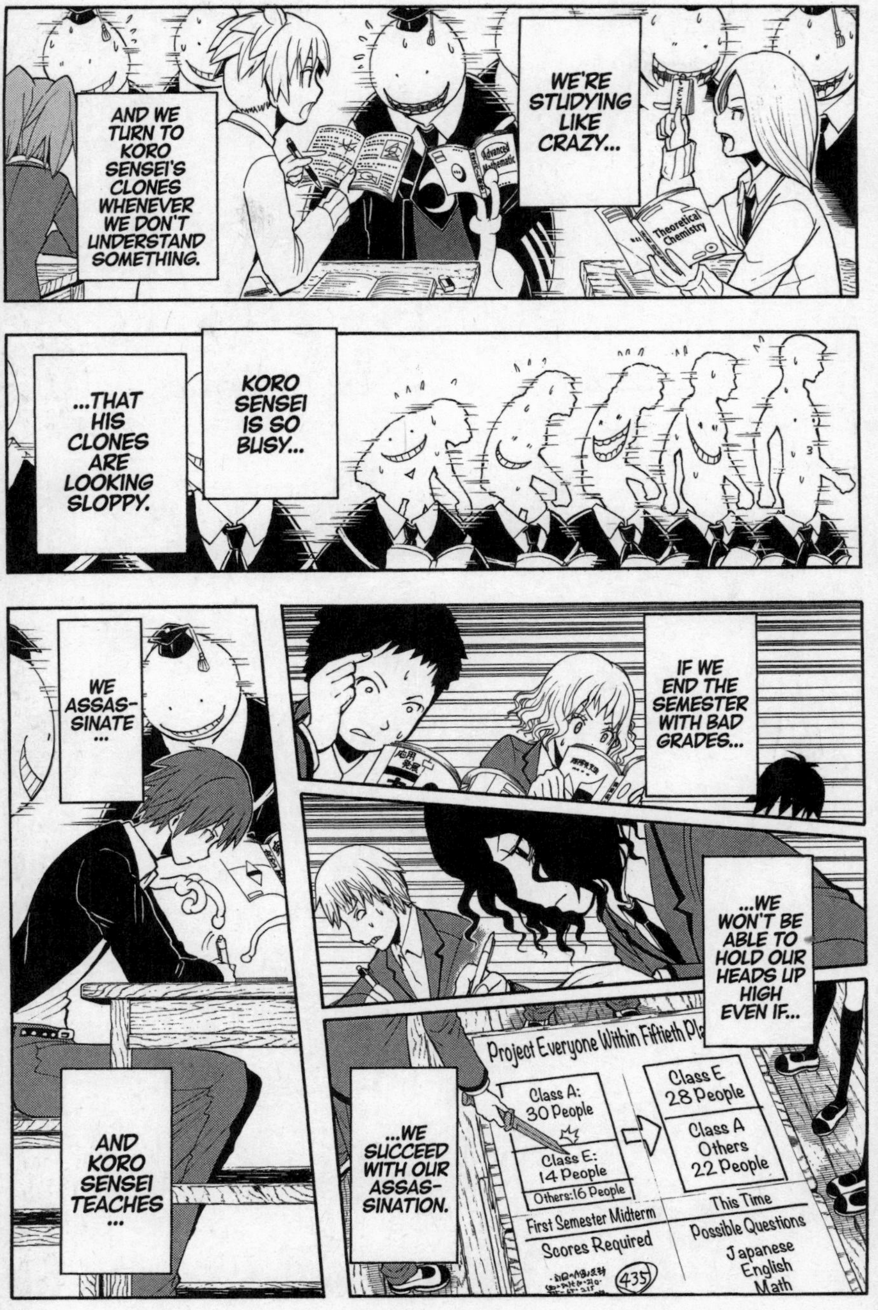
WE'RE STUDYING LIKE CRAZY...
Theoretical Chemistry
Advanced Mathematic
AND WE TURN TO KORO SENSEI'S CLONES WHENEVER WE DON'T UNDERSTAND SOMETHING.
KORO SENSEI IS SO BUSY...
...THAT HIS CLONES ARE LOOKING SLOPPY.
IF WE END THE SEMESTER WITH BAD GRADES...
...WE WON'T BE ABLE TO HOLD OUR HEADS UP HIGH EVEN IF...
Project Everyone Within Fiftieth Pla
Class A: 30 People
Class E: 14 People
Others: 16 People
Class E 28 People
Class A Others 22 People
First Semester Midterm
Scores Required
This Time
Possible Questions
Japanese
English
Math
435
...WE SUCCEED WITH OUR ASSAS-SINATION.
WE ASSAS-SINATE ...
AND KORO SENSEI TEACHES ...

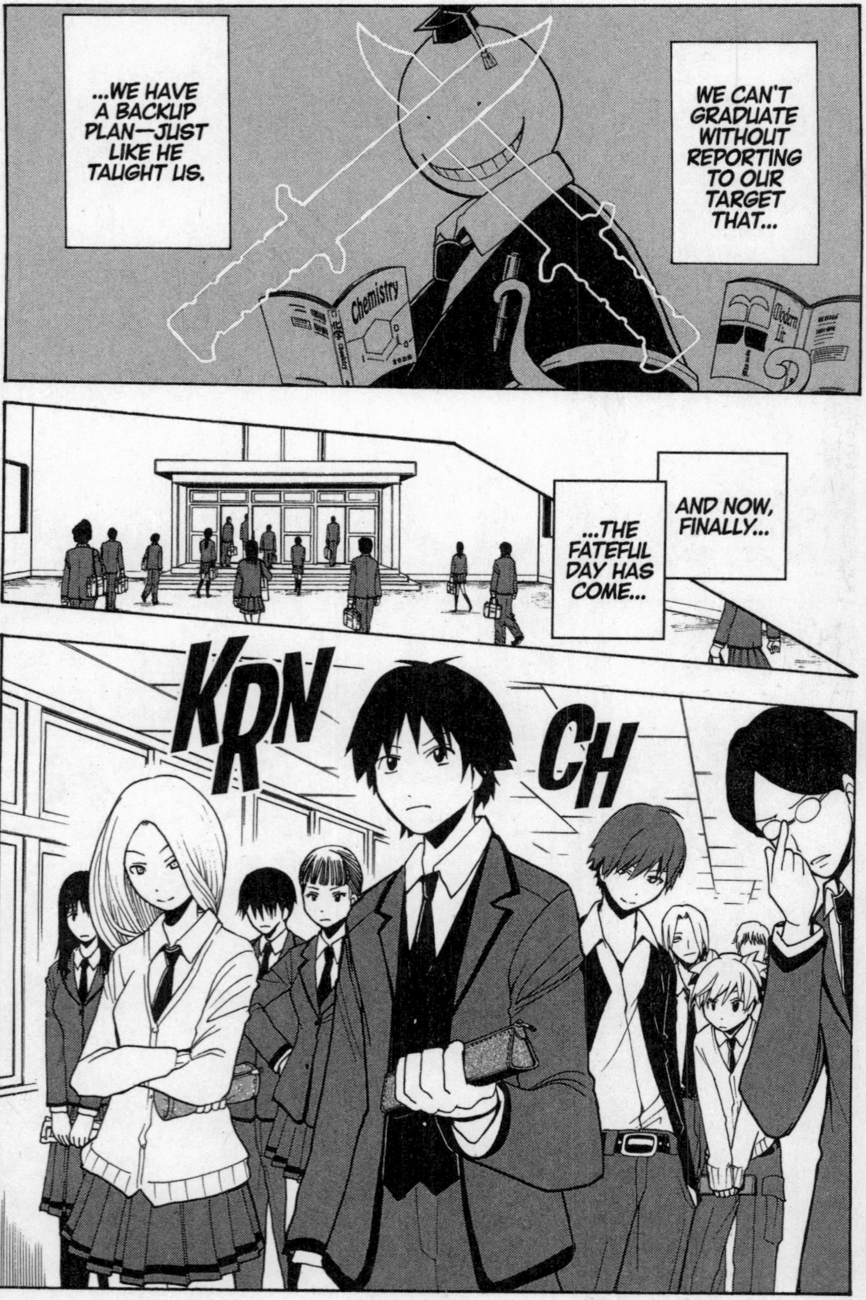
WE CAN'T GRADUATE WITHOUT REPORTING TO OUR TARGET THAT...
...WE HAVE A BACKUP PLAN—JUST LIKE HE TAUGHT US.
Chemistry
AND NOW, FINALLY...
...THE FATEFUL DAY HAS COME...
KRNCH

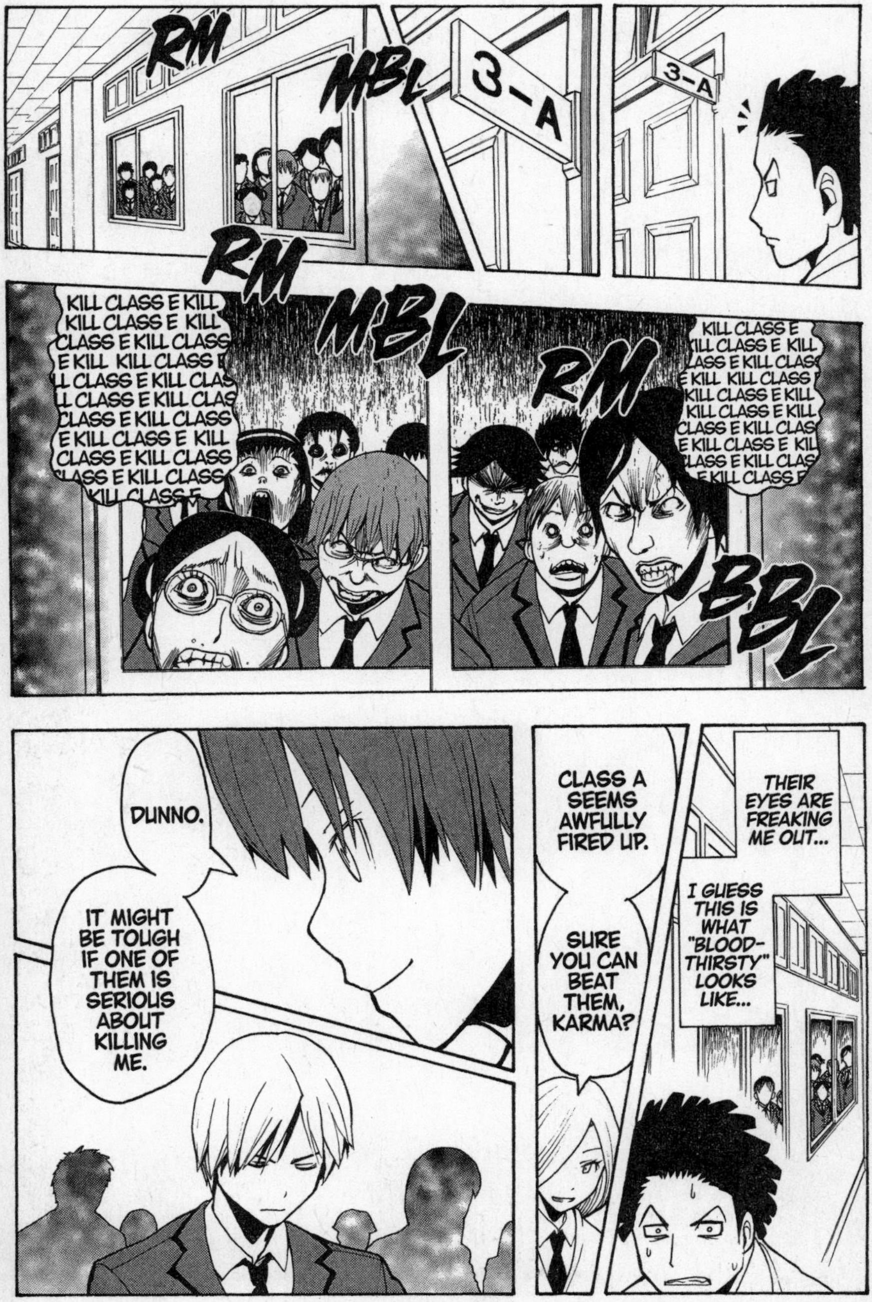
3-A
3-A
MBL
RM
RM
MBL
KILL CLASS E
ILL CLASS E KILL
ASS E KILL CLAS
E KILL KILL CLASS
ILL CLASS E KILL
KILL CLASS E KILL
CLASS E KILL CLAS
E KILL CLASS E KIL
LASS E KILL CLASS
E KILL CLASS E
RM
BBL
KILL CLASS E KILL
KILL CLASS E KILL
CLASS E KILL CLASS
E KILL KILL CLASS E
LL CLASS E KILL CLAS
LL CLASS E KILL CLAS
CLASS E KILL CLASS
E KILL CLASS E KILL
CLASS E KILL CLASS
LASS E KILL CLASS
KILL CLASS E
THEIR EYES ARE FREAKING ME OUT...
I GUESS THIS IS WHAT "BLOOD-THIRSTY" LOOKS LIKE...
CLASS A SEEMS AWFULLY FIRED UP.
SURE YOU CAN BEAT THEM, KARMA?
DUNNO.
IT MIGHT BE TOUGH IF ONE OF THEM IS SERIOUS ABOUT KILLING ME.

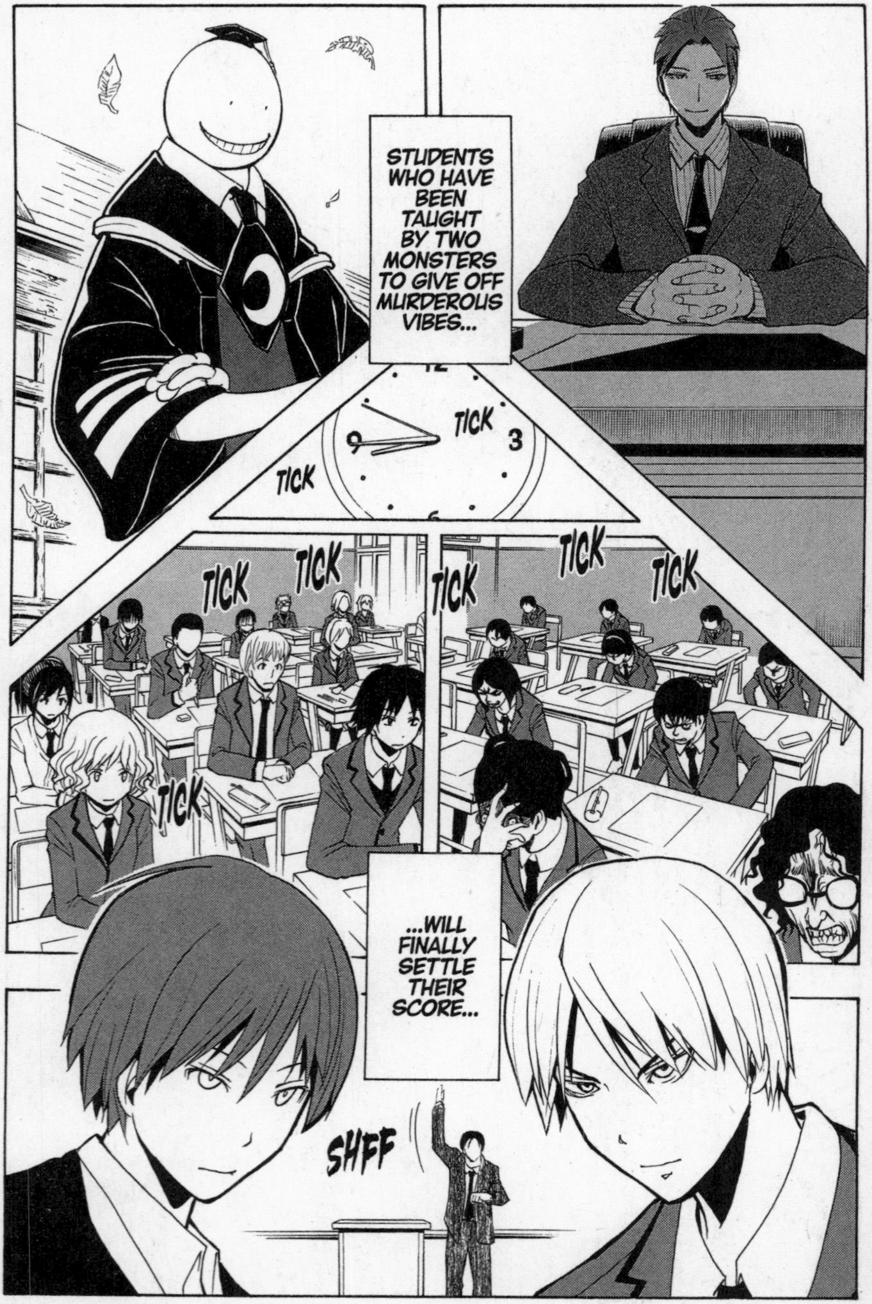
STUDENTS WHO HAVE BEEN TAUGHT BY TWO MONSTERS TO GIVE OFF MURDEROUS VIBES...
TICK
TICK
TICK
TICK
TICK
TICK
TICK
TICK
...WILL FINALLY SETTLE THEIR SCORE...
SHFF

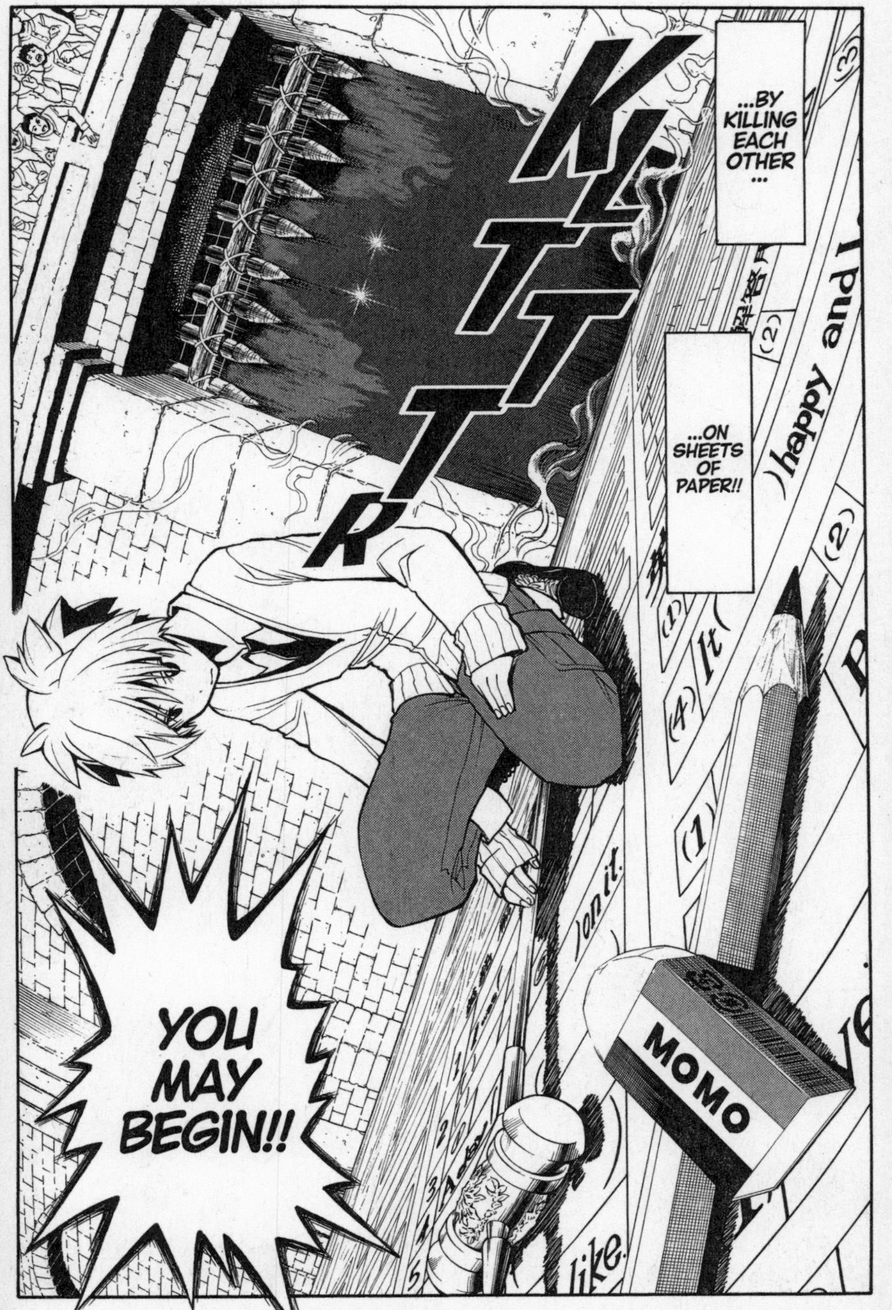

...BY KILLING EACH OTHER ...
...ON SHEETS OF PAPER!!
)happy and
)on it.
like.
MOMO
YOU MAY BEGIN!!

The Evolution of Man — The Shocking Future —

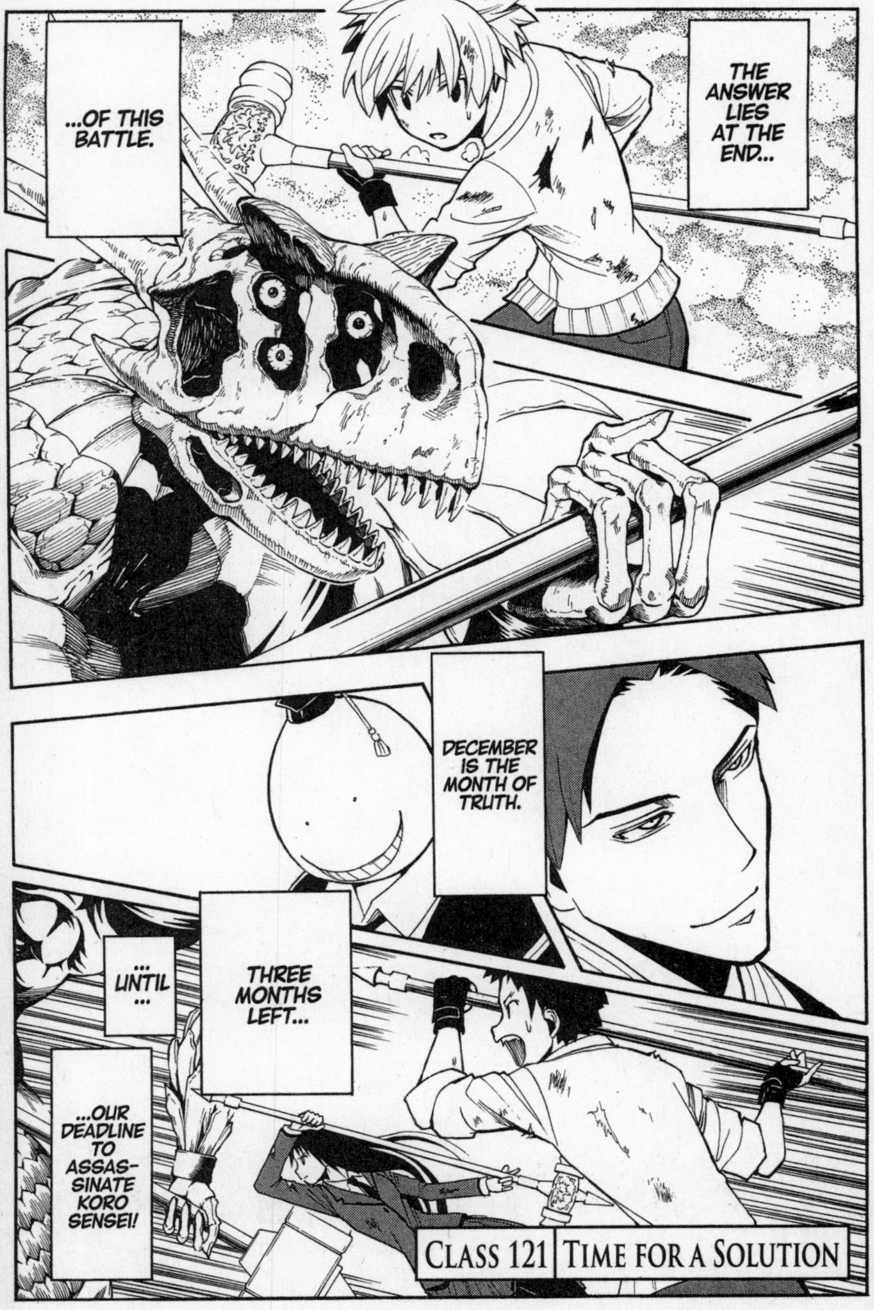
THE ANSWER LIES AT THE END...
...OF THIS BATTLE.
DECEMBER IS THE MONTH OF TRUTH.
THREE MONTHS LEFT...
... UNTIL ...
...OUR DEADLINE TO ASSAS-SINATE KORO SENSEI!
CLASS 121 TIME FOR A SOLUTION

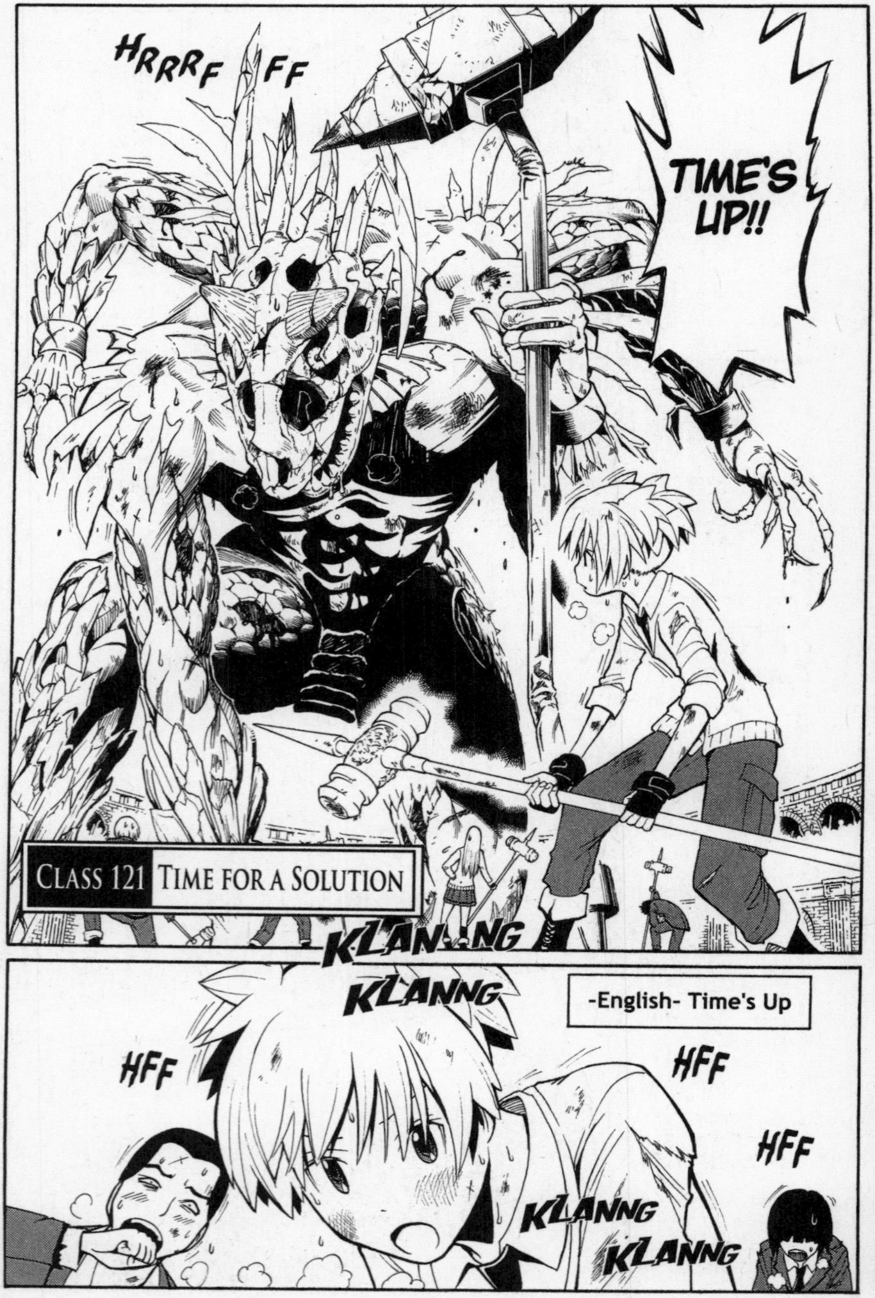
TIME'S UP!!
HRRRF FF
CLASS 121 TIME FOR A SOLUTION
KLAN-NG
-English- Time's Up
KLANNG
HFF
HFF
HFF
KLANNG
KLANNG

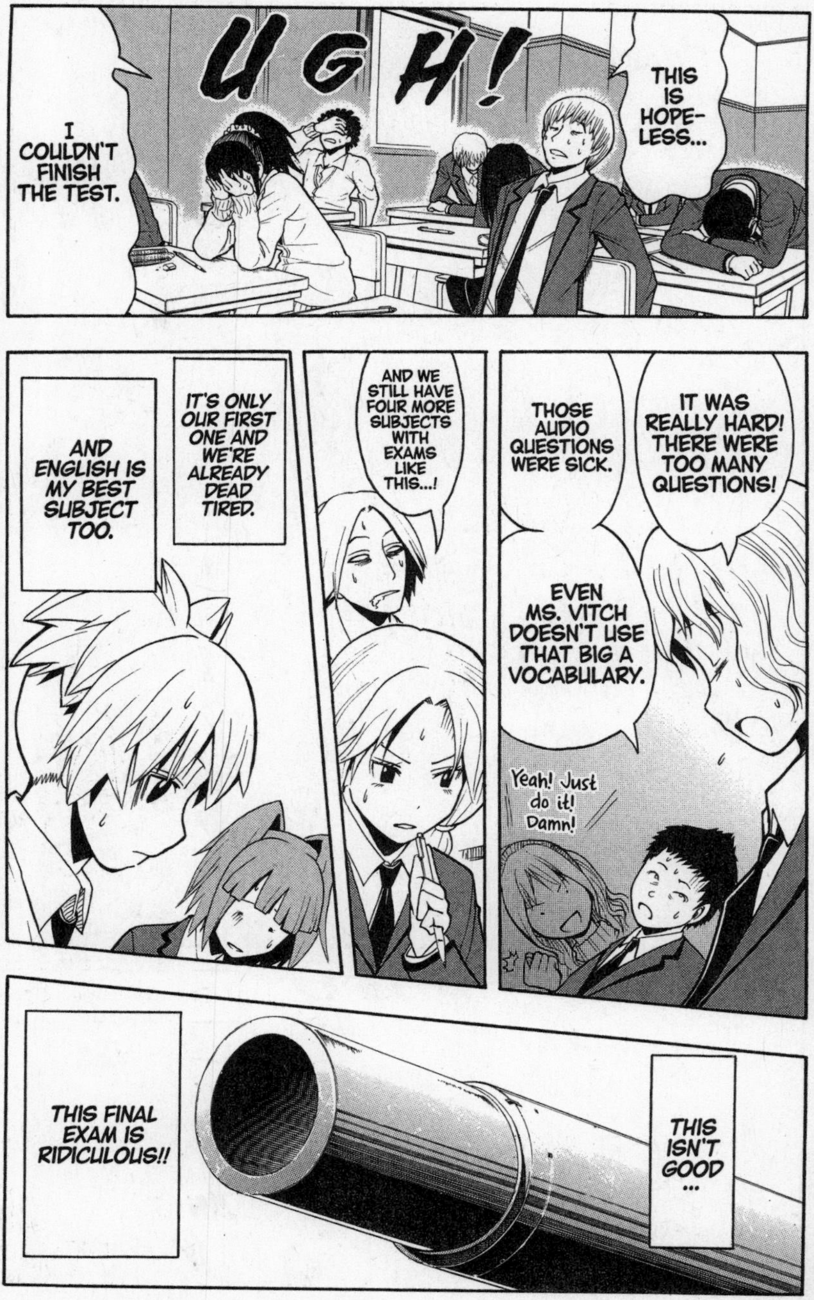
THIS IS HOPE-LESS...
UGH!
I COULDN'T FINISH THE TEST.
IT WAS REALLY HARD! THERE WERE TOO MANY QUESTIONS!
THOSE AUDIO QUESTIONS WERE SICK.
EVEN MS. VITCH DOESN'T USE THAT BIG A VOCABULARY.
Yeah! Just do it! Damn!
AND WE STILL HAVE FOUR MORE SUBJECTS WITH EXAMS LIKE THIS...!
IT'S ONLY OUR FIRST ONE AND WE'RE ALREADY DEAD TIRED.
AND ENGLISH IS MY BEST SUBJECT TOO.
THIS ISN'T GOOD ...
THIS FINAL EXAM IS RIDICULOUS!!

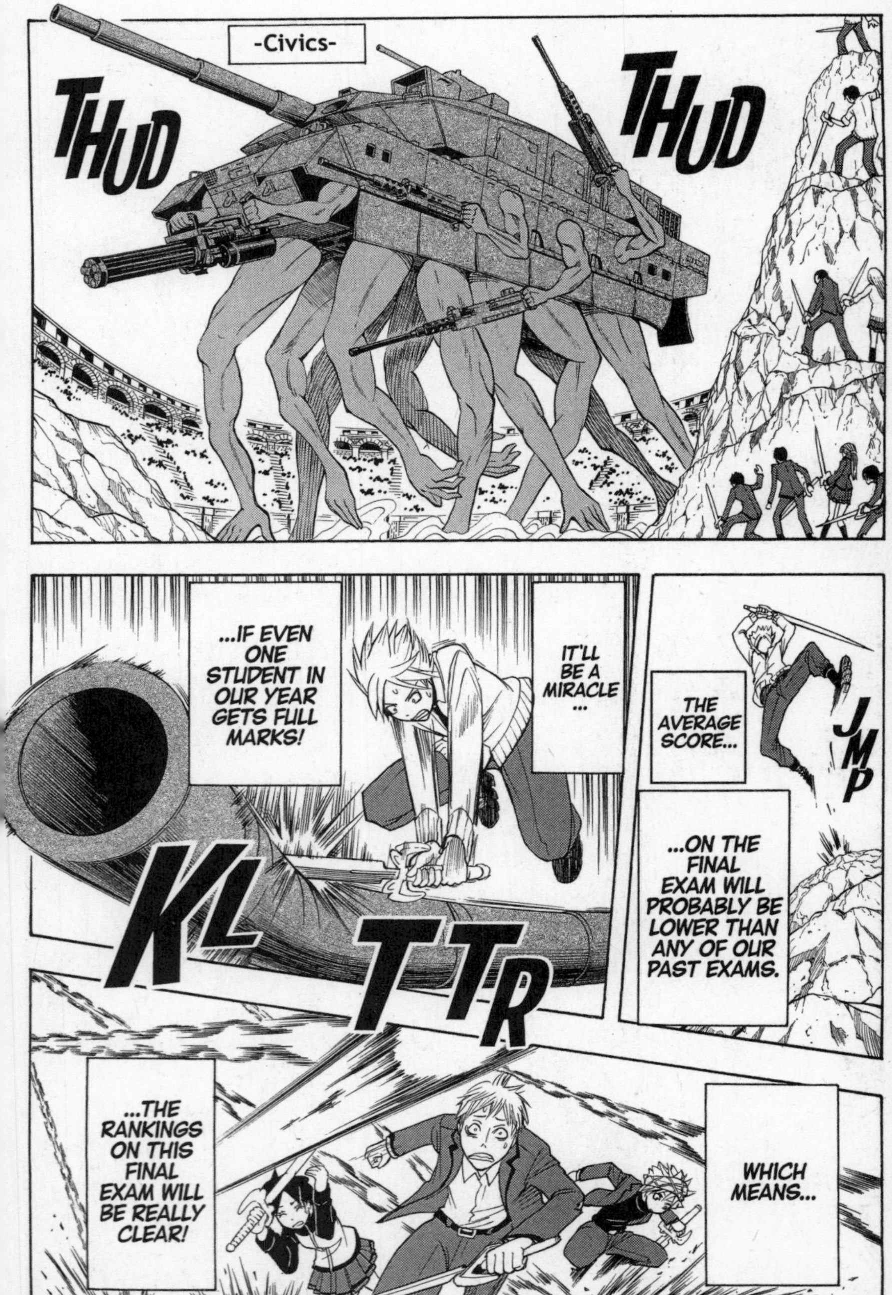
-Civics-
THUD
THUD
THE AVERAGE SCORE...
JMP
...ON THE FINAL EXAM WILL PROBABLY BE LOWER THAN ANY OF OUR PAST EXAMS.
IT'LL BE A MIRACLE ...
...IF EVEN ONE STUDENT IN OUR YEAR GETS FULL MARKS!
KLTTR
WHICH MEANS...
...THE RANKINGS ON THIS FINAL EXAM WILL BE REALLY CLEAR!

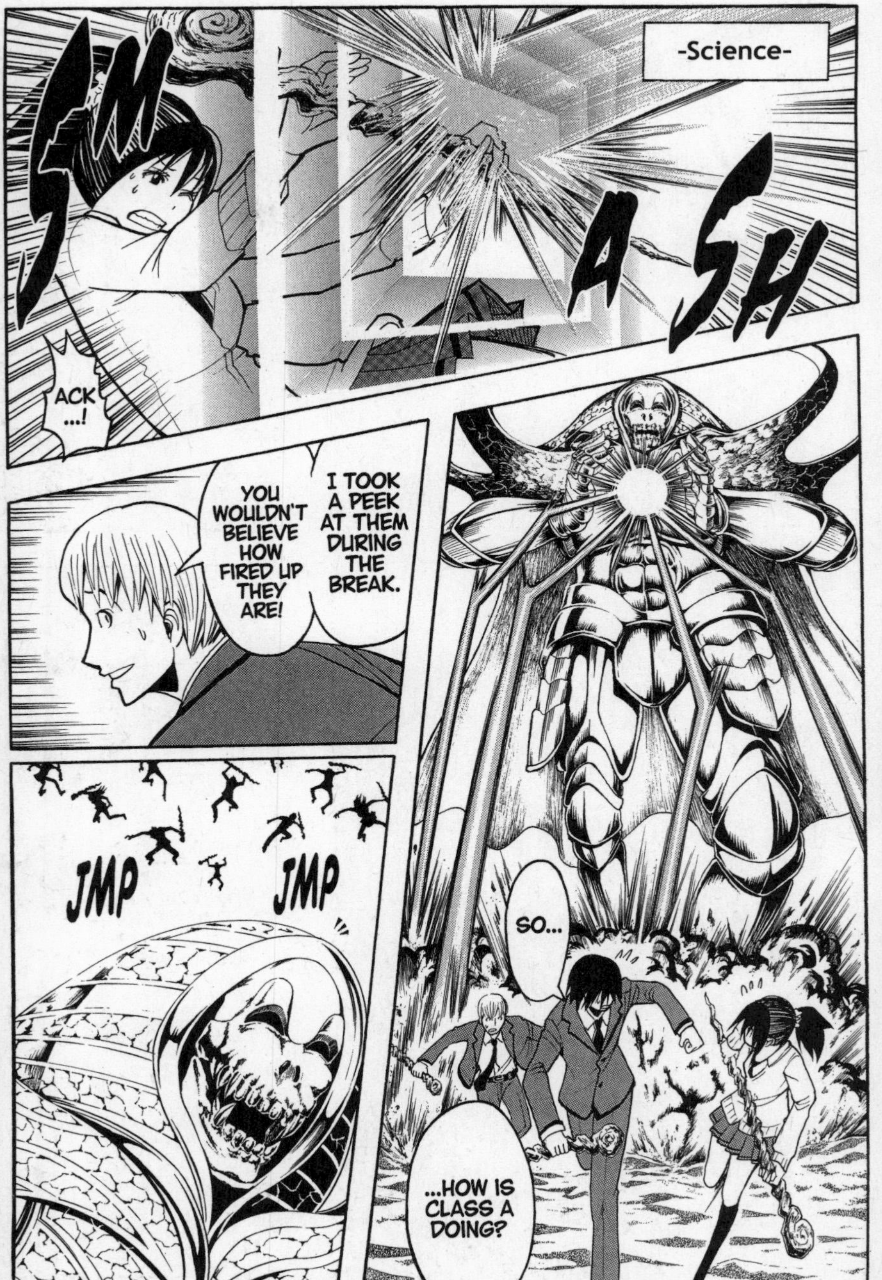
-Science-
SM
A SH
ACK ...!
SO...
...HOW IS CLASS A DOING?
I TOOK A PEEK AT THEM DURING THE BREAK.
YOU WOULDN'T BELIEVE HOW FIRED UP THEY ARE!
JMP
JMP

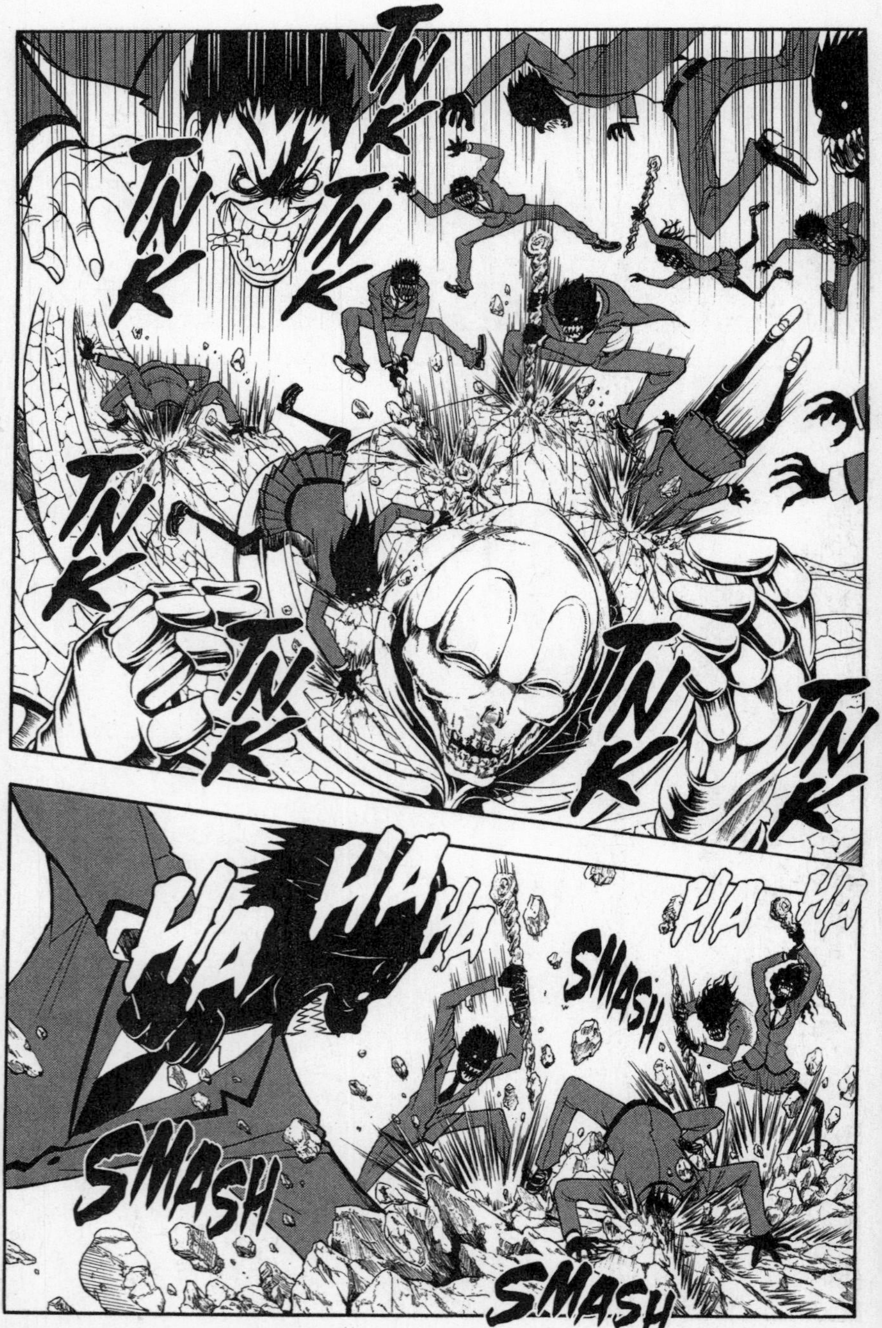
TINK
TINK
TINK
TINK
TINK
TINK
TINK
HA HA HA
HA HA HA
SMASH
SMASH
SMASH

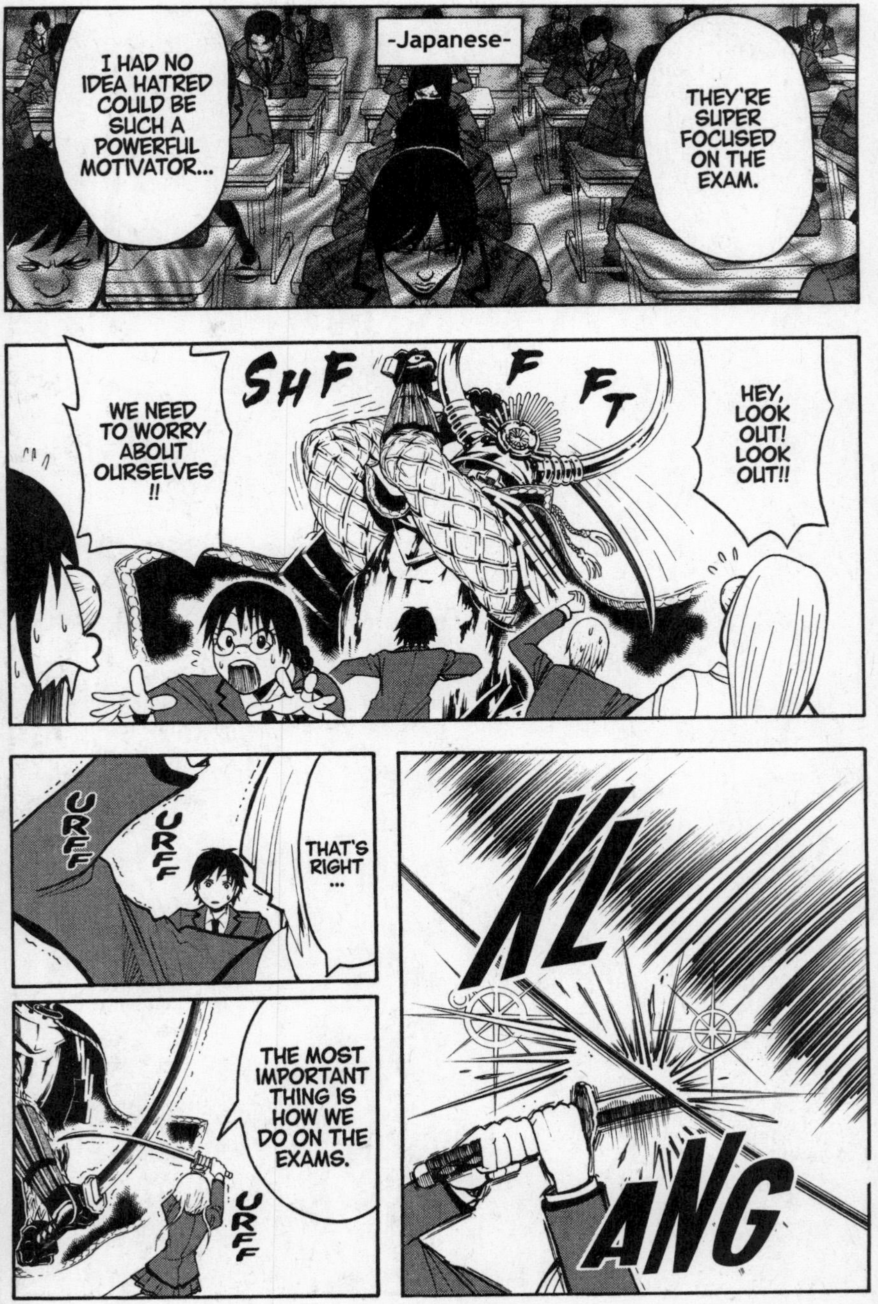

-Japanese-
THEY'RE SUPER FOCUSED ON THE EXAM.
I HAD NO IDEA HATRED COULD BE SUCH A POWERFUL MOTIVATOR...
HEY, LOOK OUT! LOOK OUT!!
SHF
F
FT
WE NEED TO WORRY ABOUT OURSELVES!!
XL
ANG
THAT'S RIGHT...
URFF
URFF
THE MOST IMPORTANT THING IS HOW WE DO ON THE EXAMS.
URFF

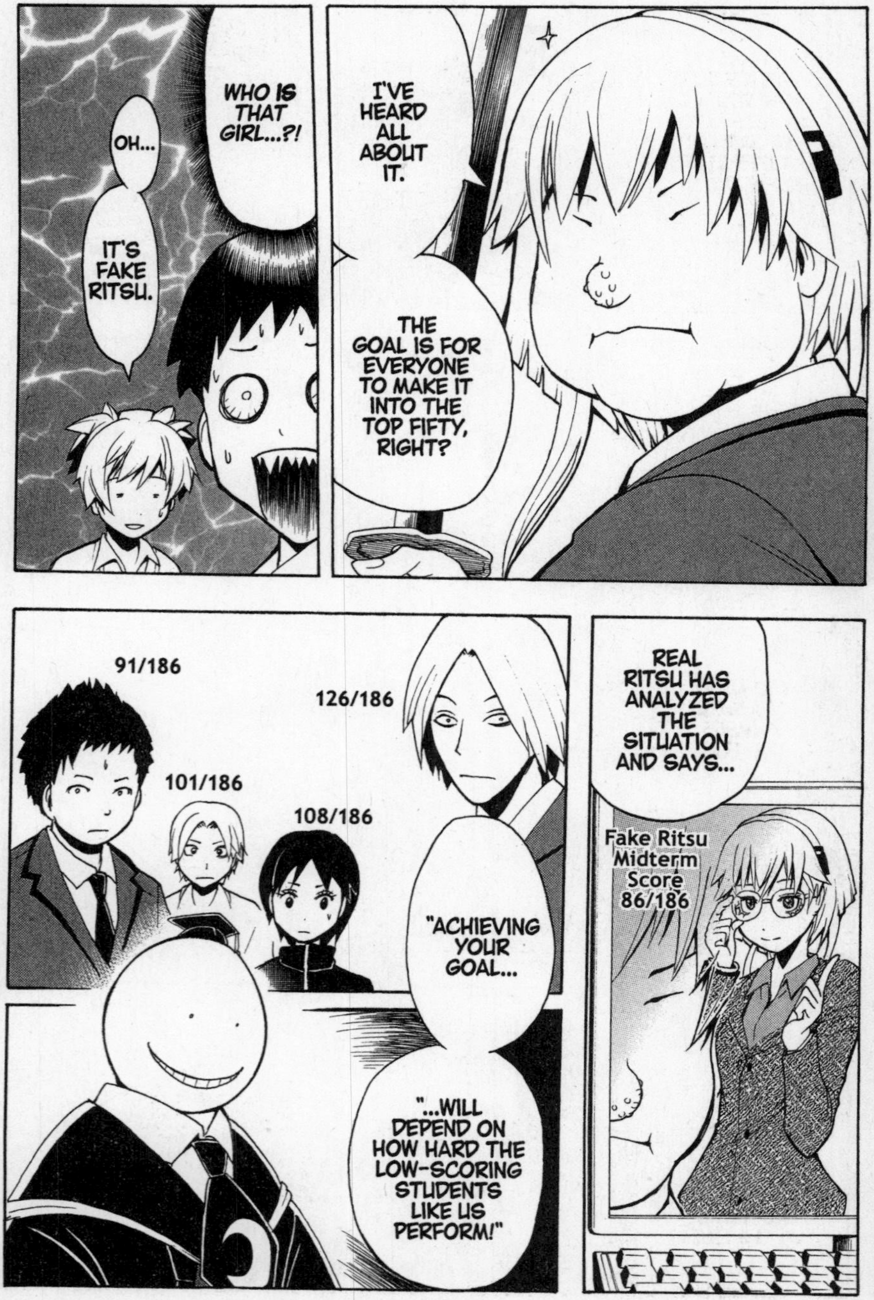
I'VE HEARD ALL ABOUT IT.
THE GOAL IS FOR EVERYONE TO MAKE IT INTO THE TOP FIFTY, RIGHT?
WHO IS THAT GIRL...?!
OH...
IT'S FAKE RITSU.
REAL RITSU HAS ANALYZED THE SITUATION AND SAYS...
Fake Ritsu Midterm Score 86/186
126/186
91/186
101/186
108/186
"ACHIEVING YOUR GOAL...
"...WILL DEPEND ON HOW HARD THE LOW-SCORING STUDENTS LIKE US PERFORM!"

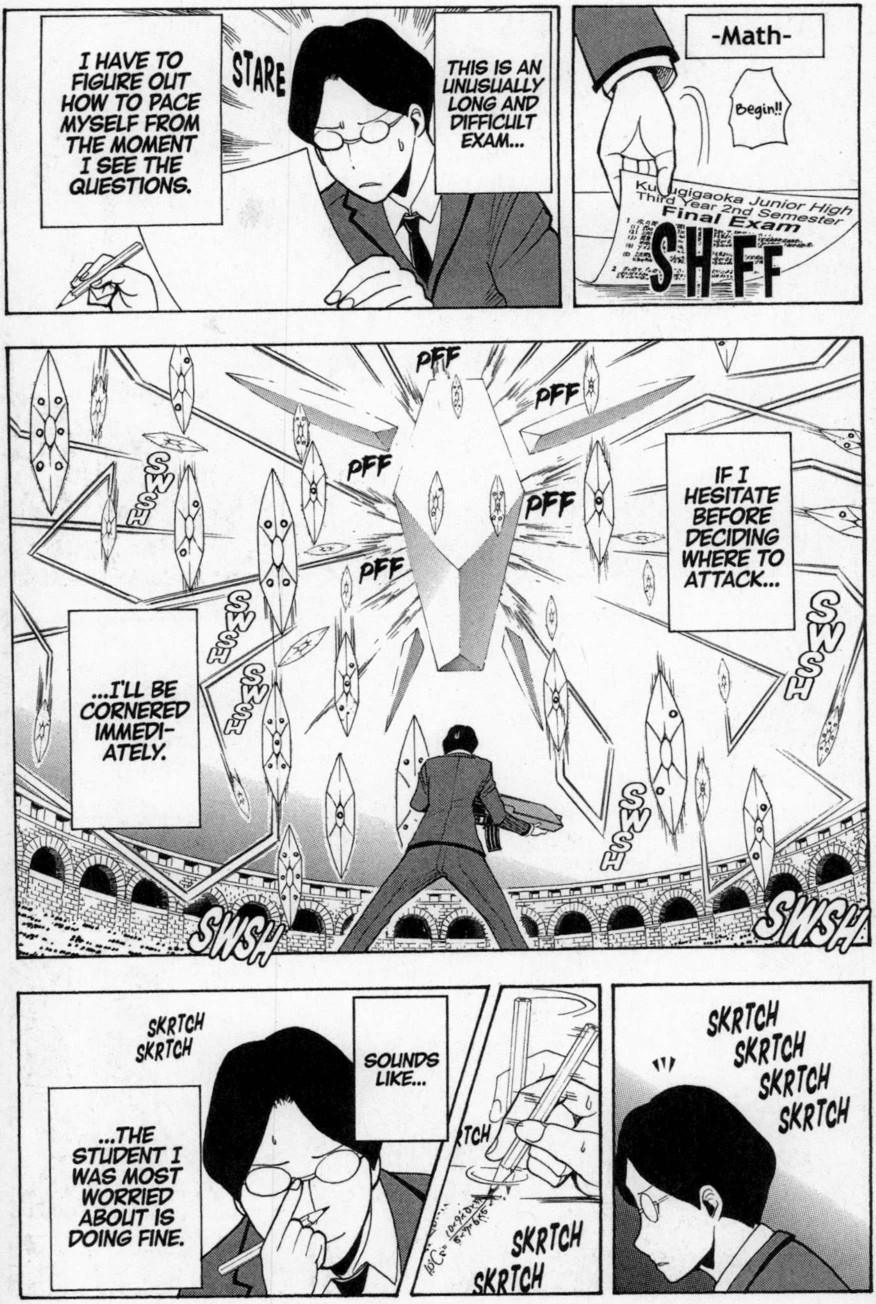
-Math-
Begin!!
Third Year 2nd Semester
Final Exam
SHFF
THIS IS AN UNUSUALLY LONG AND DIFFICULT EXAM...
STARE
I HAVE TO FIGURE OUT HOW TO PACE MYSELF FROM THE MOMENT I SEE THE QUESTIONS.
PFF
PFF
PFF
PFF
PFF
IF I HESITATE BEFORE DECIDING WHERE TO ATTACK...
SWSH
SWSH
SWSH
SWSH
SWSH
...I'LL BE CORNERED IMMEDI-ATELY.
SWSH
SWSH
SKRTCH SKRTCH SKRTCH SKRTCH
SKRTCH SKRTCH
SOUNDS LIKE...
SKRTCH SKRTCH
...THE STUDENT I WAS MOST WORRIED ABOUT IS DOING FINE.

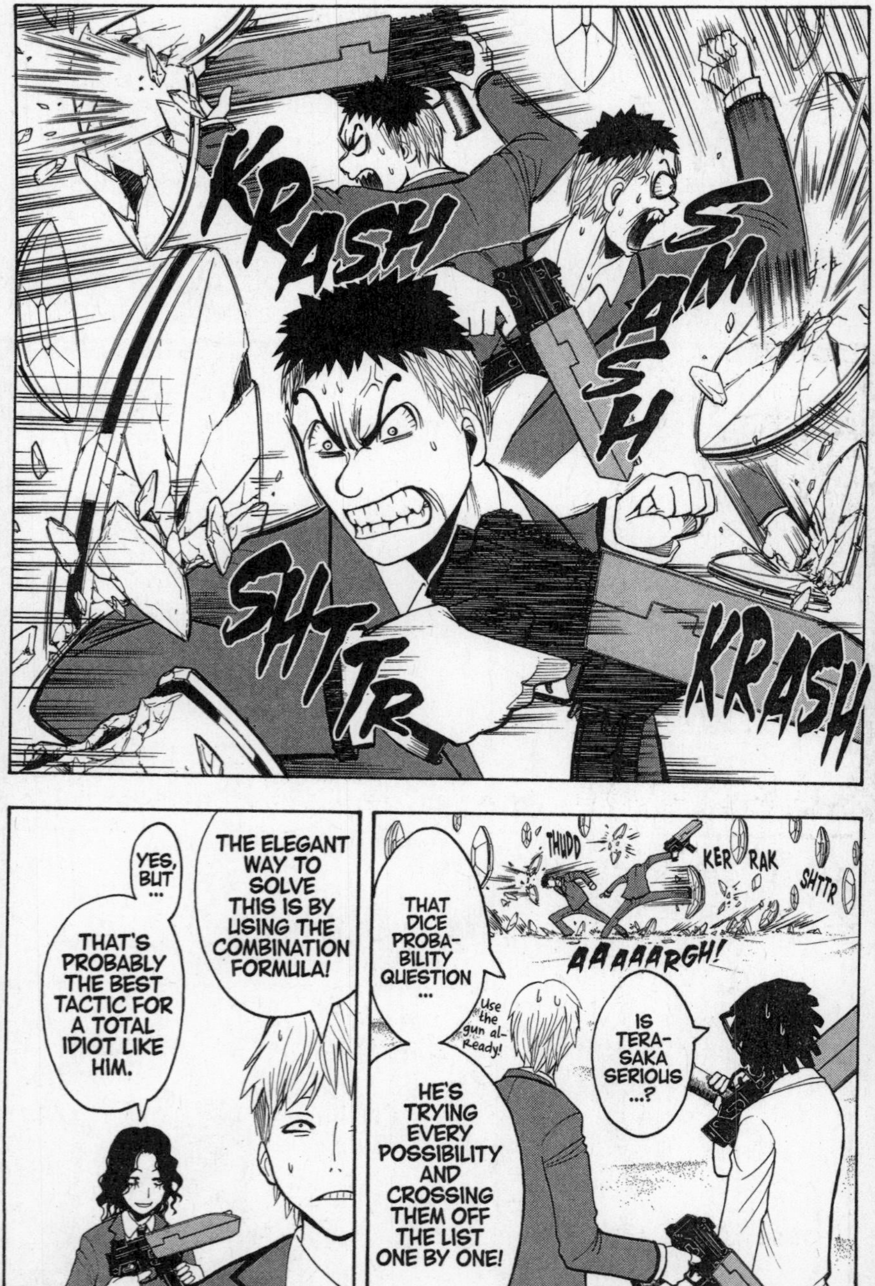
SMASH
KRASH
KRASH
SHTTR
KER RAK
SHTTR
THUDD
AAAAARGH!
IS TERA-SAKA SERIOUS ...?
Use the gun al-ready!
THAT DICE PROBA-BILITY QUESTION ...
HE'S TRYING EVERY POSSIBILITY AND CROSSING THEM OFF THE LIST ONE BY ONE!
THE ELEGANT WAY TO SOLVE THIS IS BY USING THE COMBINATION FORMULA!
YES, BUT ...
THAT'S PROBABLY THE BEST TACTIC FOR A TOTAL IDIOT LIKE HIM.

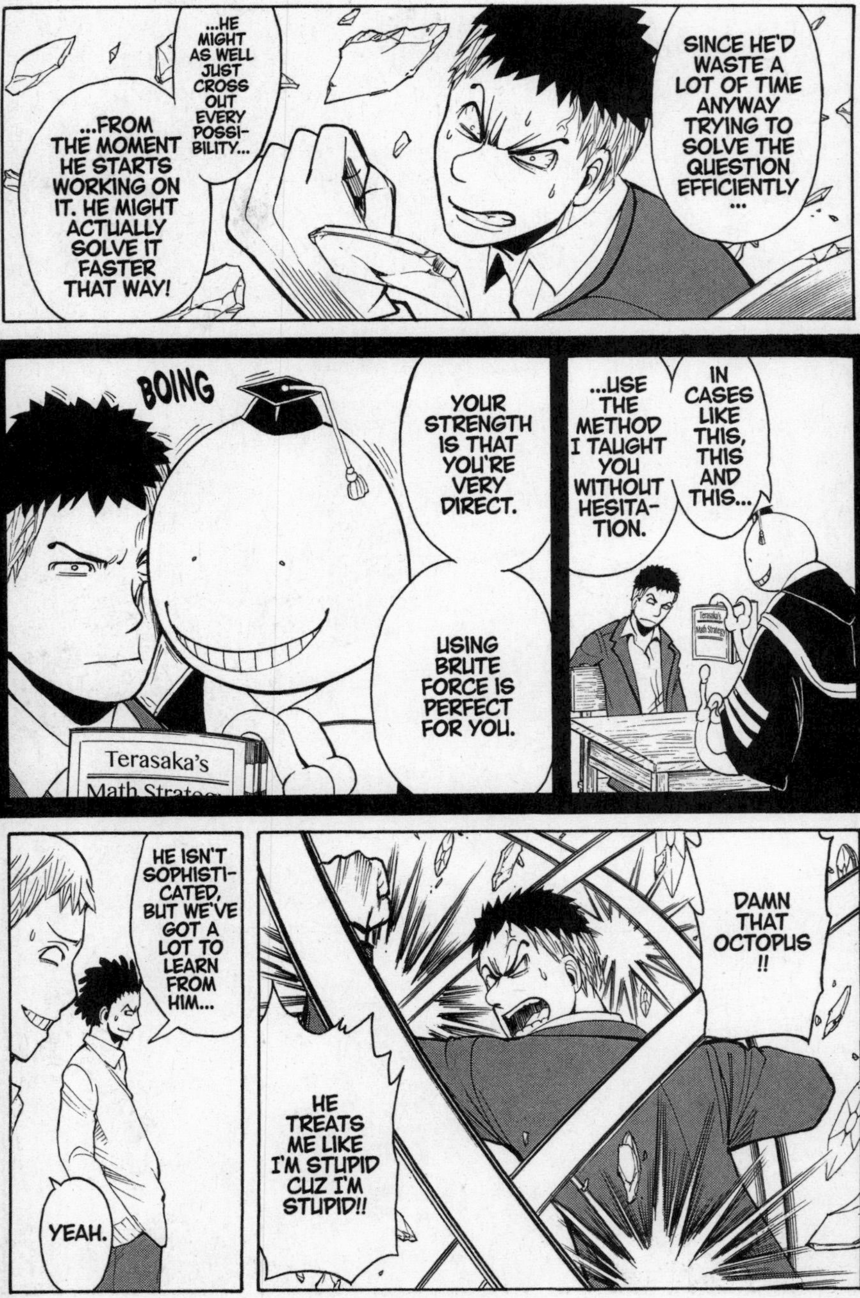

SINCE HE'D WASTE A LOT OF TIME ANYWAY TRYING TO SOLVE THE QUESTION EFFICIENTLY ...
...HE MIGHT AS WELL JUST CROSS OUT EVERY POSSIBILITY...
...FROM THE MOMENT HE STARTS WORKING ON IT. HE MIGHT ACTUALLY SOLVE IT FASTER THAT WAY!
IN CASES LIKE THIS, THIS AND THIS...
...USE THE METHOD I TAUGHT YOU WITHOUT HESITATION.
Terasaka's Math Strategy
BOING
YOUR STRENGTH IS THAT YOU'RE VERY DIRECT.
USING BRUTE FORCE IS PERFECT FOR YOU.
Terasaka's
DAMN THAT OCTOPUS !!
HE TREATS ME LIKE I'M STUPID CUZ I'M STUPID!!
HE ISN'T SOPHISTICATED, BUT WE'VE GOT A LOT TO LEARN FROM HIM...
YEAH.

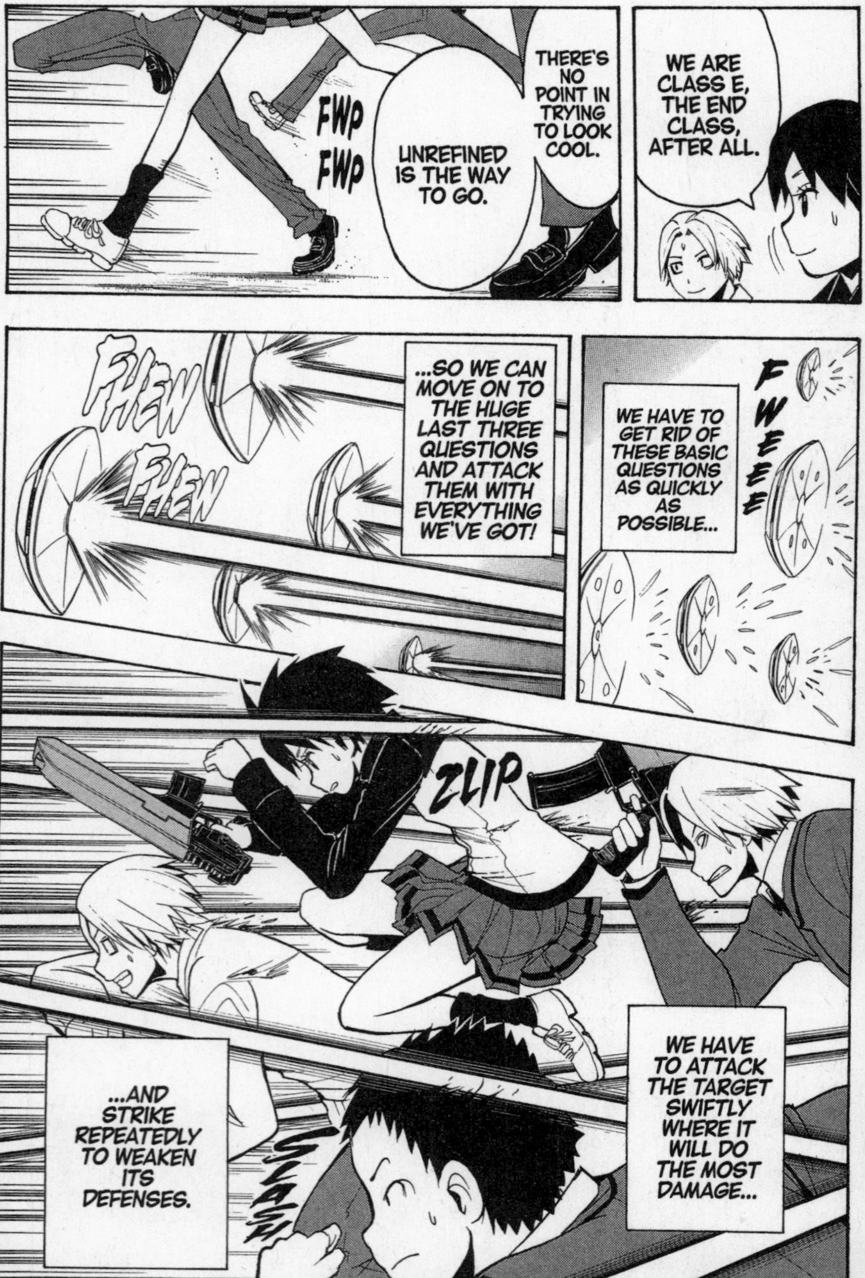
WE ARE CLASS E, THE END CLASS, AFTER ALL.
THERE'S NO POINT IN TRYING TO LOOK COOL.
UNREFINED IS THE WAY TO GO.
FWP FWP
FWEEE
WE HAVE TO GET RID OF THESE BASIC QUESTIONS AS QUICKLY AS POSSIBLE...
...SO WE CAN MOVE ON TO THE HUGE LAST THREE QUESTIONS AND ATTACK THEM WITH EVERYTHING WE'VE GOT!
FHEW FHEW
ZLIP
WE HAVE TO ATTACK THE TARGET SWIFTLY WHERE IT WILL DO THE MOST DAMAGE...
SLASH
...AND STRIKE REPEATEDLY TO WEAKEN ITS DEFENSES.

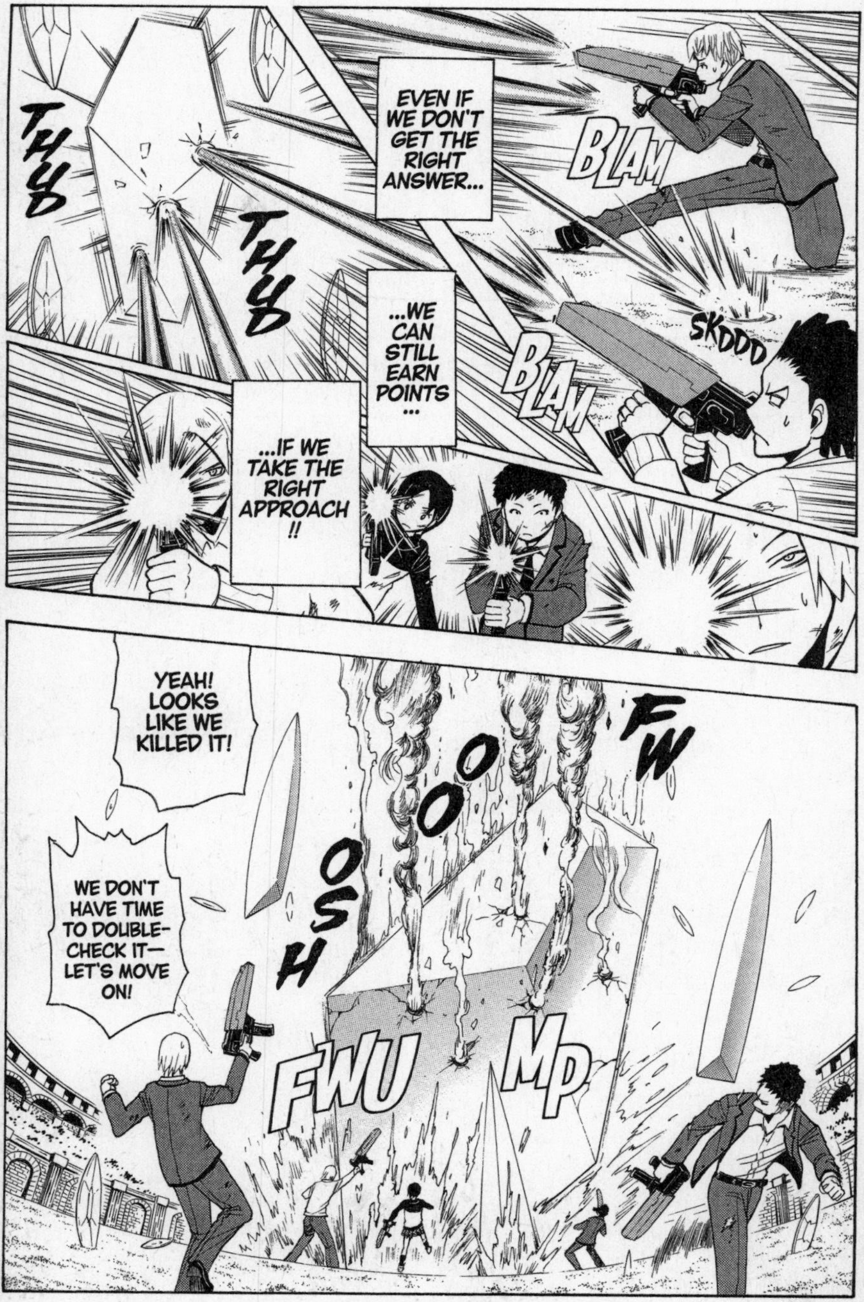

BLAM
EVEN IF WE DON'T GET THE RIGHT ANSWER...
THUD
THUD
SKDDD
BLAM
...WE CAN STILL EARN POINTS...
...IF WE TAKE THE RIGHT APPROACH!!
FWOOOOSH
YEAH! LOOKS LIKE WE KILLED IT!
WE DON'T HAVE TIME TO DOUBLE-CHECK IT—LET'S MOVE ON!
FWUMP

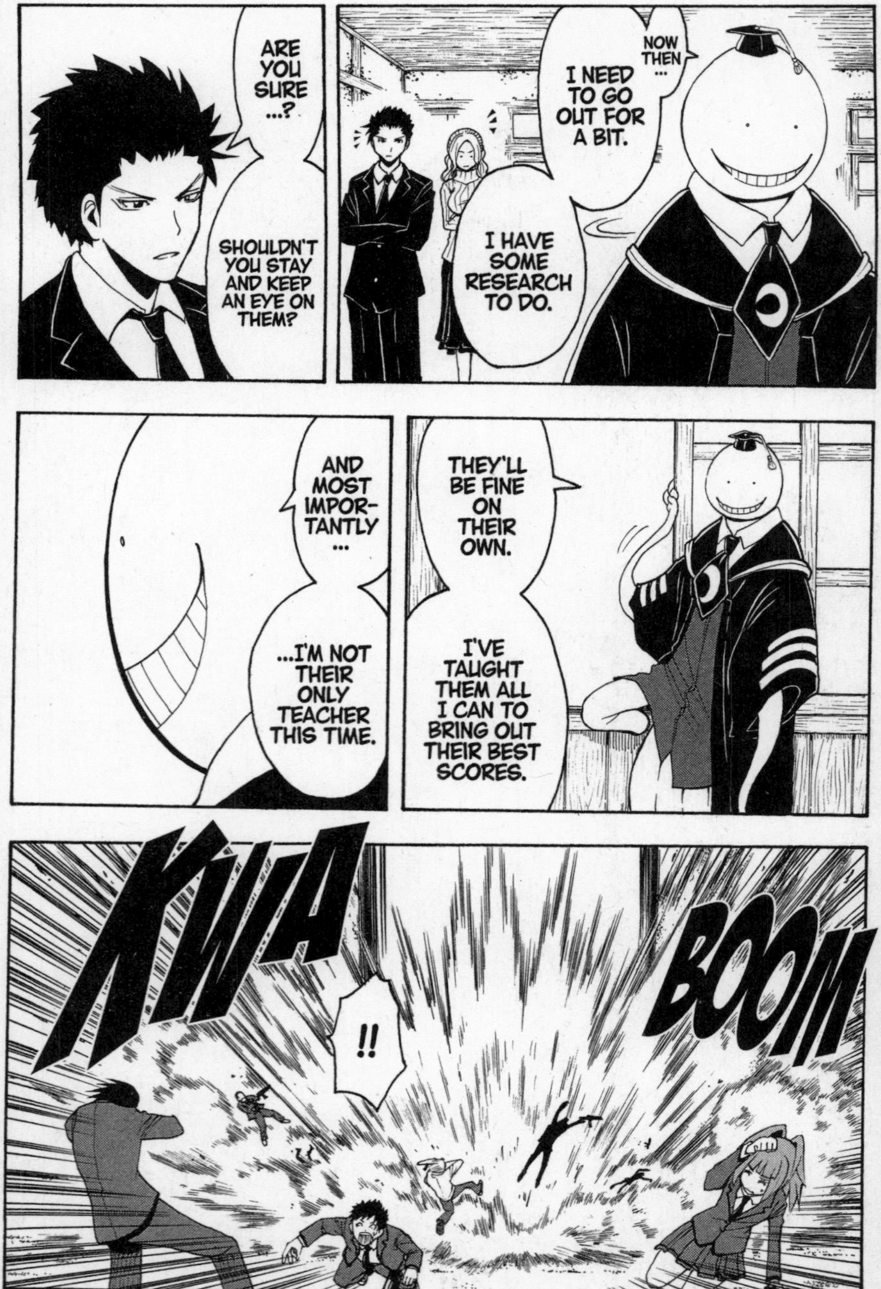
NOW THEN...
I NEED TO GO OUT FOR A BIT.
I HAVE SOME RESEARCH TO DO.
ARE YOU SURE...?
SHOULDN'T YOU STAY AND KEEP AN EYE ON THEM?
THEY'LL BE FINE ON THEIR OWN.
I'VE TAUGHT THEM ALL I CAN TO BRING OUT THEIR BEST SCORES.
AND MOST IMPOR-TANTLY...
...I'M NOT THEIR ONLY TEACHER THIS TIME.
BOOM
!!
KWA

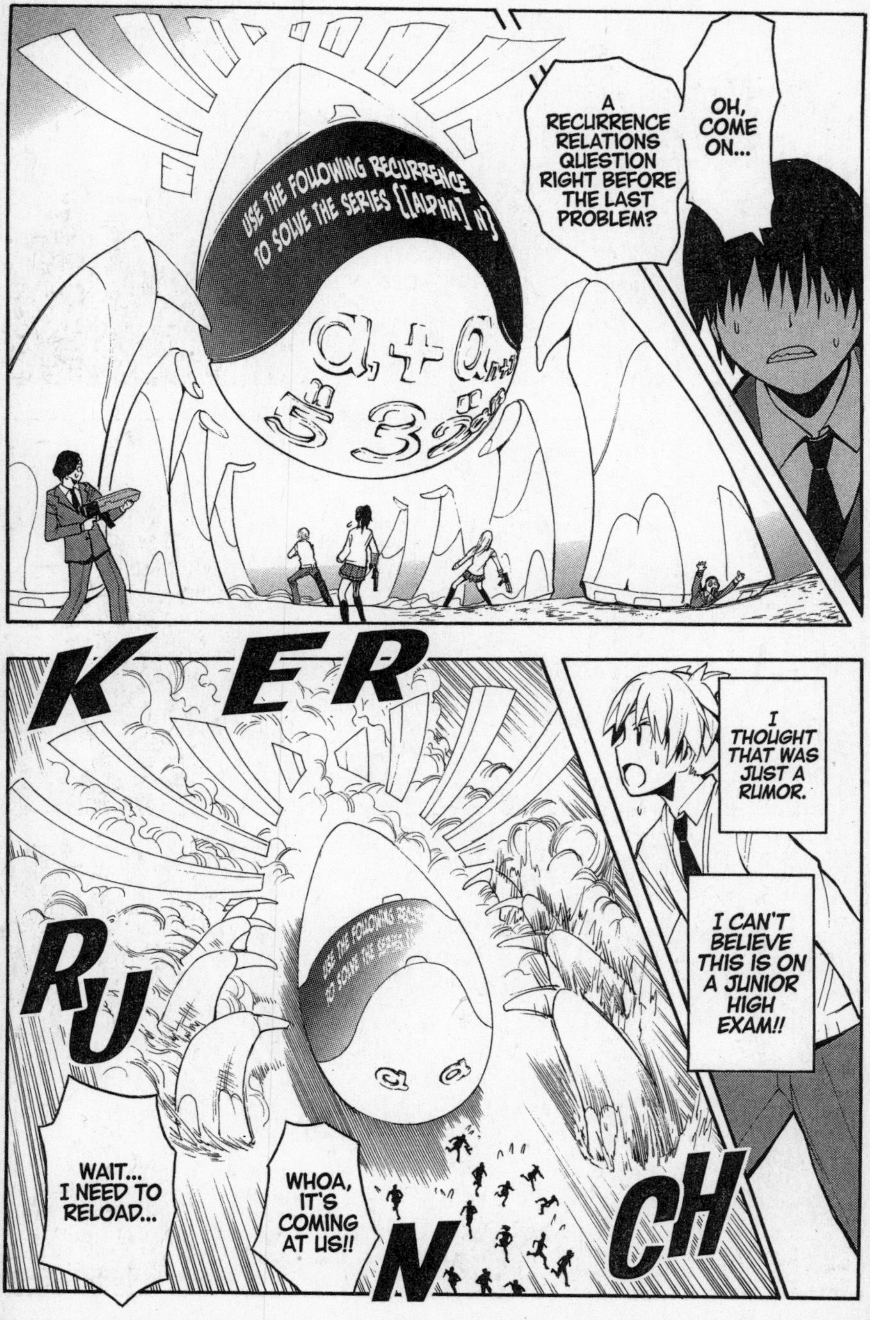

OH, COME ON...
A RECURRENCE RELATIONS QUESTION RIGHT BEFORE THE LAST PROBLEM?
USE THE FOLLOWING RECURRENCE TO SOLVE THE SERIES {[ALPHA] N}
I THOUGHT THAT WAS JUST A RUMOR.
I CAN'T BELIEVE THIS IS ON A JUNIOR HIGH EXAM!!
KERRUNCH
WHOA, IT'S COMING AT US!!
WAIT... I NEED TO RELOAD...

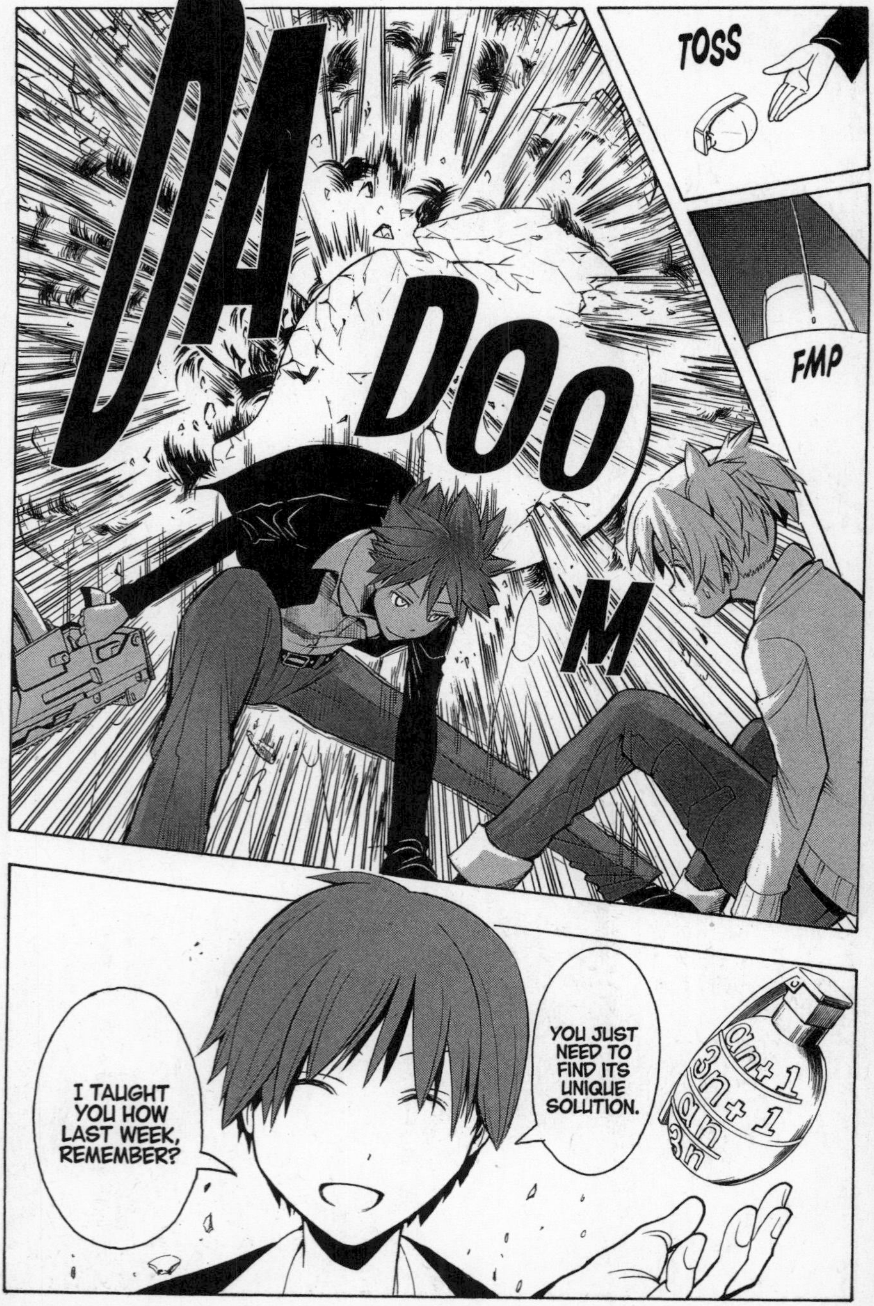
TOSS
FMP
DA DOOM
YOU JUST NEED TO FIND ITS UNIQUE SOLUTION.
I TAUGHT YOU HOW LAST WEEK, REMEMBER?

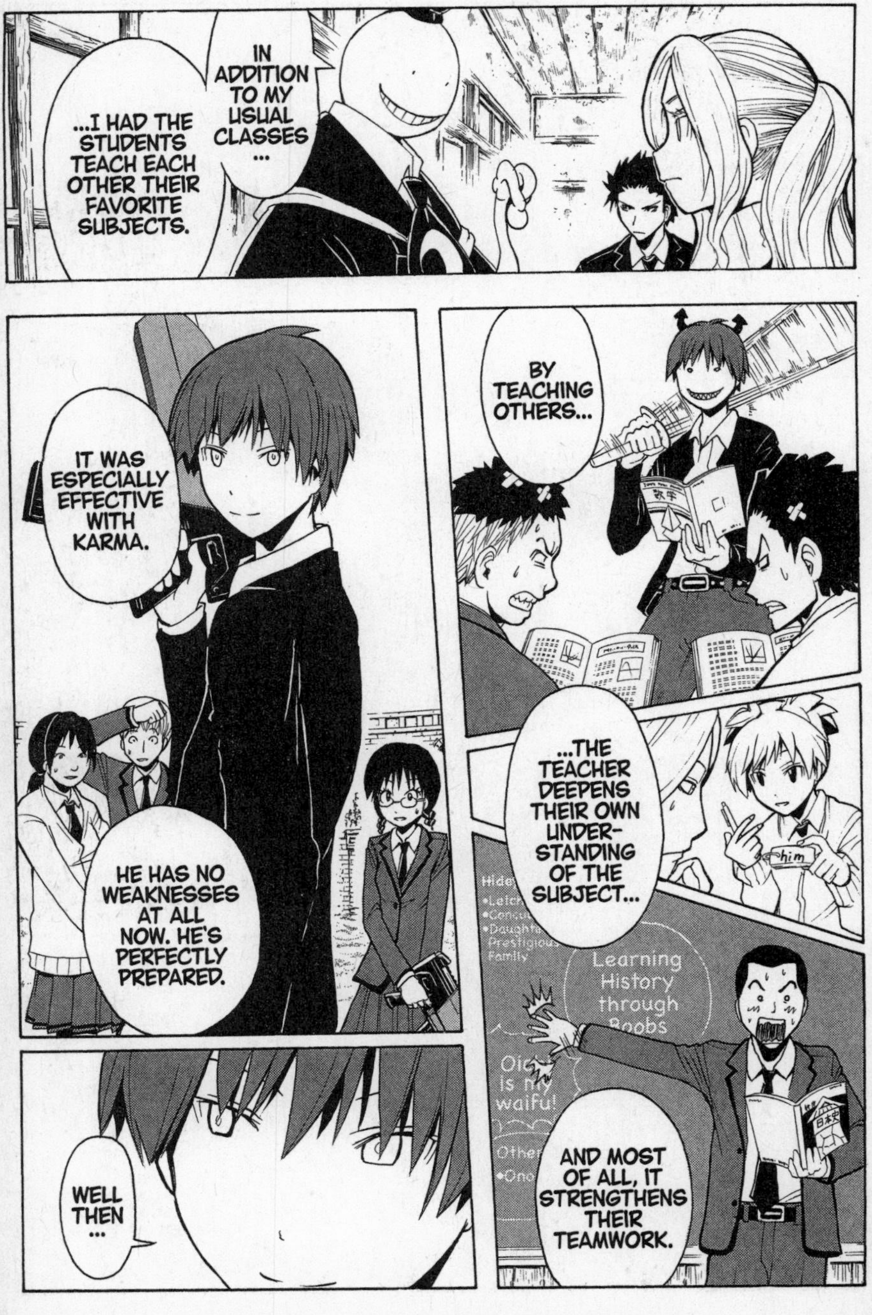
IN ADDITION TO MY USUAL CLASSES...
...I HAD THE STUDENTS TEACH EACH OTHER THEIR FAVORITE SUBJECTS.
BY TEACHING OTHERS...
...THE TEACHER DEEPENS THEIR OWN UNDER-STANDING OF THE SUBJECT...
him
Prestigious Family
Learning History through Boobs
is my waifu!
AND MOST OF ALL, IT STRENGTHENS THEIR TEAMWORK.
IT WAS ESPECIALLY EFFECTIVE WITH KARMA.
HE HAS NO WEAKNESSES AT ALL NOW. HE'S PERFECTLY PREPARED.
WELL THEN...

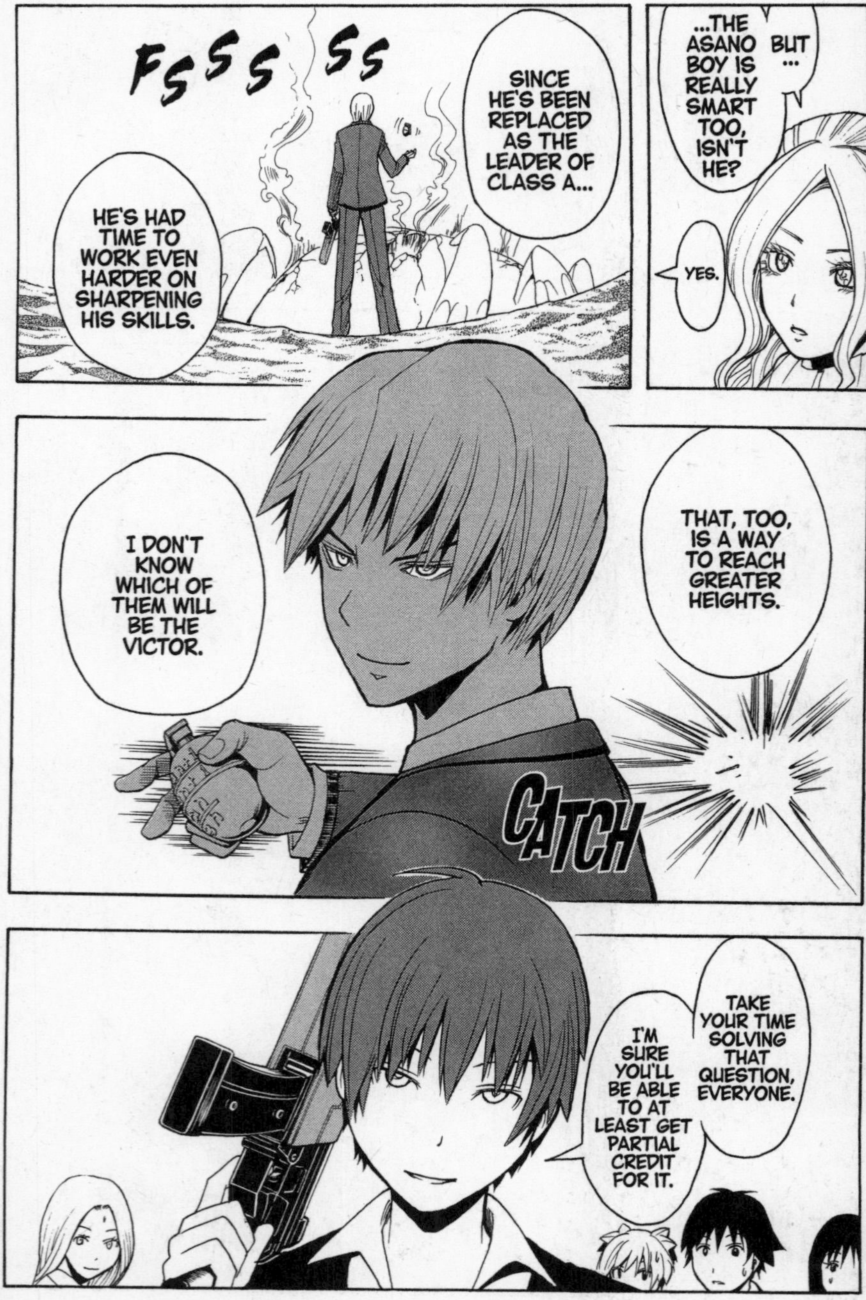
BUT...
...THE ASANO BOY IS REALLY SMART TOO, ISN'T HE?
YES.
SINCE HE'S BEEN REPLACED AS THE LEADER OF CLASS A...
FSSS SS
HE'S HAD TIME TO WORK EVEN HARDER ON SHARPENING HIS SKILLS.
THAT, TOO, IS A WAY TO REACH GREATER HEIGHTS.
I DON'T KNOW WHICH OF THEM WILL BE THE VICTOR.
CATCH
TAKE YOUR TIME SOLVING THAT QUESTION, EVERYONE.
I'M SURE YOU'LL BE ABLE TO AT LEAST GET PARTIAL CREDIT FOR IT.

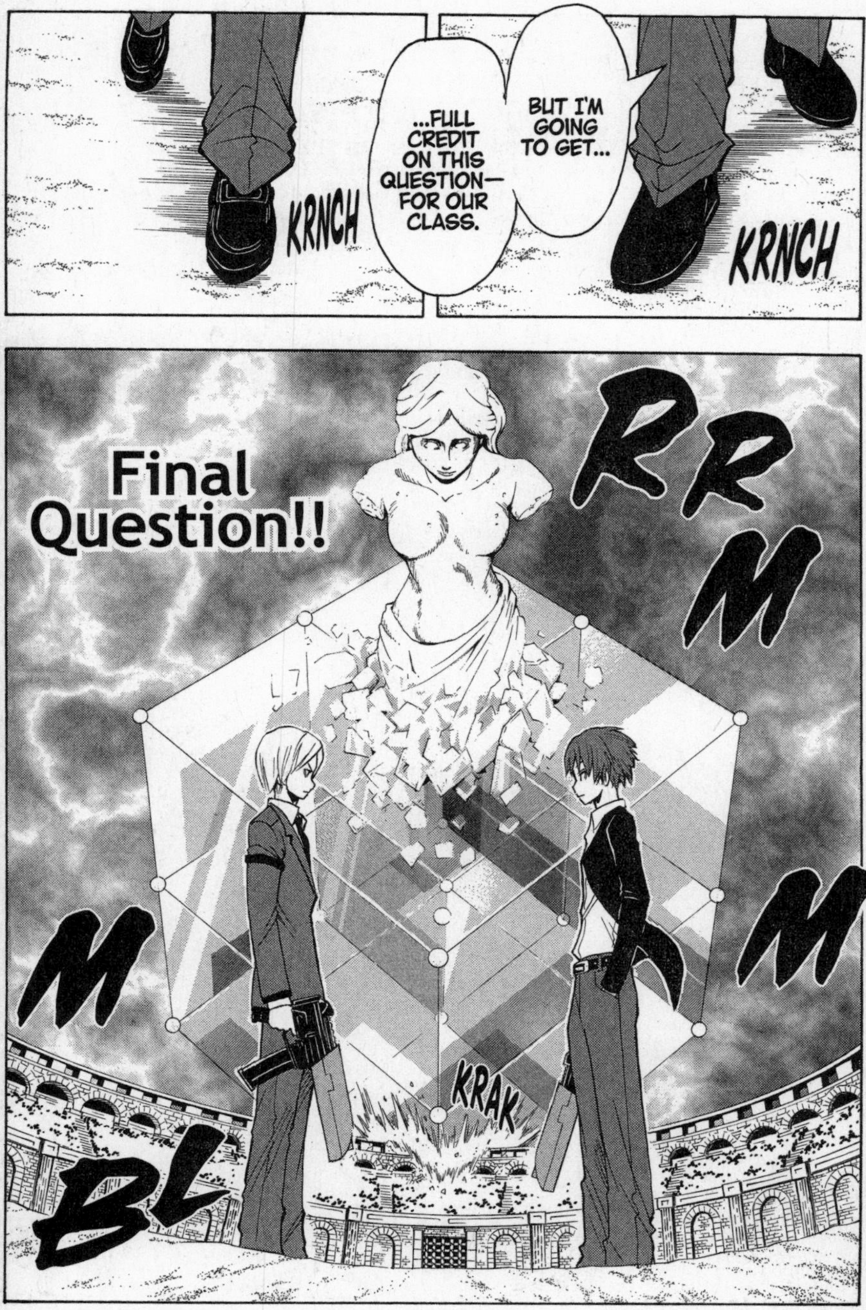
BUT I'M GOING TO GET...
KRNCH
...FULL CREDIT ON THIS QUESTION— FOR OUR CLASS.
KRNCH
RRM
Final Question!!
M
M
KRAK
BL

About the Anime

I'm writing this after watching up to episode 11. The quality of the animation in this series is wonderful. It's loyal to the manga yet fills in gaps there weren't room for. That's probably the best and most gratifying result for the fans and the original creator when creating an anime based on a manga. As the creator of the series, I strongly recommend the DVD for those who can't wait to see *Assassination Classroom* in action.

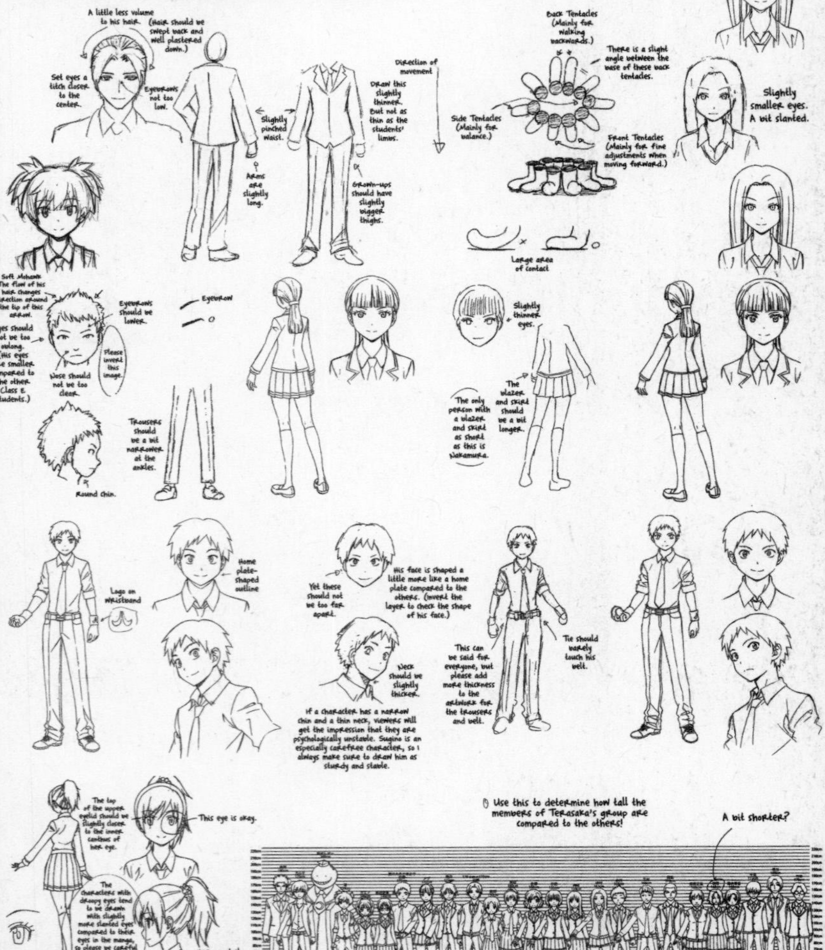
A little less volume to his hair. (Hair should be swept back and well plastered down.)
Set eyes a titch closer to the center.
Eyebrows not too low.
Slightly pinched waist.
Arms are slightly long.
Direction of movement
Draw this slightly thinner. But not as thin as the students' limbs.
Grown-ups should have slightly bigger thighs.
Back Tentacles (Mainly for walking backwards.)
There is a slight angle between the base of these back tentacles.
Side Tentacles (Mainly for balance.)
Front Tentacles (Mainly for fine adjustments when moving forward.)
Large area of contact
Slightly smaller eyes. A bit slanted.
Soft Mohawk The flow of his hair changes direction around the tip of this arrow.
Eyes should not be too oblong. (His eyes are smaller compared to the other Class E students.)
Nose should not be too clear.
Eyebrows should be lower.
Eyebrow
Please invert this image.
Trousers should be a bit narrower at the ankles.
Round chin.
Slightly thinner eyes.
The only person with a blazer and skirt as short as this is Nakamura.
The blazer and skirt should be a bit longer.
Logo on wristband
Home plate-shaped outline
Yet these should not be too far apart.
His face is shaped a little more like a home plate compared to the others. (Invert the layer to check the shape of his face.)
Neck should be slightly thicker.
If a character has a narrow chin and a thin neck, viewers will get the impression that they are psychologically unstable. Sugino is an especially carefree character, so I always make sure to draw him as sturdy and stable.
This can be said for everyone, but please add more thickness to the artwork for the trousers and belt.
Tie should barely touch his belt.
The top of the upper eyelid should be slightly closer to the inner canthus of her eye.
This eye is okay.
The characters with droopy eyes tend to be drawn with slightly more slanted eyes compared to their eyes in the manga, so please be careful about that. (Kayano, Yada, Kanzaki, Kurahashi)
Her ponytail should have a little more volume.
Use this to determine how tall the members of Terasaka's group are compared to the others!
A bit shorter?

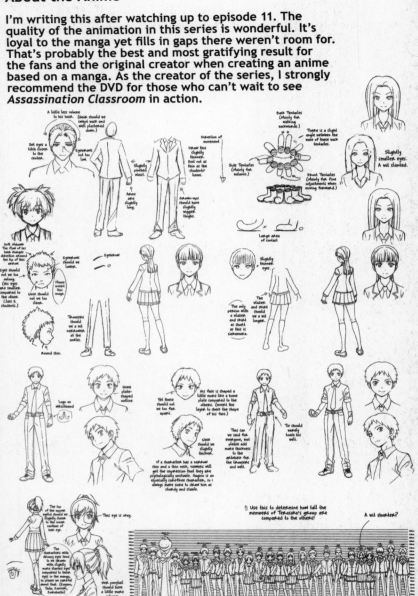

As you can see, I've been talking about all the characters in detail with the animators. But until the discussions about the anime, I hadn't really given much thought to how tall Koro Sensei actually was. (laugh)

Class 122 | Time to Think Outside the Box

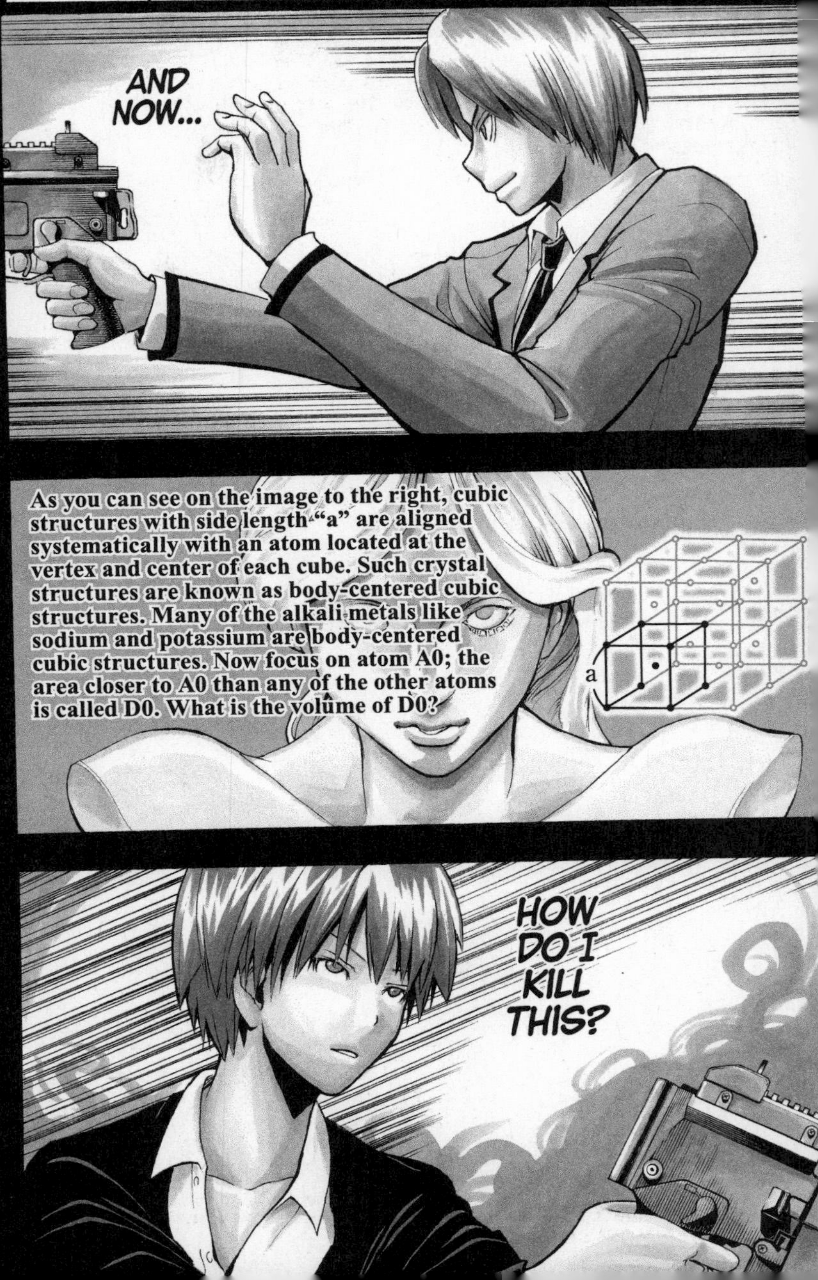
AND NOW...
As you can see on the image to the right, cubic structures with side length "a" are aligned systematically with an atom located at the vertex and center of each cube. Such crystal structures are known as body-centered cubic structures. Many of the alkali metals like sodium and potassium are body-centered cubic structures. Now focus on atom A0; the area closer to A0 than any of the other atoms is called D0. What is the volume of D0?
a
HOW DO I KILL THIS?

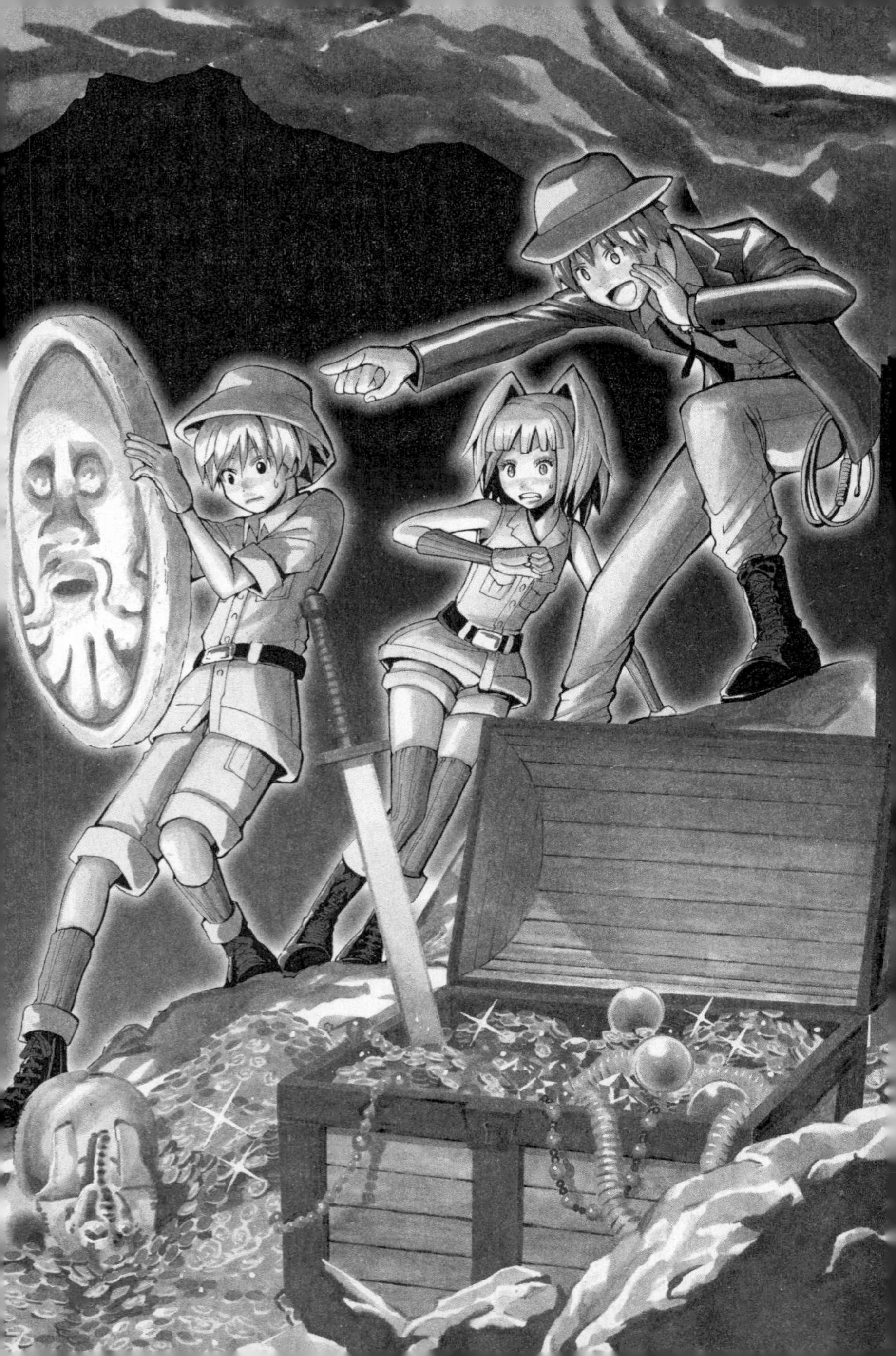

CLASS 122 TIME SQUARED

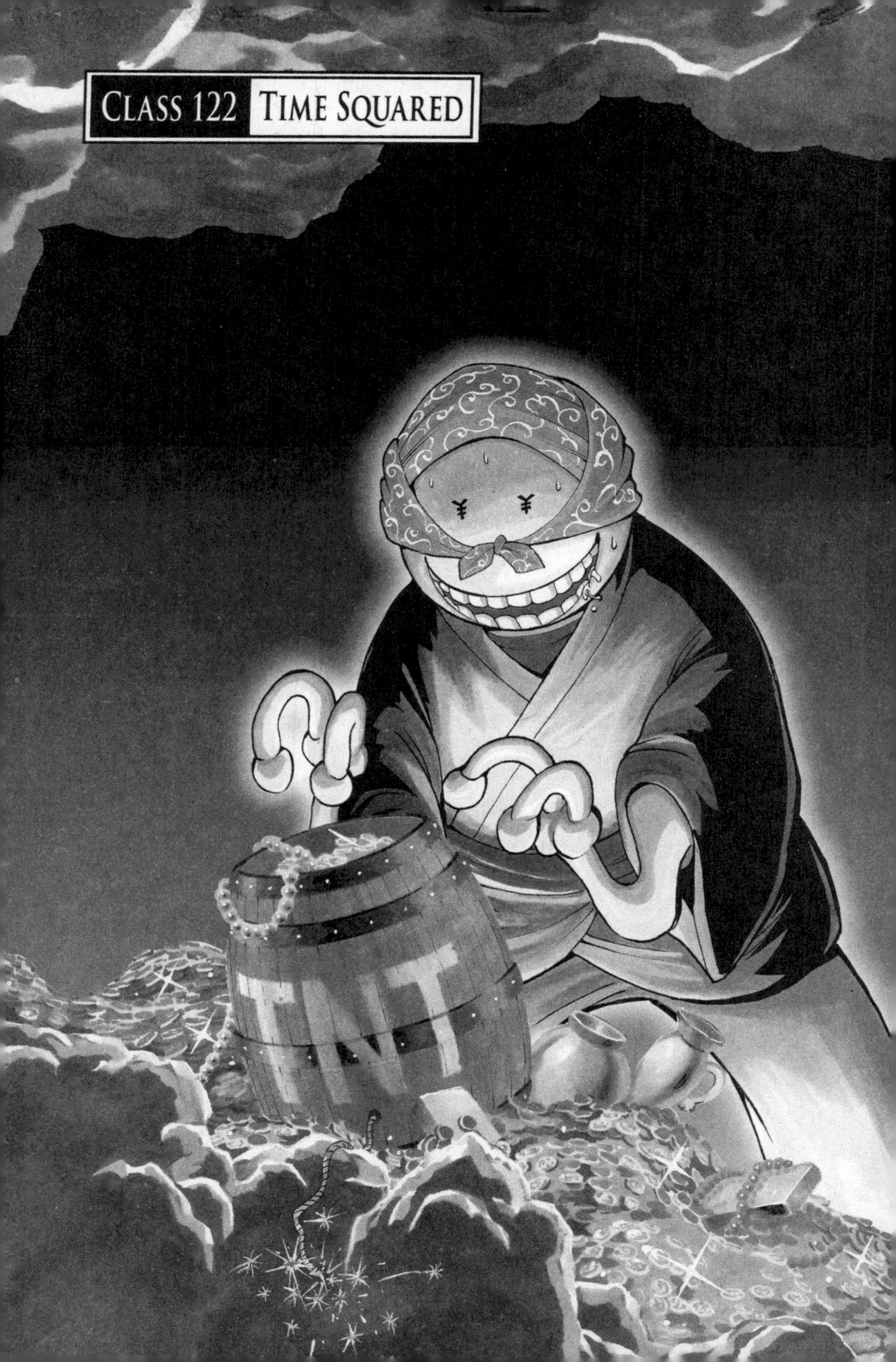
TNT

As you can see on the image to the right, cubic structures with side length "a" are aligned systematically with an atom located at the vertex and center of each cube. Such crystal structures are known as body-centered cubic structures. Many of the alkali metals like sodium and potassium are body-centered cubic structures. Now focus on atom A0; the area closer to A0 than any of the other atoms is called D0. What is the volume of D0?

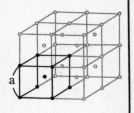

I had someone from Z-kai create this math problem for me. I asked for "college-level exam questions that could be solved with junior high knowledge" and chose the one that fit the themes of the manga.

It took me three days to understand the question so that I could explain it in simple words to heat up the story, but I thought it was a wonderfully interesting problem.

I've finally realized that people who create exam questions like this are skillful artists, and the people who can solve them are excellent game players...

Of course, you don't have to solve the question to enjoy the story, but please take a moment to try if you feel up to it.

What do you think...?

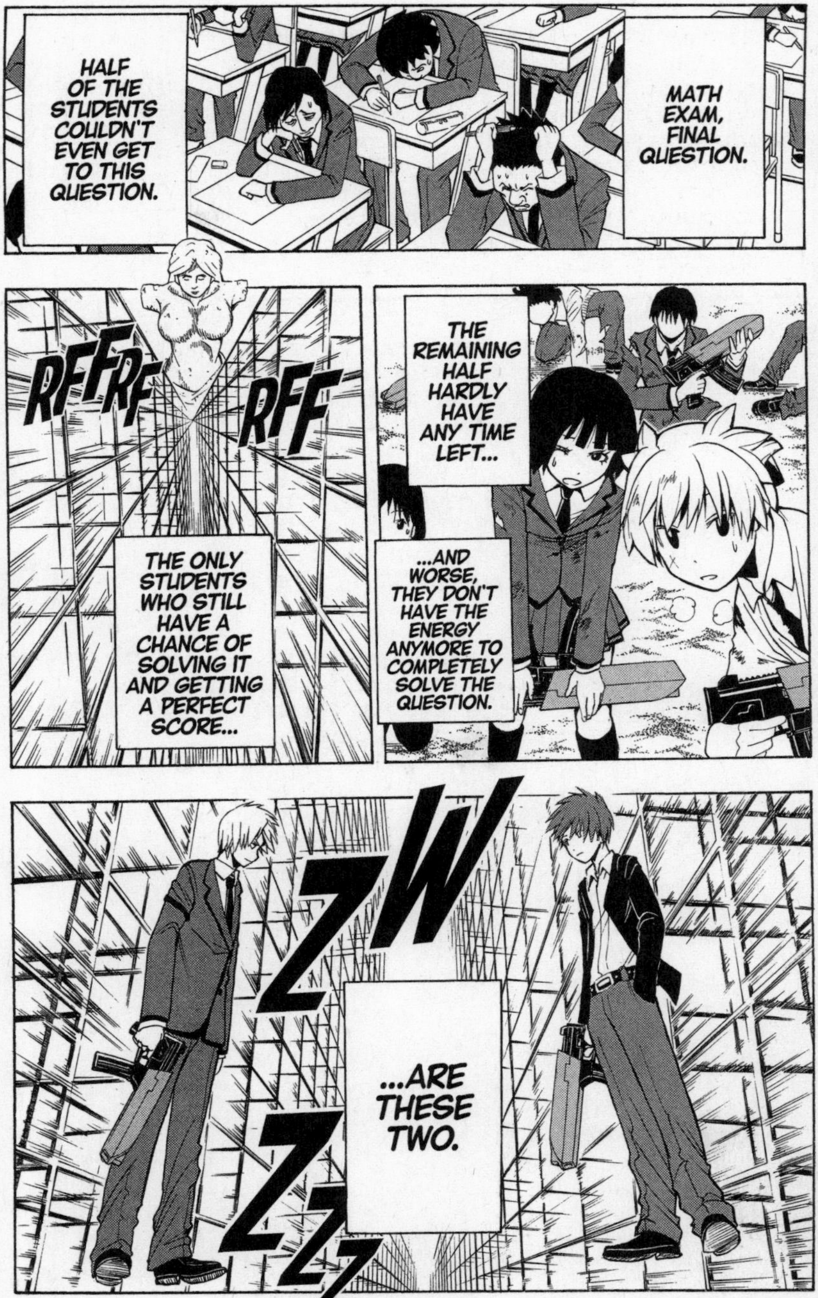
MATH EXAM, FINAL QUESTION.
HALF OF THE STUDENTS COULDN'T EVEN GET TO THIS QUESTION.
THE REMAINING HALF HARDLY HAVE ANY TIME LEFT...
...AND WORSE, THEY DON'T HAVE THE ENERGY ANYMORE TO COMPLETELY SOLVE THE QUESTION.
RFF
RFFRF
THE ONLY STUDENTS WHO STILL HAVE A CHANCE OF SOLVING IT AND GETTING A PERFECT SCORE...
ZW
...ARE THESE TWO.
ZZZ

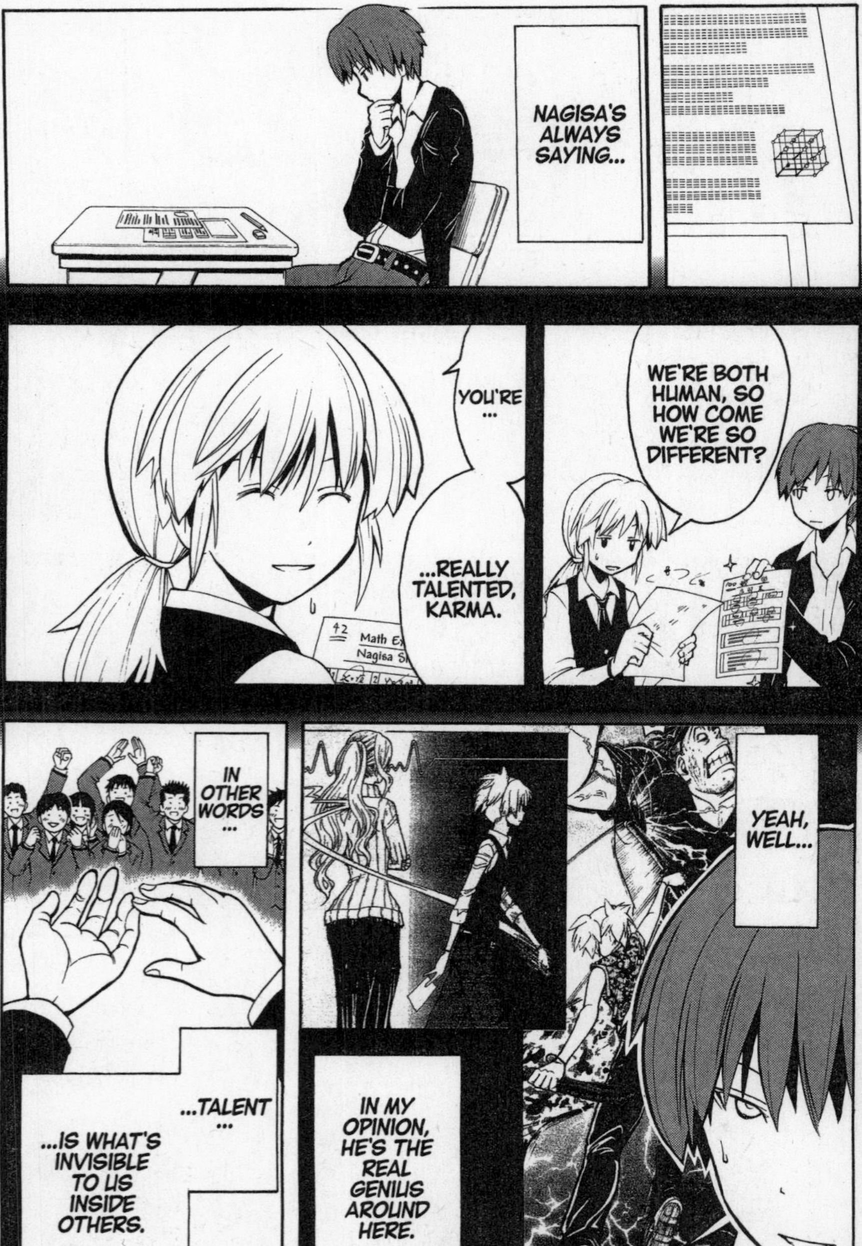
NAGISA'S ALWAYS SAYING...
WE'RE BOTH HUMAN, SO HOW COME WE'RE SO DIFFERENT?
YOU'RE ...
...REALLY TALENTED, KARMA.
YEAH, WELL...
IN MY OPINION, HE'S THE REAL GENIUS AROUND HERE.
IN OTHER WORDS ...
...TALENT ...
...IS WHAT'S INVISIBLE TO US INSIDE OTHERS.

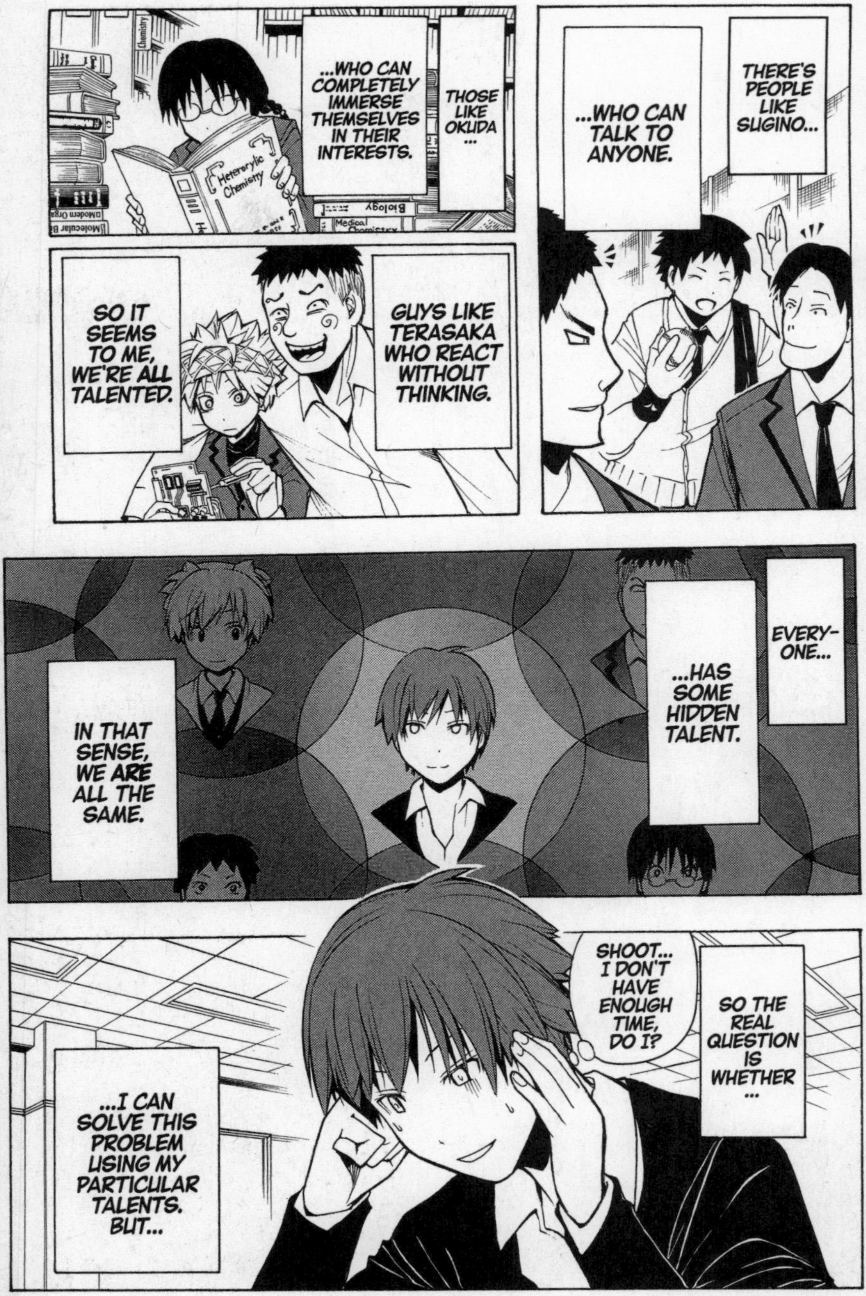
THERE'S PEOPLE LIKE SUGINO...
...WHO CAN TALK TO ANYONE.
THOSE LIKE OKUDA ...
...WHO CAN COMPLETELY IMMERSE THEMSELVES IN THEIR INTERESTS.
Chemistry
Heterorylic Chemistry
Biology
GUYS LIKE TERASAKA WHO REACT WITHOUT THINKING.
SO IT SEEMS TO ME, WE'RE ALL TALENTED.
EVERY-ONE...
...HAS SOME HIDDEN TALENT.
IN THAT SENSE, WE ARE ALL THE SAME.
SO THE REAL QUESTION IS WHETHER ...
SHOOT... I DON'T HAVE ENOUGH TIME, DO I?
...I CAN SOLVE THIS PROBLEM USING MY PARTICULAR TALENTS. BUT...

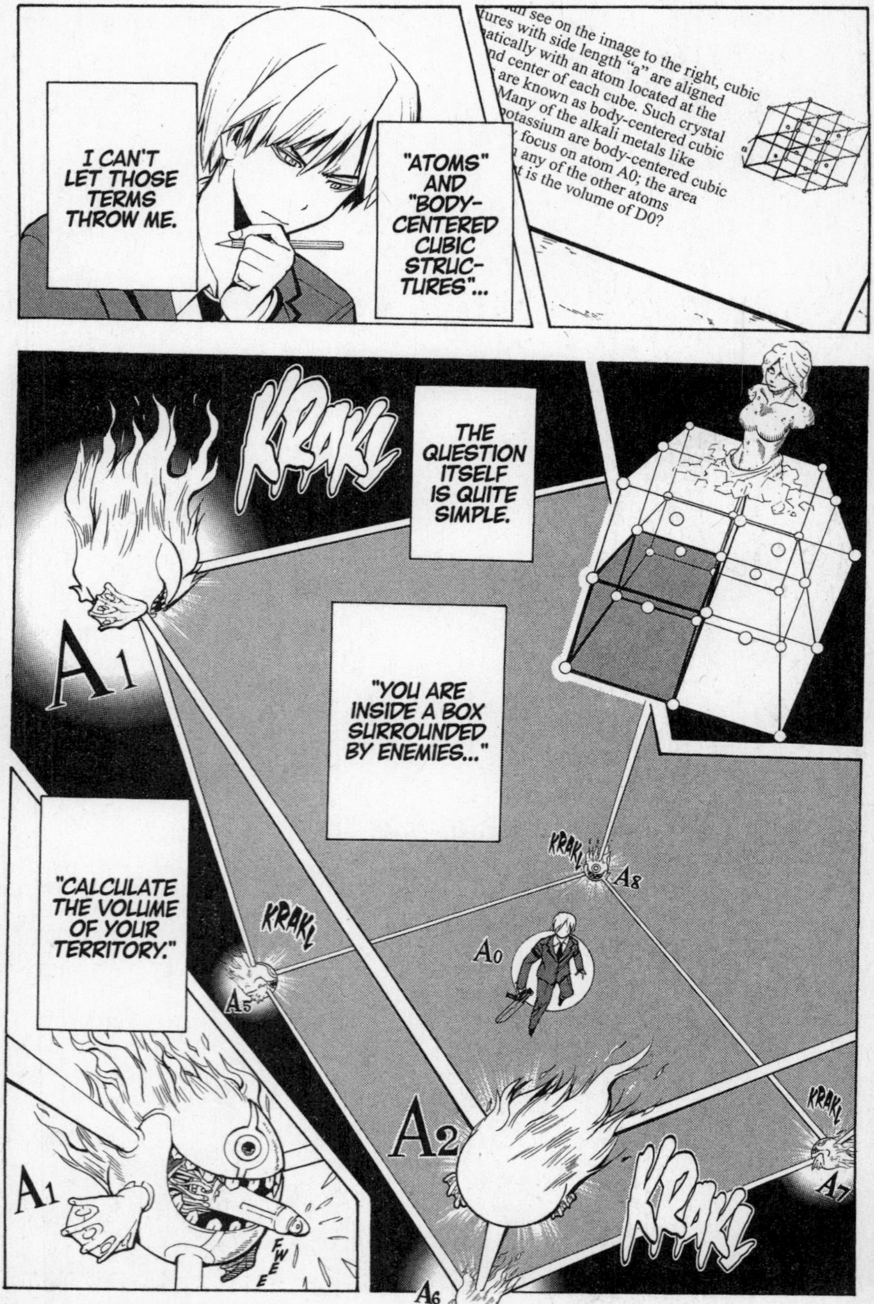

...u can see on the image to the right, cubic
...tures with side length "a" are aligned
...matically with an atom located at the
...nd center of each cube. Such crystal
... are known as body-centered cubic
Many of the alkali metals like
potassium are body-centered cubic
... focus on atom A0; the area
... any of the other atoms
...t is the volume of D0?
"ATOMS" AND "BODY-CENTERED CUBIC STRUCTURES"...
I CAN'T LET THOSE TERMS THROW ME.
THE QUESTION ITSELF IS QUITE SIMPLE.
KRAKL
A1
"YOU ARE INSIDE A BOX SURROUNDED BY ENEMIES..."
KRAKL
A8
A0
KRAKL
A5
"CALCULATE THE VOLUME OF YOUR TERRITORY."
KRAKL
A7
KRAKL
A2
A6
FWEE
A1

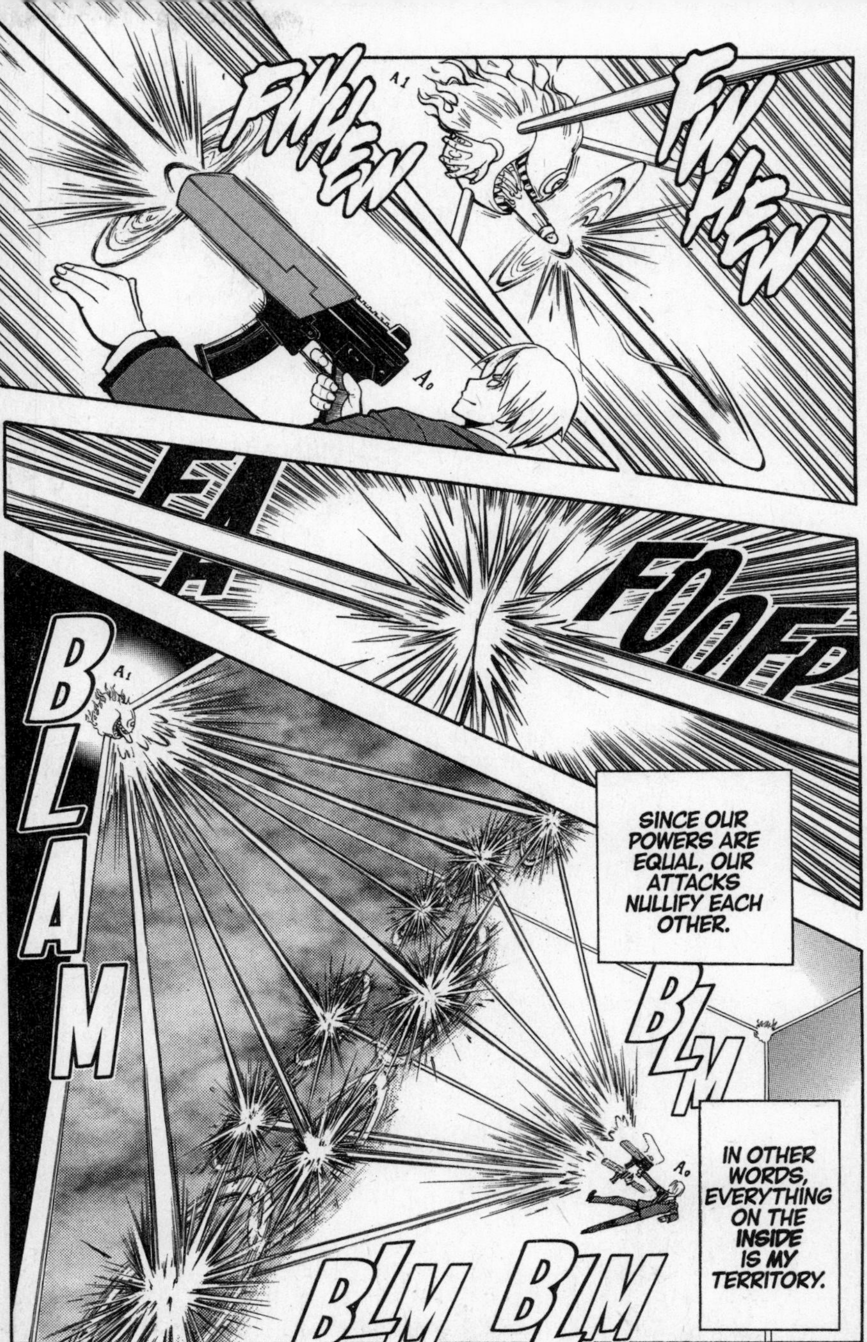
FWHEW
FWHEW
A1
A0
FOOFP
SINCE OUR POWERS ARE EQUAL, OUR ATTACKS NULLIFY EACH OTHER.
BLM
IN OTHER WORDS, EVERYTHING ON THE INSIDE IS MY TERRITORY.
A0
BLM BLM
BLAM
A1

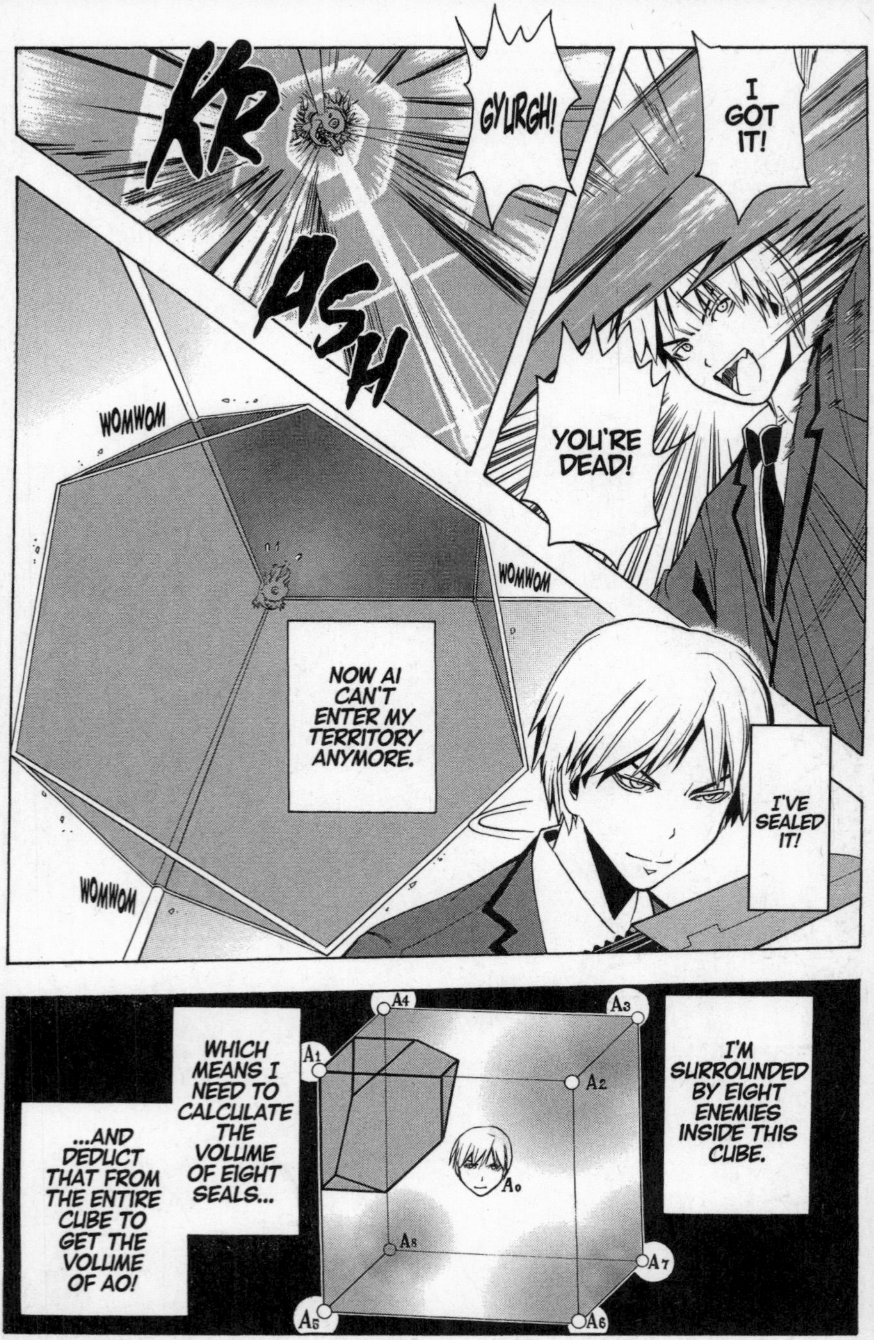
I GOT IT!
GYURGH!
KRASH
YOU'RE DEAD!
I'VE SEALED IT!
NOW AI CAN'T ENTER MY TERRITORY ANYMORE.
WOMWOM
WOMWOM
WOMWOM
I'M SURROUNDED BY EIGHT ENEMIES INSIDE THIS CUBE.
A4
A3
A1
A2
A0
A8
A7
A5
A6
WHICH MEANS I NEED TO CALCULATE THE VOLUME OF EIGHT SEALS...
...AND DEDUCT THAT FROM THE ENTIRE CUBE TO GET THE VOLUME OF AO!

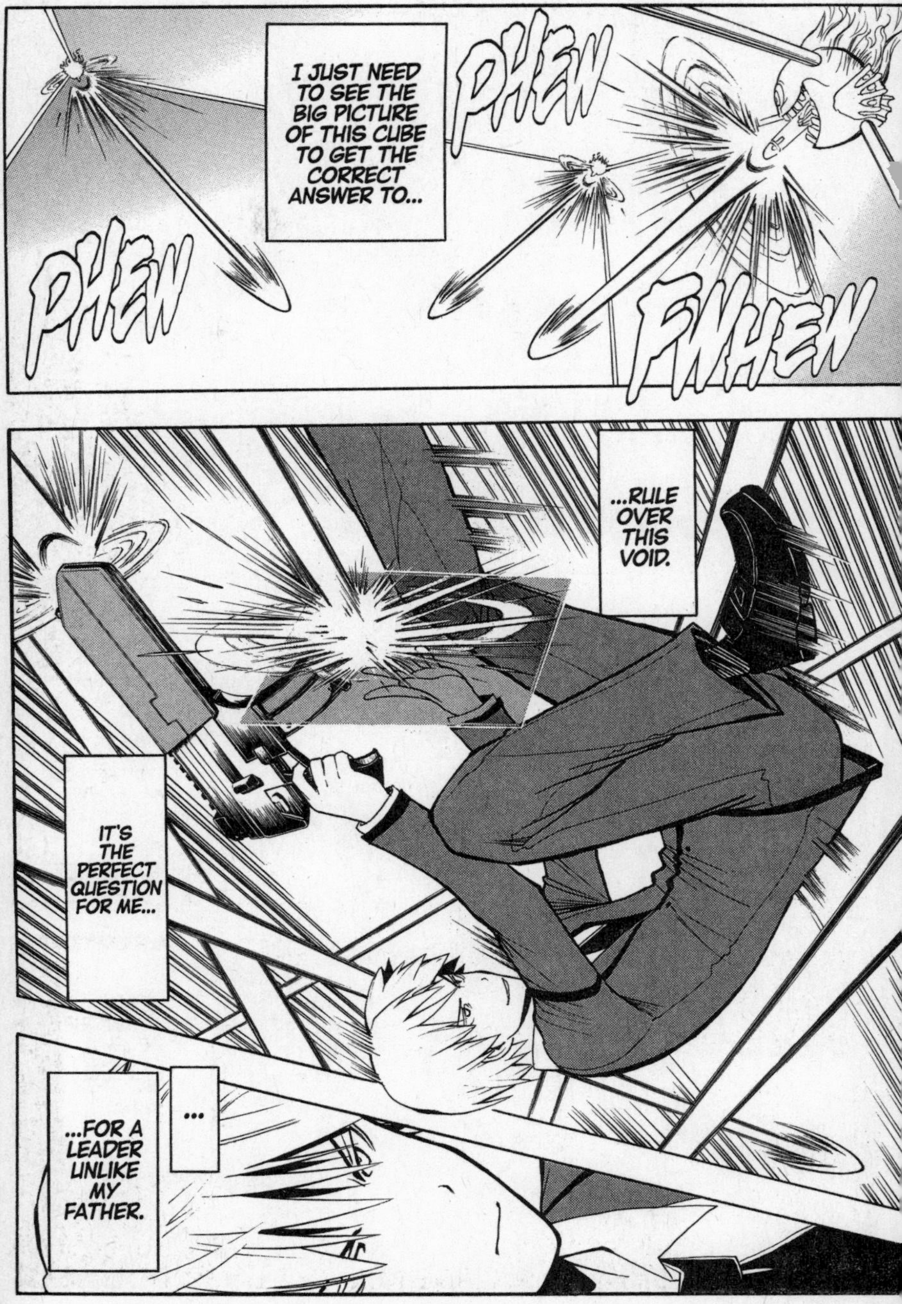
PHEW
I JUST NEED TO SEE THE BIG PICTURE OF THIS CUBE TO GET THE CORRECT ANSWER TO...
FWHEW
PHEW
...RULE OVER THIS VOID.
IT'S THE PERFECT QUESTION FOR ME...
...
...FOR A LEADER UNLIKE MY FATHER.

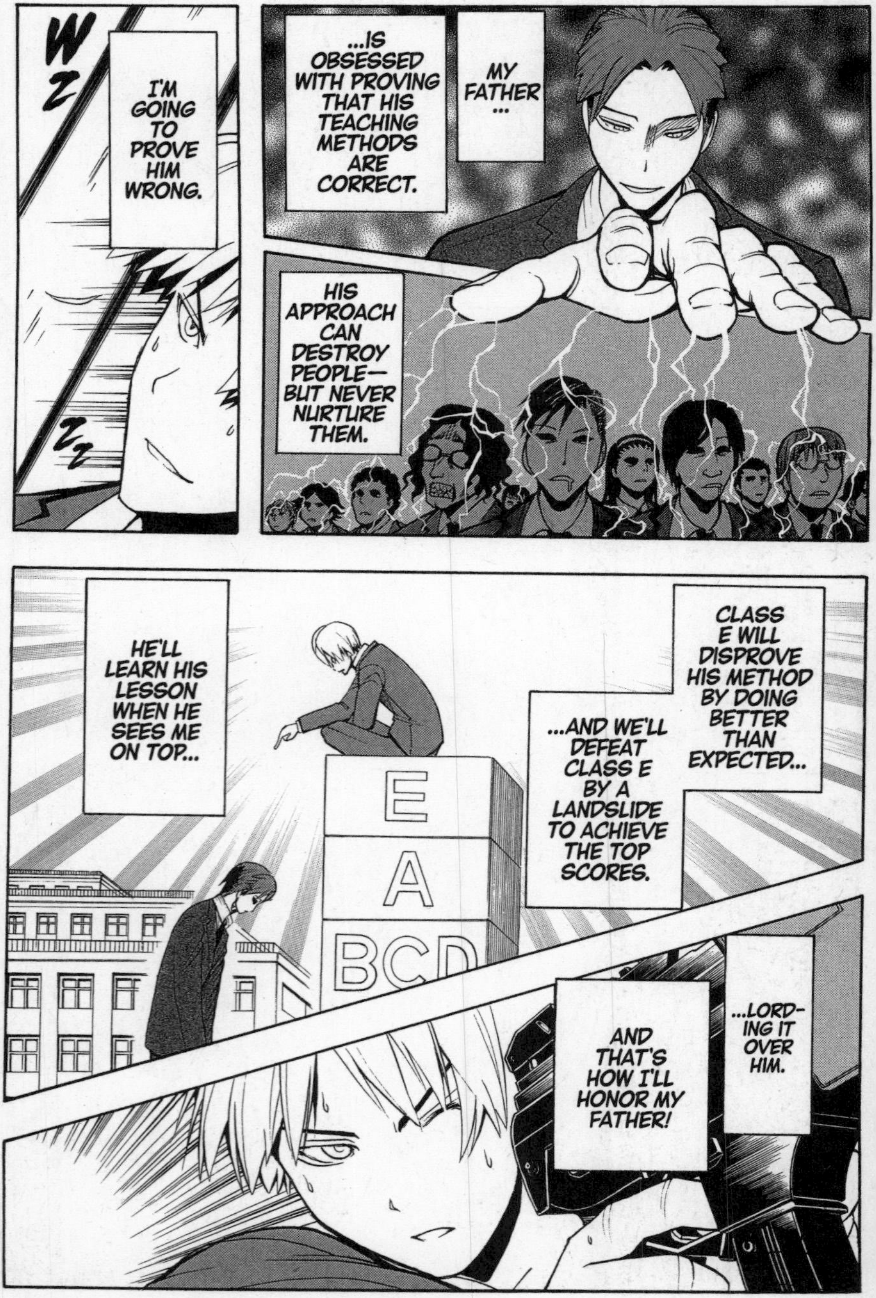
MY FATHER...
...IS OBSESSED WITH PROVING THAT HIS TEACHING METHODS ARE CORRECT.
HIS APPROACH CAN DESTROY PEOPLE—BUT NEVER NURTURE THEM.
I'M GOING TO PROVE HIM WRONG.
CLASS E WILL DISPROVE HIS METHOD BY DOING BETTER THAN EXPECTED...
...AND WE'LL DEFEAT CLASS E BY A LANDSLIDE TO ACHIEVE THE TOP SCORES.
HE'LL LEARN HIS LESSON WHEN HE SEES ME ON TOP...
E
A
BCD
...LORDING IT OVER HIM.
AND THAT'S HOW I'LL HONOR MY FATHER!

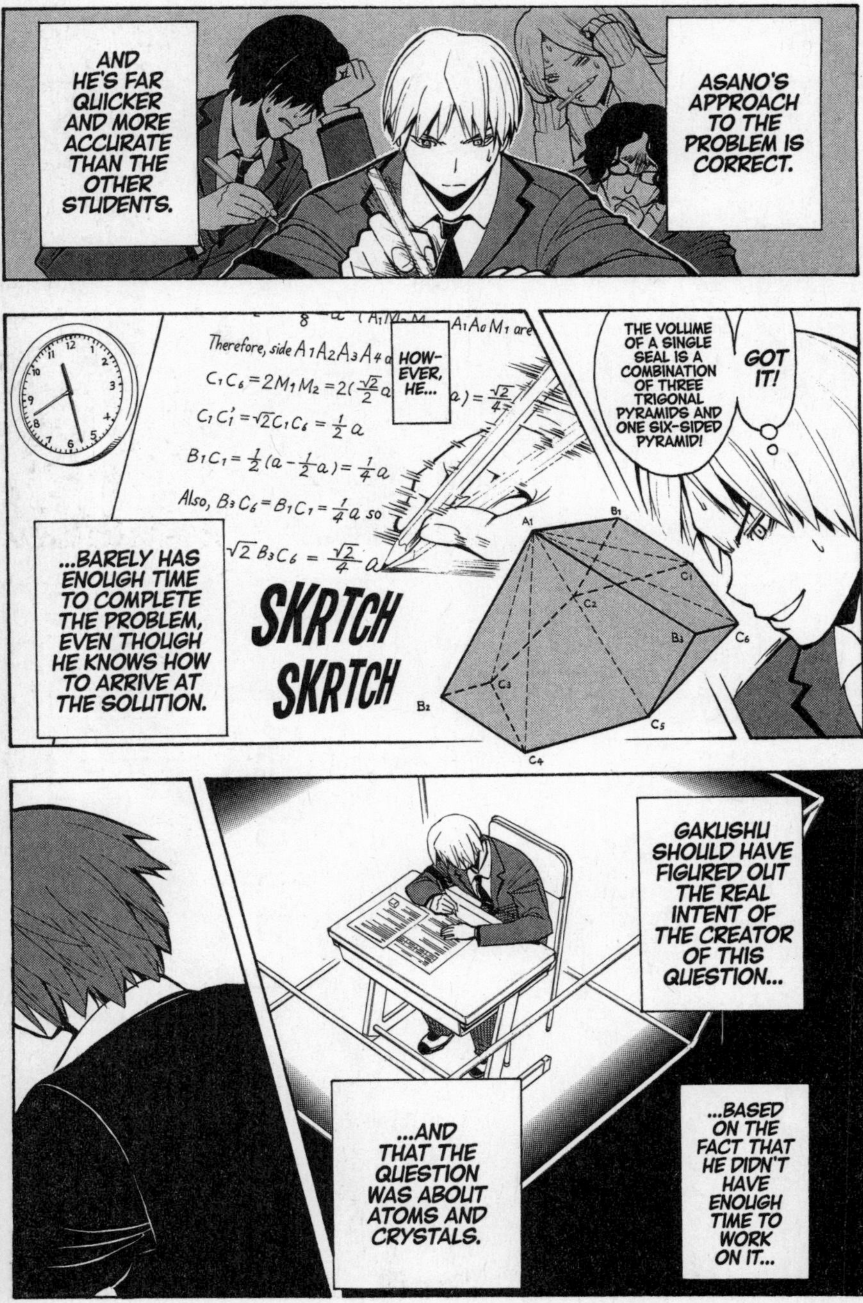
ASANO'S APPROACH TO THE PROBLEM IS CORRECT.
AND HE'S FAR QUICKER AND MORE ACCURATE THAN THE OTHER STUDENTS.
GOT IT!
THE VOLUME OF A SINGLE SEAL IS A COMBINATION OF THREE TRIGONAL PYRAMIDS AND ONE SIX-SIDED PYRAMID!
A1
B1
C1
C2
B3
C6
C3
B2
C5
C4
HOW-EVER, HE...
Therefore, side $A_1A_2A_3A_4$
$C_1C_6 = 2M_1M_2 = 2(\frac{\sqrt{2}}{2}$
$a) = \frac{\sqrt{2}}{4}$
$C_1C_1' = \sqrt{2}C_1C_6 = \frac{1}{2}a$
$B_1C_1 = \frac{1}{2}(a - \frac{1}{2}a) = \frac{1}{4}a$
Also, $B_3C_6 = B_1C_1 = \frac{1}{4}a$ so
$\sqrt{2}\,B_3C_6 = \frac{\sqrt{2}}{4}a$
...BARELY HAS ENOUGH TIME TO COMPLETE THE PROBLEM, EVEN THOUGH HE KNOWS HOW TO ARRIVE AT THE SOLUTION.
SKRTCH
SKRTCH
GAKUSHU SHOULD HAVE FIGURED OUT THE REAL INTENT OF THE CREATOR OF THIS QUESTION...
...BASED ON THE FACT THAT HE DIDN'T HAVE ENOUGH TIME TO WORK ON IT...
...AND THAT THE QUESTION WAS ABOUT ATOMS AND CRYSTALS.

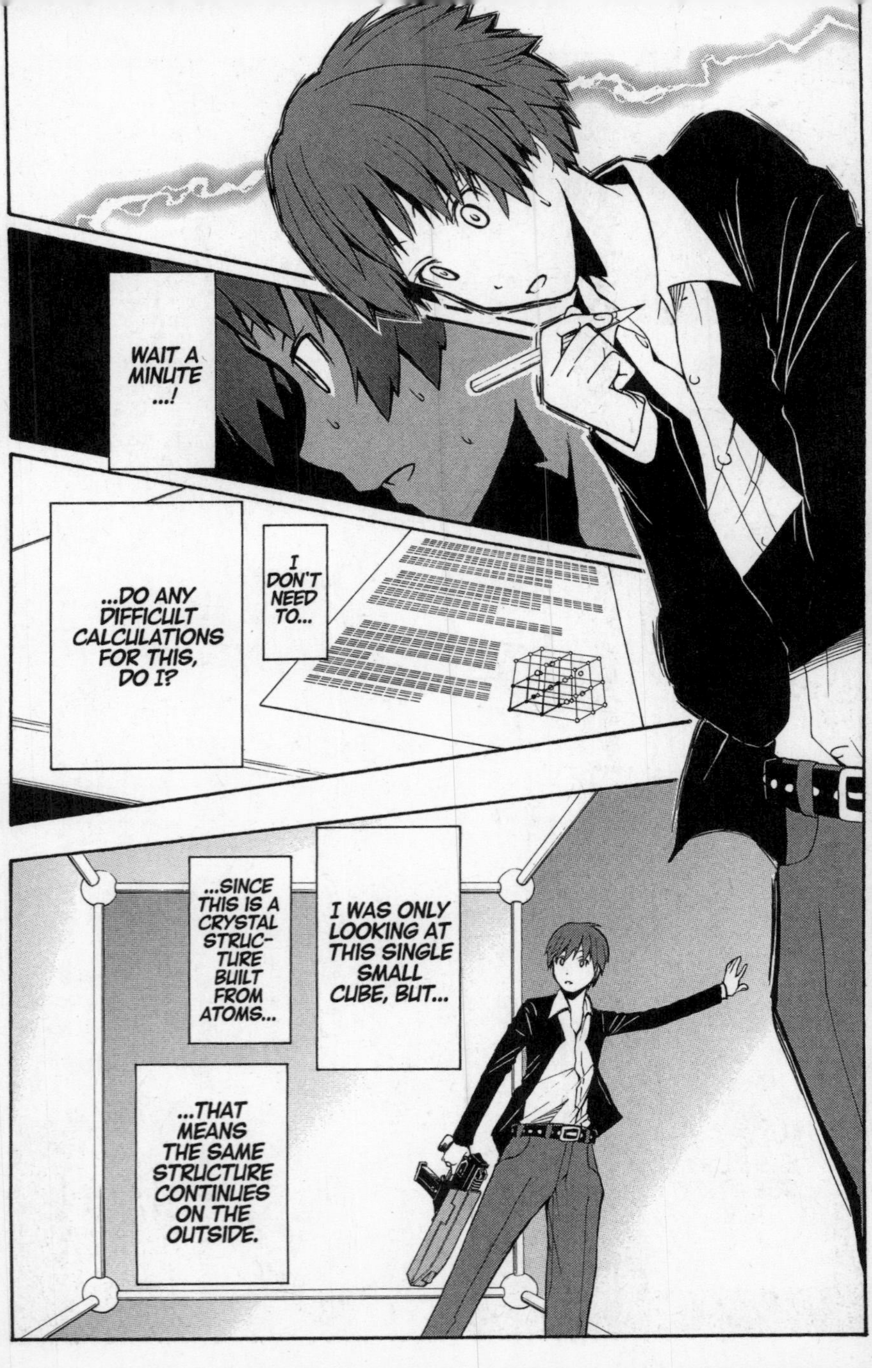
WAIT A MINUTE ...!
I DON'T NEED TO...
...DO ANY DIFFICULT CALCULATIONS FOR THIS, DO I?
I WAS ONLY LOOKING AT THIS SINGLE SMALL CUBE, BUT...
...SINCE THIS IS A CRYSTAL STRUC-TURE BUILT FROM ATOMS...
...THAT MEANS THE SAME STRUCTURE CONTINUES ON THE OUTSIDE.

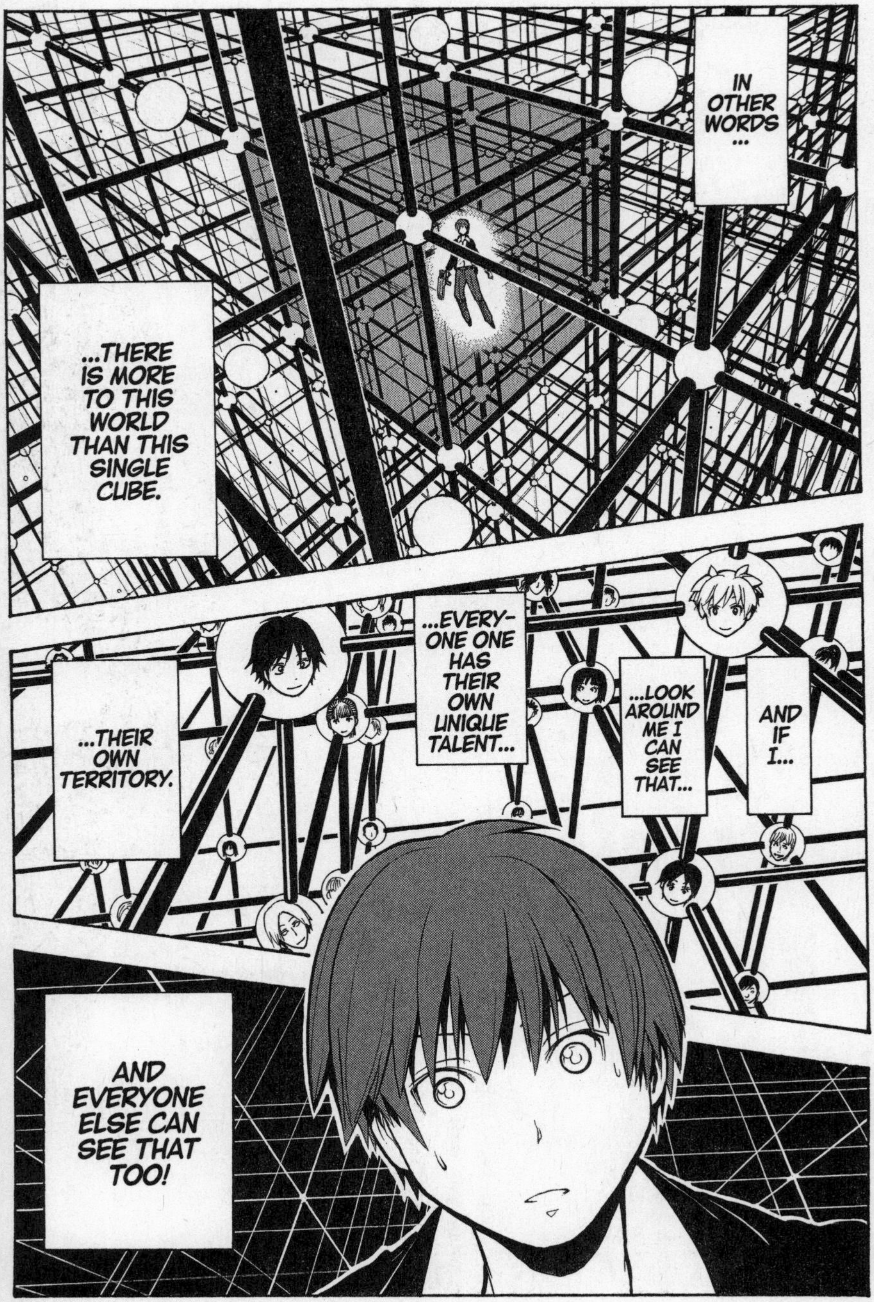
IN OTHER WORDS...
...THERE IS MORE TO THIS WORLD THAN THIS SINGLE CUBE.
AND IF I...
...LOOK AROUND ME I CAN SEE THAT...
...EVERY-ONE ONE HAS THEIR OWN UNIQUE TALENT...
...THEIR OWN TERRITORY.
AND EVERYONE ELSE CAN SEE THAT TOO!

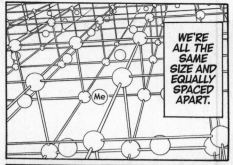

WHAT I WAS LOOKING AT FROM INSIDE THIS BOX...
...WAS JUST FRAGMENTS OF THE OTHERS.
WE'RE ALL THE SAME SIZE AND EQUALLY SPACED APART.
Me
SO IF I CUT OUT A SINGLE BOX...
...I'LL GET SOMETHING LIKE THIS.
Me
ONE EIGHTH.
THESE FRAGMENTS ARE ONE EIGHTH OF THE PEOPLE AROUND ME.
SO INSIDE THE BOX IS ME...
Me
1
...AND EIGHT ONE-EIGHTHS OF THE PEOPLE AROUND ME.
1/8 ×8
1:1
THAT MEANS THAT INSIDE THIS CUBE...
...THE RATIO...
...BETWEEN ME AND THE OTHER EIGHT PEOPLE...
...WILL ALWAYS BE ONE TO ONE!

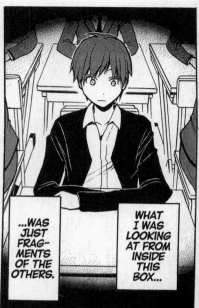

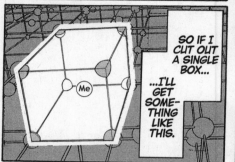

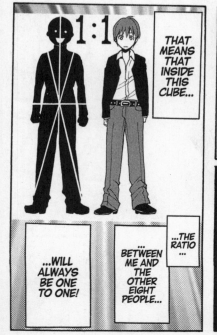

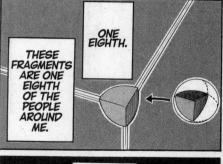

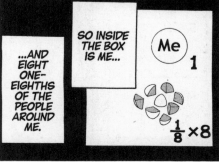

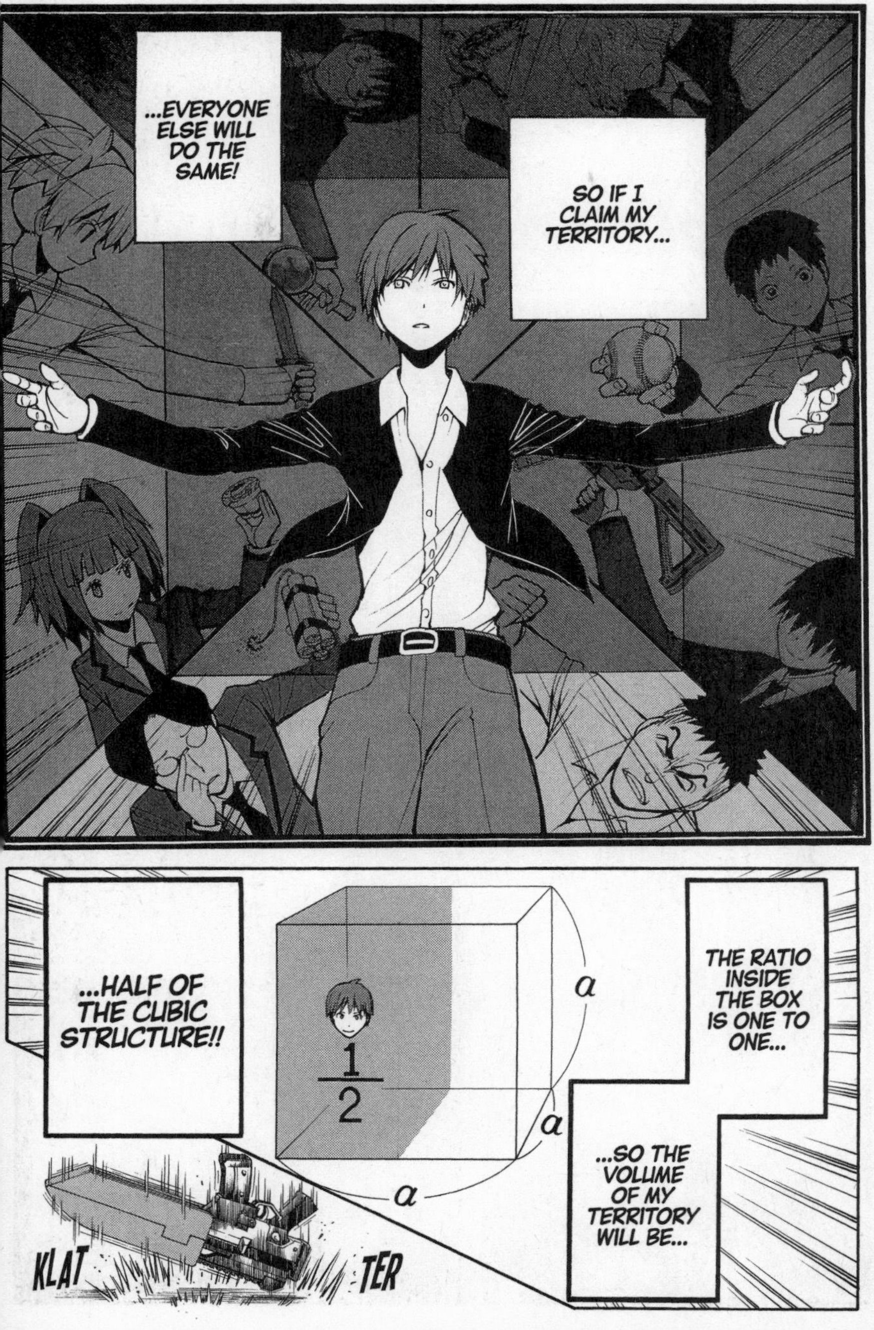
SO IF I CLAIM MY TERRITORY...
...EVERYONE ELSE WILL DO THE SAME!
THE RATIO INSIDE THE BOX IS ONE TO ONE...
...SO THE VOLUME OF MY TERRITORY WILL BE...
...HALF OF THE CUBIC STRUCTURE!!
a
a
a
1/2
KLAT
TER

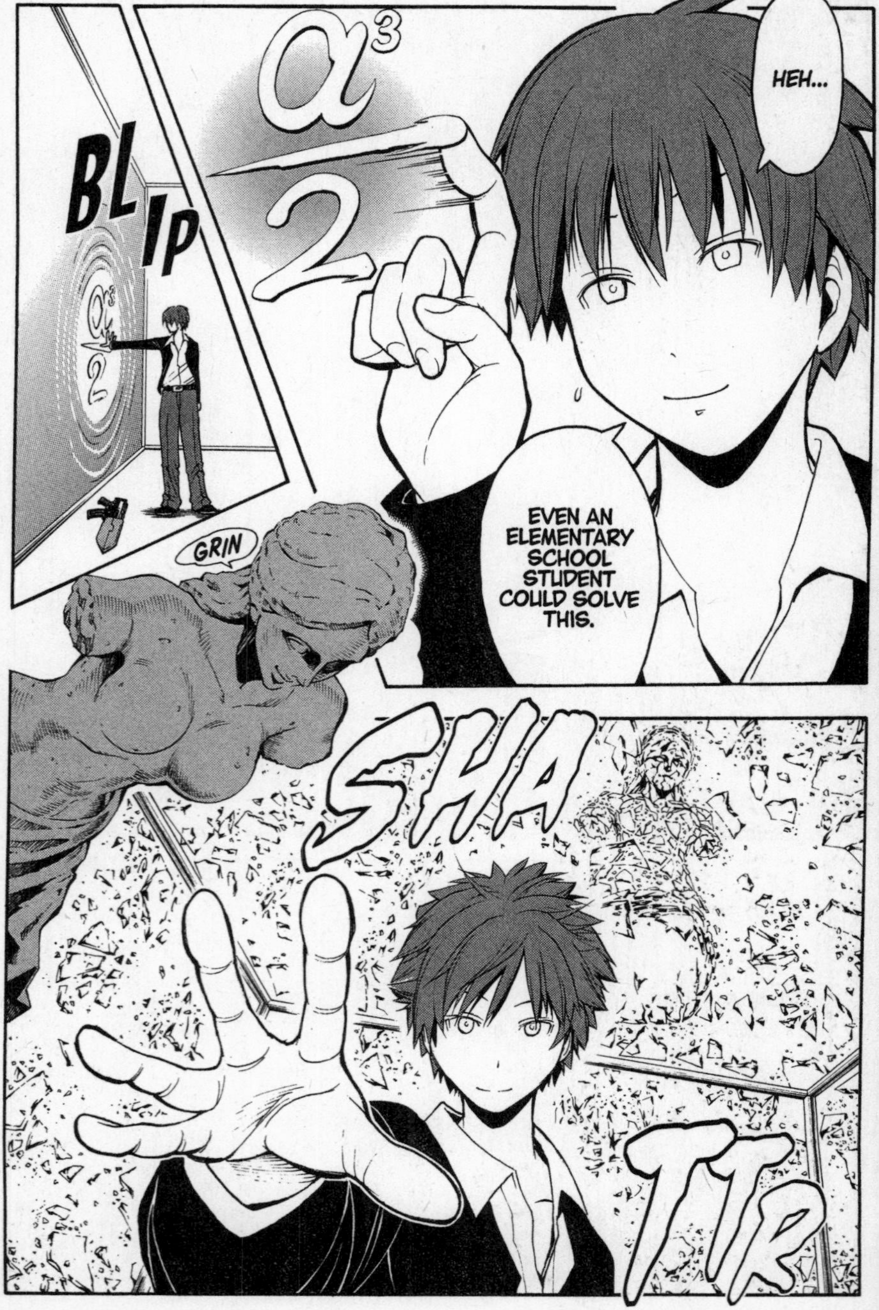
HEH...
EVEN AN ELEMENTARY SCHOOL STUDENT COULD SOLVE THIS.
BLIP
GRIN
SHA
TTR

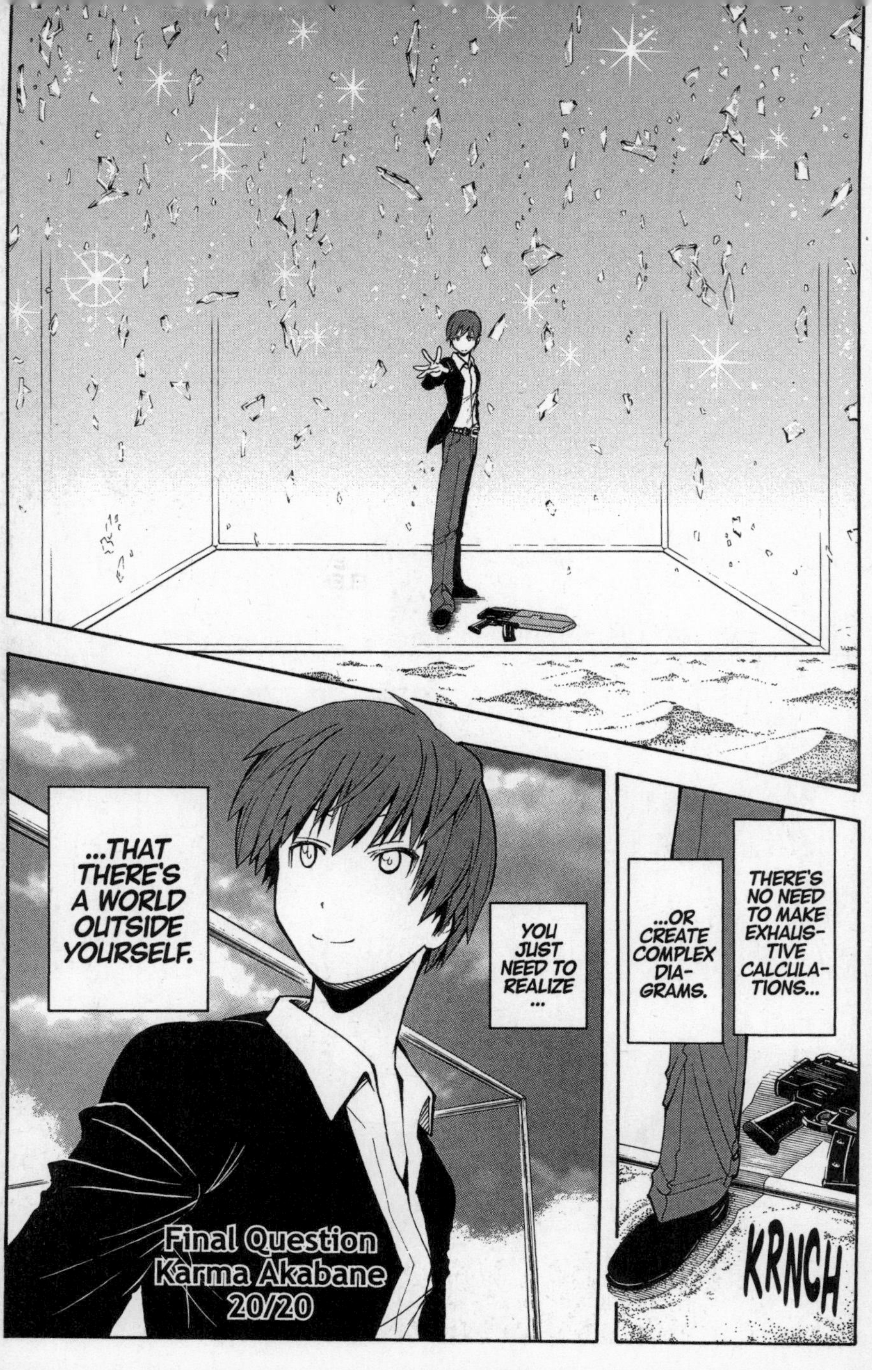
THERE'S NO NEED TO MAKE EXHAUSTIVE CALCULATIONS...
...OR CREATE COMPLEX DIAGRAMS.
KRNCH
YOU JUST NEED TO REALIZE...
...THAT THERE'S A WORLD OUTSIDE YOURSELF.
Final Question
Karma Akabane
20/20

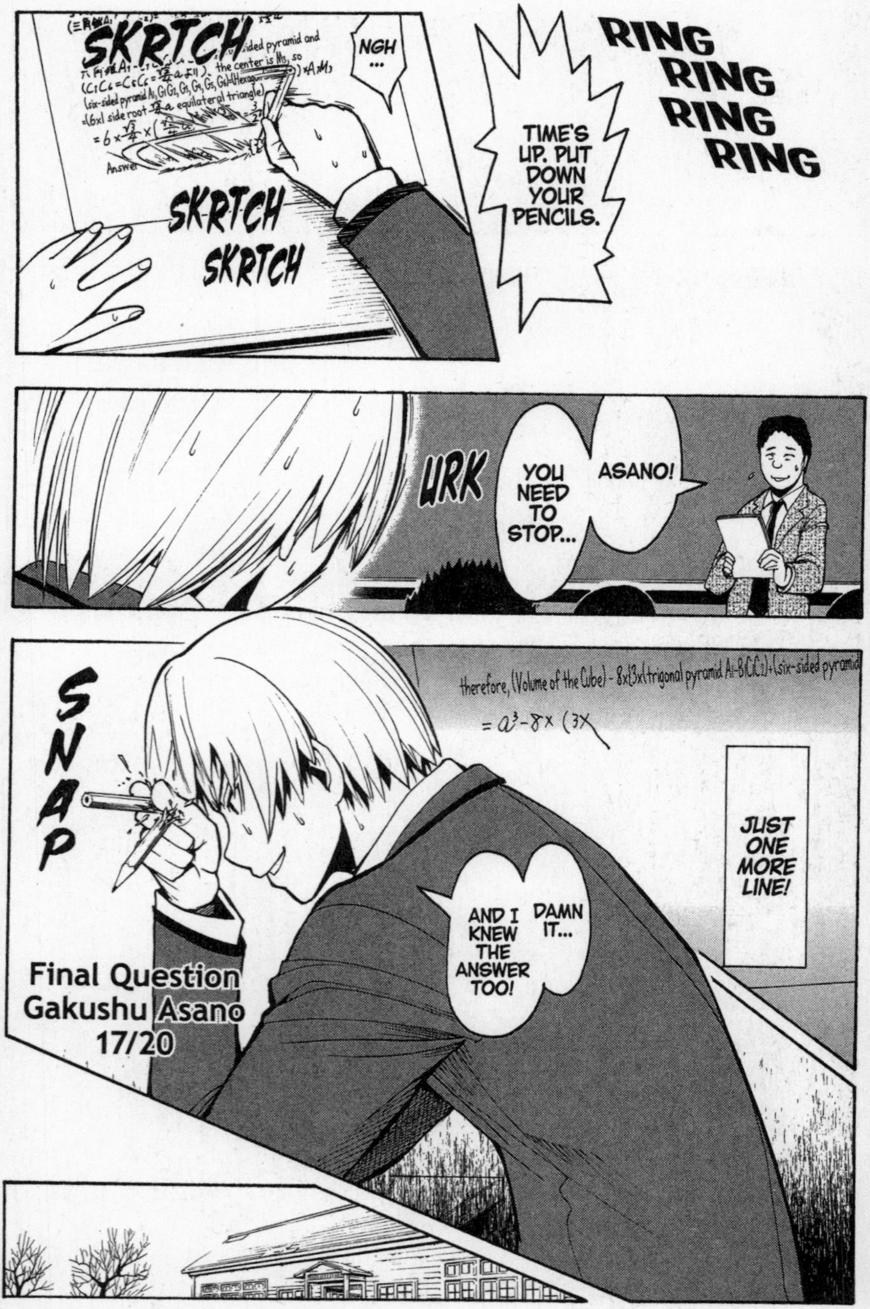

RING RING RING RING
TIME'S UP. PUT DOWN YOUR PENCILS.
NGH...
SKRTCH
SKRTCH SKRTCH
ASANO!
YOU NEED TO STOP...
URK
therefore, (Volume of the Cube) - 8x(3x(trigonal pyramid A1-B(C1C2)+(six-sided pyramid
JUST ONE MORE LINE!
DAMN IT...
AND I KNEW THE ANSWER TOO!
SNAP
Final Question
Gakushu Asano
17/20

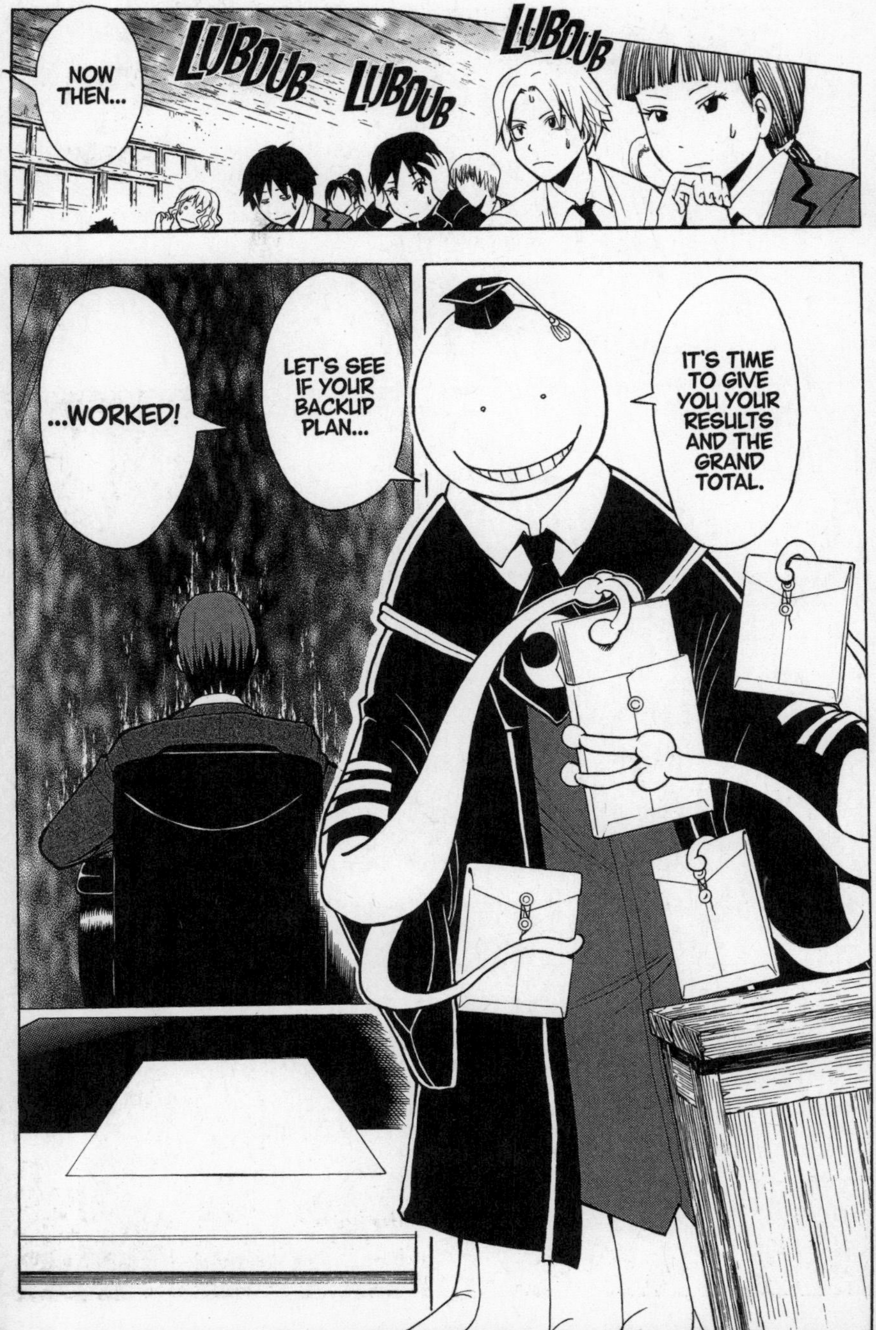
LUBDUB
LUBDUB
LUBDUB
NOW THEN...
IT'S TIME TO GIVE YOU YOUR RESULTS AND THE GRAND TOTAL.
LET'S SEE IF YOUR BACKUP PLAN...
...WORKED!

E-4 HINATA OKANO

- 😊 BIRTHDAY: APRIL 2
- 😊 HEIGHT: 5' 00"
- 😊 WEIGHT: 93 LBS.
- 😊 FAVORITE SUBJECT: PHYSICAL EDUCATION
- 😊 LEAST FAVORITE SUBJECT: ENGLISH
- 😊 HOBBY/SKILLS: CLEARING KARASUMA'S OBSTACLE COURSE
- 😊 FUTURE GOAL: PROFESSIONAL GYMNAST
- 😊 PERSONALITY: LAID-BACK
- 😊 WHEN SHE FOLDS A PAPER CRANE...
  ...THE HEAD AND TAIL ALWAYS END UP TOUCHING.

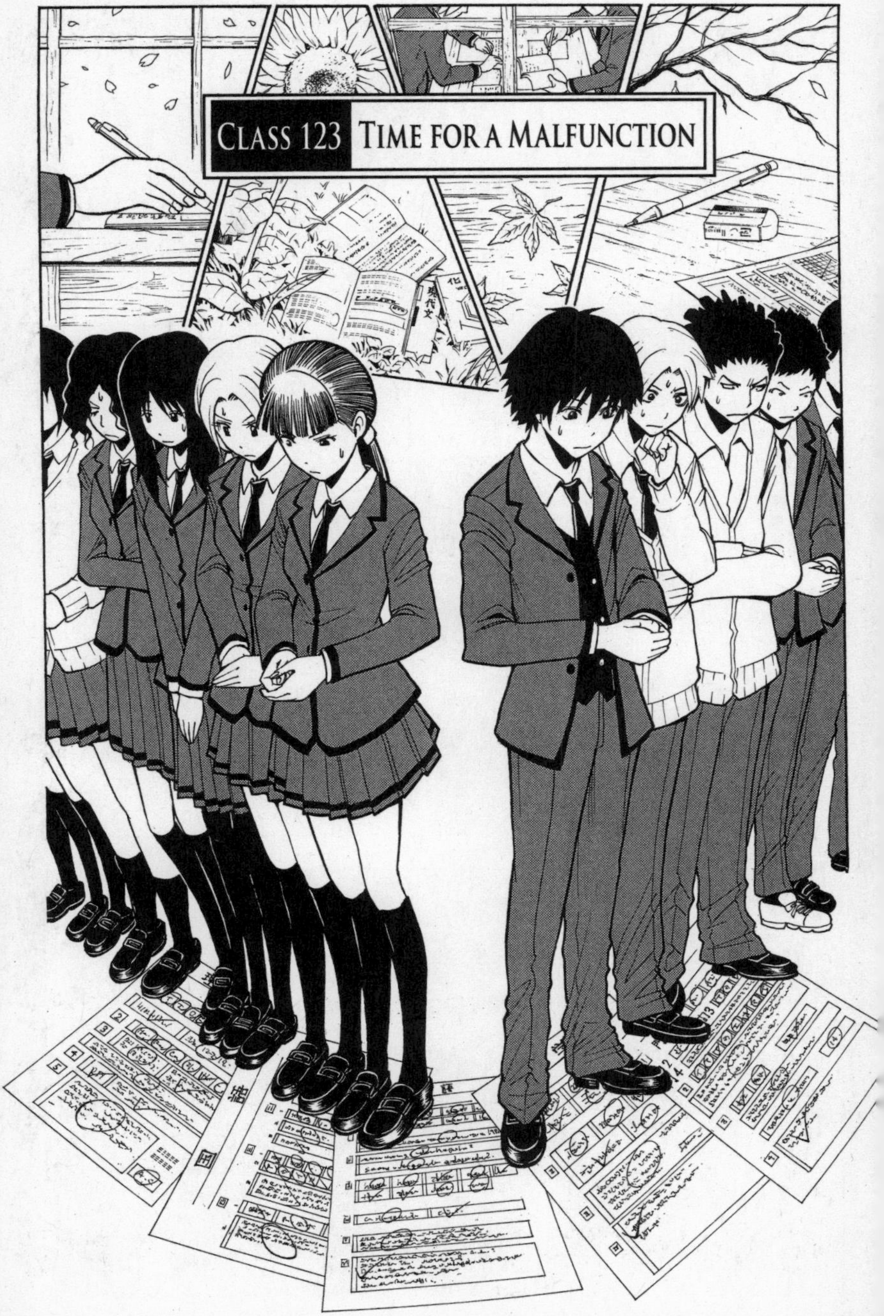
Class 123 Time for a Malfunction

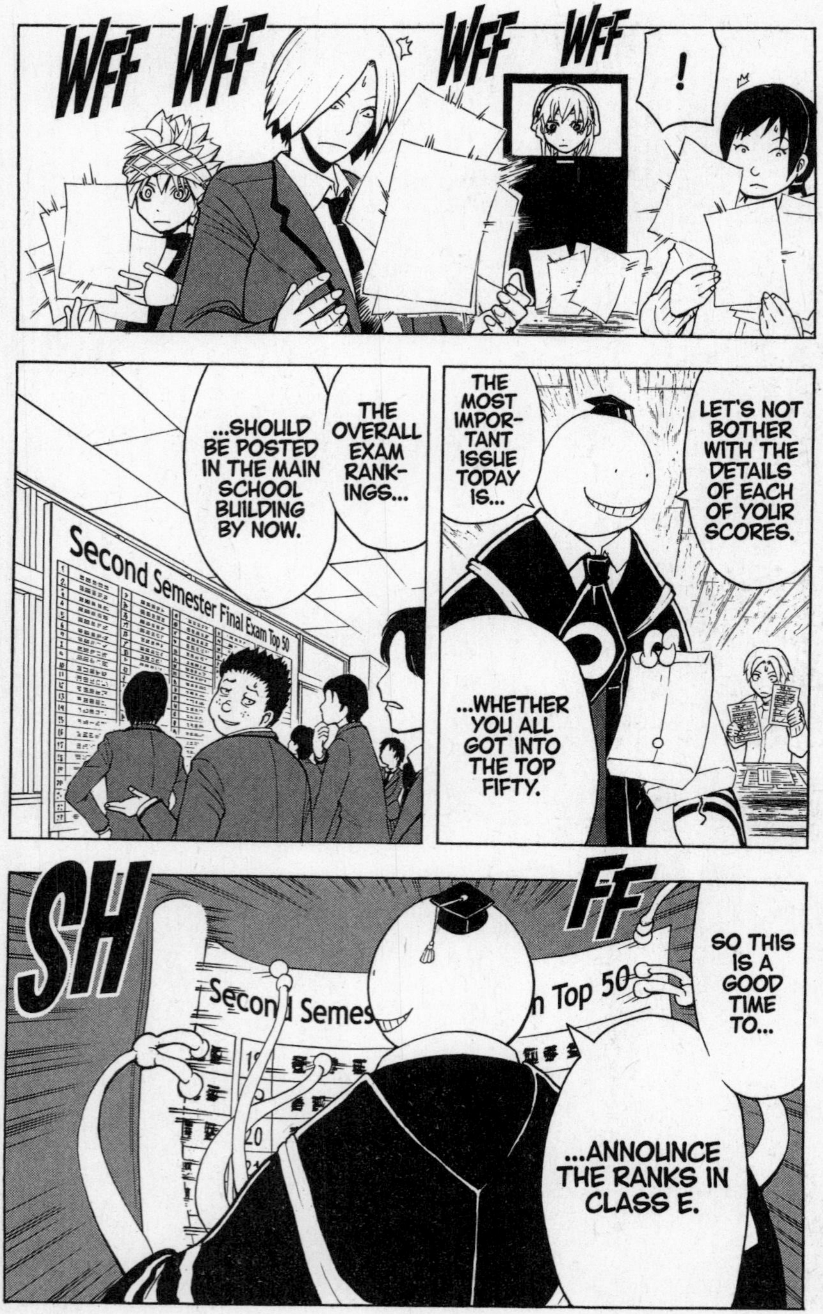
WFF WFF
!
WFF WFF
LET'S NOT BOTHER WITH THE DETAILS OF EACH OF YOUR SCORES.
THE MOST IMPORTANT ISSUE TODAY IS...
...WHETHER YOU ALL GOT INTO THE TOP FIFTY.
THE OVERALL EXAM RANKINGS...
...SHOULD BE POSTED IN THE MAIN SCHOOL BUILDING BY NOW.
Second Semester Final Exam Top 50
SH
FF
SO THIS IS A GOOD TIME TO...
...ANNOUNCE THE RANKS IN CLASS E.

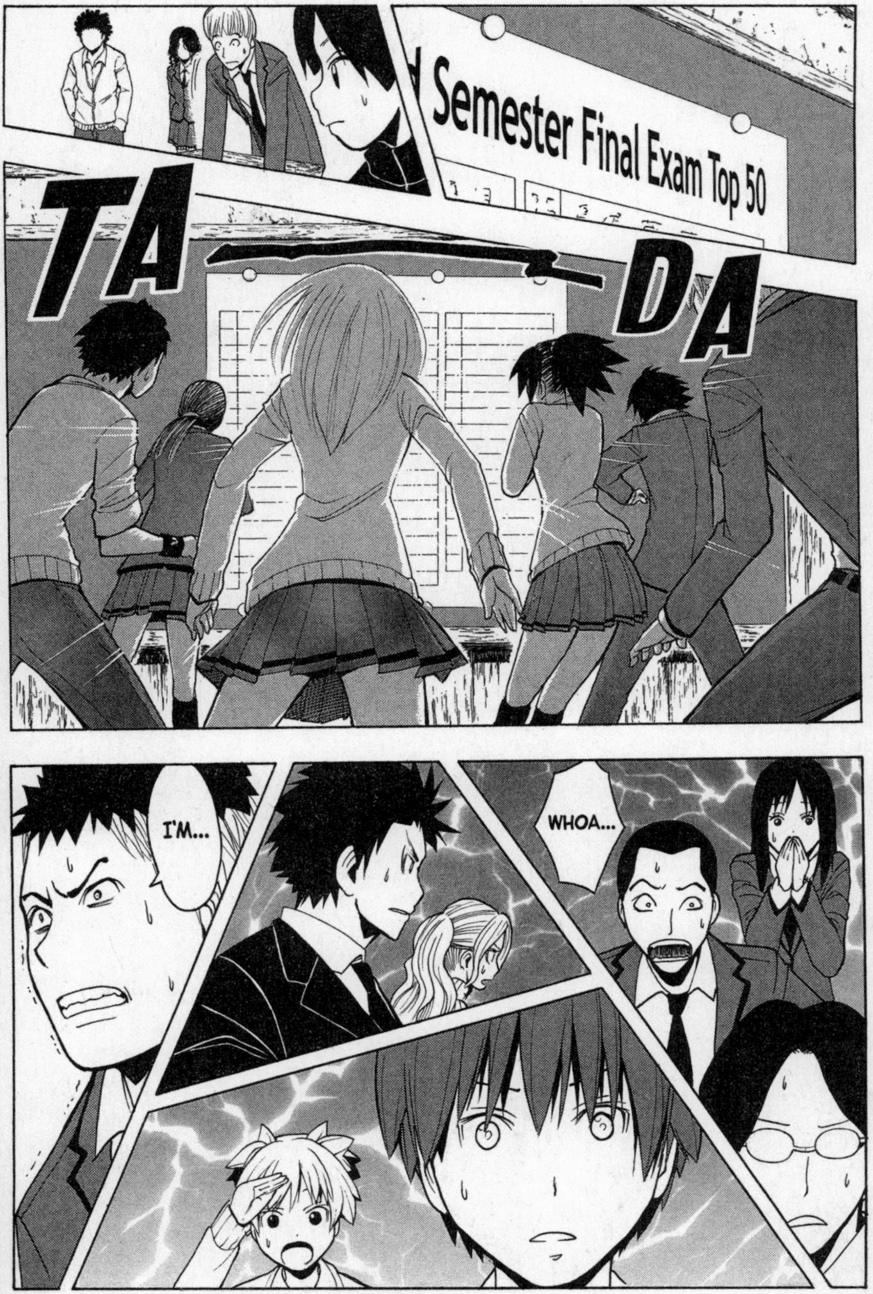

Semester Final Exam Top 50
TA
DA
WHOA...
I'M...

Second Semester Final Exam Top 50

Rank	Name	Score
1	Karma Akabane	500
2	Gakushu Asano	497
3	Rio Nakamura	461
4	Yuma Isogai	457
5	Kotaro Takebayashi	447
6	Meg Kataoka	443
7	Yukiko Kanzaki	437
8	Ren Sakakibara	435
9	Ryunosuke Chiba	429
10	Sumire Hara	426
11	Natsuhiko Koyama	421
12	Teppei Araki	418
13	Rinka Hayami	410
14	Nagisa Shiota	402
15	Tomoya Seo	401
16	Koki Mimura	392
7	Yuzuki Fuwa	389
18	Kirara Hazama	381
19	Iori Mori	379
20	Manami Okuda	377
21	Taiga Okajima	377
22	Kisho Yano	363
23	Julia Nagasawa	360
24	Kaede Kayano	356
25	Takemaru Mizuno	355
26	Takuya Muramatsu	350
27	Himeki Ito	348
28	Hakuyu Fuji	345
29	Seijiro Toda	344
30	Ji Ritsu	342
30	Keima Tamamushi	342
32	Toka Yada	340
33	Itona Horibe	339
34	Satsuki Yamaga	337
35	Eisai Tori	336
36	Gyosei Okamoto	335
37	Tomohito Sugino	333
38	Hinano Kurahashi	331
39	Taisei Yoshida	327
40	Hinata Okano	324
41	Issei Oyamada	323
41	Hiroto Maehara	323
43	Masayoshi Kimura	321
44	Kosuke Uchida	320
44	Sosuke Sugaya	320
46	Ryoma Terasaka	317
47	Mika Morikawa	308
48	Sekai Tanaka	302
49	Kazutaka Shindo	299
50	Sho Hashizume	295

WHICH MEANS...

BUT HE'S RANKED IN 46TH PLACE...

TERASAKA GETS THE LOWEST GRADES IN OUR CLASS, RIGHT...?

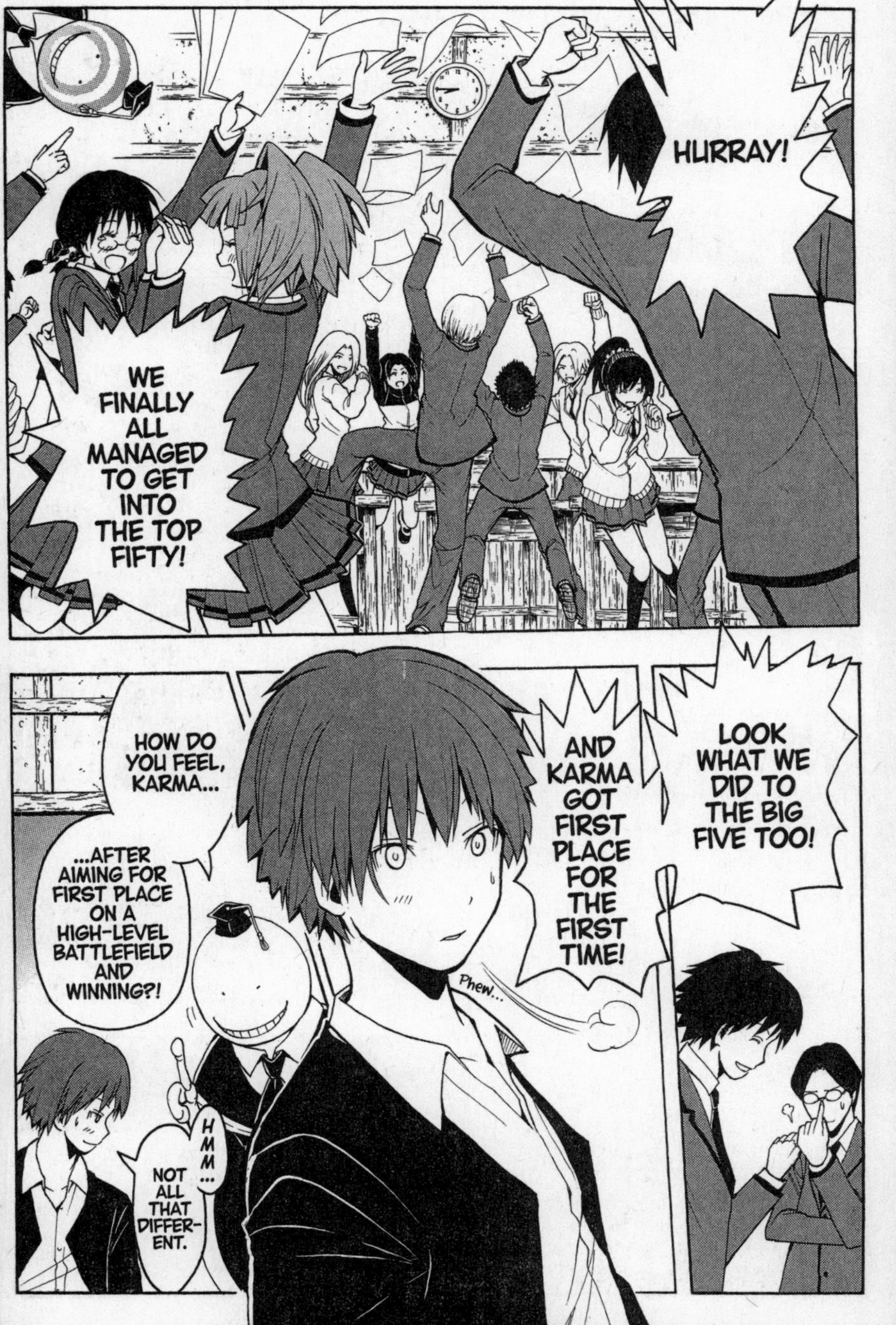
HURRAY!
WE FINALLY ALL MANAGED TO GET INTO THE TOP FIFTY!
LOOK WHAT WE DID TO THE BIG FIVE TOO!
AND KARMA GOT FIRST PLACE FOR THE FIRST TIME!
HOW DO YOU FEEL, KARMA...
...AFTER AIMING FOR FIRST PLACE ON A HIGH-LEVEL BATTLEFIELD AND WINNING?!
Phew...
HMM...
NOT ALL THAT DIFFER-ENT.

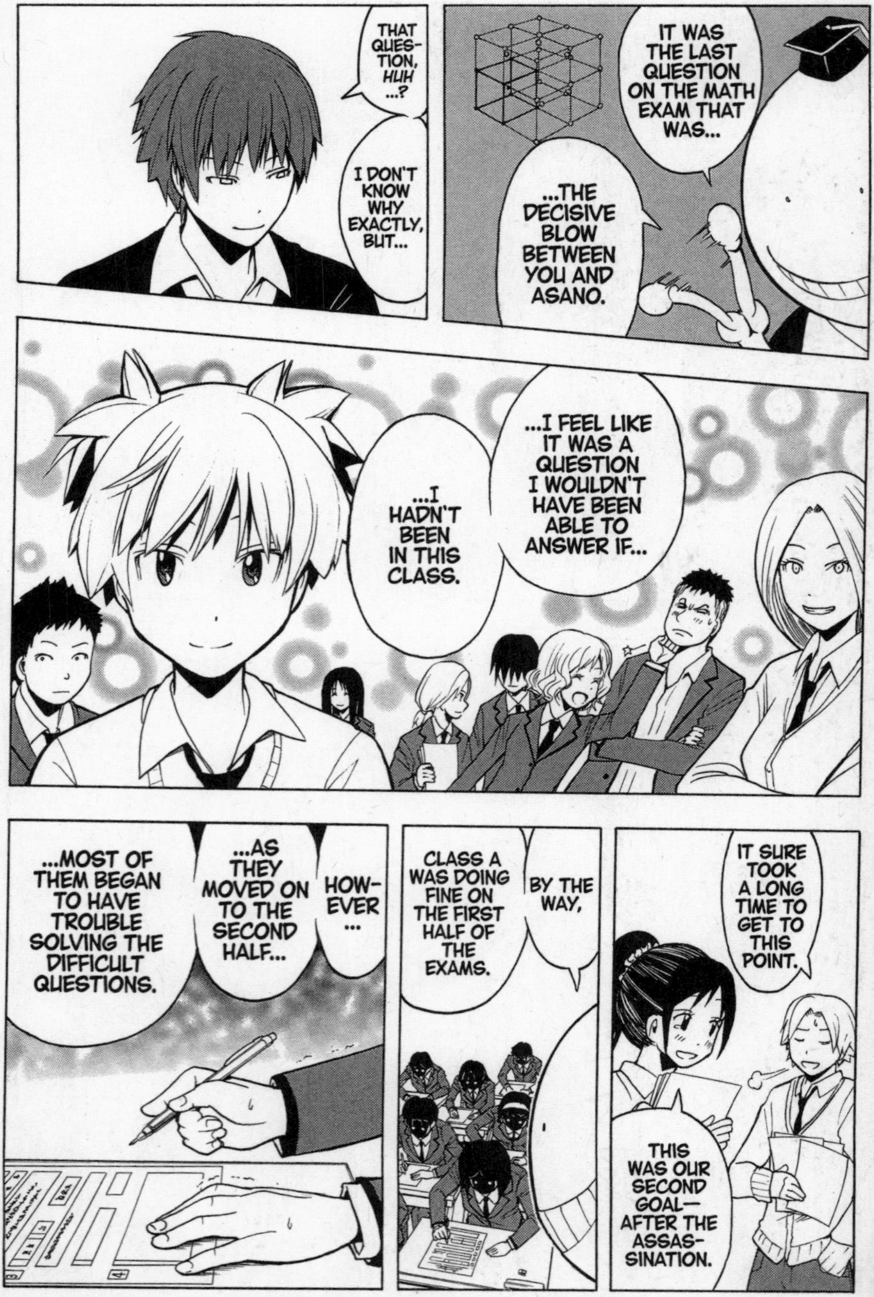
IT WAS THE LAST QUESTION ON THE MATH EXAM THAT WAS...
...THE DECISIVE BLOW BETWEEN YOU AND ASANO.
THAT QUESTION, HUH ...?
I DON'T KNOW WHY EXACTLY, BUT...
...I FEEL LIKE IT WAS A QUESTION I WOULDN'T HAVE BEEN ABLE TO ANSWER IF...
...I HADN'T BEEN IN THIS CLASS.
IT SURE TOOK A LONG TIME TO GET TO THIS POINT.
THIS WAS OUR SECOND GOAL—AFTER THE ASSASSINATION.
BY THE WAY,
CLASS A WAS DOING FINE ON THE FIRST HALF OF THE EXAMS.
HOWEVER...
...AS THEY MOVED ON TO THE SECOND HALF...
...MOST OF THEM BEGAN TO HAVE TROUBLE SOLVING THE DIFFICULT QUESTIONS.

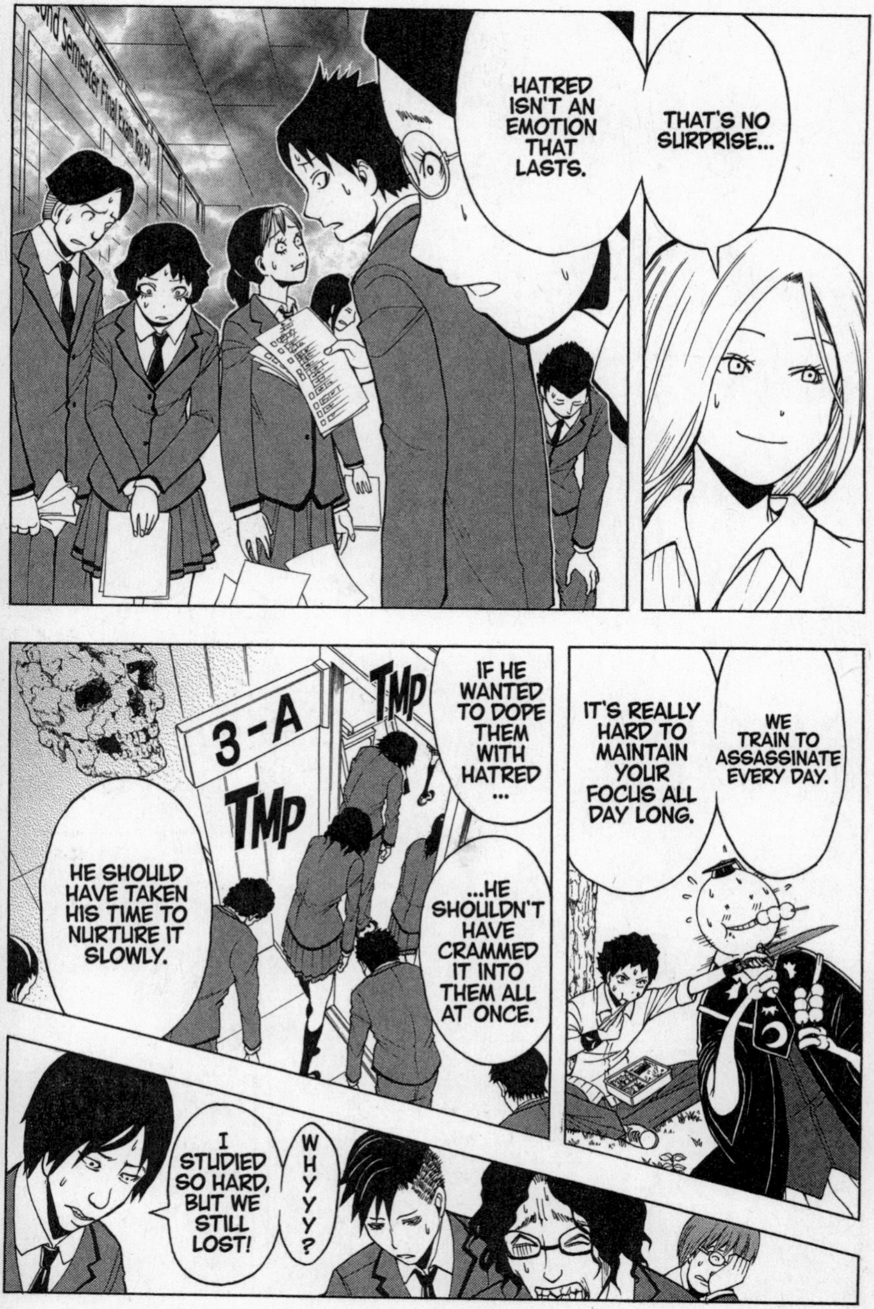
Semester Final Exam Top 50
THAT'S NO SURPRISE...
HATRED ISN'T AN EMOTION THAT LASTS.
WE TRAIN TO ASSASSINATE EVERY DAY.
IT'S REALLY HARD TO MAINTAIN YOUR FOCUS ALL DAY LONG.
3-A
TMP
TMP
IF HE WANTED TO DOPE THEM WITH HATRED ...
...HE SHOULDN'T HAVE CRAMMED IT INTO THEM ALL AT ONCE.
HE SHOULD HAVE TAKEN HIS TIME TO NURTURE IT SLOWLY.
WHYYY?
I STUDIED SO HARD, BUT WE STILL LOST!

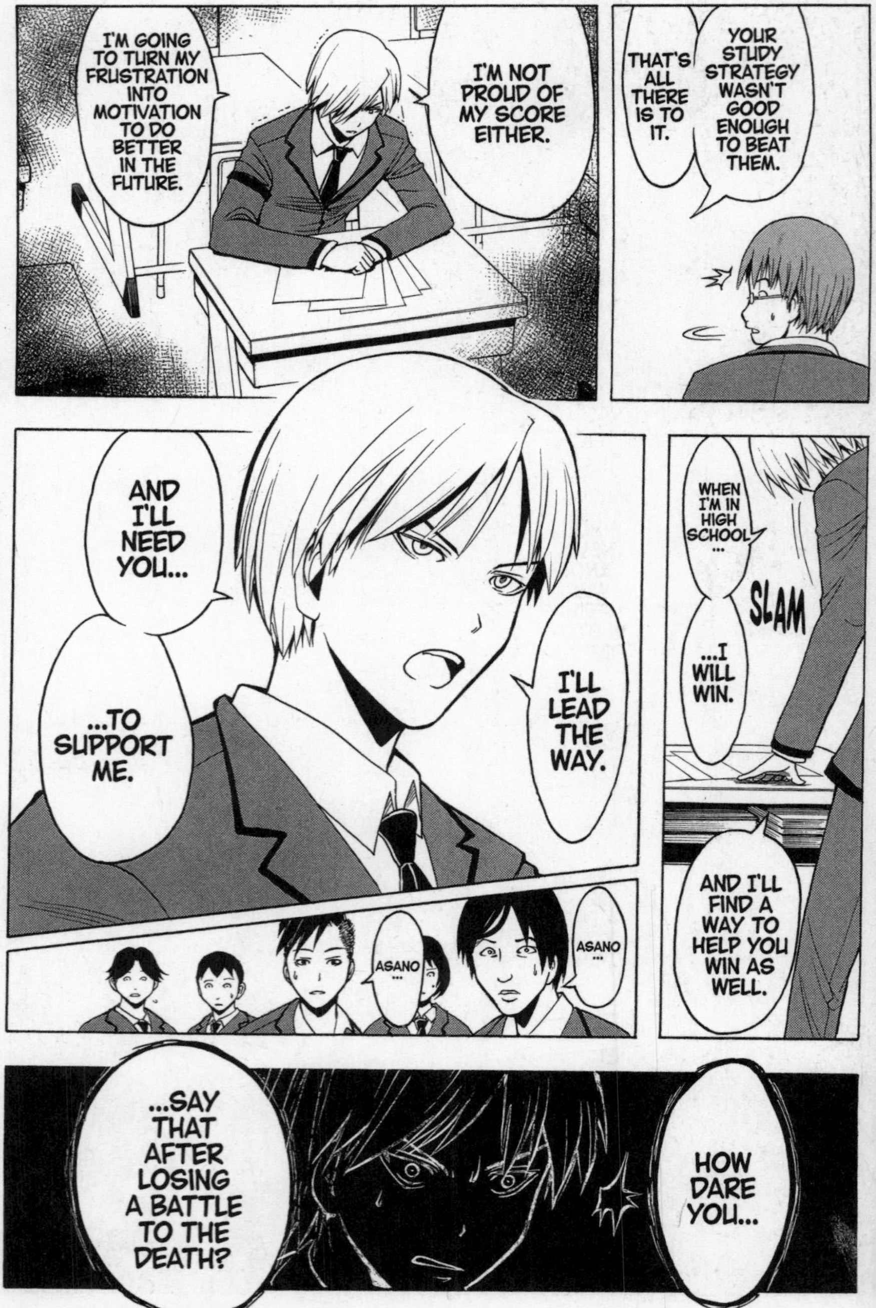
YOUR STUDY STRATEGY WASN'T GOOD ENOUGH TO BEAT THEM.
THAT'S ALL THERE IS TO IT.
I'M NOT PROUD OF MY SCORE EITHER.
I'M GOING TO TURN MY FRUSTRATION INTO MOTIVATION TO DO BETTER IN THE FUTURE.
WHEN I'M IN HIGH SCHOOL...
SLAM
...I WILL WIN.
AND I'LL FIND A WAY TO HELP YOU WIN AS WELL.
I'LL LEAD THE WAY.
AND I'LL NEED YOU...
...TO SUPPORT ME.
ASANO...
ASANO...
HOW DARE YOU...
...SAY THAT AFTER LOSING A BATTLE TO THE DEATH?

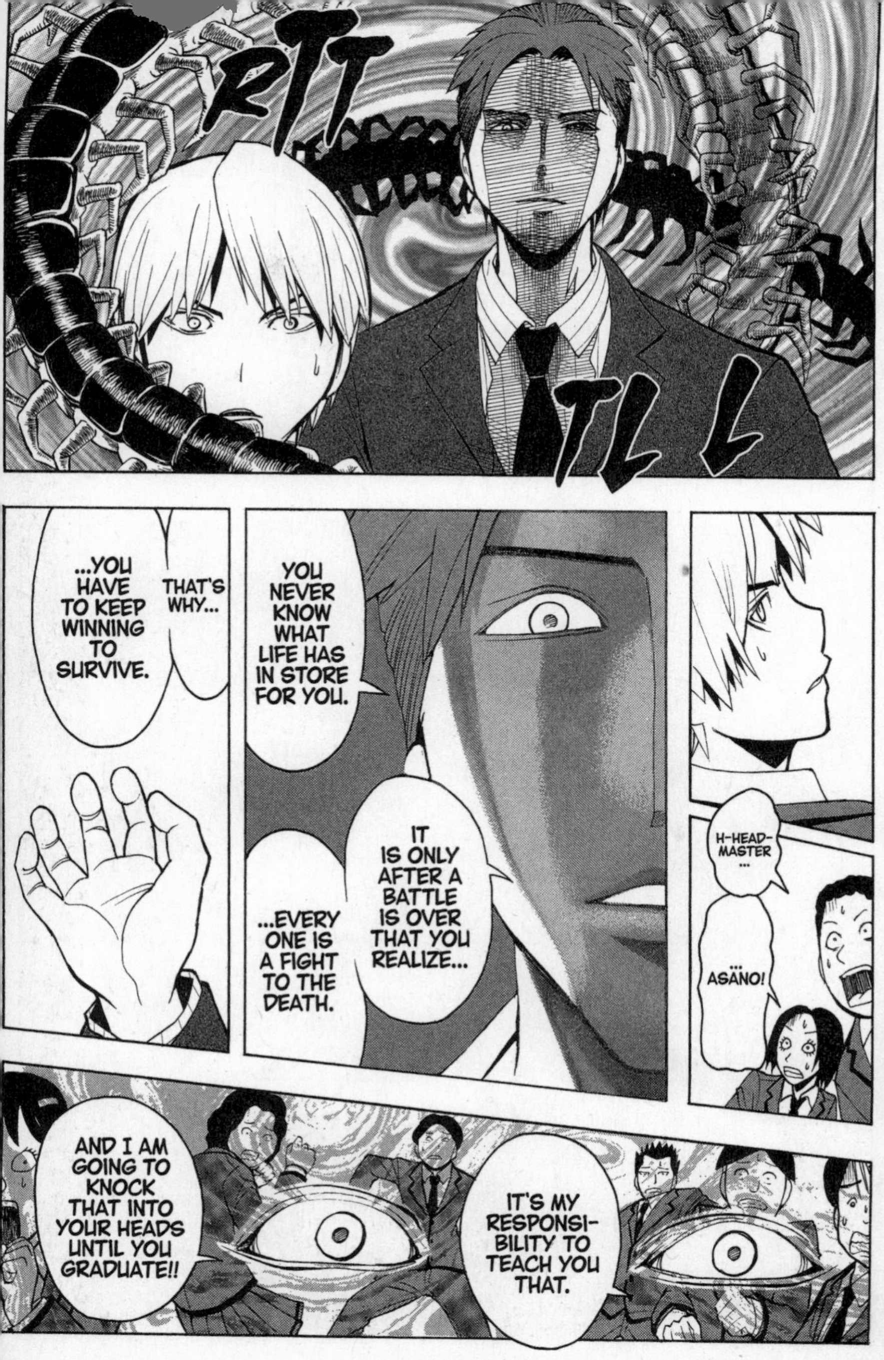
RTT
TLL
H-HEADMASTER ...
... ASANO!
YOU NEVER KNOW WHAT LIFE HAS IN STORE FOR YOU.
IT IS ONLY AFTER A BATTLE IS OVER THAT YOU REALIZE...
...EVERY ONE IS A FIGHT TO THE DEATH.
THAT'S WHY...
...YOU HAVE TO KEEP WINNING TO SURVIVE.
IT'S MY RESPONSIBILITY TO TEACH YOU THAT.
AND I AM GOING TO KNOCK THAT INTO YOUR HEADS UNTIL YOU GRADUATE!!

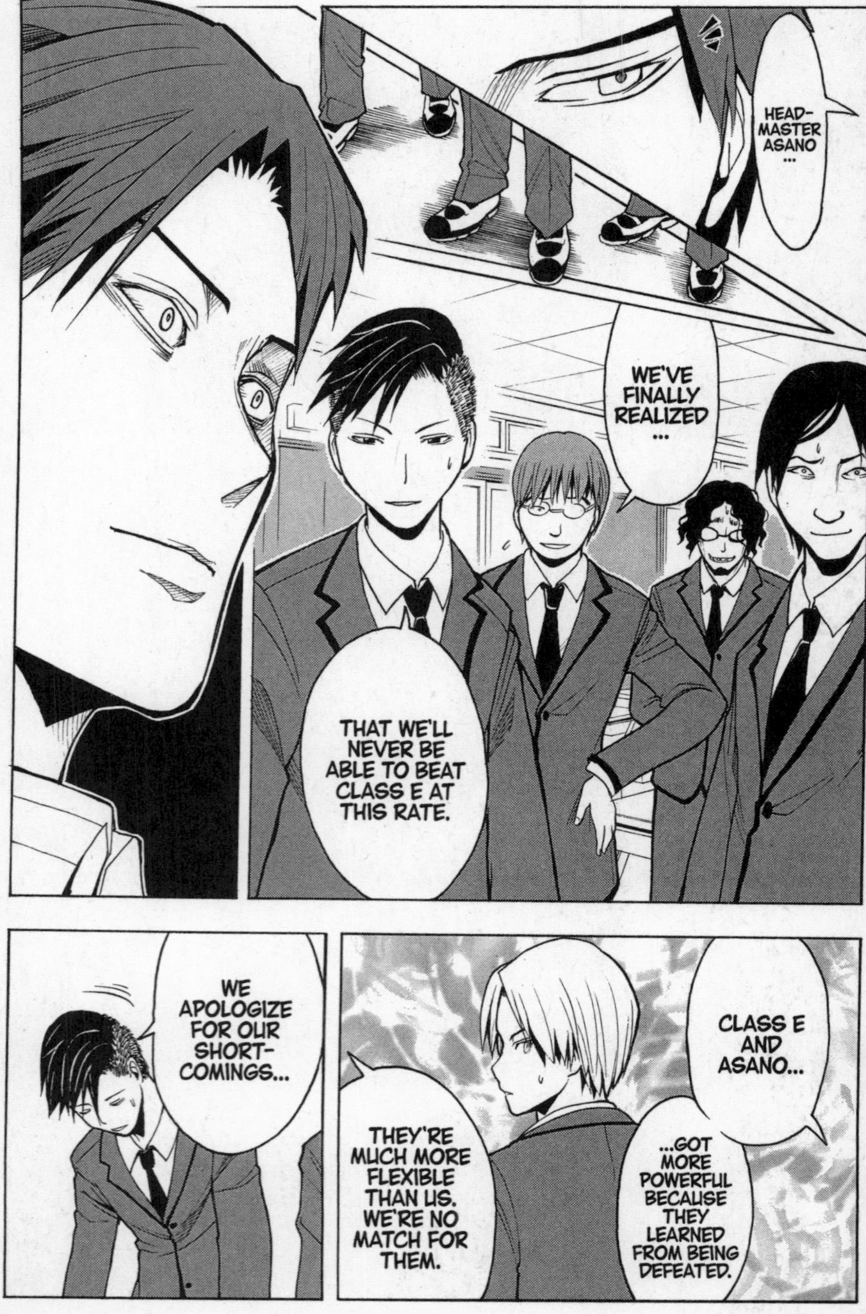
HEAD-MASTER ASANO...
WE'VE FINALLY REALIZED...
THAT WE'LL NEVER BE ABLE TO BEAT CLASS E AT THIS RATE.
CLASS E AND ASANO...
...GOT MORE POWERFUL BECAUSE THEY LEARNED FROM BEING DEFEATED.
THEY'RE MUCH MORE FLEXIBLE THAN US. WE'RE NO MATCH FOR THEM.
WE APOLOGIZE FOR OUR SHORT-COMINGS...

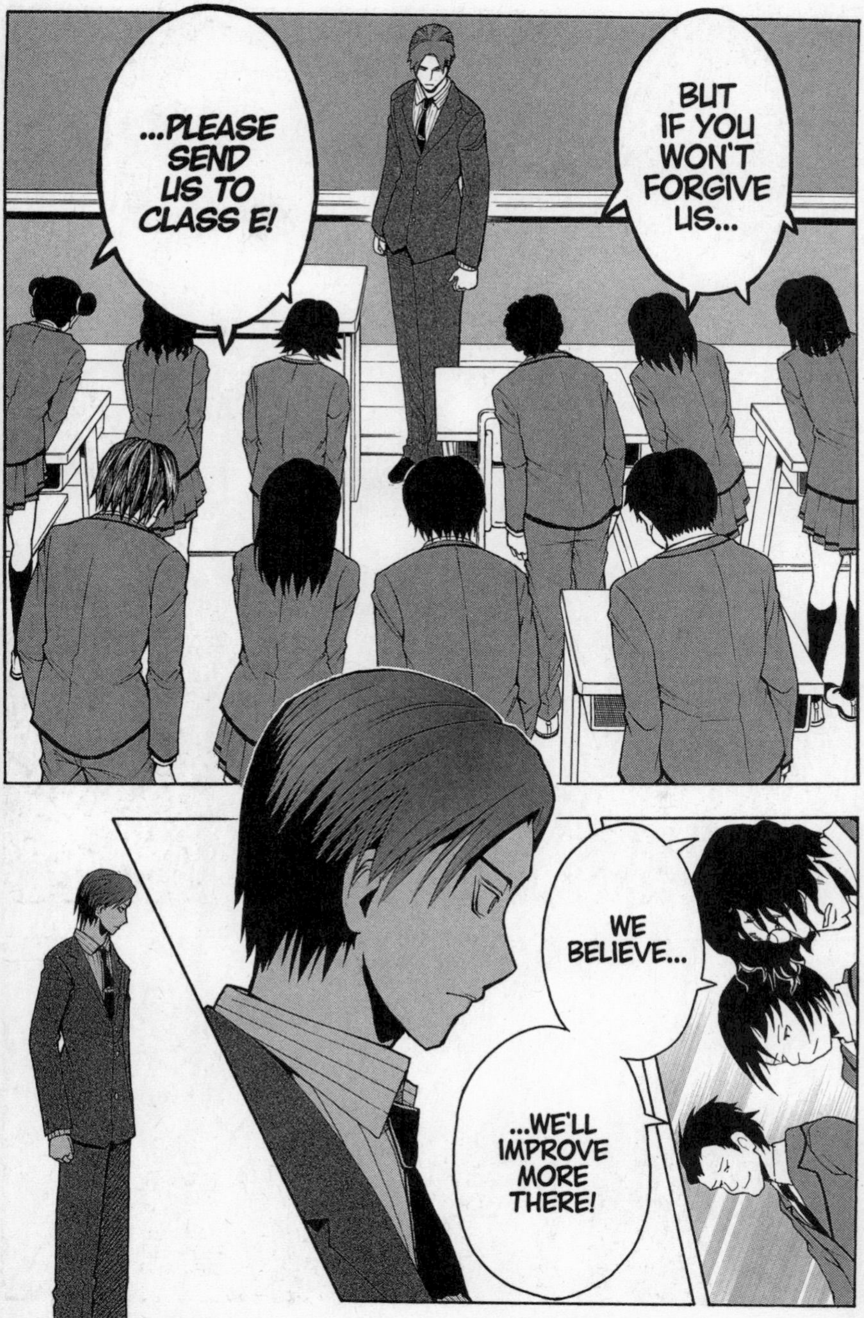
BUT IF YOU WON'T FORGIVE US...
...PLEASE SEND US TO CLASS E!
WE BELIEVE...
...WE'LL IMPROVE MORE THERE!

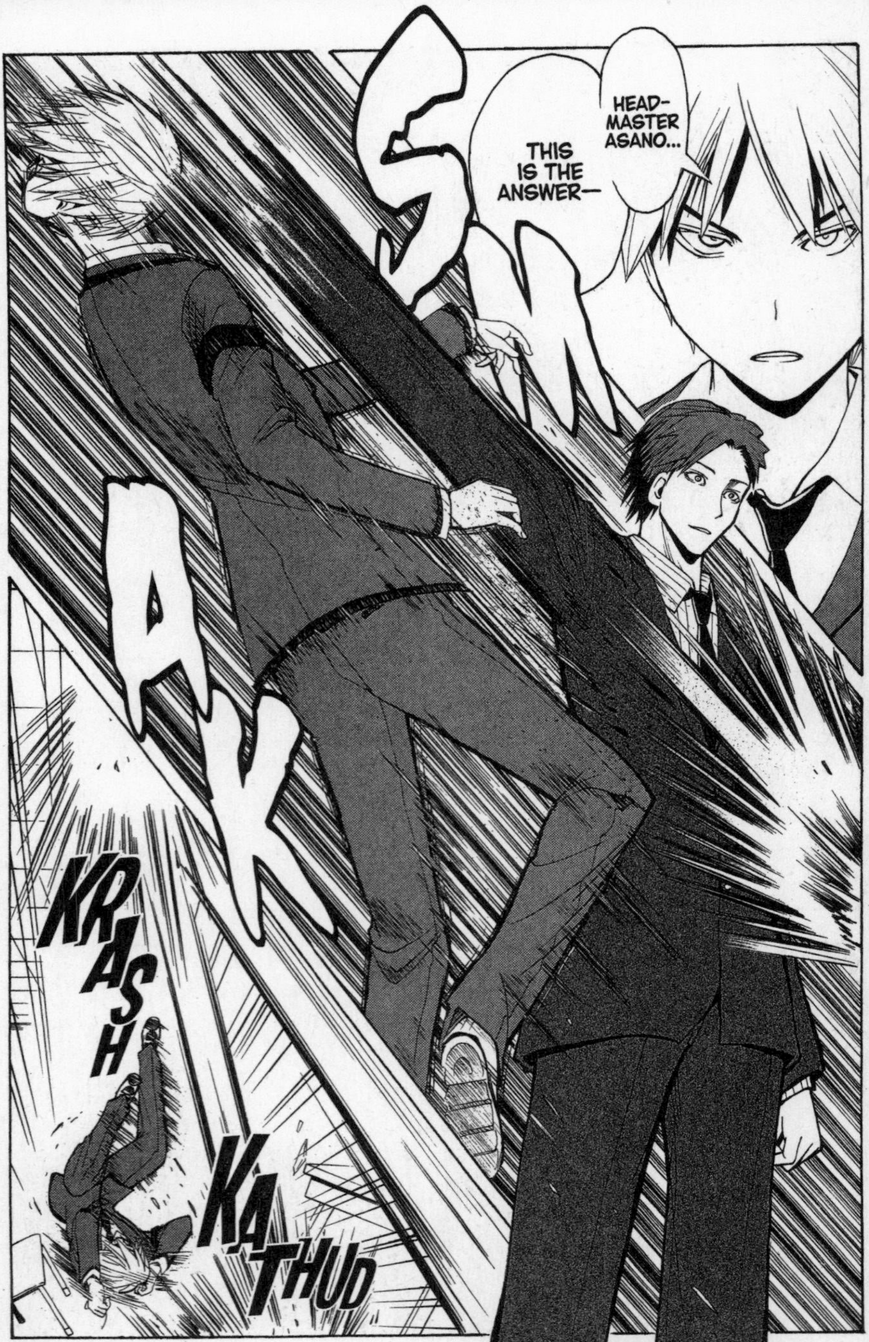
HEAD-MASTER ASANO...
THIS IS THE ANSWER—
SMAK
KRASH
KA THUD

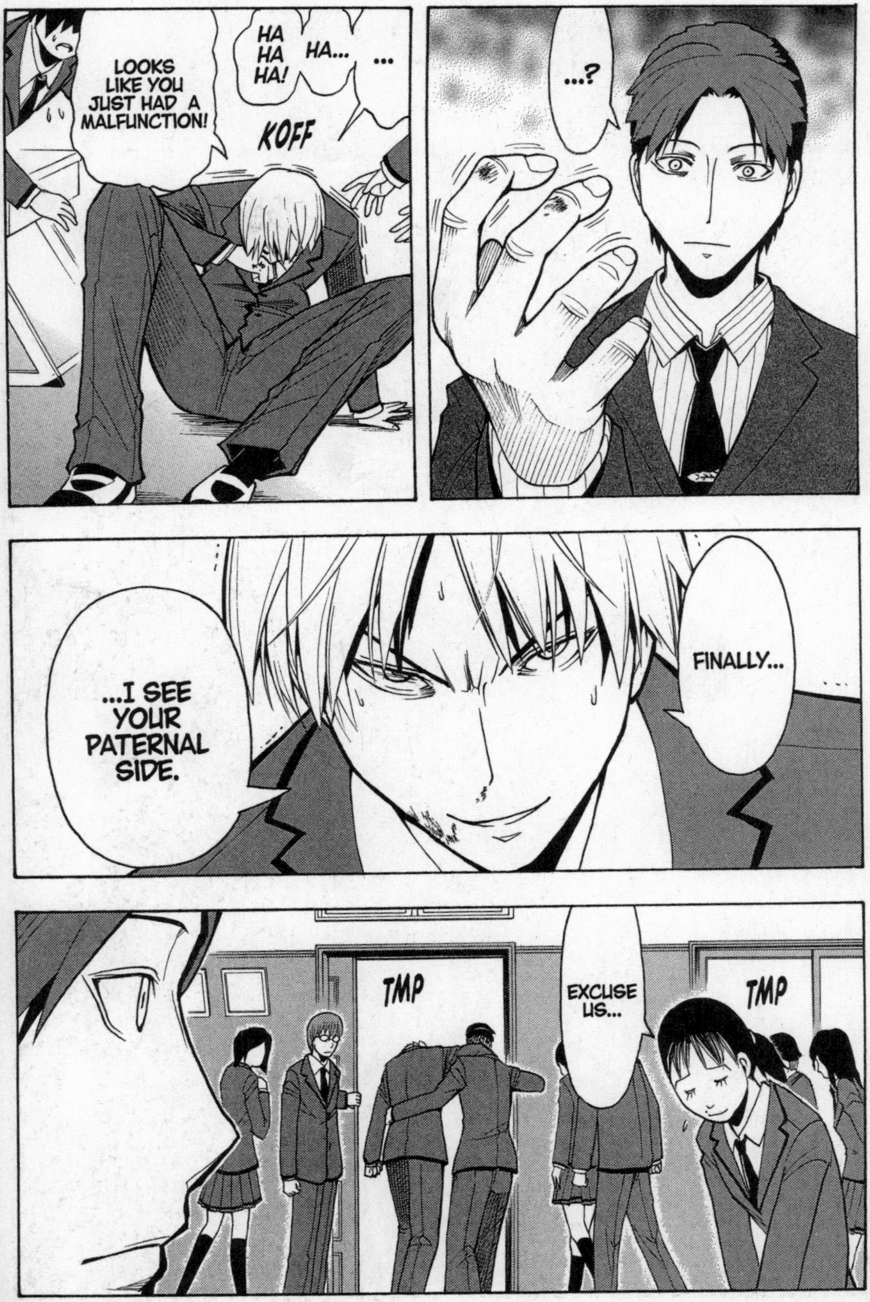
...?
HA HA HA! HA... ...
LOOKS LIKE YOU JUST HAD A MALFUNCTION!
KOFF
FINALLY...
...I SEE YOUR PATERNAL SIDE.
TMP
EXCUSE US...
TMP

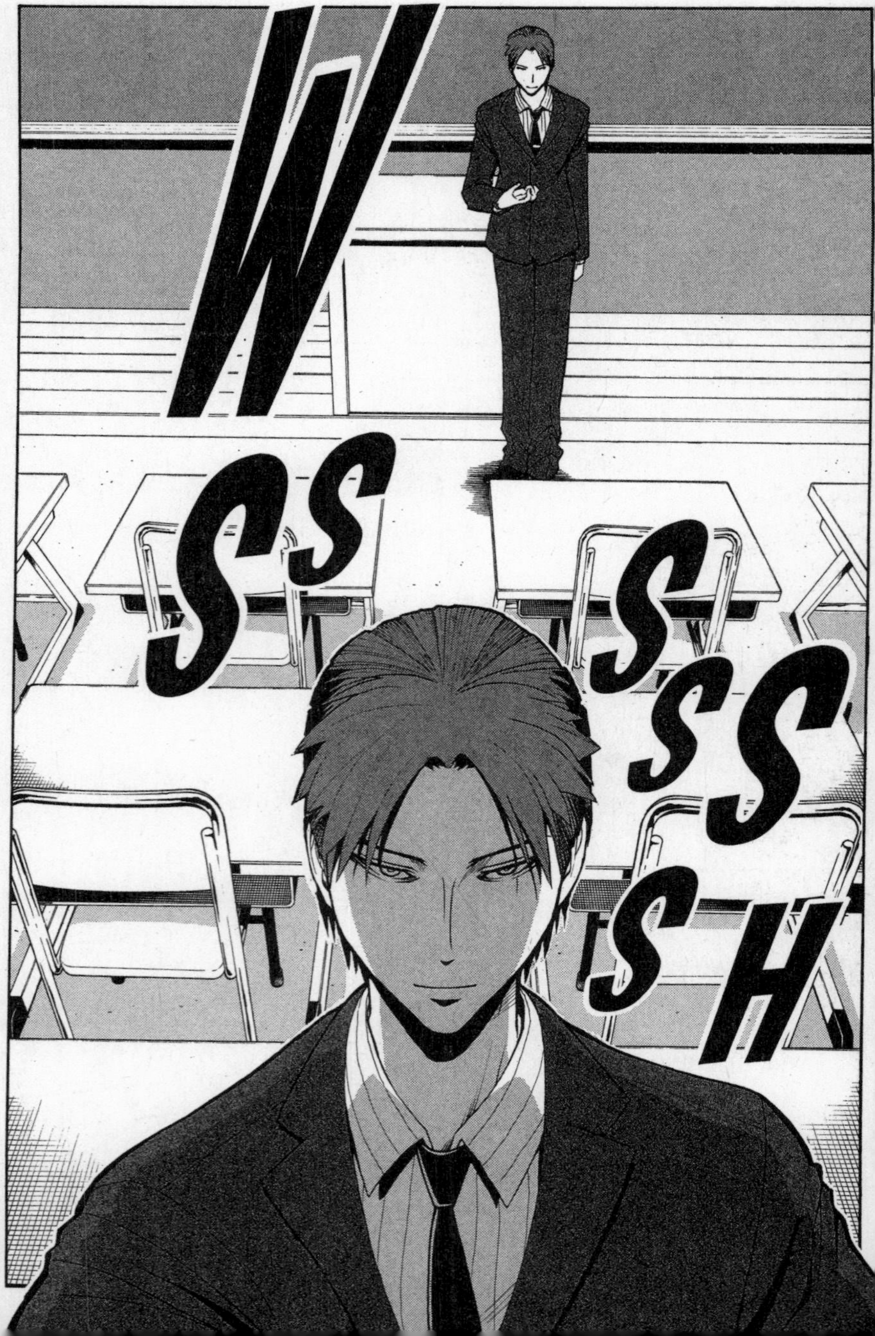
WSSSSSSH

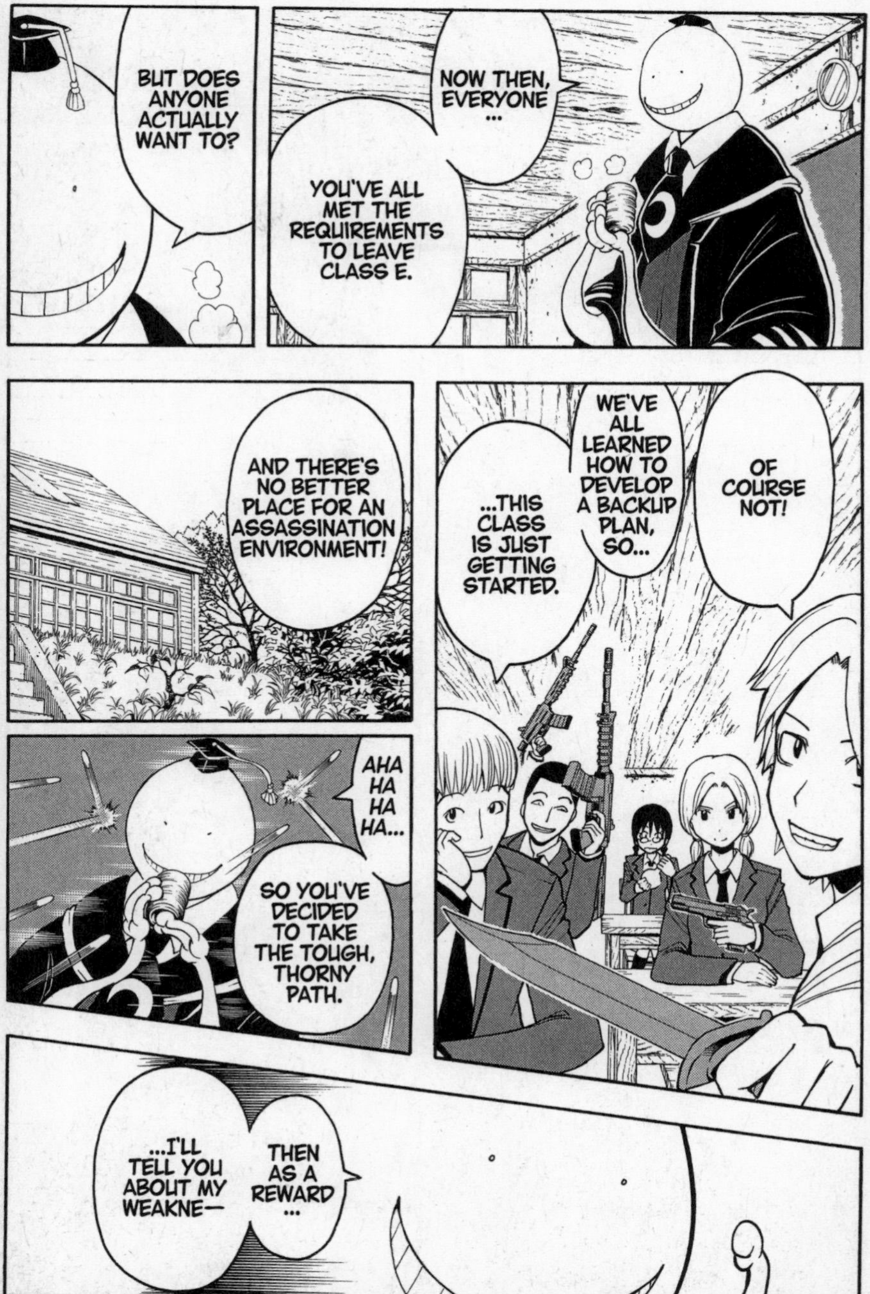
NOW THEN, EVERYONE ...
YOU'VE ALL MET THE REQUIREMENTS TO LEAVE CLASS E.
BUT DOES ANYONE ACTUALLY WANT TO?
OF COURSE NOT!
WE'VE ALL LEARNED HOW TO DEVELOP A BACKUP PLAN, SO...
...THIS CLASS IS JUST GETTING STARTED.
AND THERE'S NO BETTER PLACE FOR AN ASSASSINATION ENVIRONMENT!
AHA HA HA HA...
SO YOU'VE DECIDED TO TAKE THE TOUGH, THORNY PATH.
THEN AS A REWARD ...
...I'LL TELL YOU ABOUT MY WEAKNE—

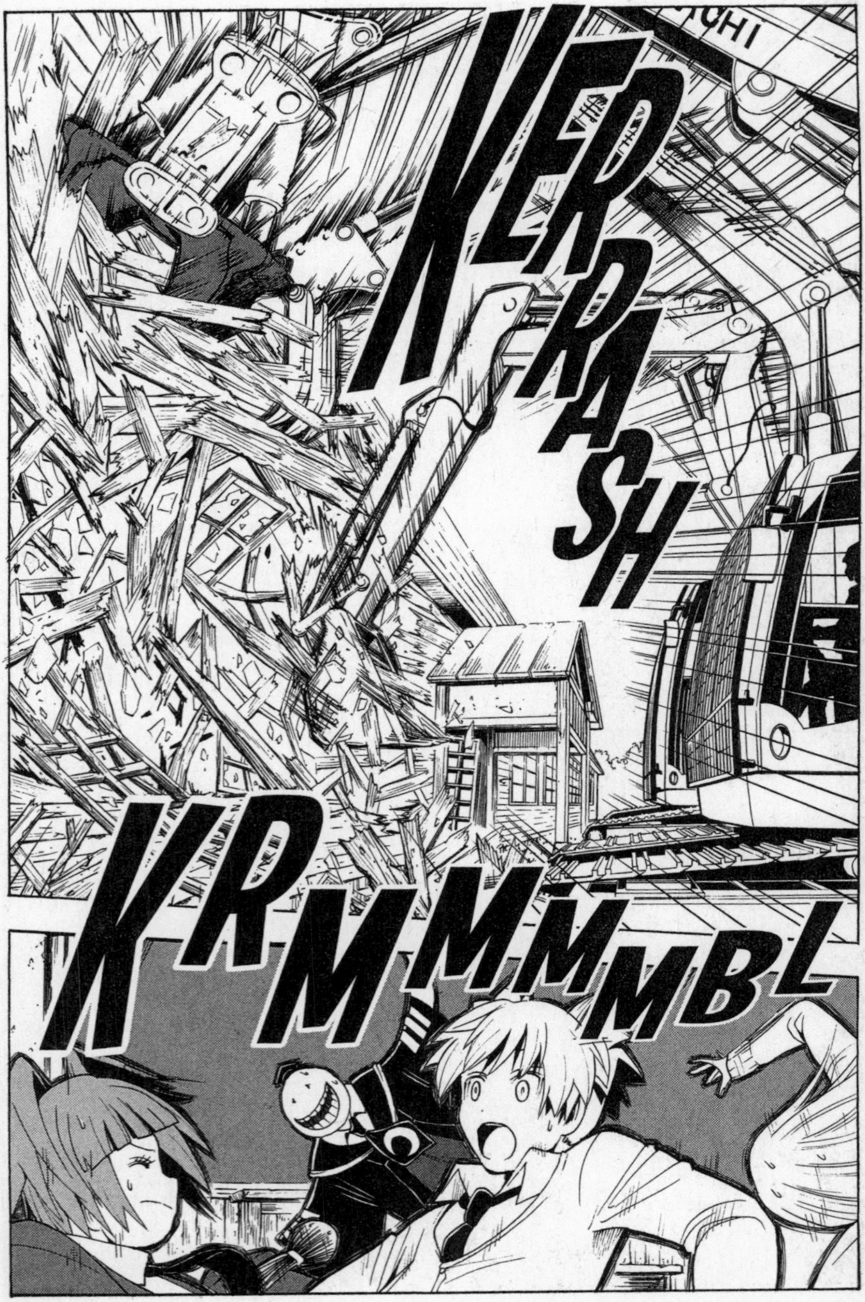
KRRASH
KRMMMMBL

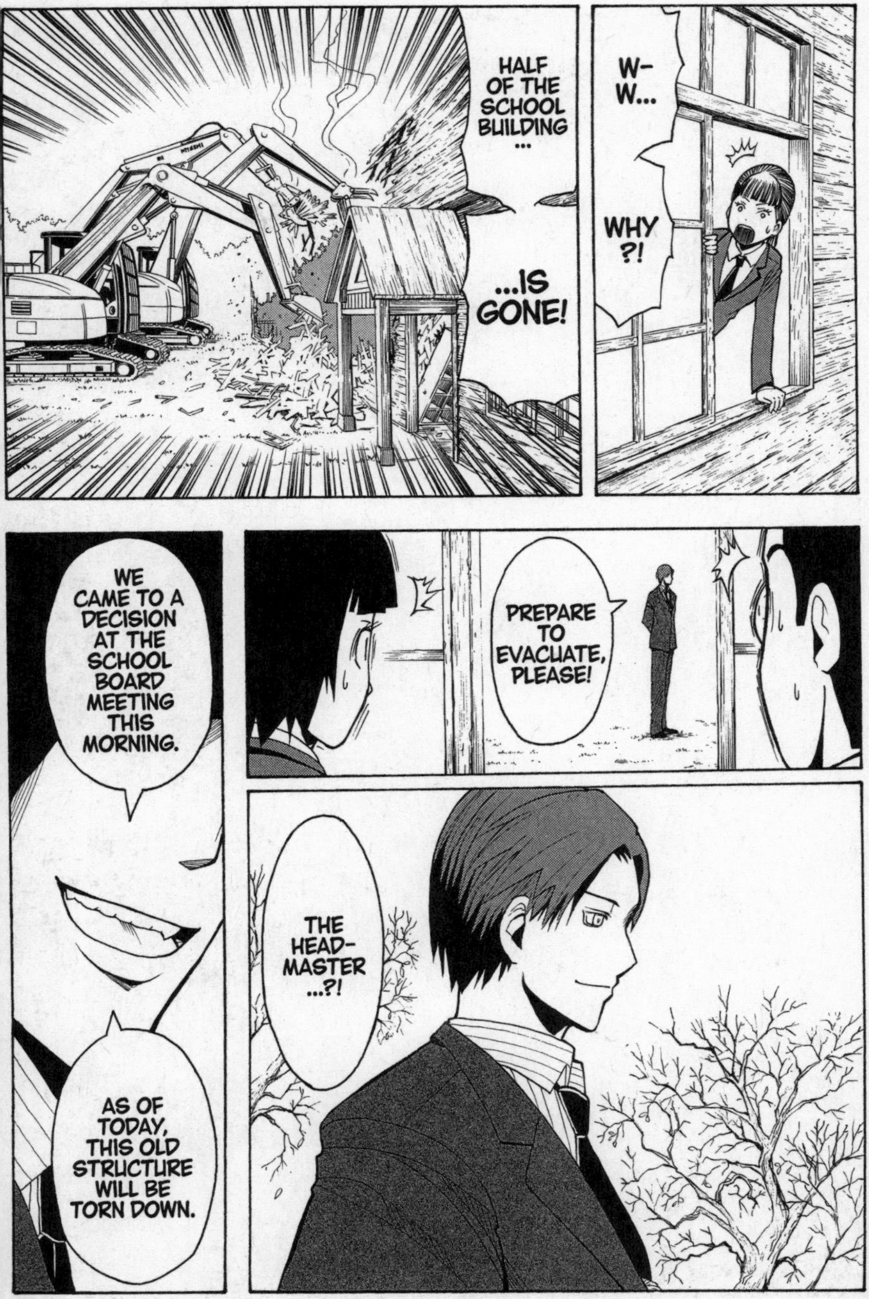
W- W...
WHY ?!
HALF OF THE SCHOOL BUILDING ...
...IS GONE!
PREPARE TO EVACUATE, PLEASE!
THE HEAD-MASTER ...?!
WE CAME TO A DECISION AT THE SCHOOL BOARD MEETING THIS MORNING.
AS OF TODAY, THIS OLD STRUCTURE WILL BE TORN DOWN.

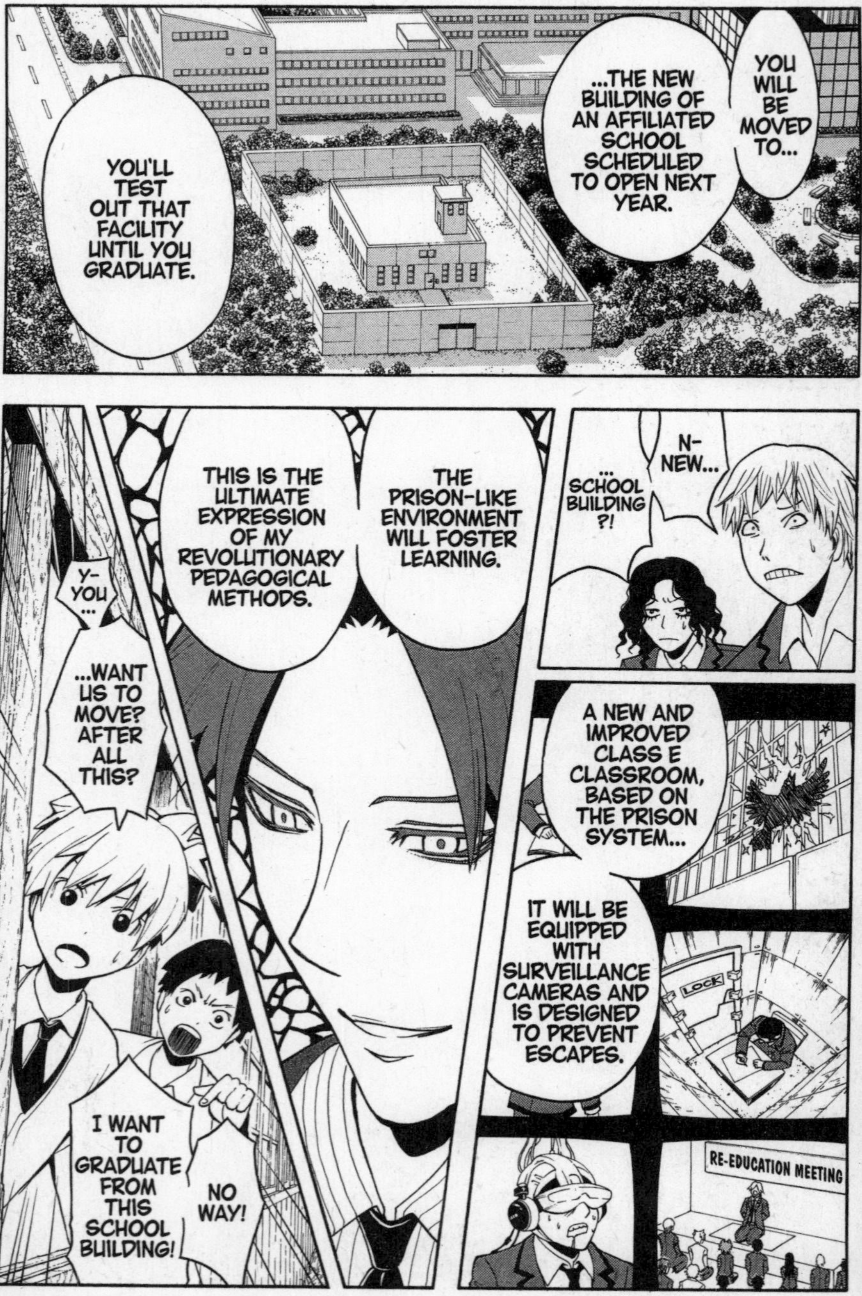

YOU WILL BE MOVED TO...
...THE NEW BUILDING OF AN AFFILIATED SCHOOL SCHEDULED TO OPEN NEXT YEAR.
YOU'LL TEST OUT THAT FACILITY UNTIL YOU GRADUATE.
N- NEW...
...SCHOOL BUILDING?!
A NEW AND IMPROVED CLASS E CLASSROOM, BASED ON THE PRISON SYSTEM...
IT WILL BE EQUIPPED WITH SURVEILLANCE CAMERAS AND IS DESIGNED TO PREVENT ESCAPES.
LOCK
RE-EDUCATION MEETING
THE PRISON-LIKE ENVIRONMENT WILL FOSTER LEARNING.
THIS IS THE ULTIMATE EXPRESSION OF MY REVOLUTIONARY PEDAGOGICAL METHODS.
Y-YOU...
...WANT US TO MOVE? AFTER ALL THIS?
NO WAY!
I WANT TO GRADUATE FROM THIS SCHOOL BUILDING!

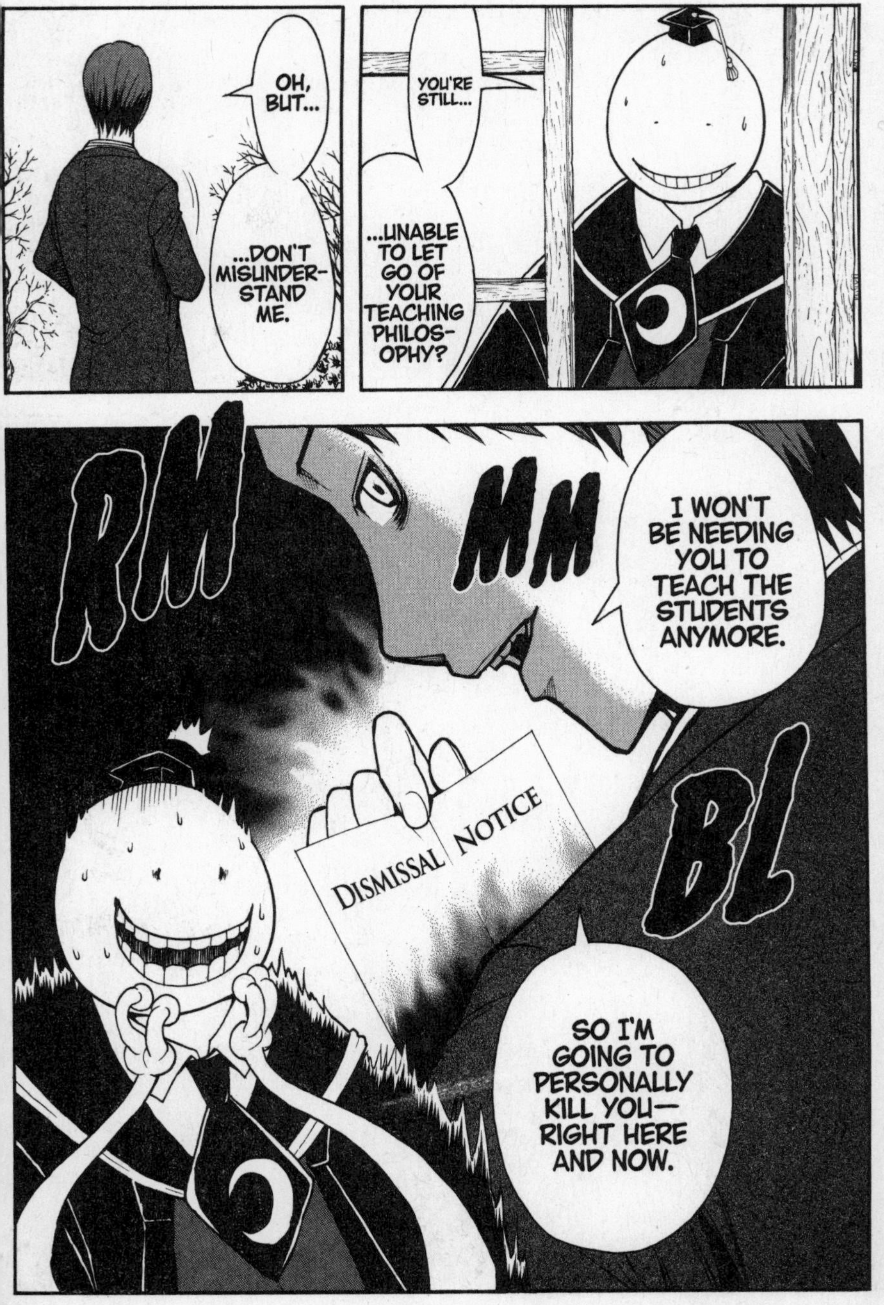
YOU'RE STILL...
...UNABLE TO LET GO OF YOUR TEACHING PHILOSOPHY?
OH, BUT...
...DON'T MISUNDERSTAND ME.
I WON'T BE NEEDING YOU TO TEACH THE STUDENTS ANYMORE.
RM MM
DISMISSAL NOTICE
BL
SO I'M GOING TO PERSONALLY KILL YOU—RIGHT HERE AND NOW.

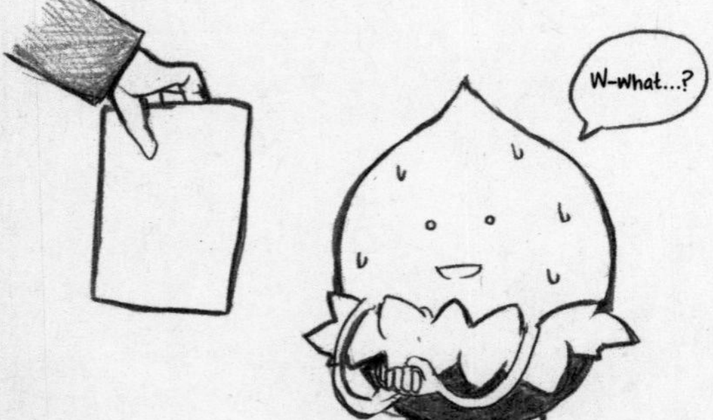
W-what...?

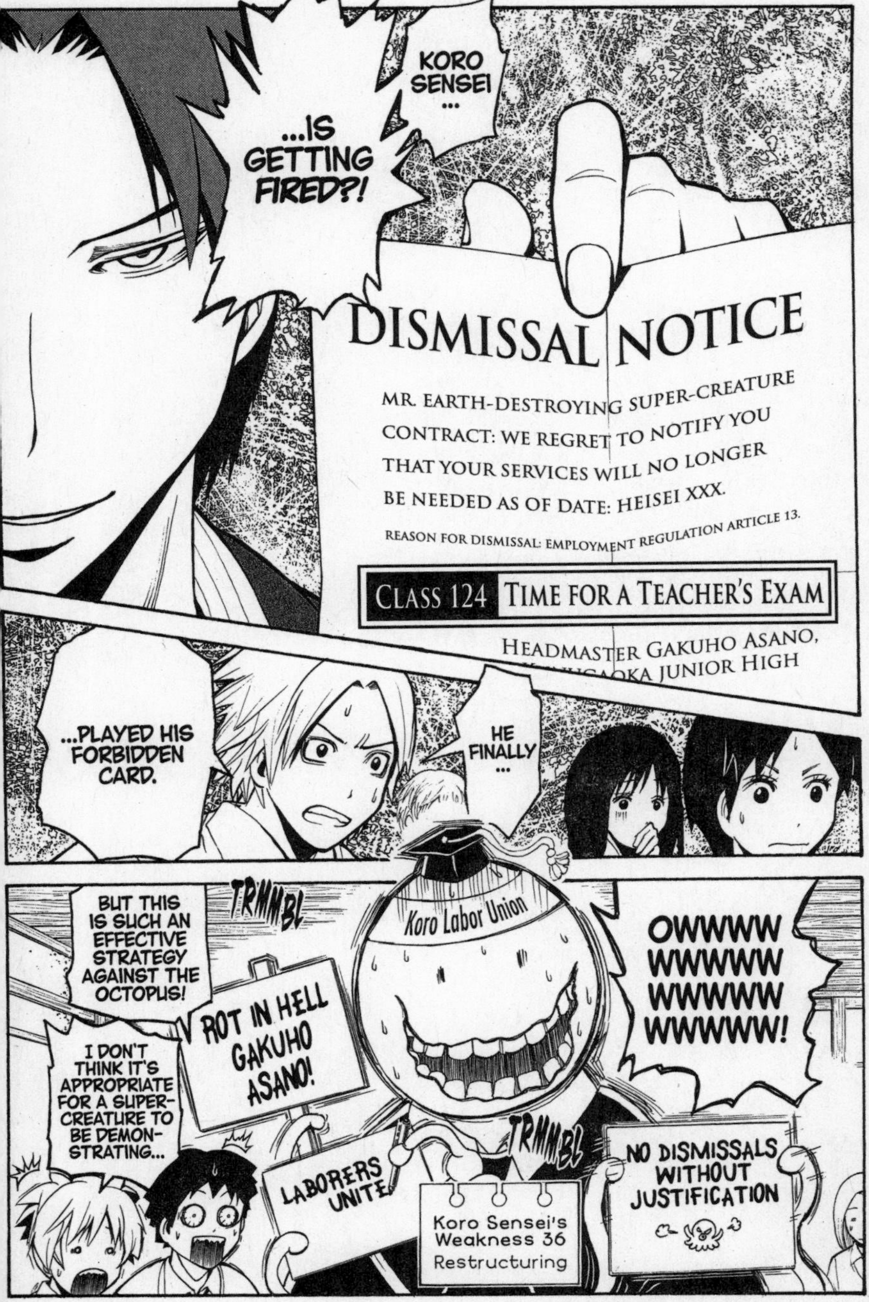
KORO SENSEI ...
...IS GETTING FIRED?!
DISMISSAL NOTICE
MR. EARTH-DESTROYING SUPER-CREATURE CONTRACT: WE REGRET TO NOTIFY YOU THAT YOUR SERVICES WILL NO LONGER BE NEEDED AS OF DATE: HEISEI XXX.
REASON FOR DISMISSAL: EMPLOYMENT REGULATION ARTICLE 13.
CLASS 124 TIME FOR A TEACHER'S EXAM
HEADMASTER GAKUHO ASANO,
HE FINALLY ...
...PLAYED HIS FORBIDDEN CARD.
OWWWWWWWWWWWWWWWWWWWWWWW!
Koro Labor Union
TRMMBL
BUT THIS IS SUCH AN EFFECTIVE STRATEGY AGAINST THE OCTOPUS!
ROT IN HELL GAKUHO ASANO!
I DON'T THINK IT'S APPROPRIATE FOR A SUPER-CREATURE TO BE DEMON-STRATING...
TRMMBL
NO DISMISSALS WITHOUT JUSTIFICATION
LABORERS UNITE
Koro Sensei's Weakness 36 Restructuring

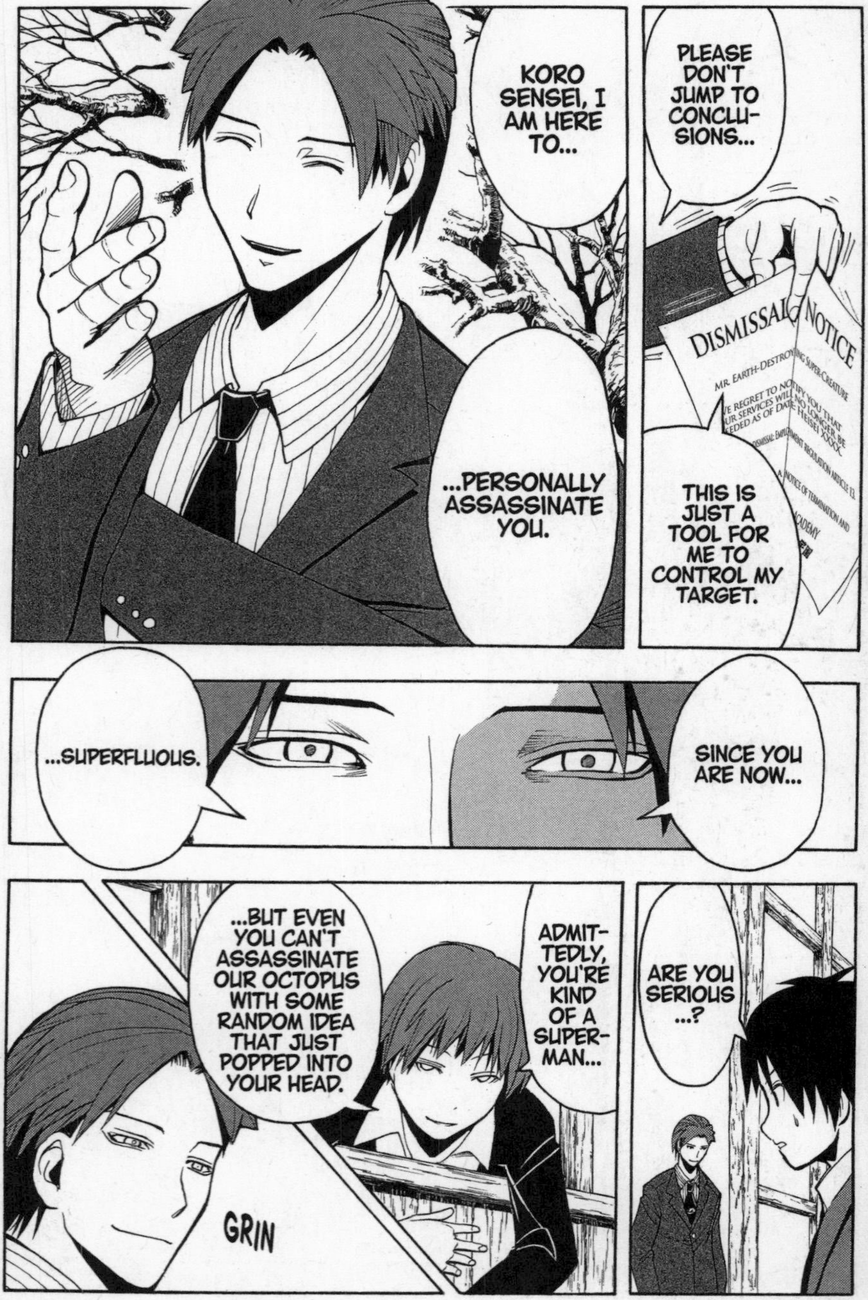
PLEASE DON'T JUMP TO CONCLUSIONS...
DISMISSAL NOTICE
MR. EARTH-DESTROYING SUPER-CREATURE
THIS IS JUST A TOOL FOR ME TO CONTROL MY TARGET.
KORO SENSEI, I AM HERE TO...
...PERSONALLY ASSASSINATE YOU.
SINCE YOU ARE NOW...
...SUPERFLUOUS.
ARE YOU SERIOUS ...?
ADMITTEDLY, YOU'RE KIND OF A SUPERMAN...
...BUT EVEN YOU CAN'T ASSASSINATE OUR OCTOPUS WITH SOME RANDOM IDEA THAT JUST POPPED INTO YOUR HEAD.
GRIN

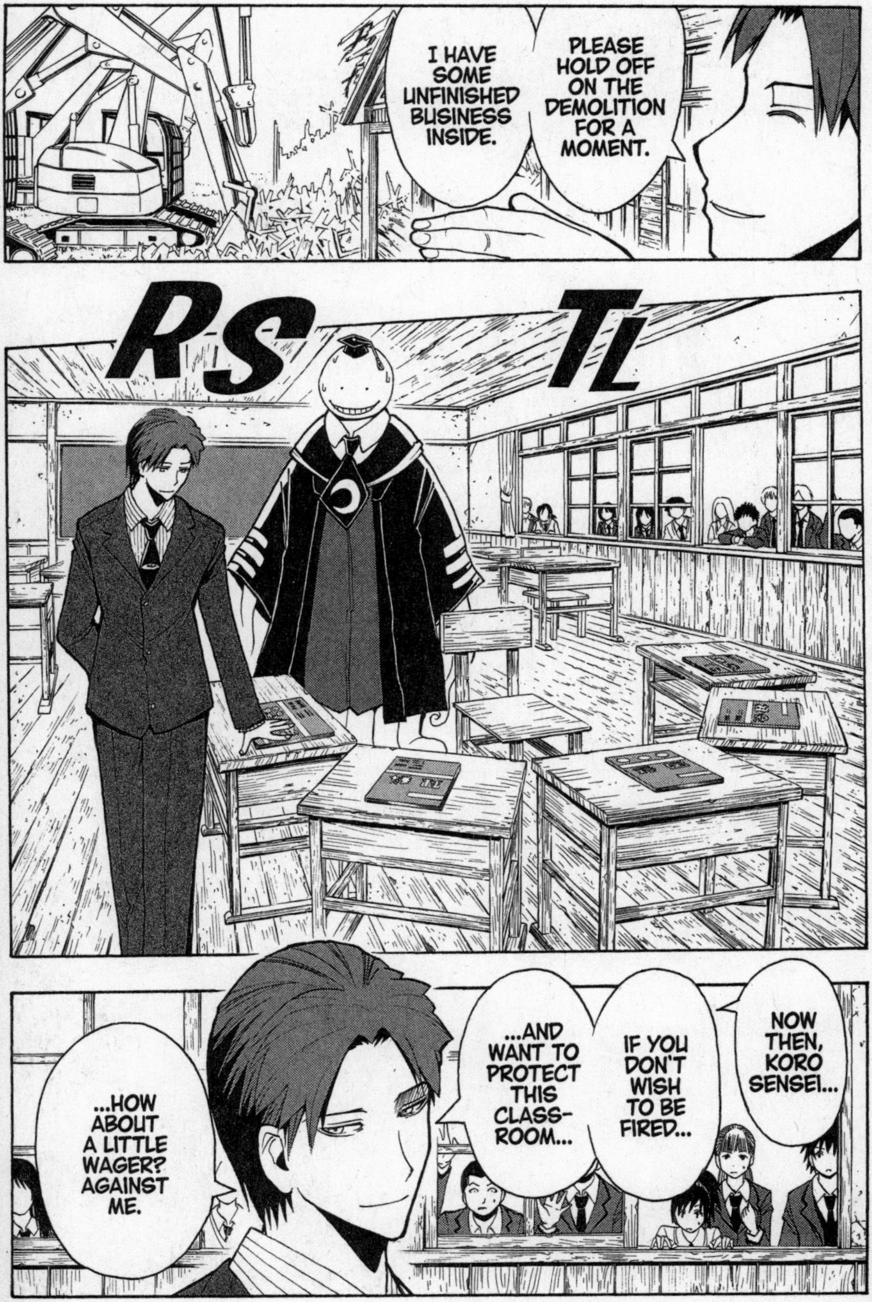
PLEASE HOLD OFF ON THE DEMOLITION FOR A MOMENT.
I HAVE SOME UNFINISHED BUSINESS INSIDE.
RS TL
NOW THEN, KORO SENSEI...
IF YOU DON'T WISH TO BE FIRED...
...AND WANT TO PROTECT THIS CLASS-ROOM...
...HOW ABOUT A LITTLE WAGER? AGAINST ME.

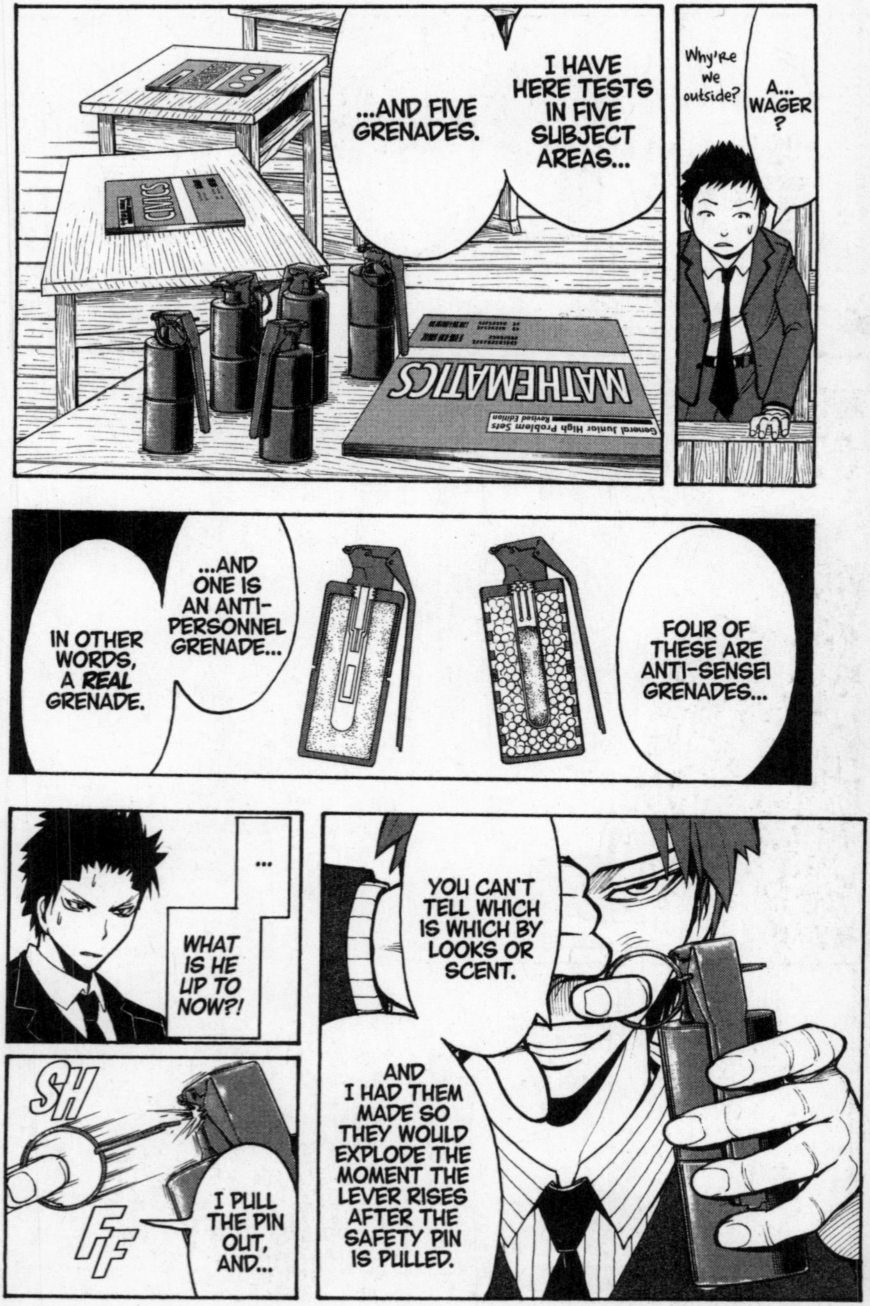
A... WAGER?
Why're we outside?
I HAVE HERE TESTS IN FIVE SUBJECT AREAS...
...AND FIVE GRENADES.
CIVICS
MATHEMATICS
General Junior High Problem Sets
Revised Edition
FOUR OF THESE ARE ANTI-SENSEI GRENADES...
...AND ONE IS AN ANTI-PERSONNEL GRENADE...
IN OTHER WORDS, A *REAL* GRENADE.
YOU CAN'T TELL WHICH IS WHICH BY LOOKS OR SCENT.
AND I HAD THEM MADE SO THEY WOULD EXPLODE THE MOMENT THE LEVER RISES AFTER THE SAFETY PIN IS PULLED.
...
WHAT IS HE UP TO NOW?!
SHFF
I PULL THE PIN OUT, AND...

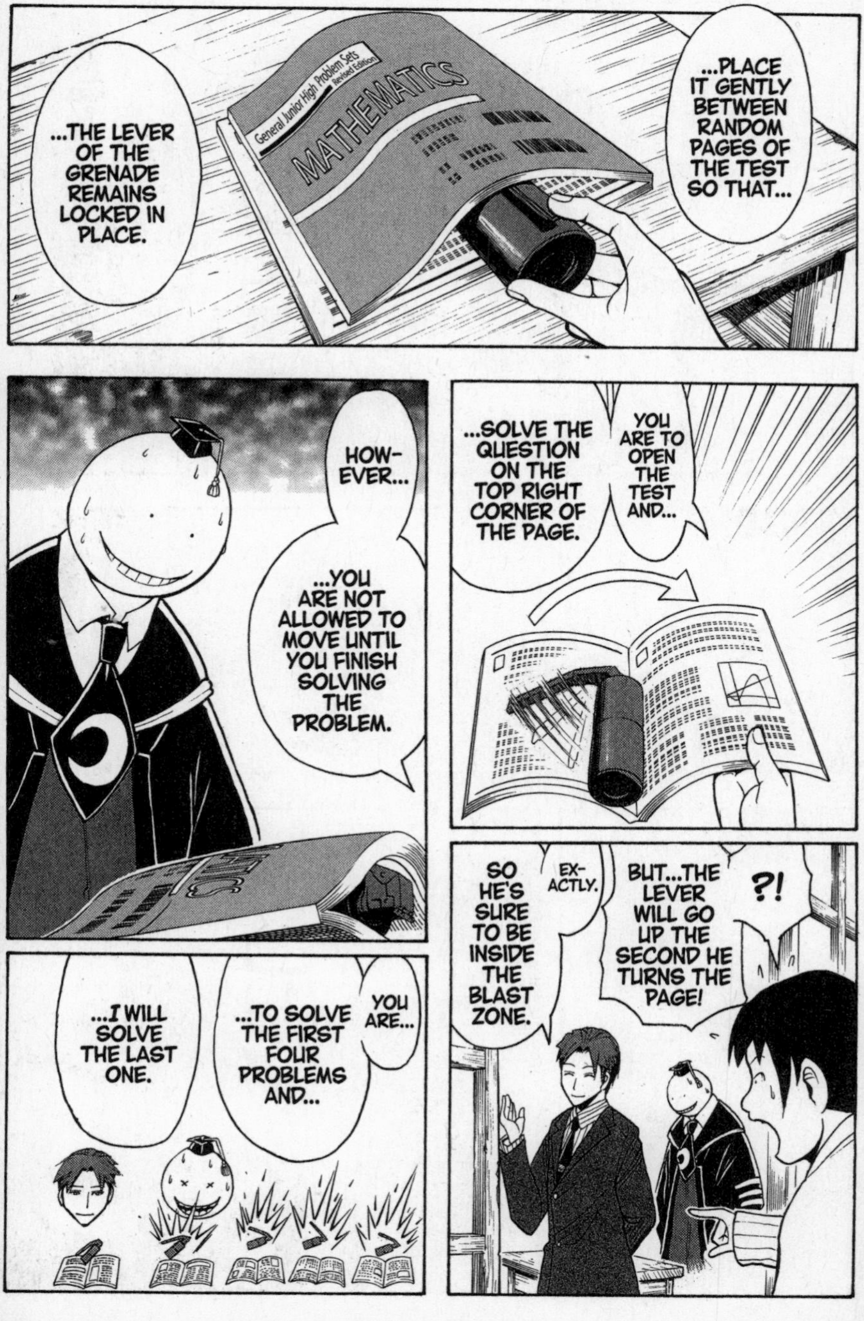
...PLACE IT GENTLY BETWEEN RANDOM PAGES OF THE TEST SO THAT...
General Junior High Problem Sets
Revised Edition
MATHEMATICS
...THE LEVER OF THE GRENADE REMAINS LOCKED IN PLACE.
YOU ARE TO OPEN THE TEST AND...
...SOLVE THE QUESTION ON THE TOP RIGHT CORNER OF THE PAGE.
HOW-EVER...
...YOU ARE NOT ALLOWED TO MOVE UNTIL YOU FINISH SOLVING THE PROBLEM.
?!
BUT...THE LEVER WILL GO UP THE SECOND HE TURNS THE PAGE!
EX-ACTLY.
SO HE'S SURE TO BE INSIDE THE BLAST ZONE.
YOU ARE...
...TO SOLVE THE FIRST FOUR PROBLEMS AND...
...I WILL SOLVE THE LAST ONE.

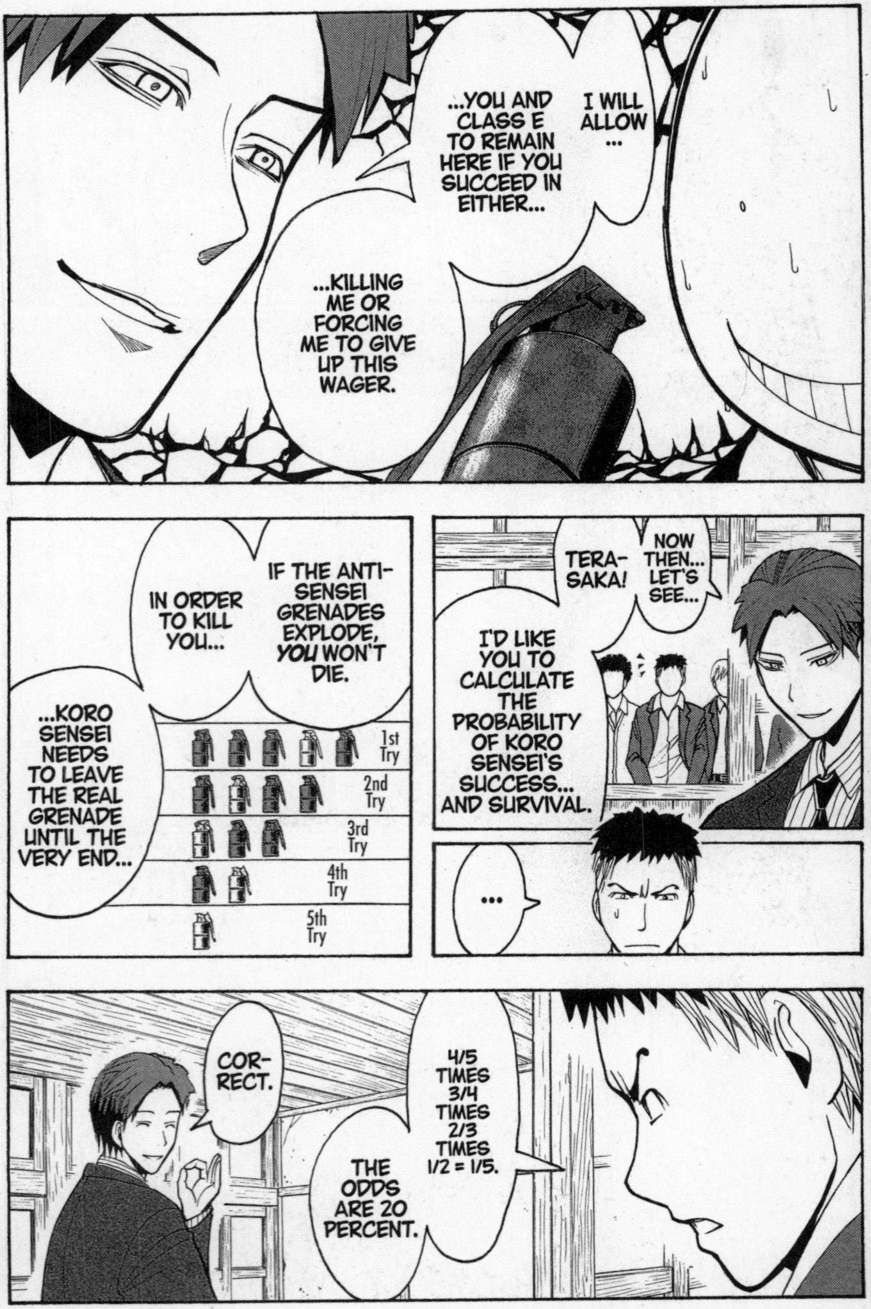
I WILL ALLOW ...
...YOU AND CLASS E TO REMAIN HERE IF YOU SUCCEED IN EITHER...
...KILLING ME OR FORCING ME TO GIVE UP THIS WAGER.
NOW THEN... LET'S SEE...
TERA-SAKA!
I'D LIKE YOU TO CALCULATE THE PROBABILITY OF KORO SENSEI'S SUCCESS... AND SURVIVAL.
...
IF THE ANTI-SENSEI GRENADES EXPLODE, YOU WON'T DIE.
IN ORDER TO KILL YOU...
...KORO SENSEI NEEDS TO LEAVE THE REAL GRENADE UNTIL THE VERY END...
1st Try
2nd Try
3rd Try
4th Try
5th Try
4/5 TIMES 3/4 TIMES 2/3 TIMES 1/2 = 1/5.
THE ODDS ARE 20 PERCENT.
COR-RECT.

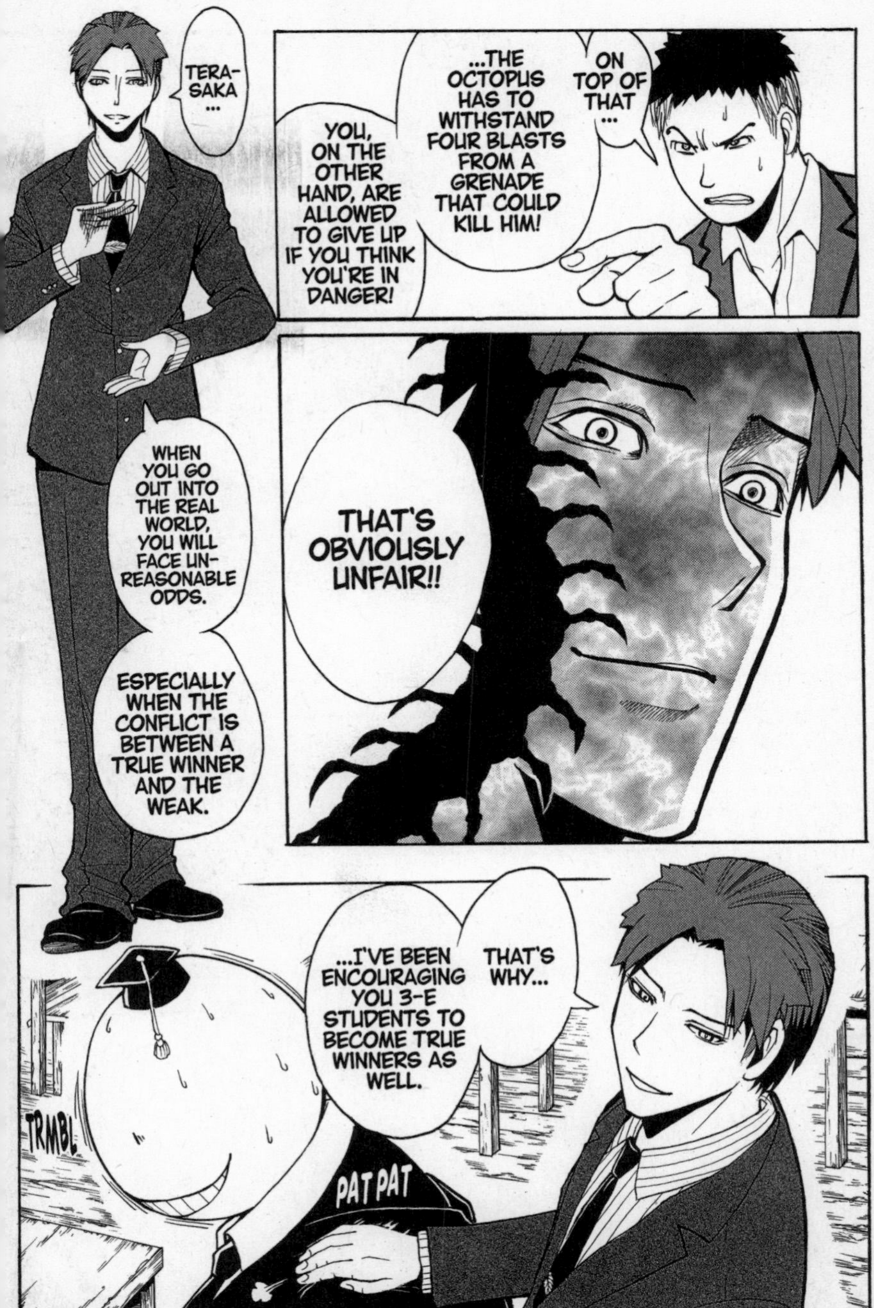
ON TOP OF THAT...
...THE OCTOPUS HAS TO WITHSTAND FOUR BLASTS FROM A GRENADE THAT COULD KILL HIM!
YOU, ON THE OTHER HAND, ARE ALLOWED TO GIVE UP IF YOU THINK YOU'RE IN DANGER!
THAT'S OBVIOUSLY UNFAIR!!
TERA-SAKA...
WHEN YOU GO OUT INTO THE REAL WORLD, YOU WILL FACE UN-REASONABLE ODDS.
ESPECIALLY WHEN THE CONFLICT IS BETWEEN A TRUE WINNER AND THE WEAK.
THAT'S WHY...
...I'VE BEEN ENCOURAGING YOU 3-E STUDENTS TO BECOME TRUE WINNERS AS WELL.
PAT PAT
TRMBL

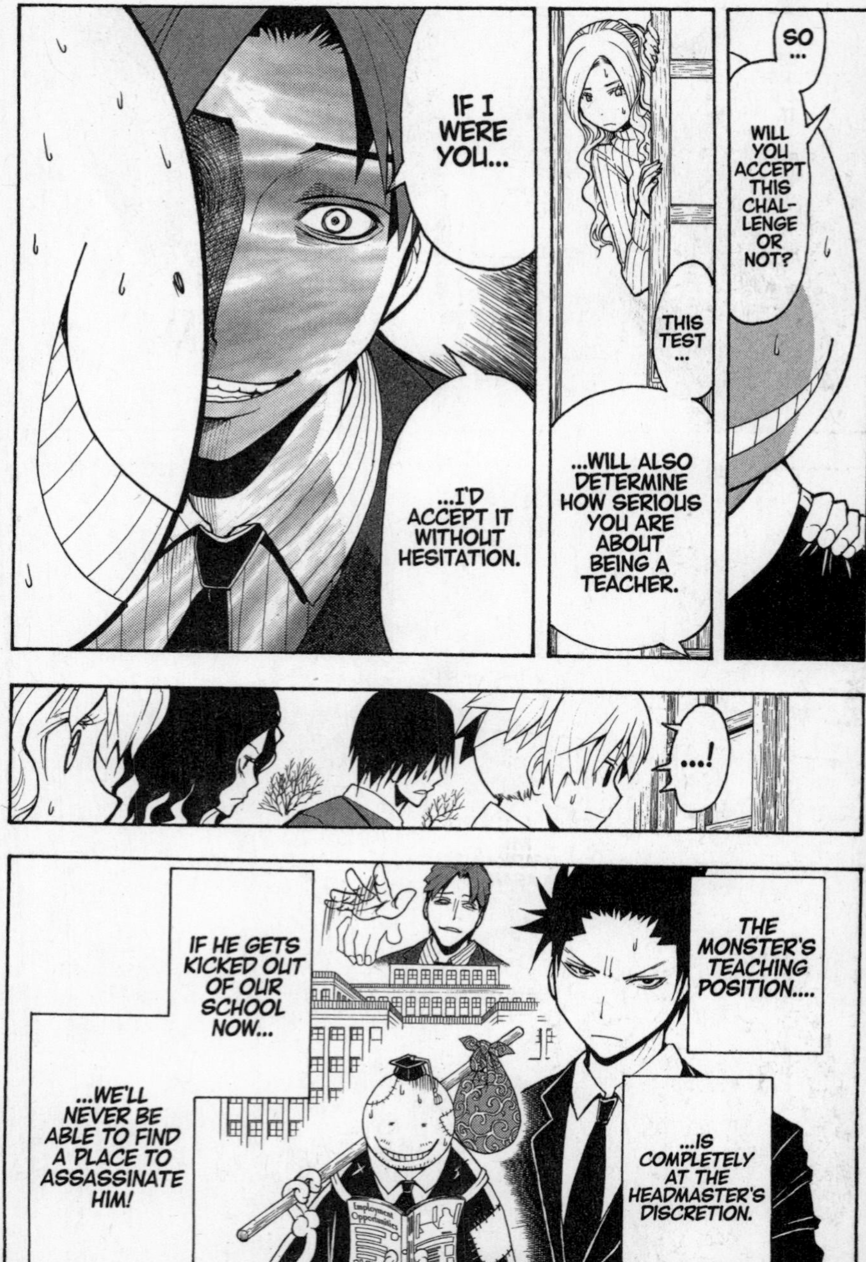
SO...
WILL YOU ACCEPT THIS CHAL-LENGE OR NOT?
THIS TEST...
...WILL ALSO DETERMINE HOW SERIOUS YOU ARE ABOUT BEING A TEACHER.
IF I WERE YOU...
...I'D ACCEPT IT WITHOUT HESITATION.
....!
THE MONSTER'S TEACHING POSITION....
...IS COMPLETELY AT THE HEADMASTER'S DISCRETION.
IF HE GETS KICKED OUT OF OUR SCHOOL NOW...
...WE'LL NEVER BE ABLE TO FIND A PLACE TO ASSASSINATE HIM!
Employment Opportunities

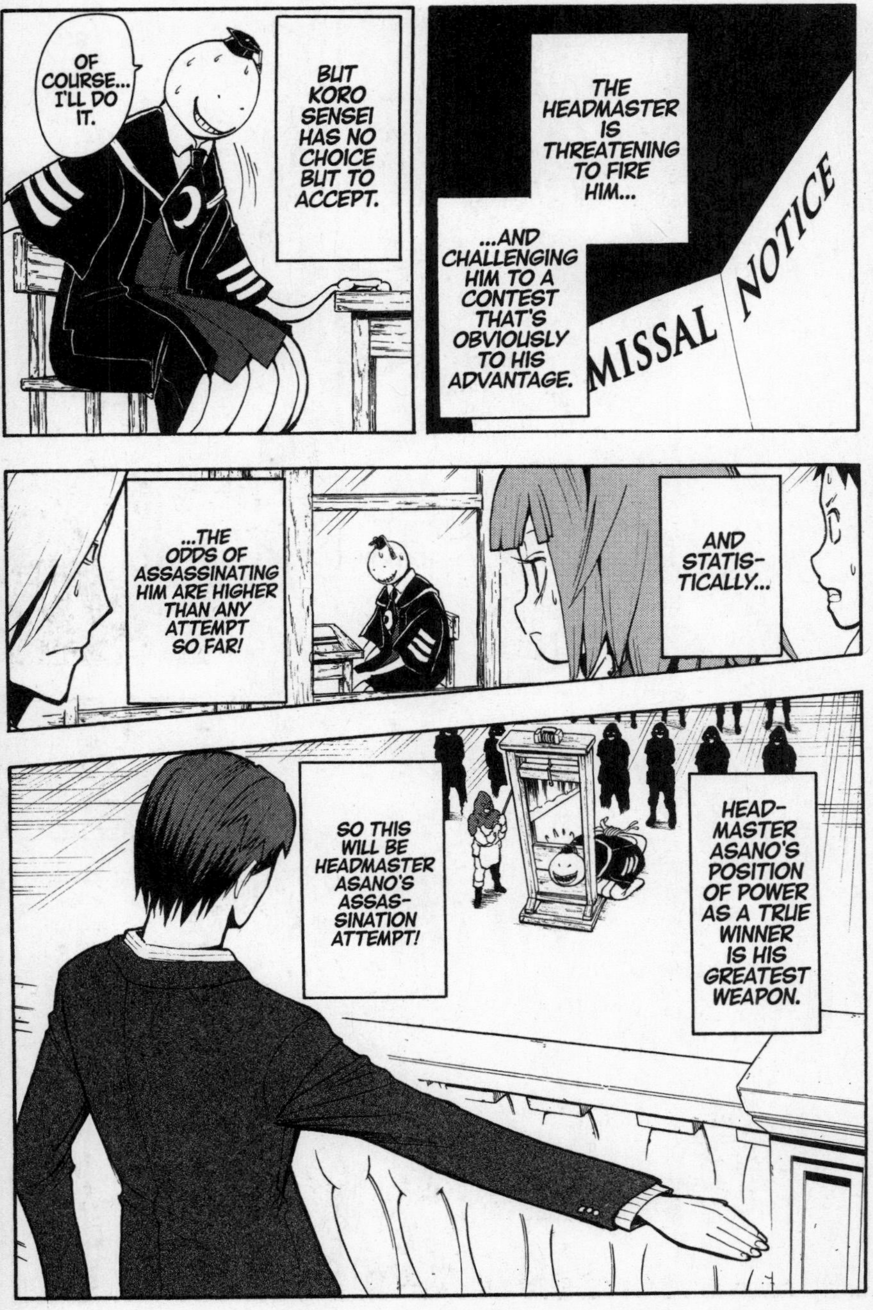
THE HEADMASTER IS THREATENING TO FIRE HIM...
...AND CHALLENGING HIM TO A CONTEST THAT'S OBVIOUSLY TO HIS ADVANTAGE.
MISSAL NOTICE
BUT KORO SENSEI HAS NO CHOICE BUT TO ACCEPT.
OF COURSE... I'LL DO IT.
AND STATISTICALLY...
...THE ODDS OF ASSASSINATING HIM ARE HIGHER THAN ANY ATTEMPT SO FAR!
HEADMASTER ASANO'S POSITION OF POWER AS A TRUE WINNER IS HIS GREATEST WEAPON.
SO THIS WILL BE HEADMASTER ASANO'S ASSASSINATION ATTEMPT!

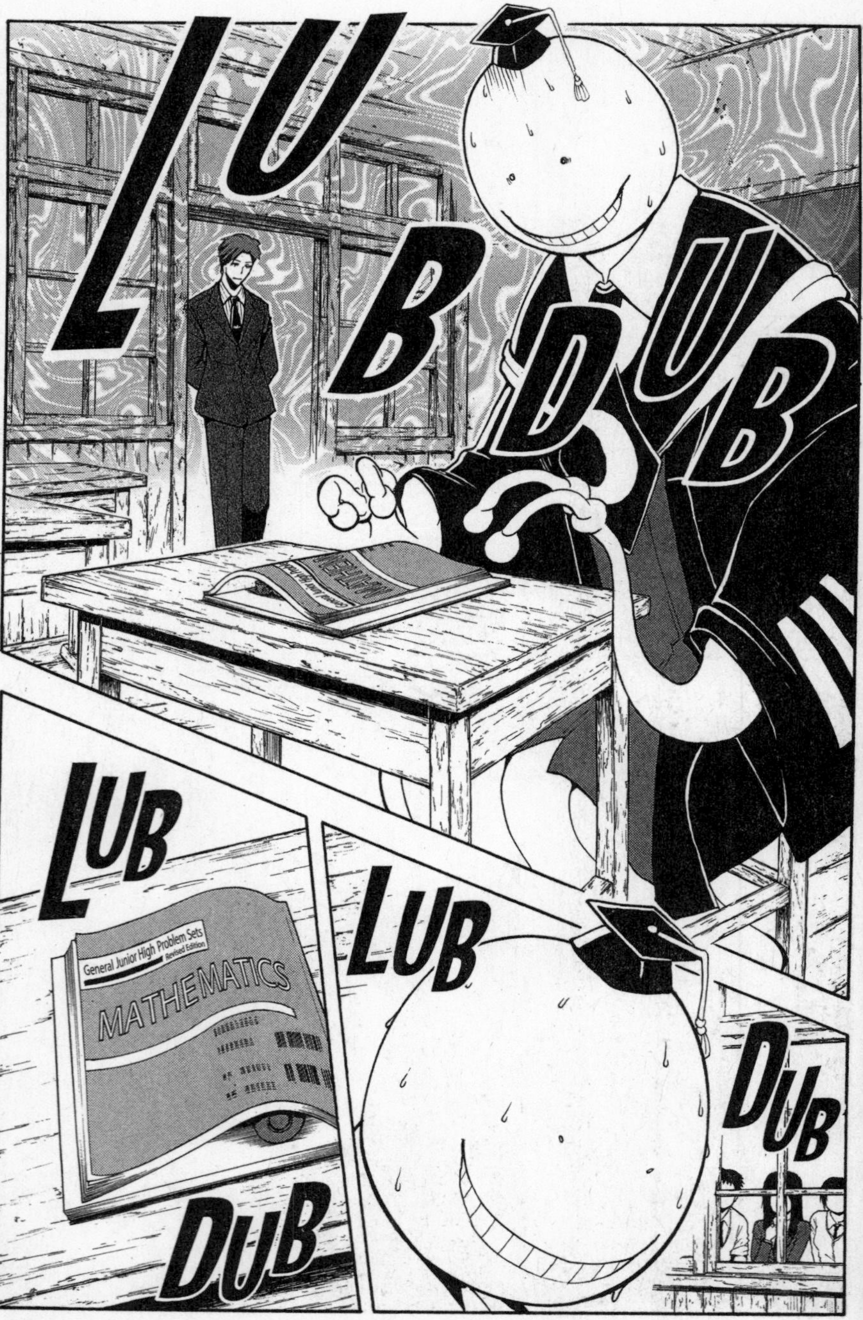

LUB
DUB
DUB
LUB
DUB
LUB
DUB
General Junior High Problem Sets
Revised Edition
MATHEMATICS

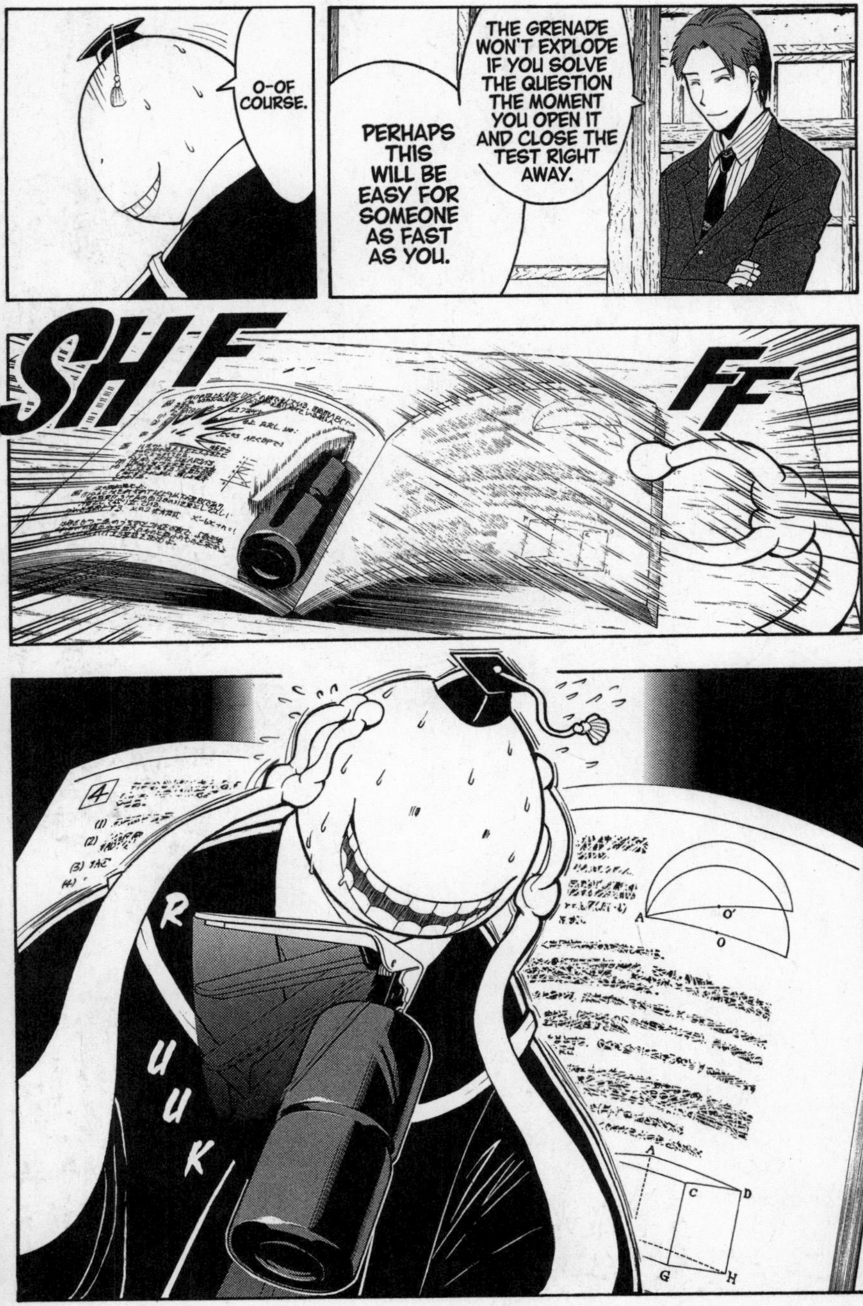
THE GRENADE WON'T EXPLODE IF YOU SOLVE THE QUESTION THE MOMENT YOU OPEN IT AND CLOSE THE TEST RIGHT AWAY.
PERHAPS THIS WILL BE EASY FOR SOMEONE AS FAST AS YOU.
O-OF COURSE.
SHF
FF
RUUK

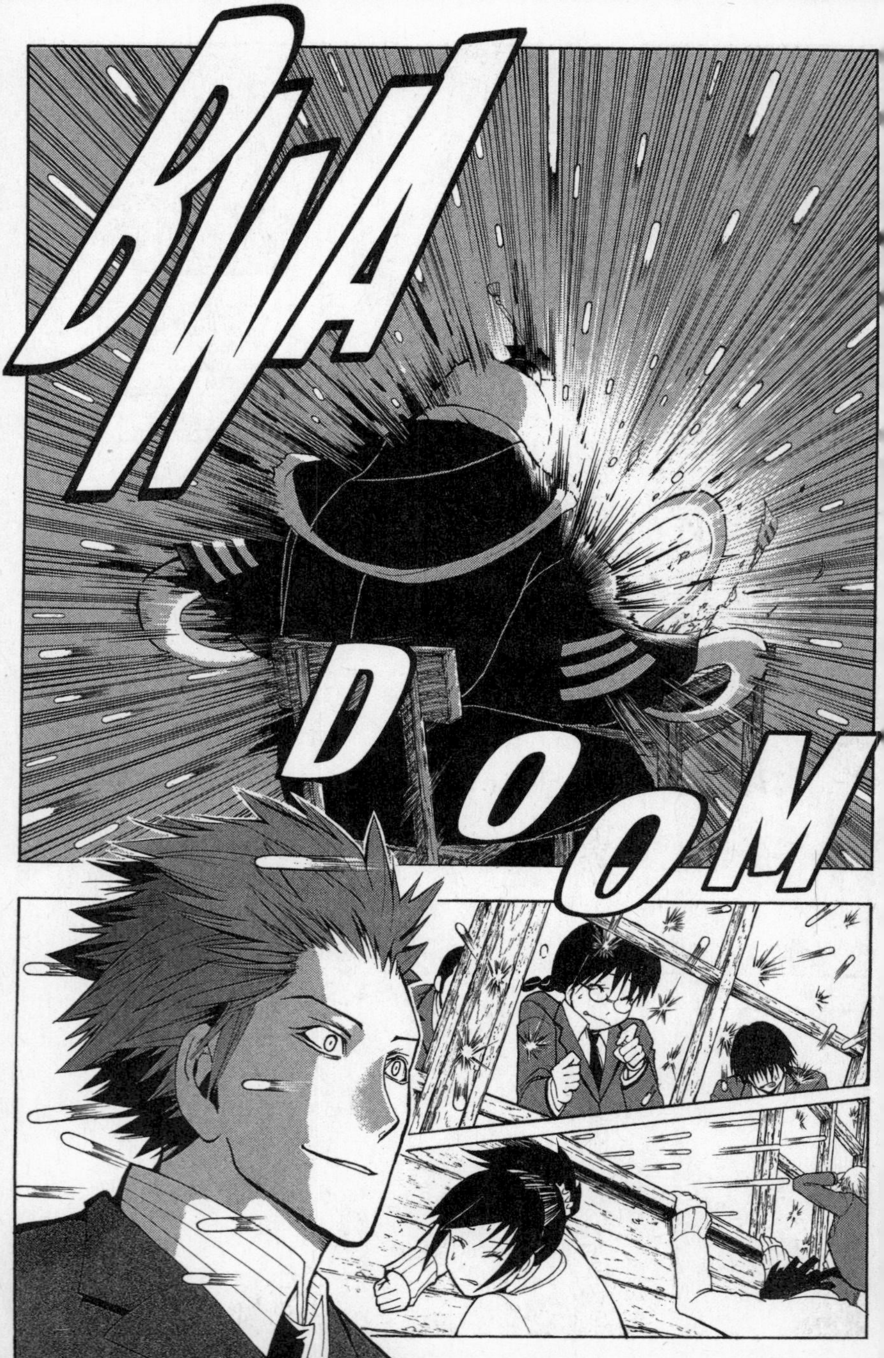
BWA
DOOM

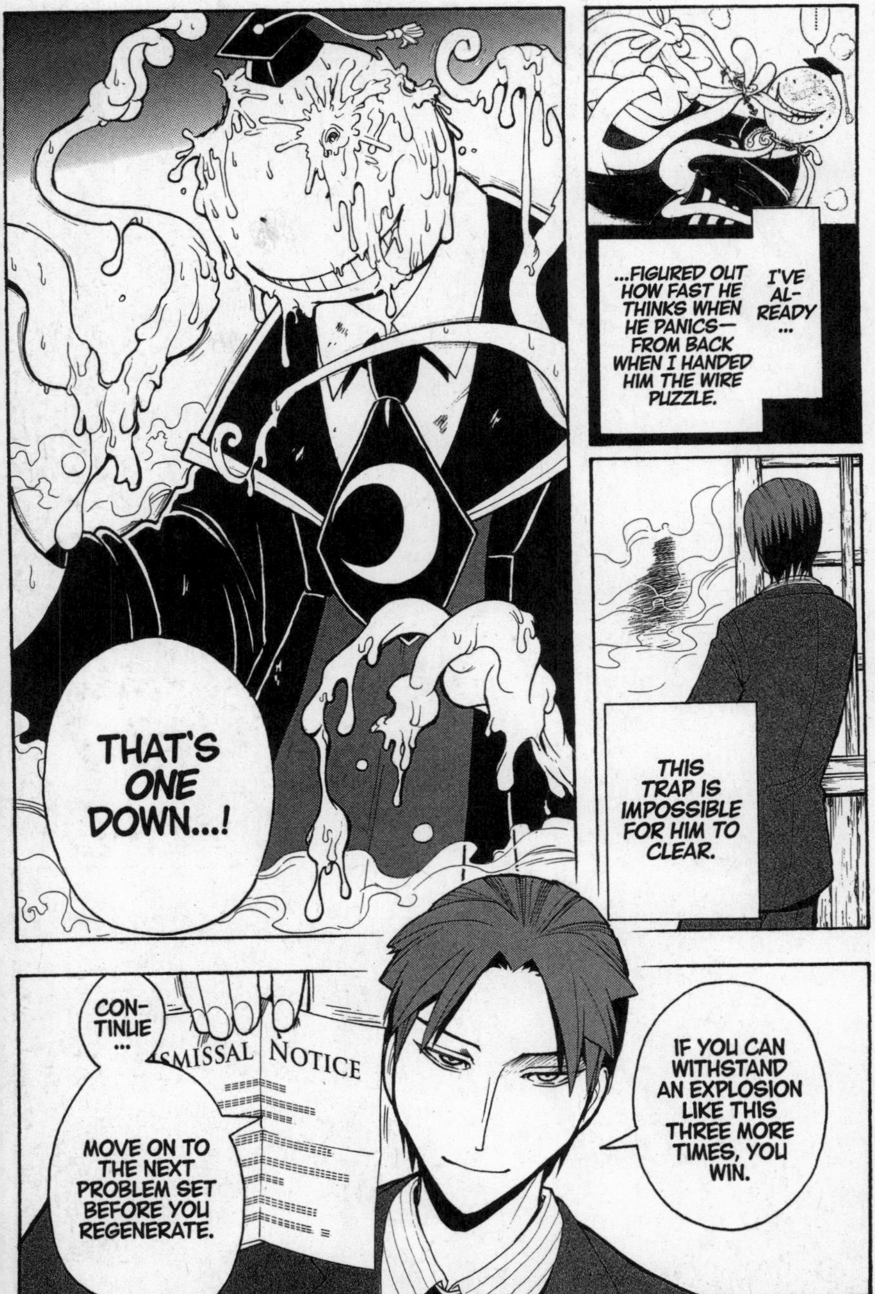
I'VE ALREADY...
...FIGURED OUT HOW FAST HE THINKS WHEN HE PANICS—FROM BACK WHEN I HANDED HIM THE WIRE PUZZLE.
THIS TRAP IS IMPOSSIBLE FOR HIM TO CLEAR.
THAT'S ONE DOWN...!
IF YOU CAN WITHSTAND AN EXPLOSION LIKE THIS THREE MORE TIMES, YOU WIN.
SMISSAL NOTICE
CONTINUE...
MOVE ON TO THE NEXT PROBLEM SET BEFORE YOU REGENERATE.

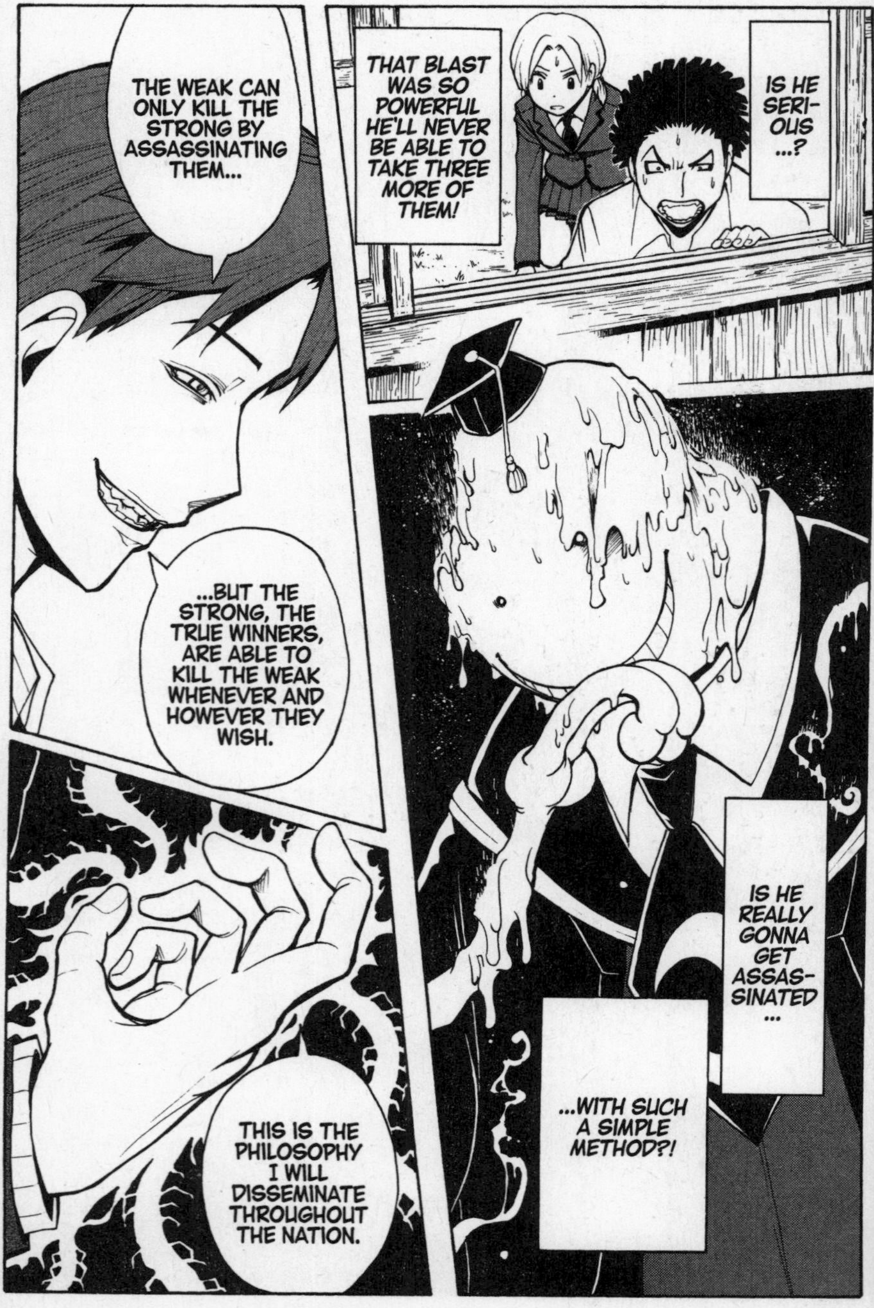
IS HE SERI-OUS ...?
THAT BLAST WAS SO POWERFUL HE'LL NEVER BE ABLE TO TAKE THREE MORE OF THEM!
THE WEAK CAN ONLY KILL THE STRONG BY ASSASSINATING THEM...
...BUT THE STRONG, THE TRUE WINNERS, ARE ABLE TO KILL THE WEAK WHENEVER AND HOWEVER THEY WISH.
IS HE REALLY GONNA GET ASSAS-SINATED ...
...WITH SUCH A SIMPLE METHOD?!
THIS IS THE PHILOSOPHY I WILL DISSEMINATE THROUGHOUT THE NATION.

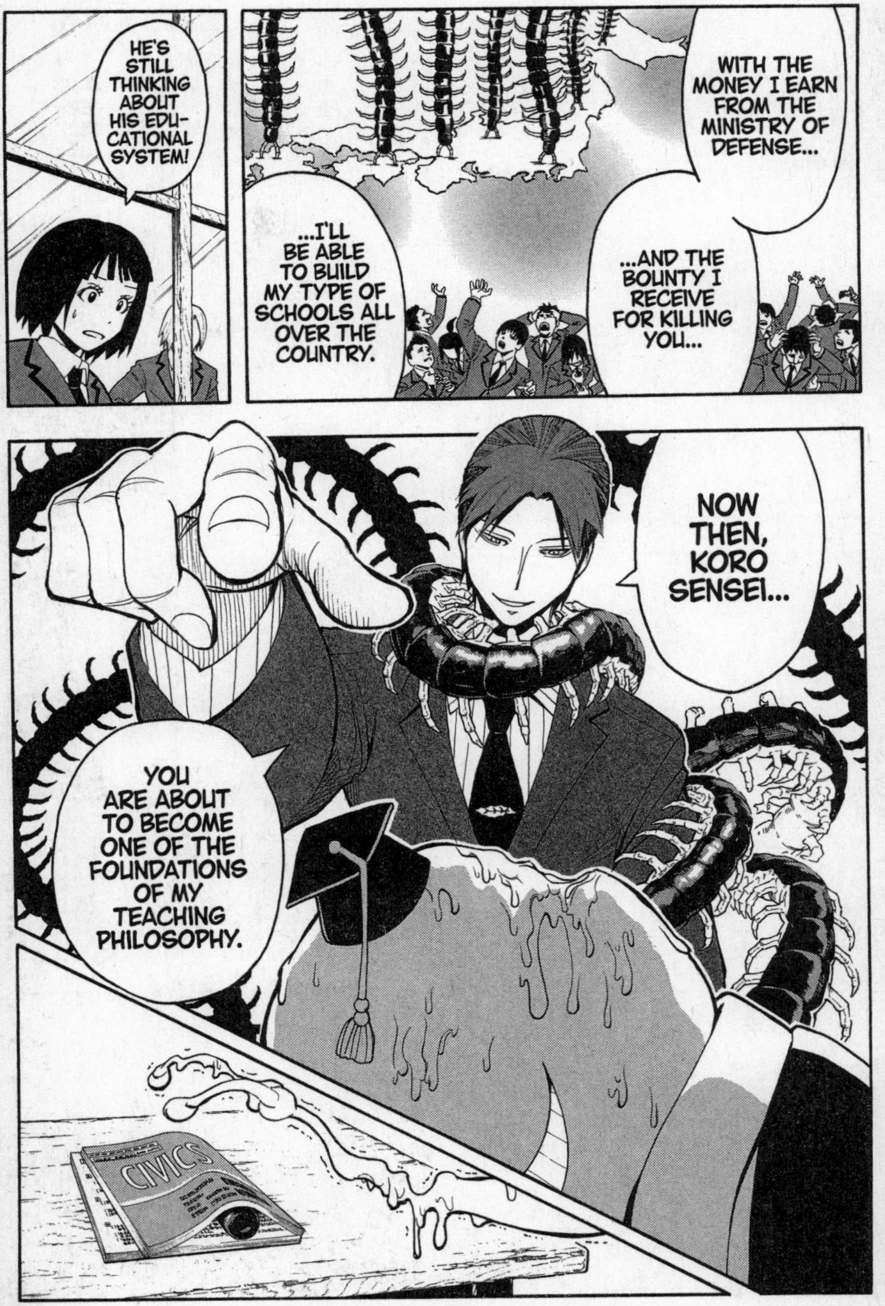
WITH THE MONEY I EARN FROM THE MINISTRY OF DEFENSE...
...AND THE BOUNTY I RECEIVE FOR KILLING YOU...
...I'LL BE ABLE TO BUILD MY TYPE OF SCHOOLS ALL OVER THE COUNTRY.
HE'S STILL THINKING ABOUT HIS EDU-CATIONAL SYSTEM!
NOW THEN, KORO SENSEI...
YOU ARE ABOUT TO BECOME ONE OF THE FOUNDATIONS OF MY TEACHING PHILOSOPHY.
CIVICS

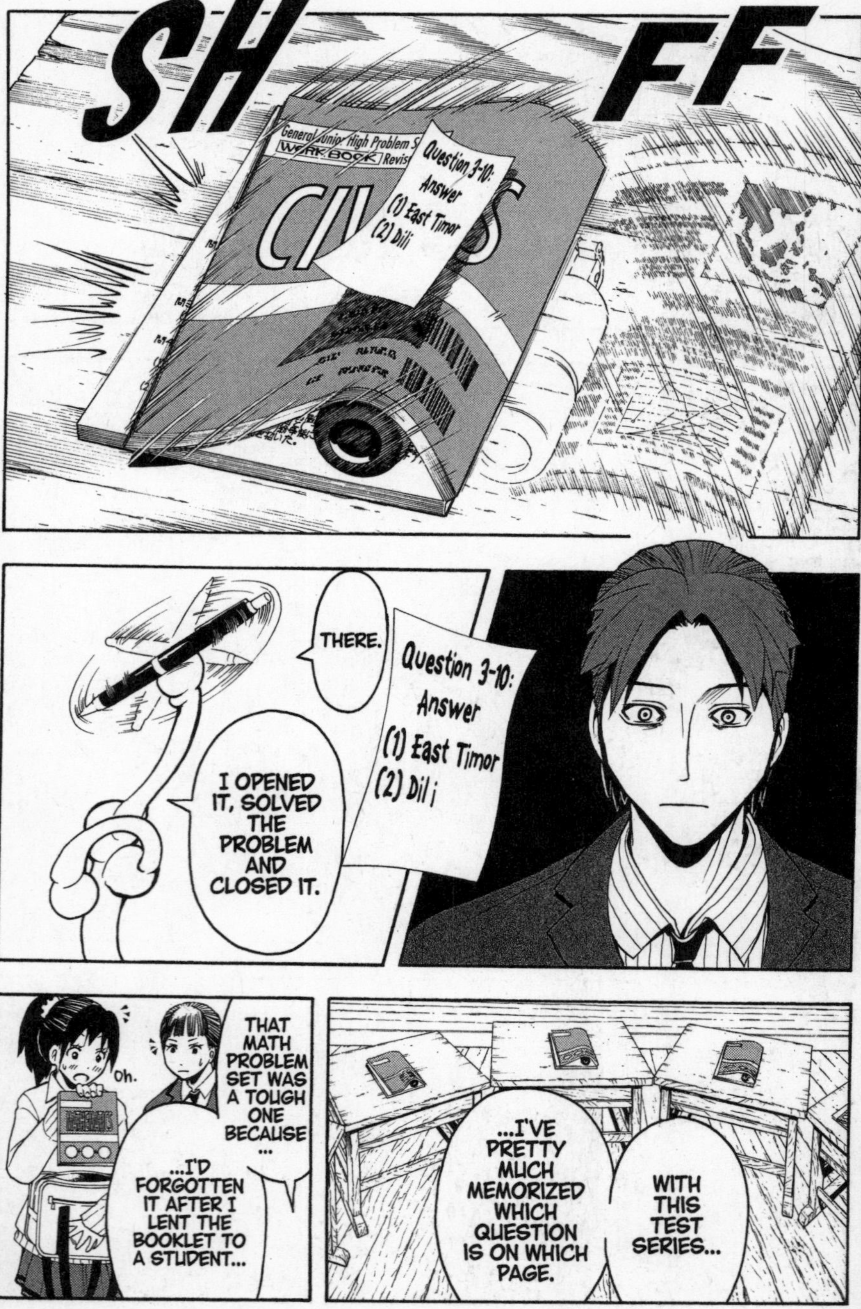
SH FF
General Junior High Problem S
WORK BOOK Revis
Question 3-10: Answer (1) East Timor (2) Dili
THERE.
Question 3-10: Answer (1) East Timor (2) Dili
I OPENED IT, SOLVED THE PROBLEM AND CLOSED IT.
WITH THIS TEST SERIES...
...I'VE PRETTY MUCH MEMORIZED WHICH QUESTION IS ON WHICH PAGE.
THAT MATH PROBLEM SET WAS A TOUGH ONE BECAUSE ...
...I'D FORGOTTEN IT AFTER I LENT THE BOOKLET TO A STUDENT...
Oh.

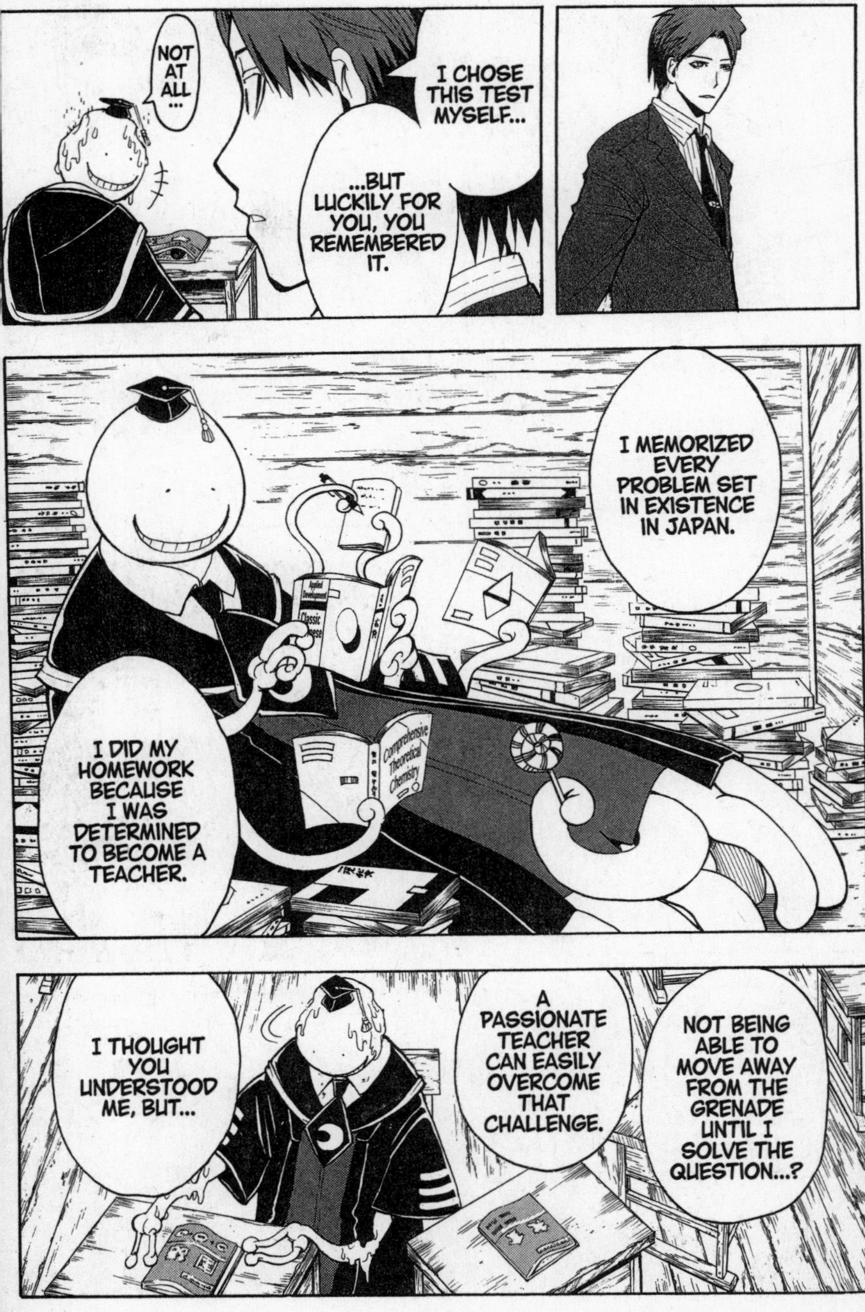
I CHOSE THIS TEST MYSELF...
...BUT LUCKILY FOR YOU, YOU REMEMBERED IT.
NOT AT ALL...
I MEMORIZED EVERY PROBLEM SET IN EXISTENCE IN JAPAN.
Applied Development
Comprehensive Theoretical Chemistry
I DID MY HOMEWORK BECAUSE I WAS DETERMINED TO BECOME A TEACHER.
NOT BEING ABLE TO MOVE AWAY FROM THE GRENADE UNTIL I SOLVE THE QUESTION...?
A PASSIONATE TEACHER CAN EASILY OVERCOME THAT CHALLENGE.
I THOUGHT YOU UNDERSTOOD ME, BUT...

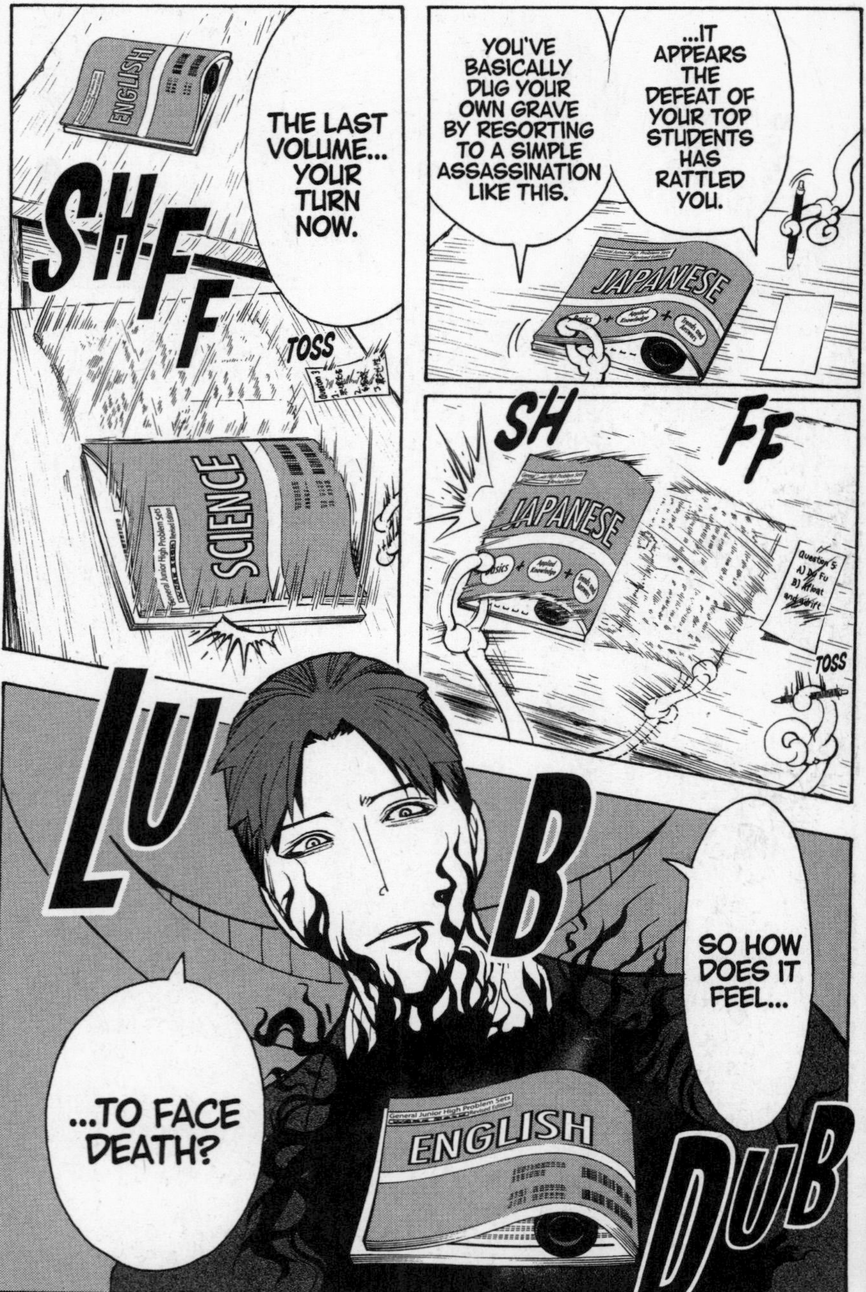
...IT APPEARS THE DEFEAT OF YOUR TOP STUDENTS HAS RATTLED YOU.
YOU'VE BASICALLY DUG YOUR OWN GRAVE BY RESORTING TO A SIMPLE ASSASSINATION LIKE THIS.
General Junior High Problem Sets
JAPANESE
Basics + Applied Knowledge + Trends and Answers
SH
FF
JAPANESE
TOSS
THE LAST VOLUME... YOUR TURN NOW.
ENGLISH
SH-F-F
TOSS
Question 3
SCIENCE
General Junior High Problem Sets Revised Edition
LU
B
SO HOW DOES IT FEEL...
...TO FACE DEATH?
General Junior High Problem Sets Revised Edition
ENGLISH
DUB

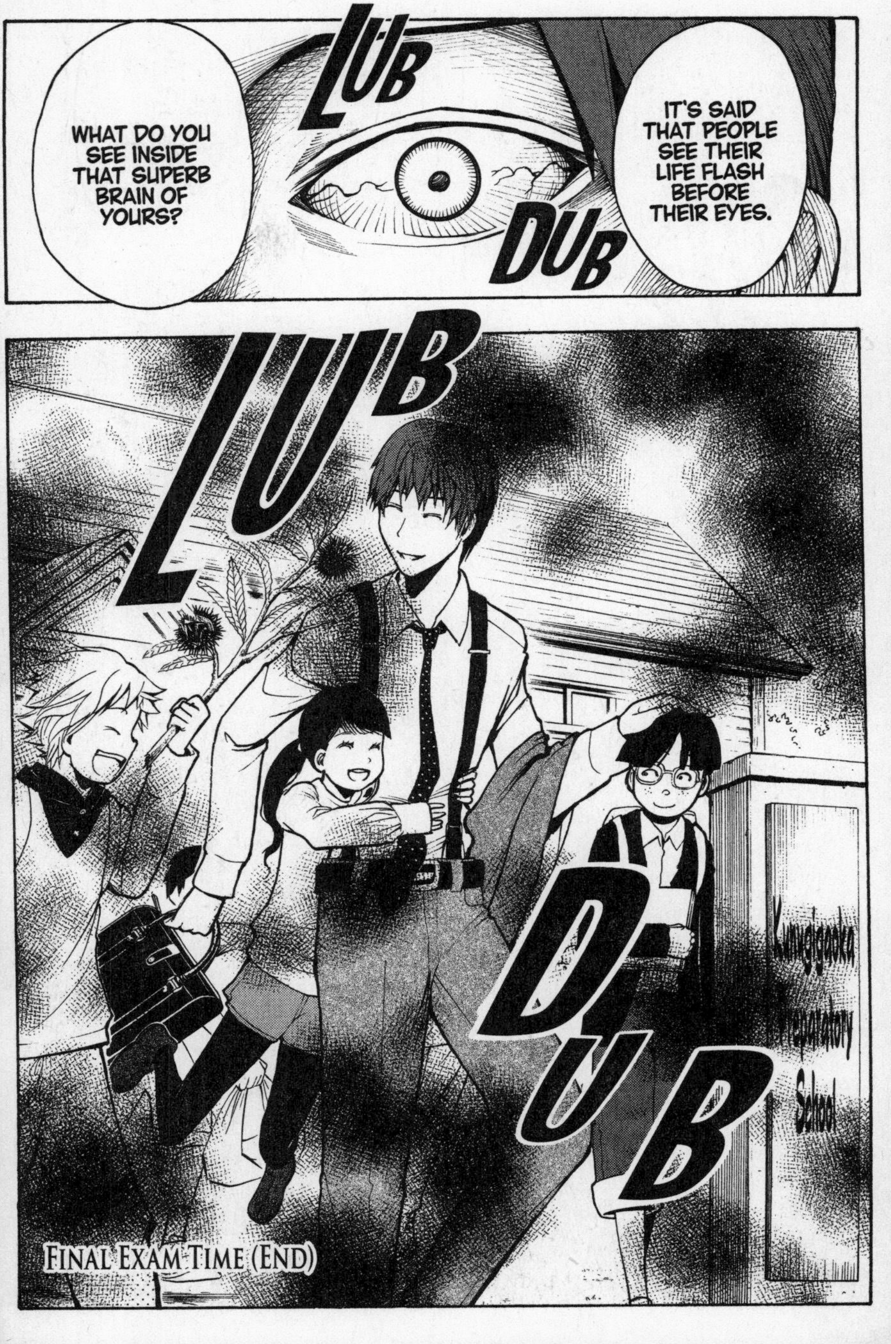
IT'S SAID THAT PEOPLE SEE THEIR LIFE FLASH BEFORE THEIR EYES.
LUB
DUB
WHAT DO YOU SEE INSIDE THAT SUPERB BRAIN OF YOURS?
LUB
DUB
Kunugigaoka Preparatory School
FINAL EXAM TIME (END)

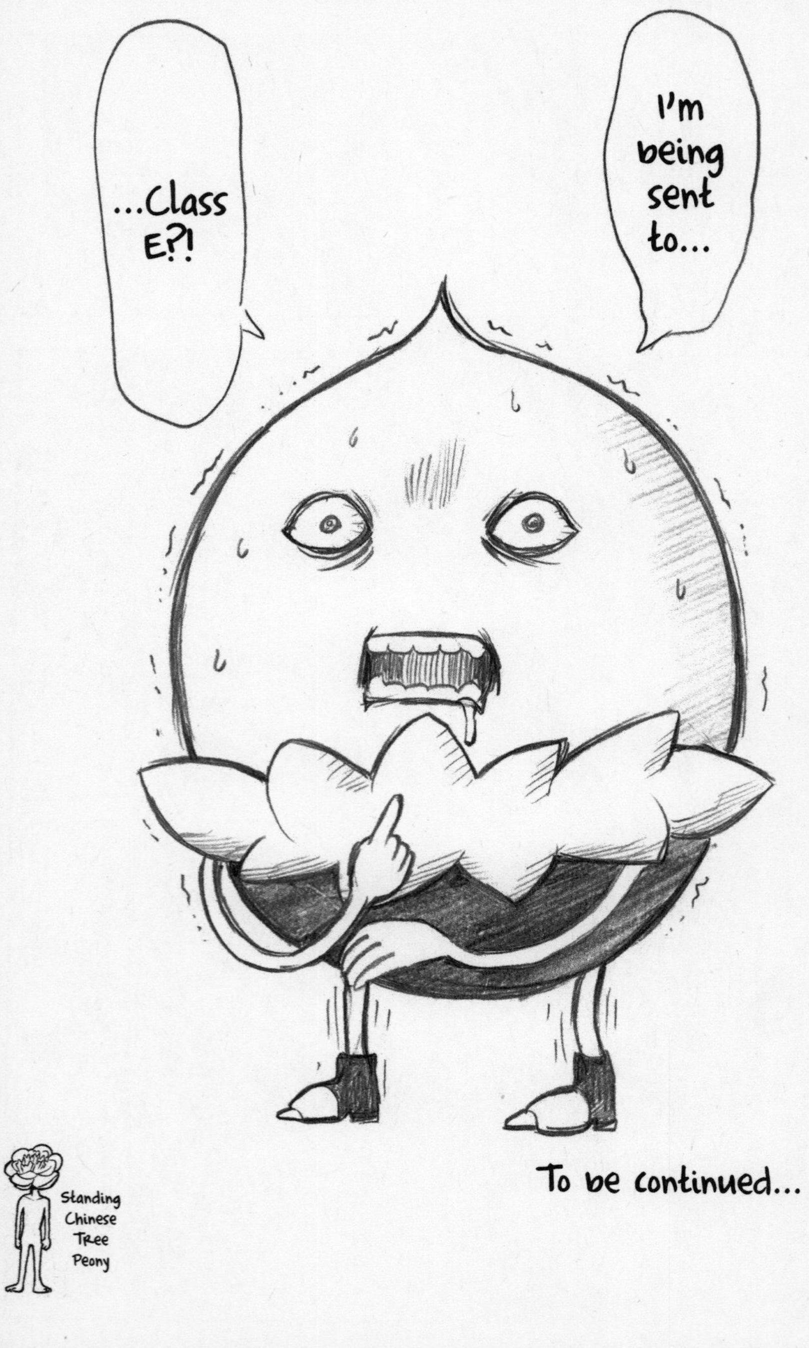
I'm being sent to...
...Class E?!
To be continued...
Standing Chinese Tree Peony

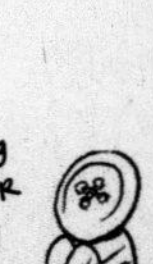

Sitting
Regular
Peony

Like many other manga artists, I'm sure, I personally supervise everything related to the *Assassination Classroom* series—such as the anime, live-action movie, English vocabulary/grammar books, and character books—time permitting.

I often propose a variety of projects and provide comments and many specifics about what we should do and how, in hopes of enhancing fans' experience.

I bet the creators and editors are sick and tired of me butting in, but I can't thank them enough for their dedication to fulfilling my vision.

—Yusei Matsui

Yusei Matsui was born on the last day of January in Saitama Prefecture, Japan. He has been drawing manga since elementary school. Some of his favorite manga series are *Bobobo-bo Bo-bobo*, *JoJo's Bizarre Adventure* and *Ultimate Muscle*. Matsui learned his trade working as an assistant to manga artist Yoshio Sawai, creator of *Bobobo-bo Bo-bobo*. In 2005, Matsui debuted his original manga *Neuro: Supernatural Detective* in *Weekly Shonen Jump*. In 2007, *Neuro* was adapted into an anime. In 2012, *Assassination Classroom* began serialization in *Weekly Shonen Jump*.

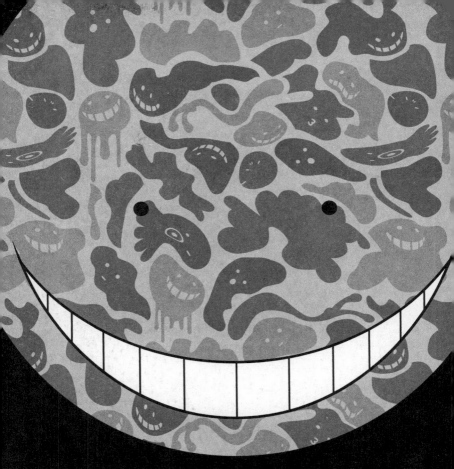

How do you like this new pattern? The "Koro Camo" is a camouflage design made up of a variety of faces that hide you from detection by all types of enemies. And if liquefied Koro Sensei happens to be hidden inside the pattern...there's nothing you can do about that!

ASSASSINATION CLASSROOM

YUSEI MATSUI

TIME FOR A TEACHER'S EXAM

A MOMENT OF TENTACLE ZEN

Koronda, the power of tentacles.

ASSASSINATION CLASSROOM

Volume 14
SHONEN JUMP ADVANCED Manga Edition

Story and Art by YUSEI MATSUI

Translation/Tetsuichiro Miyaki
English Adaptation/Bryant Turnage
Touch-up Art & Lettering/Stephen Dutro
Cover & Interior Design/Sam Elzway
Editor/Annette Roman

ANSATSU KYOSHITSU © 2012 by Yusei Matsui
All rights reserved.
First published in Japan in 2012 by SHUEISHA Inc., Tokyo.
English translation rights arranged by SHUEISHA Inc.

The stories, characters and incidents mentioned in this
publication are entirely fictional.

No portion of this book may be reproduced or
transmitted in any form or by any means without
written permission from the copyright holders.

Printed in the U.S.A.

Published by VIZ Media, LLC
P.O. Box 77010
San Francisco, CA 94107

10 9 8 7 6 5 4 3 2 1
First printing, February 2017

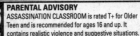

www.viz.com

www.shonenjump.com

RATED T+

PARENTAL ADVISORY
ASSASSINATION CLASSROOM is rated T+ for Older
Teen and is recommended for ages 16 and up. It
contains realistic violence and suggestive situations.
FOR OLDER TEEN

ratings.viz.com

WELLESLEY FREE LIBRARY
WELLESLEY, MASS. 02482

Several secret pasts are revealed this volume: the tragedy that led Principal Asano to develop his harsh—some would say brutal, sadistic, and inhumane—pedagogical methods, the personal relationship that motivates one student to assassinate their teacher, and even the origin of Koro Sensei! Will his students be more or less motivated to assassinate him now? And to what lengths will shy Nagisa go to sway a certain classmate from going down the dark path of vengeance? Then, it's time for class 3–E lunch theater! Who will be the star?

Available April 2017!

A PREMIUM BOX SET OF THE FIRST TWO STORY ARCS OF ONE PIECE!

A PIRATE'S TREASURE FOR ANY MANGA FAN!

STORY AND ART BY EIICHIRO ODA

Comes with
EXCLUSIVE POSTER
and the
ROMANCE DAWN
mini-comic!

As a child, Monkey D. Luffy dreamed of becoming King of the Pirates. But his life changed when he accidentally gained the power to stretch like rubber...at the cost of never being able to swim again! Years later, Luffy sets off in search of the "One Piece," said to be the greatest treasure in the world...

This box set includes VOLUMES 1-23, which comprise the EAST BLUE and BAROQUE WORKS story arcs.

EXCLUSIVE PREMIUMS and GREAT SAVINGS
over buying the individual volumes!

WWW.SHONENJUMP.COM

ONE PIECE © 1997 by Eiichiro Oda/SHUEISHA Inc.

RATED **T** FOR TEEN
ratings.viz.com

VIZ media
www.viz.cor

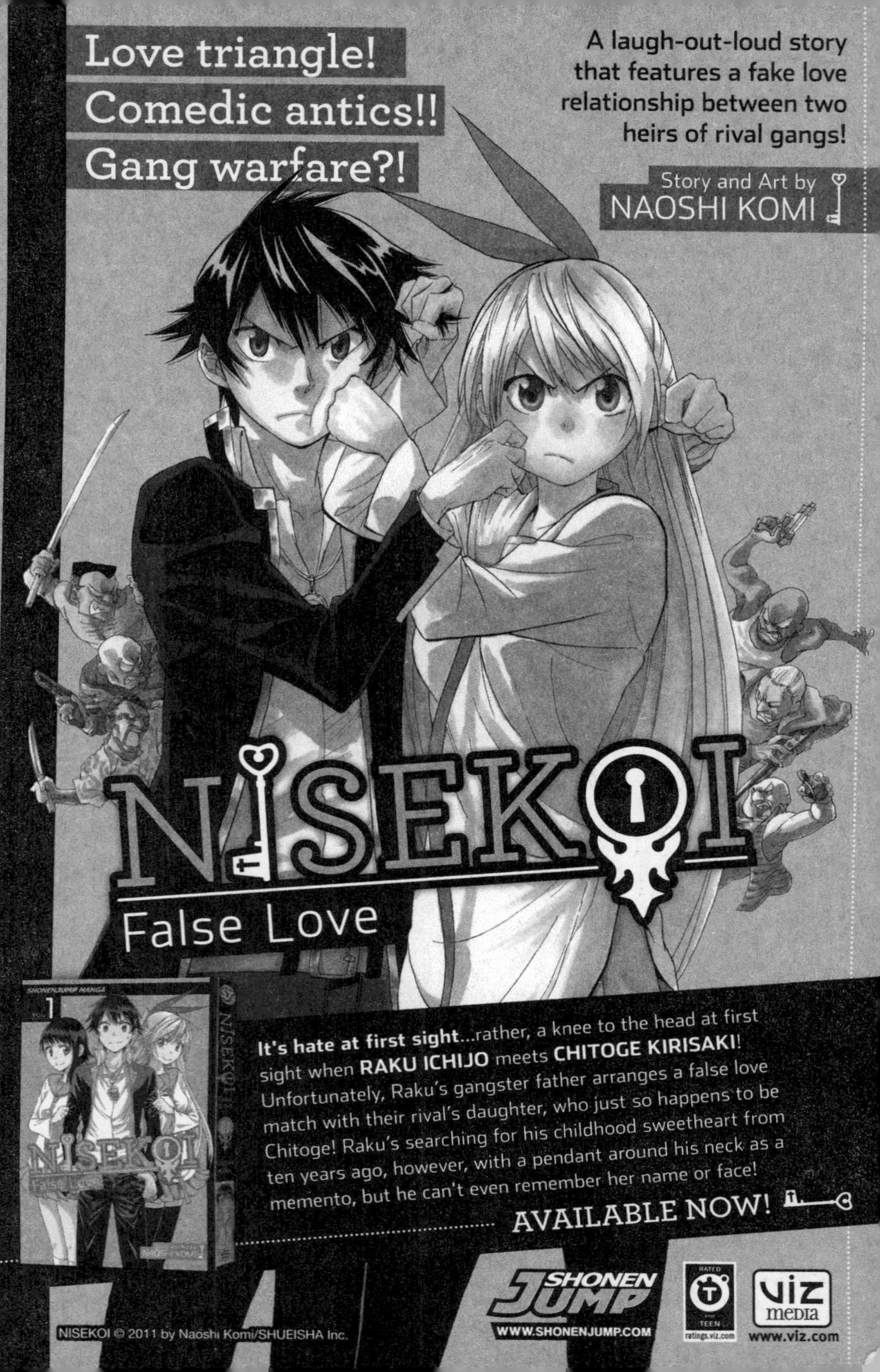
Love triangle!
Comedic antics!!
Gang warfare?!
A laugh-out-loud story that features a fake love relationship between two heirs of rival gangs!
Story and Art by
NAOSHI KOMI
NISEKOI
False Love
SHONENJUMP MANGA
It's hate at first sight...rather, a knee to the head at first sight when RAKU ICHIJO meets CHITOGE KIRISAKI! Unfortunately, Raku's gangster father arranges a false love match with their rival's daughter, who just so happens to be Chitoge! Raku's searching for his childhood sweetheart from ten years ago, however, with a pendant around his neck as a memento, but he can't even remember her name or face!
AVAILABLE NOW!
SHONEN JUMP
WWW.SHONENJUMP.COM
RATED T TEEN
ratings.viz.com
viz media
www.viz.com
NISEKOI © 2011 by Naoshi Komi/SHUEISHA Inc.

FROM THE CREATOR OF
DEATH NOTE

School Judgment

Judgment

GAKKYU HOTEI

STORY BY Nobuaki Enoki
ART BY Takeshi Obata

At Tenbin Elementary, there is only one way to settle a dispute—in a court of law! All quarrels bypass the teachers and are settled by some of the best lawyers in the country...who also happen to be elementary school students.

SHONEN JUMP   viz media   RATED T FOR TEEN
www.viz.com   ratings.viz.com

GAKKYU HOTEI © 2014 by Nobuaki Enoki, Takeshi Obata/SHUEISHA Inc.

You're Reading in the Wrong Direction!!

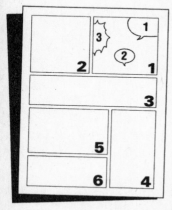

Whoops! Guess what? You're starting at the wrong end of the comic!

...It's true! In keeping with the original Japanese format, **Assassination Classroom** is meant to be read from right to left, starting in the upper-right corner.

Unlike English, which is read from left to right, Japanese is read from right to left, meaning that action, sound effects and word-balloon order are completely reversed... something which can make readers unfamiliar with Japanese feel pretty backwards themselves. For this reason, manga or Japanese comics published in the U.S. in English have sometimes been published "flopped"—that is, printed in exact reverse order, as though seen from the other side of a mirror.

By flopping pages, U.S. publishers can avoid confusing readers, but the compromise is not without its downside. For one thing, a character in a flopped manga series who once wore in the original Japanese version a T-shirt emblazoned with "M A Y" (as in "the merry month of") now wears one which reads "Y A M"! Additionally, many manga creators in Japan are themselves unhappy with the process, as some feel the mirror-imaging of their art skews their original intentions.

We are proud to bring you Yusei Matsui's **Assassination Classroom** in the original unflopped format.

For now, though, turn to the other side of the book and let the adventure begin...!

—Editor